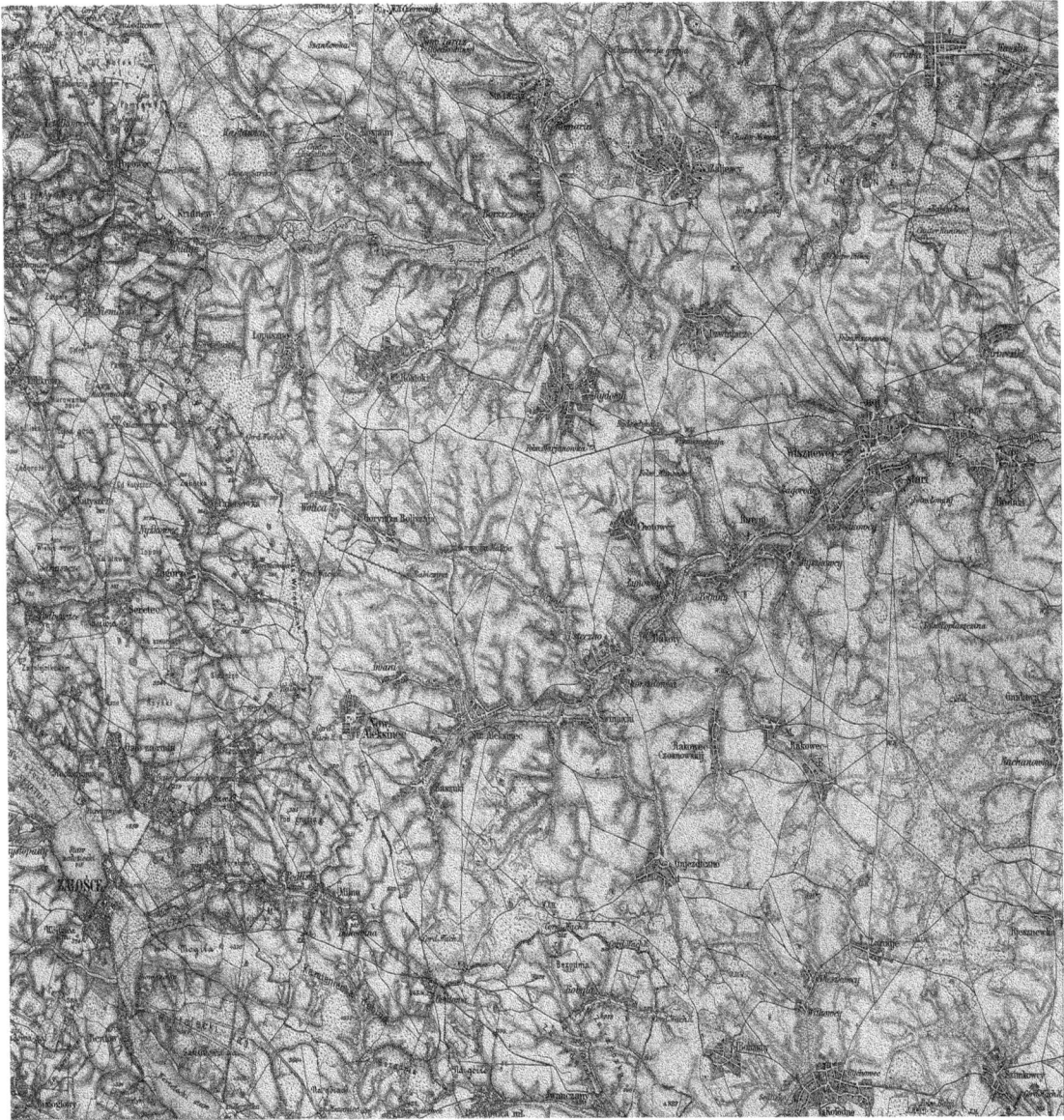

Zalosce Area 1877

Memorial Book of Vishnevets
(Vishnevets, Ukraine)

Translation of
Sefer Vishnivits: Sefer zikaron likedoshei
Vishnivits shenispu besho'at hanatsim

Memorial Book to the Martyrs of Vishnivits Who Perished
in the Nazi Holocaust

Original Yizkor Book Edited by: Chayim Rabin
Published by Organization of Vishnevets Immigrants
Published in Tel Aviv, 1970

Published by JewishGen

**An Affiliate of the Museum of Jewish Heritage—A Living Memorial to the Holocaust
New York**

Memorial Book of Vishnevets
(Vishnevets, Ukraine)
Translation of: *Sefer Vishnivits:*
Sefer zikaron likedoshei Vishnivits shenispu besho'at hanatsim
Memorial Book to the Martyrs of Vishnivits Who Perished in the Nazi Holocaust

Editor of the original Yizkor Book: Chayim Rabin
Translation Project Coordinator: Ellen Garshick
Translators: Lucas Bruyn, Tina Lunson, Sara Mages, and Aviv Small.
Layout: Jonathan Wind
Cover Design: Nina Schwartz, Impulse Graphics
Name Indexing: Jonathan Wind

Published by JewishGen, Inc.
An Affiliate of the Museum of Jewish Heritage
A Living Memorial to the Holocaust
36 Battery Place, New York, NY 10280

JewishGen, Inc. is not responsible for inaccuracies or omissions in the original work and makes no representations regarding the accuracy of this translation. Digital images of the original book's contents can be seen online at the New York Public Library website.

The mission of the JewishGen organization is to produce a translation of the original work, and we cannot verify the accuracy of statements or alter facts cited.

Printed in the United States of America by Lightning Source, Inc.

Library of Congress Control Number (LCCN): 2020941940
ISBN: 978-1-939561-93-0 (hard cover: 438 pages, alk. paper)

Cover Credits:

Front Cover:

Top:

Family of Mordechai (Mordko) and Rochel Kroun, circa 1927. Photo courtesy of Barbara Hirsch. The Krouns are flanked by daughters Faegel (called Shayna) at far left, Laike, Surrel and Mincha in back row (the eldest shown with her husband and child), and Frieda, at far right.

Bottom:

Kiddush after services, circa 1934, unknown location, extended family of Dubcia Press (nee Shridnik) of Vishnevets. Photo courtesy of Graham Michaels. Press emigrated to London with her three children in 1902.

Back Cover:

Top left:

Ruin of mill near bridge. The mill may have been Jewish-owned (see p. 41).

Top right:

The town viewed from the Palace. Photos ©2000 by Sandra and Alan Eisen, courtesy of Sandra Eisen.

Bottom right:

The orphanage, spring 1929. Photo courtesy of Barbara Hirsch. In 1929 Hirsch's father, Nathan Wirsch (second row center) returned to Vishnevets after 7 years in America, to marry his fiancée Frieda Kroun. During the trip he visited the orphanage supported by the Vishnevets Benevolent Society in New York (see p. 388).

Background:

Map of the town with Jewish and other landmarks during the early Nazi era, 1941-1942. Drawn from memory by Moshe Segal.

JewishGen and the Yizkor Books in Print Project

This book has been published by the **Yizkor Books in Print Project**, as part of the **Yizkor Book Project** of JewishGen, Inc.

JewishGen, Inc. is a non-profit organization founded in 1987 as a resource for Jewish genealogy. Its website [www.jewishgen.org] serves as an international clearinghouse and resource center to assist individuals who are researching the history of their Jewish families and the places where they lived. JewishGen provides databases, facilitates discussion groups, and coordinates projects relating to Jewish genealogy and the history of the Jewish people. In 2003, JewishGen became an affiliate of the **Museum of Jewish Heritage — A Living Memorial to the Holocaust** in New York.

The **JewishGen Yizkor Book Project** was organized to make more widely known the existence of Yizkor (Memorial) Books written by survivors and former residents of various Jewish communities throughout the world. Later, volunteers connected to the different destroyed communities began cooperating to have these books translated from the original language — usually Hebrew or Yiddish — into English, thus enabling a wider audience to have access to the valuable information contained within them. As each chapter of these books was translated, it was posted on the JewishGen website and made available to the general public.

The **Yizkor Books in Print Project** began in 2011 as an initiative to print and publish Yizkor Books that had been fully translated, so that hard copies would be available for purchase by the descendants of these communities and also by scholars, universities, synagogues, libraries, and museums.

These Yizkor books have been produced almost entirely through the volunteer effort of researchers from around the world, assisted by donations from private individuals. The books are printed and sold at near cost, so as to make them as affordable as possible. Our goal is to make this important genre of Jewish literature and history available in English in book form, so that people can have the personal histories of their ancestral towns on their bookshelves for themselves and for their children and grandchildren.

A list of all published translated Yizkor Books in the project with prices and ordering information can be found at:
http://www.jewishgen.org/Yizkor/ybip.html

Binny Lewis, Yizkor Book Project Manager
Joel Alpert, Yizkor-Book-in-Print Project Coordinator

JewishGen
Yizkor Book Project

This book is presented by the
Yizkor-Books-In-Print Project
Project Coordinator: Joel Alpert

Part of the Yizkor Books Project of JewishGen. Inc.
Project Manager: Binny Lewis

These books have been produced solely through efforts of volunteers
from around the world. The books are printed using the Print-on-Demand technology and sold at
near cost, to make them as affordable as possible.

Our goal is to make this intimate history of the destroyed Jewish shtetls
of Eastern Europe available in book form in English, so that people can
experience the near-personal histories of their ancestral town on their
bookshelves and those of their children and grandchildren.

All donations to the Yizkor Books Project, which translated the books,
are sincerely appreciated.

Please send donations to:

Yizkor Book Project
JewishGen, Inc.
36 Battery Place
New York, NY, 10280

JewishGen, Inc. is an affiliate of the
Museum of Jewish Heritage
A Living Memorial to the Holocaust

Acknowledgment

We are indebted to the following translators for their work on this yizkor book: Lucas Bruyn, Tina Lunson, Sara Mages, and Aviv Small. I take full responsibility for changes I have made and any damage done to their work.

In transliterating Hebrew and Yiddish, we followed the guidelines used for all Kremenets-area translation projects, which are based generally on the ANSI Z39.25-1975 General Purpose Standard for Hebrew, YIVO's transliteration schema for Yiddish, and Alexander Beider's *Ashkenazic Given Names.* For an explanation of these guidelines, please see:

https://kehilalinks.jewishgen.org/Kremenets/webpages/documents/transliteration /Transliteration%20Guidelines,%20Hebrew%20&%20Yiddish.pdf

In the original Yizkor book, some articles appeared in both Hebrew and Yiddish. In this version of the book, such articles appear only once.

Ellen Garshick (KremenetsDRG@gmail.com)
Editor, Kremenets Yizkor Book Translation Project

Kremenets Shtetl CO-OP/Jewish Records Indexing—Poland
https://kehilalinks.jewishgen.org/Kremenets/web-pages/index.html
an activity of the Kremenets District Research Group
Ellen Garshick, Ronald D. Doctor, and Sheree Roth, Co-coordinators

Notes to the Reader:

We apologize ahead of time for the poor quality of images in the book. Often these images had been scanned from the original Yizkor books which were of poor quality to begin with, being copies of old photographs. Each transfer results in loss of quality. We have done the best we could, given the original material and the resources and technology at hand. Even though images often appear of higher quality on computer screens, that does not transfer to high quality images in print. A reader can view the original scans on the web sites listed below.

Within the text the reader will note "{34}" standing ahead of a paragraph. This indicates that the material translated below was on page 34 of the original book. However, when a paragraph was split between two pages in the original book, the marker is placed in this book after the end of the paragraph for ease of reading.

Also please note that all references within the text of the book to page numbers, refer to the page numbers of the original Yizkor Book.

The original book can be seen online at the New York Public Library site:

https://digitalcollections.nypl.org/items/881daa00-2e3b-0133-2ff8-58d385a7bbd0

or at the Yiddish Book Center web site:

https://www.yiddishbookcenter.org/collections/yizkor-books/yzk-nybc314092/rabin-chaim-vishnivits-sefer-zikaron-li-kedoshe-vishnivits-she-nispu

In order to obtain a list of all Shoah victims from Vishnevets, the reader should access the Yad Vashem web site listed below; one can also search for specific family names using family name option. These lists are continually updated by Yad Vashem, so it is worthwhile to periodically search these lists.

There is much valuable information available on this web site, including the Pages of Testimony, etc.
http://yvng.yadvashem.org

A list of this book and all books available in the Yizkor-Book-In-Print Project along with prices is available at:
http://www.jewishgen.org/Yizkor/ybip.html

Geopolitical Information:

Vishnevets, Ukraine
The town is located at 49°54' N 25°45' E, 214 miles W of Kyyiv

Period	Town	District	Province	Country
Before WWI (c. 1900):	Vishnevets	Kremenets	Volhynia	Russian Empire
Between the wars (c. 1930):	Wiśniowiec	Krzemieniec	Wołyń	Poland
After WWII (c. 1950):	Vishnevets			Soviet Union
Today (c. 2000):	Vyshnivets'			Ukraine

Alternate names for the town: Vishnevets [Rus], Wiśniowiec [Pol], Vishnivits [Yid], Vyshnivets' [Ukr], Vishnevits, Vishniets, Vishnivitz, Vishnyovyets, Wisnievicze, Wiśniowiec Nowy, Wisnowiec, Vysnivec

Nearby Jewish Communities:

- Katerynivka 9 miles NE
- Podlesnoye 10 miles N
- Novyy Oleksinets 12 miles WSW
- Vyshhorodok 13 miles SE
- Kremenets 14 miles N
- Pochayev 14 miles NW
- Lanivtsi 15 miles E
- Velikiye Berezhtsy 15 miles NNW
- Zbarazh 16 miles S
- Zaliztsi 19 miles WSW
- Pidkamin 19 miles W
- Stryyivka 21 miles S
- Belozërka 21 miles ESE
- Shums'k 22 miles NE
- Rakhmanov 22 miles NE
- Yampil 23 miles ENE
- Ternopil 25 miles SSW
- Ozerna 26 miles SW
- Kam'yanky 27 miles SSE
- Verba 27 miles NNW
- Radyvyliv 27 miles NW
- Kozin 28 miles NNW
- Ozhyhivtsi 28 miles SE
- Brody 30 miles WNW
- Teofipol 30 miles E
- Kozliv 30 miles SW
- Bilohirya 30 miles ENE

Jewish Population: 2,825 (in 1897)

MAP OF UKRAINE IN 2014

Location of Vishnevets indicated

Hebrew Title Page of Original Hebrew/Yiddish Book

וישניביץ

ספר־זכרון לקדושי וישניביץ
שנספו בשואת הנאצים

העורך
חיים רבין

חברי מערכת :
מאיר אור, הנציה זק, משה סגל, יהושע רון

Translation of the Title Page of the Original Hebrew Book

Vishnevits

Memorial Book to the Martyrs of Vishnevits Who Perished in the Nazi Holocaust

Editor: Chayim Rabin

Editorial Board:
Meir Or, Hentsye Zak, Moshe Segal, Yehoshua Ron

הוצא ע"י ארגון עולי וישניביץ

עיצוב השער והעטיפה ש מ ו א ל   ב ר נ ר

נדפוס בדפוס גאות בע"מ

Translation of previous page

Published by the Organization of Former Residents of Vishnevets

Graphic Design of Title Page and Book Cover: Shmuel Brand

Printed by Naot Printing

Table of Contents

Translation Project Editor's Note   2

List of Illustrations   3

Town Locator   5

Name Index   9

Map of Vishnevets – Moshe Segal   25

Part One (Hebrew)

Note from the Editorial Board   27

Note from the Organization of Vishnevets Immigrants   28

Vishnevets

Vishnevets in Original Sources and Sefer Vishnivits – Chayim Rabin   29

Guide to Volin – Dr. Mstislav Orlovich   34

Vishnevets (History and Description) – Encyklopedia Powszechna   37

Vishnevets in Ruins and Her Annihilated Jewry – Meir Or   39

Our Town

Cradle of Our Childhood – Yakov Ayzenberg   40

When I Remember Vishnevets – Sonya (Shats) Levanon   41

Opening Remarks at the Adoption Ceremony – Moshe Kahan   44

Vishnevets as We Saw It – Children of Binyamina   45

The Hole in the Synagogue (from tales of Vishnevets) – Avraham Rozenberg 51

Poem – Chayim Elyovich   52

Poem – Nurit Sheyner   53

Oy, Mama (Poem) – Nitse Biv   53

Vishnevets through Its Institutions – Various photos   54

In the Tempest of the Holocaust (Survivors' Testimonies)

History Will Not Repeat Itself – Edna Yafe   61

The Vishnevets Ghetto – Zev Sobol   61

Nazi Atrocities in Vishnevets – A Survivor   72

In the Sea of Human Madness – Sore Kitaykesher (Kirshenboym)   83

I Was a Girl in the Vishnevets Ghetto – Rachel Sobol (Fuks)   92

The Destruction of Vishnevets, Volin – Mendel Zinger   98

A 12-Year-Old under Nazi Rule – Gdalye Rozenberg   108

From Inferno to Inferno – Moshe Segal   112

Jewish Communism in Vishnevets – Yehuda Margalit   123

Jewish Communism in Vishnevets – G. Nudel   127

Years of Senseless Horror – Chayim Korin   129

With the Soviets in Vishnevets and Afterward – Y. Mazur   135

The Victims We Sacrificed... – Sonye Shats   143

Under Justice-Perverted Regimes – Yerachmiel Servetnik   146

Russia, Which Was My Undoing – Menashe Tsvik   149

An Answer to a Grandson (Poem) – Meir Or   154

My Trip to Vishnevets in 1956 – M. Meliv (Frayer)   155

Institutions and Movements

Tarbut and Culture – Chayim Tsvi Mazur   157

A Hebrew Kindergarten in Vishnevets – Tsipora (Shlayen) Kornfeld   161

General Zionist and General Zionist Pioneer Representatives in Vishnevets – Y. Ron   163

A Treasured Memory of Vishnevets – Hentsye Zak (Zeyger)   166

Young People in Vishnevets – Moshe Shteynberg   168

The Founding of Young Pioneer in Our Town – Yakov Chatski   170

How I Came to Immigrate – Chayim Verdi   174

Youth Guard and More in Vishnevets – Moshe Leshed (Markhbeyn)   176

Betar in Vishnevets – Sore Kitaykisher (Kirshenboym)   179

In a Training Detachment in Vishnevets – Tsipora (Shlayen) Kornfeld   180

Drama Circles in Vishnevets – Yone Ron   183

An Anti-Semitic Judge's Verdict in Vishnevets – Yehoshue Ron (Shike Geler)   185

From Cheder to the Northern Fence – Yitschak Verdi (Reyzels)   188

How Yitschak Reyzels (Verdi) Was Wounded   191

The Northern Fence Builders – B. Chabas   191

Notes and Letters

Letter from Kopel Dobrovitker   192

Letter from D. Balmelakhe to Yakov Chachkis   194

Letter from Leybtsi Fefer   195

Leybtsi (Arye Leyb) Fefer, of Blessed Memory   198

People We Remember

Grandma Chane-Malke – Yone Ron   200

Azriel (Son of Moshe Aharon) Kubrik – A. Barak   202

Shimon Ayzenberg – Lipa Goldberg   205

Something about Shimon Ayzenberg – Yitschak Kecholy   207

Duvid Roynik – Lipa Goldberg   208

The Spirit of Nachum Beren – Sore Or   210

In Memory of My Beloved Parents and My Friend, Avraham Bisker, of Blessed Memory – Eliezer Tsinberg   213

Something about Dad, of Blessed Memory – Tsvi Katz   215

In Memory of Mr. Avraham Vitels, of Blessed Memory – Y. N-S   217

R' Mordekhay Kechum – Y. Ron (Shike der Geler)   218

Gdalye "Gedoyle" – Y. Ron   220

On the Nation's Stage

Betsalel Mishne – Batye Derbarimdiker   222

Ben-Tsion (Bentsi) Tsur, of Blessed Memory – His Parents   224

Neta Hadari – Yakov Chachkis   226

Our Dead in the Nation

Azriel Kubrik – Yitschak Ben-Tsvi (the President)   228

Duvid Roynik, of Blessed Memory – Meir Or   229

More about Shimon Ayzenberg   230

A Time to Mourn – Meir Or   231

Chayim Zev Barkay – Meir Or   235

Simche Zak, of Blessed Memory – Meir Or   237

Yitschak Rabin – Meir Or   238

Moshe Goldshub, of Blessed Memory – Meir Or   239

My Father, Yehuda, and My Mother, Sore – Tikve (Rozental) Sklod   241

Sore, Duvid Roynik's Daughter – Mikhael Goldberg   242

The Sofer Brothers

About Yosef Sofer – Hentsye Zak   245

Yakov Sofer, of Blessed Memory – Meir Or   247

Asher Sofer – Ts. R.   249

Collection (Contributions Received after Typesetting)

Those Who Are No Longer – Y. N.-S.   250

Among Russian Citizens and on Its Frontiers – Mikhael Valdman   252

From a Survivor's Diary – A. Y. Teyer   255

The Story of Asher Sofer – Cherne (Katz) Rabin   280

R' Simche Ayzik Rotman – M. M.   284

Loving Friends (Poem) – Simche Ayzik Rotman   287

On The Enlightenment (Poem) – Simche Ayzik Rotman   290

My Parents, Some of the First Immigrants from Vishnevets – Shlome Rachmani   290

Bat-Sheve and Zalman Chazan, of Blessed Memory – Meir   291

In Memory of the Martyrs of Vishnevets – Chayim Rabin   293

Part Two (Yiddish)

Horror and Death

The Last Rabbi of Vishnevets – Edna Yafe   294

Let Us Not Forget – Mordekhay Fishman   294

Mama (Poem) – Avraham Lev   297

My Mother Is Off to Ponar (Poem) – Avraham Lev   298

Vishnevets 1944 – Simche Hirsh Boytener's   298

Our Poor Town

Vishnevets–Historical Dates – Chayim Rabin   303

Guide to Volhynia – Mstislav Orlovich   305

A Treasure of Memories – Avraham Blum   307

Vishnevets – Avraham Averbukh   311

Vishnevets, My Town – Yehoshue Zeyger   312

I See My Vishnevets – Zeyde Kamtsen   315

Synagogues in Vishnevets – Meir Or   317

My Contribution to the Memorial Book – Misha Koren   321

Vishnevets in a Trick Mirror – M. Averbukh   340

Episodes and Legends

Face Down – Sh. Ayzenberg   349

The Rabbi and the Police Chief – Louis Ratman   350

Vishnevets Demons – Yakov Sheyngold   351

Hometown Memories – M. Fishman   352

The False Accusation against the Great Saint R' Yosele Radiviler – M. Chazan 354

Jewish Benefactors – A. Freylekh   360

A Favor for a Favor – M. Chazan   362

Characters

Chane Malke – M. Or (Averbukh)   366

Three Generations of Pedigree – Alef   368

R' Levi Yitschak of Berdichev's Grandchildren in Vishnevets – M. Averbukh   371

Hersh Bisker, of Blessed Memory – Chayim Baral   373

Avraham Yehuda Katz – Yoel Akiva Zusman   375

Fund for the Sick in Vishnevets, or History of an Institution – Miryam Maliv (Frayer)   377

Mikhel Fishman, of Blessed Memory – From Newspapers   380

Idel Shapiro – The Editors   382

A Story with Duvid Roynik – Sh. Sheyner   383

Makhlye Vaynman (Kremenetski), of Blessed Memory – M. Alef   384

Society

History of the Vishnevets Society – Avraham Freylikh   386

Vishnevets–Adopted – Meir   390

The Vishnevetsers' Good Name – Yosef Shatski   391

Vishnevetsers in Israel and America – Avraham Averbukh   393

With Brethren from Argentina (February 1961) – M. Alef   395

Vishnevets Townspeople Societies in America and Israel – The Organization   398

A Last Word

Vishnevets 1956 – M. Malev (Frayer)   402

Shoshana Zak (Agsi), of Blessed Memory – From a memorial booklet   404

Name Index   406

Sefer Vishnevets
A Memorial Book to the Vishnevets Martyrs
Who Perished in the Nazi Holocaust

ספר וישנביץ

Translation Project Editor's Note

Sefer Vishnevets has in two major sections: one in Hebrew, beginning on page I, and one in Yiddish, beginning in page on p. 287. As is clear from the table of contents, much of the material is presented in both languages.

In translating Hebrew and Yiddish, we followed the guidelines used for all Kremenets-area translation projects, which are based generally on the ANSI Z39.25-1975 General Purpose Standard for Hebrew, YIVO's transliteration schema for Yiddish, and Alexander Beider's book, Ashkenazic Given Names. For an explanation of these guidelines, please see

https://kehilalinks.jewishgen.org/Kremenets/web-pages/transliteration.html

We are indebted to the following translators for their work on this yizkor book: Sara Mages, Lucas Bruyn, and Aviv Small. I take full responsibility for changes I have made and any damage done to their work. Please keep in mind that this is an ongoing project. Additions and revisions to this translation will be made available as they are completed.

The Vishnevets Yizkor Book Translation Project is a project of the Kremenets Shtetl CO-OP/Jewish Records Indexing-Poland, an activity of the Kremenets District Research Group.

Ellen Garshick
Editor, Vishnevets Yizkor Book Translation Project
Kremenets Shtetl CO-OP/Jewish Records Indexing-Poland

http://www.shtetlinks.jewishgen.org/Kremenets
An activity of the Kremenets District Research Group

Ronald D. Doctor, Co-Coordinator
Kremenets Shtetl CO-OP/Jewish Records Indexing-Poland
An activity of the Kremenets District Research Group
Portland, Oregon USA

List of Illustrations

Based on Pagination in the original Yizkor book, not this translation

	Page
Map of the Town of Vishnevets	Flyleaf
Bat-Sheve Chazan	27
The Trade School and the Palace	31
Tarbut	42
Artistry	43
Reading: Founders and Administrators of the Vishnevets Municipal Library, 5687-5692	44
Prayer ...	45
Financial Activities	45
Youth Guard Exhibit at the Jewish National Fund Bazaar in Vishnevets	46
Organization and Immigration	47
Orphan Care	48
Worker Protection	48
Rabbi Meir Nachum Yingerleyb, Last Rabbi of Vishnevets	51
Remaining of All of Vishnevets ...	117
Nothing Remained of Vishnevets but Mass Graves	124
In the Valley of Skeletons	138
Board of Directors of Tarbut in Vishnevets, with I. Shapiro in the Center	143
First Kindergarten in Vishnevets	146
General Zionist Activists	148
Freedom Movement in Vishnevets during the 1920s	150
Youth, Nature, and Relaxation	152
Pioneer and Young Pioneer Federation in Vishnevets	155
Dreaming of Immigration in Vishnevets	158
Youth Guard in Vishnevets	161
Pioneer Training in Vishnevets, 1934	164
Soccer in Vishnevets—Players and Their Proud Supporters	169

Fence Builders in the North   172

Landsberg Camp with L. Fefer as President   182

Leybtsi (Arye Leyb) Fefer   184

Grandmother Chane-Malke with Her Husband, Yakov
  Barukh   189

Azriel Kubrik   191

Shimon Ayzenberg   194

Duvid Roynik as a Fruit Picker   198

Avraham Bisker   202

Avraham Yehuda Katz   204

Betsalel Mishne   213

Ben-Tsion (Bentsi) Tsur   214

Neta Hadari   216

Duvid Roynik, of Blessed Memory   220

Chayim Zev Barkay, of Blessed Memory   226

Simche Zak, of Blessed Memory   228

Moshe Goldshub, of Blessed Memory   230

Yehuda and Sore Rozental   231

Yosef Sofer   237

Yakov Sofer   238

Asher Sofer   240

R' Simche Ayzik Rotman   275

Tel Aviv: Greetings from Israel 5691   282

Town Locator

[**Translation Editor's Note**: The translation of Sefer Vishnevets uses common English names of well-known cities and towns (e.g., Haifa, Jerusalem, Moscow, New York, Petersburg, Warsaw). Names of other European cities and towns are transliterated as they appear in the text. This locator shows those transliterations, likely standard names in the U.S. Board on Geographic Names (BGN) as of January 2012 (see http://http://earth-info.nga.mil/gns/html/bgn.htm), the location, and the distance from Vishnevets.]

Town Name as Transliterated in Sefer Vishnevets	Probable Standard Name in BGN Database (in Ukraine unless otherwise Indicated)	Probable Location and Distance from Vishnevets (49°54' N 25°45' E)
Akmolinsk	Astana, Kazakhstan	51°11' N 71°26' E, 1,973.9 miles ENE
Aktyubinsk	Aktobe, Kazakhstan	50°18' N 57°11' E, 1,382.0 miles ENE
Alma Ata	Almaty, Kazakhstan	43°15' N 76°57' E, 2,424.0 miles E
Ashkhabad	Aşgabat, Turkmenistan	37°57' N 58°23' E, 1801.0 miles ESE
Bielozerka	Belozėrka	49°46' N 26°11' E, 21.4 miles ESE
Berdichev	Berdychiv	49°54' N 28°35' E, 126.0 miles E
Berestechko	Berestechko	50°21' N 25°07' E, 41.8 miles NW
Berezits	Velikiye Berezhtsy	50°06' N 25°37' E, 15 miles NNW
Bialo-krinitse, Bialokrinitsi	Belaya Krinitsa	50°09' N 25°45' E, 17.3 miles N
Bilotserkov	Bila Tserkva	49°47' N 30°07' E, 194.6 miles E
Charkov	Kharkiv	50°00' N 36°15' E, 466.2 miles E
Cheliabinsk	Chelyabinsk, Russia	55°09' N 61°26' E, 1,524.0 miles ENE
Chichinits	Chaychintsy	49°51' N 25°52' E, 6.2 miles ESE
Chortkov	Chortkiv	49°01' N 25°48' E, 61.0 miles S
Chodorov	Khodorov	49°24' N 24°19' E, 72.8 miles WSW
Debaltsova	Debal'tsevo	48°20' N 38°24' E, 581.0 miles E

Dnepropetrovsk	Dnipropetrovs'k	48°27' N 34°59' E, 428.3 miles E
Dubno	Dubno	50°25' N 25°45' E, 35.7 miles N
Eyshishuk	Eišiškės, Lithuania	54°10' N 25°00' E 296.3 miles N
Grodno	Hrodna, Belarus	53°41' N 23°50' E, 273.3 miles NNW
Horenka, Horinka	Gorynka	49°59' N 25°47' E, 5.9 miles NNE
Horodok	Gorodok, Belarus	54°09' N 26°55' E, 298.0 miles N
Horyn	Horyn, Belarus	52°09' N 27°17' E, 168.5 miles NNE
Kagan	Kogon, Uzbekistan	39°43' N 64°33' E, 1,999.8 miles E
Karagander	Karaganda, Kazakhstan	49°48' N 73°06' E, 2,072.2 miles ENE
Katerburg	Katerinovka	50°00' N 25°53' E, 9.1miles NE
Katovits	Katowice, Poland	50°16' N 19°01' E, 299.3 miles W
Kelts	Kielce, Poland	50°50' N 20°40' E, 232.9 miles WNW
Kishinyuv	Chişinău (Moldova)	47°00' N 28°51' E, 245.3 miles SE
Klevan	Klevan	50°45' N 25°59' E, 59.6 miles N
Klosov, Klosova	Klesov	51°20' N 26°56' E, 111.7 miles NNE
Kniazshe	Knyazhe	49°50' N 24°48' E, 42.5 miles W
Kolodne	Kolonoye	48°10' N 23°36' E, 149.6 miles SW
Kolomiya	Kolomyya	48°32' N 25°02' E, 99.8 miles SSW
Korets, Korits	Korets	50°37' N 27°10' E, 79.7 miles NE
Kornochevka	Karnachovka	49°47' N 25°54' E, 10.5 miles SE
Kovne	Kaunas, Lithuania	54°54' N 23°54' E, 353.9 miles NNW
Kozin	Kozin	50°16' N 25°28' E, 28.3 NNW
Krasilov	Krasyliv	49°39' N 26°58' E, 56.9 miles ESE
Kremenets	Kremenets	50°06' N 25°43' E, 15.0 miles NNE
Kuybishev	Samara, Russia	53°12' N 50°09' E, 1,066.5 miles ENE
Lanevits, Lanovits	Lanivtsi	49°52' N 26°05' E, 15 miles E
Lida	Lida, Belarus	53°54' N 25°18' E, 276.6 miles N
Lopushna	Lopushnoye	49°55' N 25°28' E, 12.7 miles W
Lublin	Lublin (Poland)	51°15' N 22°34' E, 167.8 miles NW
Ludmir	Volodymyr-Volyns'kyy	50°51' N 24°20' E, 90.5 miles NW
Lutsk	Luts'k	50°45' N 25°20' E, 61.5 miles NNW

Malogolovsk	Malyy Golovskiy, Russia	50°34' N 42°20' E, 732.3 miles E
Melinovits	Mlinovtsy	49°53' N 25°38' E, 5.3 miles WSW
Munkachivo	Mukacheve	48°27' N 22°43' E , 169.6 miles SW
Myed	Med', Russia	58°21' N 60°03' E, 1,484.9 miles NE
Nalchik	Nal'chik, Russia	43°30' N 43°37' E, 951.3 miles ESE
Novaya Uralsk	Ural'sk, Russia	51°35' N 58°39' E, 1,429.7 miles ENE
Novograd Velinsk	Novohrad-Volyns'kyy	50°36' N 27°37' E, 95.5 miles ENE
Ostitsek	Ustechko	49°52' N 25°37' E, 6.4 miles WSW
Ostra, Ostrog	Ostroh	50°20' N 26°31' E, 45.2 miles NE
Penza	Penza, Russia	56°08' N 54°10' E, 1,245.6 miles ENE
Pochayev	Pochayiv	50°01' N 25°29' E, 14.3 miles NW
Poltava	Poltava	49°35' N 34°34' E, 393.8 miles E
Priluk	Pryluky	50°36' N 32°24' E, 297.5 miles ENE
Proskurov	Khmel'nyts'kyy	49°25' N 27°00' E, 65.1 miles ESE
Radishkovits	Radoshkovichi, Belarus	54°09' N 27°15' E, 300.5 miles NNE
Rakov	Rakov, Belarus	53°58' N 27°04' E, 286.3 miles N
Rizh	Ryzh, Russia	57°48' N 56°10' E, 1,339.1 miles NE
Rovne, Rovno	Rivne	50°37' N 26°15' E, 54.2 miles NNE
Shavli	Šiauliai (Lithuania)	55°56' N 23°19' E, 427.1 miles NNW
Shepetovka	Shepetivka	50°11' N 27°04' E, 61.6 miles ENE
Shlonsk	Słońsk, Poland	52°54' N 18°47' E, 364.4 miles NW
Sokola	Sokolya	50°04' N 24°30' E, 56.7 miles WNW
Stanislavov	Ivano-Frankivs'k	48°55' N 24°43' E, 82.1 miles SW
Stary Lovechne	Lavochnoye	48°49' N 23°22' E, 130.7 miles SW
Starykonstantin	Starokostyantyniv	49°45' N 27°13' E, 66.1 miles E
Stolin	Stolin, Belarus	51°53' N 26°51' E, 145.5 miles NNE
Strigum	Støehom, Czech Republic	50°28' N 15°08' E, 470.6 miles W
Sverdlovsk	Yekaterinburg, Russia	56°51' N 60°37' E, 1,495.1 miles ENE
Svinyoche	Dzvinyacha	49°56' N 25°40' E, 4.4 miles WNW
Tashkent	Toshkent, Uzbekistan	41°19' N 69°15' E, 2,149.9 miles E
Teofipol	Teofipol'	49°50' N 26°25' E, 30.0 miles E
Ternopol	Ternopil'	49°33' N 25°35' E, 24.9 miles SSW

Tshan: see Teofipol

Tshernigov	Chernihiv	51°30' N 31°18' E, 266.6 miles ENE
Tshernovits	Chernivtsi	48°18' N 25°56' E , 110.8 miles S
Valbezhikh	Wałbrzych, Poland	50°46' N 16°17' E, 421.2 miles WNW
Verbovits	Verbovets	48°44' N 27°26' E, 382.7 miles W
Vinitse	Vinnytsya	49°14' N 28°29' E, 130.8 miles ESE
Vyshgorodok	Vyshgorodok	49°46' N 25°58' E, 13.3 miles SE
Vitkovits	Vitkovichi	51°03' N 26°46' E, 91.1 miles NNE
Yampoli	Yampil'	49°58' N 26°15' E, 22.7 miles ENE
Yanove	Jonava, Lithuania	55°05' N 24°17' E, 363.1 miles N
Yuzefuv	Yuzefuv	50°18' N 24°36' E, 57.9 miles WNW
Zaloshtshe	Zaliztsi	49°47' N 25°22' E, 18.9 miles WSW
Zagorodzye	Zagar'ye	49°52' N 25°25' E, 15.0 miles W
Zarudi	Zarud'ye	49°47' N 25°45' E, 8.1 miles S
Zaslav	Izyaslav	50°07' N 26°48' E, 48.9 miles ENE
Zbaraz, Zbarazh	Zbarazh	49°40' N 25°47' E,16.2 miles S
Zborov	Zboriv	49°40' N 25°09' E, 31.2 miles WSW
Zolsk	Khutor Zol'skiy, Russia	44°18' N 43°52' E, 932.3 miles ESE
Zvinatsh	Dzvynyach	48°45' N 24°25' E, 95.2 miles SW

Name Index

Please note that the page numbers are the page numbers of the original Yizkor Book, not this translation. That index is the very last section of this translation.

Name	Page number(s)
Aharonson, Aharon	192
Alef, M.	496, 530
Algirdas (Grand Duke of Lithuania)	16
Anotova	125
Asher-Yoel (father of Rabbi Moshe)	172
Averbukh, Avraham	418, 527
Averbukh, Eliyahu	276
Averbukh, Meir (see also Or, Meir)	10, 21, 136, 155, 220, 222, 228, 229, 238, 282, 428, 455, 493, 499, 523
Averbukh, Todros	418
Averbukh, Yosef	389
Avraham Yenkel (doctor)	389
Avrumche (cheder teacher)	160
Aytsikel, Chayim, R'	29, 160, 172
Ayzenberg	197
Ayzenberg, Shimon	25, 194 (photo), 194-195, 196, 197, 221, 469
Ayzenberg, Shlome	68, 145
Ayzenberg, Yakov	29, 180, 181
Ayzik (blacksmith)	101

Badasiuk, Gnadke	250, 251
Badasiuk, Yashke	391, 392
Balch, Shmuel	137
Balmelakhe, Duvid	155
Barak, A.	191
Baral, Chayim	501
Barbak, Berel	168
Barkay*, Leyeke (née Shpigelman)	226, 227
Barkay, Chayim Zev (see also Brik, Chayim Volf)	25, 147, 203, 226 (photo), 226-227
Barlas	273
Beker, Yente	167
Ben Yeshurun, Yakov (see also Kitaykesher, Yakov)	155, 161, 163
Benari	180
Ben-Chayim (husband of Sore Roynik)	233
Ben-Tsvi*, Sime (née Chachkis)	222, 224, 225
Ben-Tsvi, Azriel	225
Ben-Tsvi, Mordekhay, Rabbi (see also Blekh, Mordekhay)	224, 228
Ben-Tsvi, Yitschak (see also Shimshelevits, Yitschak)	191, 192, 219
Berel, son of Moshe Aron	124
Beren, Levi	168
Beren, Nachum	25, 111, 142, 155, 166, 168, 182, 199-201
Bernad, Shmuel	2
Berstovski	89
Betshinsky	171
Binyamin, Dvosi	98
Bisker (flourmill owner)	107
Bisker, Avraham	202 (photo), 202-203,
Bisker, Hirsh	499
Biteners, Mordekhay	391
Biteners, Simche Hirsh	387
Biv, Nitse	41

Blekh, Mordekhay, Rabbi (see also Ben-Tsvi, Mordekhay)	224, 228
Blinder, Azriel	155
Blum, Avraham	413
Brik*, Leye (née Shpigelman)	226, 227
Brik, Chayim Volf (see also Barkay, Chayim Zev)	25, 147, 203, 226 (photo), 226-227
Brimer, Menashe	52
Chabas, B.	175
Chachki	142
Chachkis, Henye	222, 224
Chachkis, Sime	222, 224, 225
Chachkis, Yakov	137, 154, 173, 180, 216
Chatski, Leyb	97
Chatski, Tova	155
Chatski, Yakov	137, 154, 173, 180, 216
Chaye-Tove (butcher's wife)	266
Chazan*, Bat-Sheve	27, 27 (photo), 282 (photo), 282-283
Chazan, M.	476, 486
Chazan, Yakov	93
Chazan, Zalman	27, 282 (photo), 282-283
Chezkelyovna (sisters)	141
Chinik	89
Choish, Kalman (see also Nek, Kalman)	107, 108, 109, 129, 247
Demidov, General	18
Derbarimdiker*, Nechame	281
Derbarimdiker, Batye	213
Derbarimdiker, Chayim	281
Derbarimdiker (family)	141
Derbarimdiker, Meir	54, 302
Derbarimdiker, Moshe, R'	281
Derbarimdiker, Yisrael	52
Dmitro	57
Dobrovitker, Kopel	142, 167, 179, 180

Dzhigen	121
Egosi*, Shoshana (née Zak)	540
Elyovich, Chayim	40
Emden (grandson of Yakov)	123
Emden, Yakov	123
Epshteyn, Yakov	243
Epshteyn, Zalman	243
Erlikh, Yosef (rabbi of Vishnevets)	53, 54, 62, 142, 143, 148, 182, 251
Fayerman, Avraham	167, 168
Fefer, Arye Leyb (Leybtsi)	167, 168, 181,183, 184 (photo), 184-185
Fefer, Rivke	167
Feldman*, Hentsi	251
Feldman (carpenter)	243
Feldman, Duvid	64, 257
Feldman, Hershel Duvid	58
Feldman, Moshe	251
Feldman, Niume	243
Feyge	165
Fishman, Kalman	109, 110
Fishman, Mikhel	510, 510 (photo)
Fishman, Mordekhay	296, 474
Fishman, Moshe	117
Fishman, Yakov	148
Frayer, Miryam	137, 507, 538
Frenkel, Ester	81, 82
Freylikh, Avraham Hirsh	484, 517
Freylikh, Yontel	517
Fridland (family)	191
Fridland, Sore (Sonye)	192
Froyke (teacher)	141, 142
Fuks*, Rachel (née Sobol)	79, 326
Furman	243

Gdalye "Gedoyle"   209

Geler, Avraham   156

Geler, Moshe Yosef   115, 117, 124

Geler, Shike (see also Ron, Yehoshue)   169, 207

Geler, Zeyde   163

Gilboa   194

Girany, Mengli   18

Gnip   111, 112

Gnip, Duvid   137

Gnip, Yisrael   53

Goldberg, Lipa   194, 197

Goldberg, Mikhael   232

Goldberg, Mordekhay   154, 194

Goldman, Aharon   154, 155, 243

Goldshteyn (public health nurse)   120

Goldshub, Moshe   60, 230 (photo), 230

Gomen, Commander   206

Gordon (flourmill owner)   221

Gorenshteyn   182

Gosol*, Batye (née Derbarimdiker)

Grenovski   26

Grinberg* (née Shimkovits)   64

Grinberg, Motye   64

Grinberg, Shimon (the Soldier)   64

Grinboym   148

Grinboym*, Fride (née Yakira)   73, 74

Grinboym, Shike   73

Grocholski   259

Grocholski, Baron   17

Grozinov (flourmill owner)   107, 108, 109, 168

Gruber, Avraham   107, 109, 110, 111, 112, 114, 129

Gruber, Chana   111, 112

Grubian, Motel   123

Guber, Avraham   107, 109, 110, 111, 112, 114, 129

Guber, Shmuel	107, 110
Gun, Idil (see also Hun, Idil)	124
Gur, Arye	135
Hadari*, Rachel (née Rozen)	216
Hadari, Izye	216
Hadari, Neta	216, 216 (photo)
Harpaz, Neta	192
Heker, Yitschak	174
Heler, Yom Tov Lipman (rabbi of Ludmir)	19
Hershel, son of Sender	170, 391
Hirsh Lekales	168
Holtser, Rozye	120
Honerchuk, Holanda	83
Hun, Idil (see also Gun, Idil)	124
Ingel (author)	123
Ivan	73
Ivan the Terrible	18
Jabotinsky, Zev	163
K., Yakov	153
Kagan, Reyzi	168
Kahan, Moshe	33
Kaminska, Ester-Rachel	167
Kamtsan, Y.	124
Kamtsen, Zeyde	425
Kantor, Shmuel	123
Kardash	120
Katsnelson, Dr.	19
Katz, Avraham Leyb	142, 142, 167
Katz, Avraham Yehuda	204 (photo), 204-205, 504
Katz, Cherne	271
Katz, Hershel	168
Katz, Tsvi	204
Katz, Yosef	205
Kecholy, Yitschak	196

Kechum, Mordekhay, R'   207-208

Kirshenboym*, Sore (née Kitaykesher)   72, 163, 336

Kirshenboym, Henik   77

Kitaykesher, Duvid   265

Kitaykesher, Gitel   168

Kitaykesher, Hersh   72

Kitaykesher, Sore   72, 163, 336

Kitaykesher, Yakov (see also Ben Yeshurun, Yakov)   155, 161, 163

Kitsis   192

Klayn, Yente   56

Kleynboym   148

Klinman, Aba   66

Koler, Tsvi   155

Kolmbren   86, 87

Koniecpolski, Mikolai, Count   18

Kopel   182

Koren, Mishe   8, 167, 291, 433, 438 (photo)

Korenfeld, Mendel   204

Korin   142, 182

Korin, Avraham Leyb   168

Korin, Chayim   114

Korin, Leyb   142

Kornfeld   142

Kornfeld*, Tsipora (née Shlayen)   145, 148 (photo), 164

Kornfeld, Chayim   391

Kornfeld, Shalom   155

Korybut, Dymitr   16, 18

Kovalski   251

Kovilis, Idel   70

Koylenberner (Judenrat leader)   68, 80, 254

Krasnov, Zev   25

Kraus   74

Kremenetski, Makhlye   515, 515 (photo)

Krigsehver, Mitye   110

Krigsehver, Yakov   110

Kubrik*, Miryam Leye (née Shatski)   191

Kubrik*, Sore (Sonye) (née Fridland)   192

Kubrik, Azriel   191 (photo), 191-193, 197, 219

Kubrik, Moshe Aharon   191

Kuts (family)   267

Landesberg, Dr.   65, 253

Landoy, Dr.   26

Layter, Alter   68, 81, 256

Layter, Malke   167

Layter, Noske   130

Lerer   243

Lerer, Duvid   142

Lerner   137, 243

Leshed, Moshe (see also Markhbeyn, Moshe)   160, 161 (photo)

Lev, Avraham   335, 352

Levanon*, Sonya (née Shats)   30, 126, 393

Levi Yitschak, Rabbi   141, 281

Leyzer (barber)   120

Lifishuv   82

Lifshits   85, 111

Lifshits (brothers)   112

Lifshits (family)   111

Lifshits, Shimon   107, 109

Lintil   182

Livushke (cheder teacher)   160

Losgos, Yehoshue   120

Lyoyita   154

M., M.   275

Maltseyev   388

Marchbeyn, Chaye   222

Marchbeyn, Hirsh   244

Marchbeyn, Yakov (Yekil)   67, 68, 256, 265,267, 268

Margaliot, Hershel   68, 267, 389, 390, 391

Margaliot, Tsvi	265
Margalit, Yehuda	107, 382
Markhbeyn*, Eti Rachel	267
Markhbeyn, F.	155
Markhbeyn (family)	267
Markhbeyn, Moshe (see also Leshed, Moshe)	160, 161 (photo)
Markhbeyn, Yakov (Yekil)	67, 68, 256, 265, 267, 268
Matis (son of Rivke)	111, 112
Mazur	124
Mazur, Beni	68, 268
Mazur, Chayim Hirsh (Tsvi)	141, 168
Mazur, Y.	119, 353
Mazur, Zisa	256
Meir	182, 185
Meliv*, Miryam (née Frayer)	137, 507, 538
Melksnits (tailor)	266
Mendelboym, Duvid	168
Mikhilo	73
Mikolski	74, 77
Miler	87, 112
Miler, Tsvi	124
Mindzar, Vasil	268
Mishne, Avitsur	213
Mishne, Betsalel	213, 213 (photo)
Mniszech, Marina	17
Mniszech, Michal Wandalin	17
Mofshit*, Dora	145, 146
Mofshit, Chave	243
Mofshit, Chayke	168
Mofshit, Ozer	145
Mofshit, Yisrael	168
Monomakh, Prince	11
Mormits, Zigmunt, Dr.	16
Moshe (training kibbutz member)	165

Moshe Aharon (yeshiva teacher)	160
Moshe Aron, father of Berel	124
Moshe, R' (son of Asher-Yoel)	172
Nek, Kalman (see also Choish, Kalman)	107, 108, 109, 129, 247
N--s, Y.	206, 243
Nudel, G.	111, 379
Nudel, Yakov	173
Ochitel	123
Olshteyn*, Bat-Sheve	281
Or, Meir (see also Averbukh, Meir)	1, 10, 21, 136, 155, 220, 222, 228, 229, 238, 282, 287, 428, 455, 493, 499, 523
Or, Sore	199
Orlovich, Mstislav, Dr.	16
Osherovits, Hirsh	123
Osterer, Sore	207, 208
Osterers, Duvid (see also Rotenberg, Duvid)	142
Ostrovski, Yakub	54, 60, 61, 113, 137, 251, 302
Parnas, Louis	516 (photo)
Pawel I	17, 18
Piotrkovski, Yozef, Dr.	16
Plater, Andrzhei, Baron	16
Plotkin, Yakov	219
Poslevski	60
Presman	182
R., Ts.	240
Rabin*, Cherne (née Katz)	271
Rabin, Chayim	1, 11, 12, 284, 287, 401, 408
Rabin, Moshe	181
Rabin, Yitschak	181, 222, 229
Rachmani, Shlome (see also Derbarimdiker, Shlome)	281
Radiviler, Yosele, Rabbi	14, 34, 275
Ratman, Louis	471

Remez, Duvid   194

Reyzels, Chayim   173, 181

Reyzels, Shmuel   124

Reyzels, Yitschak (see also Verdi, Yitschak)   155, 172, 175, 181

Rivke (fish seller)   111

Romel   85

Ron, Y.   147, 207, 209

Ron, Yehoshue (see also Geler, Shike)   1, 169, 287

Ron, Yone   10, 167, 189, 272

Rotenberg, Duvid (see also Osterers, Duvid)   142

Rotman, Simche Ayzik, R'   22, 224, 275 (photo), 275-277, 278, 280

Roynik*, Zelde (née Shniribeker)   197

Roynik, Duvid   25, 197-198, 198 (photo), 220 (photo), 220-221, 231, 514

Roynik, Sore   232-234

Roynik, Tsvi   141

Roytkoytel, Niuni   117

Roytman, Louis   25

Rozen, Rachel   216

Rozenberg, Avraham   39, 137

Rozenberg, Gdalye   93-96, 346

Rozenberg, Manya   94, 95

Rozenberg, Mendel   93, 94, 95

Rozenboym, Avraham   124

Rozenhek, Sh.   25, 143

Rozental*, Chane Malke, Grandma   189 (photo), 189-190, 493

Rozental*, Ester (née Zbarizher)   189

Rozental*, Sore   231, 231 (photo)

Rozental, Moshe   391

Rozental, Tikve   231

Rozental, Tova   168

Rozental, Yankel-Barukh   189, 189 (photo)

Rozental, Yehuda   231, 231 (photo)

Rozental, Yisrael 189

Rozental, Yitschak 149

Rozin, Yehuda 204

Rozumny (Torah reader) 208

Ruach, Alter 61, 247

Ruach, Makhtsi 61, 247

Sana (see also Kleynboym) 148

Schiffer, Y., Dr. 11, 12

Segal, Hersh Matis 97

Segal, Moshe 1, 10, 97, 287, F380363

Senders, Elkane 149

Sendler, Rachel 64, 252

Servetnik, Nisan 154, 181

Servetnik, Yerachmiel 129, 130, 168

Shag (flourmill owner) 107, 112

Shag, Eliezer 181

Shag, Yudke 56

Shapiro 137

Shapiro (ritual slaughterer) 79

Shapiro, Chayke (ritual slaughterer's daughter) 79

Shapiro, Rozye 168, 181

Shapiro, Yehuda (Idel) 25, 142, 143, 143 (photo), 147, 203, 513, 513 (photo)

Shapiro, Yosef 67, 111

Shapoval (chief of police) 251, 254

Shats, Eliezer 126, 127

Shats, Sonya 30, 126, 393

Shatski, Miryam Leye 191

Shatski, Yosef 525

Sherer, Bentsi 266

Sheyner, Nurit 41

Sheyner, Sh. 514

Sheyngold, Yakov 472

Sheynke, Feyge 168

Shimkovits, Avraham	64
Shimon Chayim Shimon's	388, 391
Shimshelevits, Tsvi	191
Shimshelevits, Yitschak (see also Ben-Tsvi, Yitschak)	191
Shlayen, Tsipora	145, 164
Shniribeker, Moshe, R'	197
Shniribeker, Zelde	197
Shpigelman, Leye	226, 227
Shpiglman (family)	111
Shpilberg	273
Shprintsak	273
Shtayger	26, 55
Shteyn, Shike	119
Shteynberg, Moshe	152
Shulder, Feyge	168
Shumakher	121
Shvarts, Shaul	84-92
Shvats (teacher)	155
Shvedki, Yevdokim	59
Sirota, Gershon	208
Sklod*, Tikve (née Rozental)	231
Slutski	273
Sobol, Hene	56
Sobol, Motel	53
Sobol, Rachel	79, 326
Sobol, Rivke	56
Sobol, Zev	52, 137, 138, 298
Sofer*, Lola	237
Sofer (brothers)	235
Sofer, Asher	163, 240, 240 (photo), 240, 271-274
Sofer, Dov	173
Sofer, Issakher	62, 238, 247, 272

Sofer, Leyb   115
Sofer, Moshe   115
Sofer, Motil   115 130
Sofer, Shlome   273
Sofer, Yakov   238 (photo), 238-239
Sofer, Yoel   273
Sofer, Yosef   237, 237 (photo), 273
Sore   10
Spirt, Yosef   271
Stanislaw August, King   12, 17, 18
Storozh   113
Sudman   243
Tabenkin   154
Tenenboym   168, 243
Tenenboym, Barukh   53
Tenenboym, Moshe   53
Tenenboym, Sender   53
Tenenboym, Yakov   129, 168
Ternikov (see also Tirnikov)   141, 168
Teslier, Yokil   266
Teyer, A. Y.   247
Tirnikov (see also Ternikov)   141, 168
Todros (family)   111
Tsimberg, Lusik   149
Tsimbler, Avraham   67, 68, 86, 250, 252
Tsimbler, Yone   64
Tsinberg, Eliezer   148, 148 (photo), 202-203
Tsinberg, T.   111
Tsinberg, Yosef, Dr.   53, 54
Tsitrin, Yenkel   387
Tsizen   243
Tsur, Ben-Tsion (Bentsi)   214 (photo), 214-215
Tsvik, Avraham   132
Tsvik, Menashe (Moisey Abramovits)   132, 244

Valdman, Mikhael   244

Valdman, Moshe   245

Vanka (the redhead)   105

Vasye   64, 65, 71

Vaynman*, Makhlye (née Kremenetski)   515, 515 (photo)

Vays, Zioma   79

Vaytsman (family)   250

Veloshin   67

Venshil, Moshe   264

Venshitska-Kreshitska, Yohana   72, 76, 77

Verdi, Chayim   157-159

Verdi, Yitschak (see also Reyzels, Yitschak) 155, 157, 172, 175

Vilinski   113

Vilsker, Leybel   155

Vitels, Avraham   206

Volinsky, Ivan   389

Volk (school principal)   142, 168

Wisniowiecki, Jeremi   16, 17

Wisniowiecki, Korybut   18

Wisniowiecki, Michal Serwacy   18

Wisniowiecki, Oginska   18

Wisniowiecki, Prince   35

Wisniowiecki, Soltan   18

Witold, Prince   18

Wojtskovski (president of Poland)   26

Y., Ch.   179

Yafe, Dr.   192

Yafe, Edna   49, 295

Yakira, Efraim   170

Yakira, Fride   73, 74

Yakira, Shike   85, 251, 265

Yakira, Yakov   168

Yakov (son of Rabbi Yitschak)   39

Yanko   76

Yehoshue	112
Yenkevits	75
Yentil	183
Yingerleyb, Meir Nachum (last rabbi of Vishnevets)	49, 51 (photo)
Yisrael Feygeles (town judge)	70
Yitschak (brother of Leyzer the barber)	120
Yitschak, Rabbi	39
Yonitsman, Dr.	273
Yuger, Tsvi	60, 138
Zak*, Hentsye (née Zeyger)	1, 150, 237, 287,
Zak, Shoshana	149, 540
Zak, Simche	147, 228 (photo), 228-229
Zaltsman (family)	165
Zamoyska, Urszula	17
Zbarizher, Ester	189
Zelber, Pati	243
Zelber, Zelde	243
Zeyger, Chaskel	168
Zeyger, Fanye Chaskelovna	168
Zeyger, Hentsye	149, 540
Zeyger, Mordekhay	151
Zeyger, Yehoshue	222, 223, 224, 420, 420 (photo)
Zimbel, Moti	64
Zinger, Kopel	208
Zinger, Mendel	84
Zinger, Yehuda	168

[flyleaf]

Map of the Town of Vishnevets

Reconstructed from memory by Moshe Segal (son of Hersh Matis)

[**Translation Editor's Note:** This map, which appears on the flyleaf of Sefer Vishnevets, shows the town with Jewish and other landmarks during the early Nazi era, around 1941-1942.]

Key

Ghetto gate   Ghetto boundaries

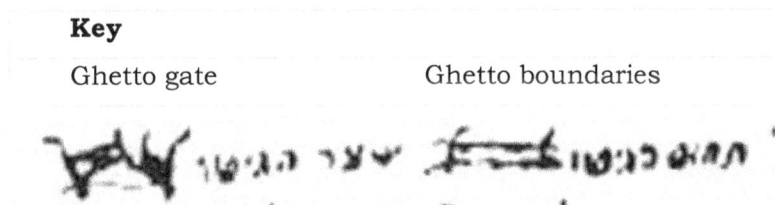

(1) The Great Synagogue

(2) Synagogues

(3) The rabbi's house and the yeshiva

(4) Tarbut School

(5) Talmud Torah school

(6) Hekdesh (poor house)

(7) Little bridge

(8) Bathhouse

(9) Cemetery

(10) Small cemetery

(11) Butcher shop

(12) Boulevard

(13) Guards

(14) Flourmill

(15) Town Hall

(16) Church

(17) Community center (Polish: gamine)

(18) Post office

(19) Castle

(20) Embankment/dam

(21) Old town

(22) Mass grave

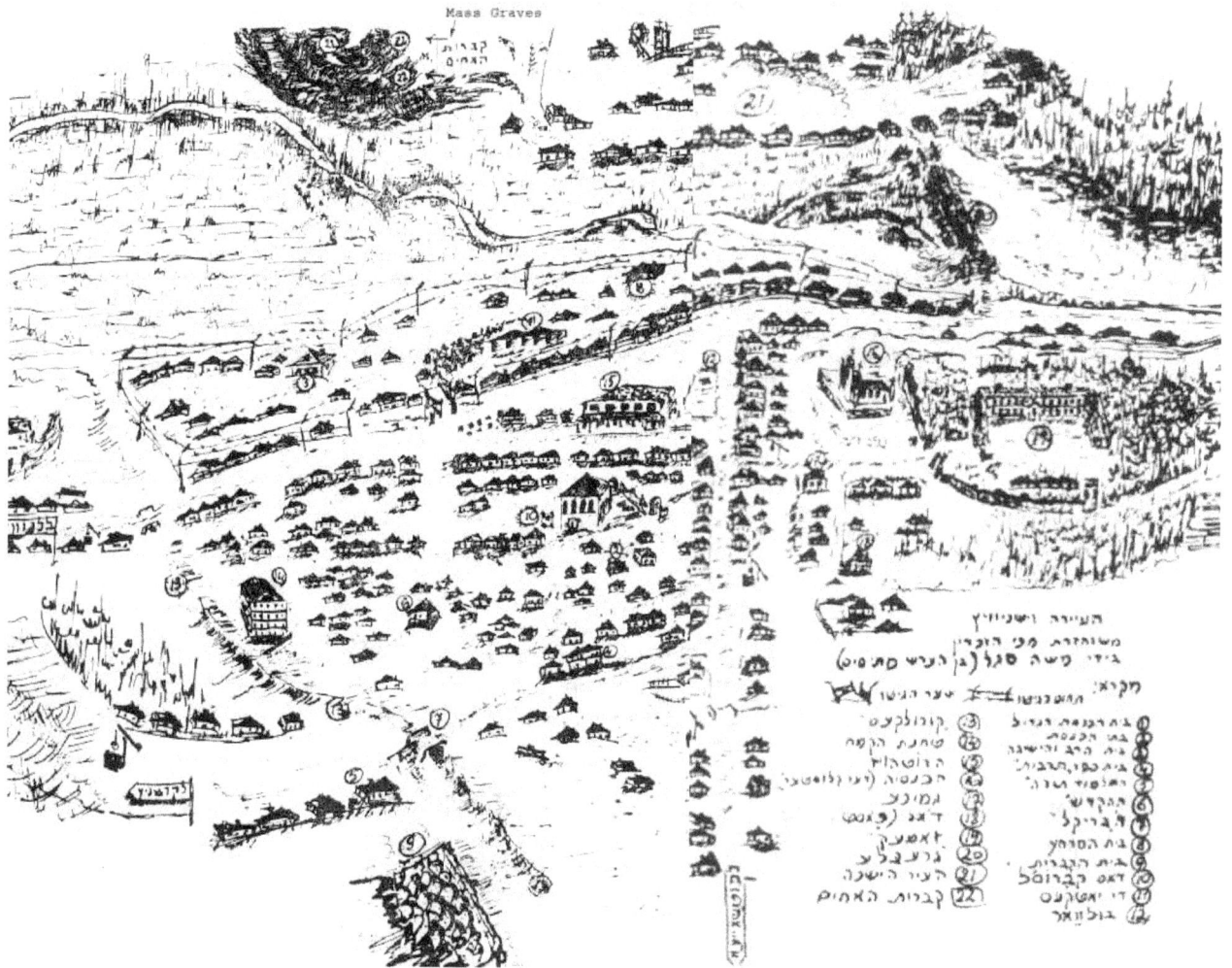

[**Translator's Note**: The Hebrew text at the top middle of the left page, *kvarot achim*, means "brothers' graves", a mass burial site. The map shows the location of the mass graves. The sign at the bottom left of the left page shows the road to Kremenets. The sign about 1/3 of the way up from the left bottom of the left page points to Lanovits. The sign at the bottom of the right page shows the road to Pochayev.]

[Page 7]

Note from the Editorial Board
English Translation by Aviv Small

For a year and a half, we worked to bring the idea of this book to fruition.

We attempted to cover all aspects of Vishnevets and its martyrs so that the book will illuminate the town and its people, who envisioned a good and fruitful society and established its institutions for the betterment of that society.

We wanted to bring to light ...

[Translation Editor's Note: The remainder of this page has not been translated.]

[Page 8]

Several sections of the book relate the history of the village as it is known through historical research and its beloved citizens' lives. Among them are people whose characters represent the jewels of values and ethics – a certain purity of soul that lived and walked in Vishnevets and lent the town the human charm that characterized the last days before its destruction. Those were the days in which death was imminent and unavoidable. Thus, this book becomes the last testimony of the holy community of Vishnevets, which should never be forgotten, as well as an enduring blemish on those who helped bring down the butcher's knife on it – those who found pleasure and delight in torturing the finest of people.

This book will be useful to researchers of communities, history, and society as a meticulous and comprehensive diary.

As a testimony written in blood and tears, the book will also serve those who research the annals of the hideous crime perpetrated by one nation against another.

Nor have we forgotten to include sections that perpetuate the memory of those who died for the sake of our nation.

We would like to thank everyone who participated in this venture and helped overcome its difficulties. Thanks to these individuals, this book has become a treasure of combined effort, and all credit is due to them.

We would like to ask forgiveness in advance for any mistakes or oversights that have inevitably found their way into the book, as those are part and parcel of a venture that is the work of many and that encompasses so many pages and such a broad scope of time.

We, in turn, forgive those witnesses of the disaster who could not participate in the making of this book; we understand their reasons, and they are excused.

Finally, we thank Mishe Koren, a Vishnevets survivor living in Argentina, who contributed his memories of Vishnevets and, in so doing, contributed a dimension of its spiritual splendor. His role in the book is of the utmost importance.

We also would like to thank our colleagues in the Vishnevets Society of the United States, who made every effort to facilitate our financial needs in publishing the book and also presented us with a unique chapter for the book, without which the picture of Vishnevets would not have been complete.

Bravo to the people of Vishnevets in America; you have shown us that Vishnevets and its people are still alive in your hearts even after so many decades. Thank you for enabling us to build this tome of remembrance to our martyrs.

It is not an easy undertaking to ask people who must do the daily chores of human existence to add hours upon hours of work recounting and remembering in order to bring our village, its people, and its society to life through these pages. It was even more difficult to convince those who witnessed the Holocaust – those who experienced firsthand in their souls and on their bodies the very things they long to forget – to go back and tell their story. Those moments of remembrance brought waves of shock, fear, and horror along with them.

For all who put their shoulders to the task of making this book happen, this has been a period of much effort and soul searching. But a deep consciousness of the need for the book helped us along our difficult path. Finally, we see the book as a culmination of much effort and many questions that at times seemed to be more difficult to answer than …

[Translation Editor's Note: The remainder of this page has not yet been translated.]

[Page 9]

Note from the Organization of Vishnevets Immigrants
English Translation by Sara Mages

[Translation Editor's Note: This section has not yet been translated.]

[Page 10]

***

A person who engages in the creation of a memorial book immerses himself in a continually painful autumn that separates him from the reality of life in our country's spring, and melancholy is his constant companion.

Therefore, a memorial book is created only by talented individuals with a deep sense of responsibility to their generation – a generation of children to the destroyed generation of parents, and we bless their emotions.

One individual whose excellent work is in this book is Meir Or, who showed initiative and energy and did not rest until he had found material on all the topics covered here. Thanks to him, the fearful, majestic book project began, and thanks to him, it ended.

As an editor, I want to thank him for helping me, but as a man who has invested many years in creating a memorial to those who conceal their painful memories, I send all the best wishes of all our organization's members to Meir, a beloved man from Vishnevets who is loyal to her memory.

And Yehoshue Ron, who provided his services to this book and took part in our mission, is also counted among the blessed.

And along with those two, blessings to Moshe Segal, whose gifts and talent added a personal touch and substance to the book.

To the women who brought about this book, Sore and Yone, a special blessing for their efforts and for understanding the importance of the book.

Those who assume the lead in and dedicate themselves to such a weighty, intense mission are few. Therefore, in keeping with public opinion and in the names of the martyrs memorialized by this book, we are inspired to bless them in the pages of this book, since their part in it is the reason for its existence and a part of its contents.

[Page 11 - Hebrew] [Page 11 - Yiddish]

Vishnevets

Vishnevets in Original Sources and Sefer Vishnivits
By Chayim Rabin

Introduction

Everything written about Vishnevets in the source material applies to New Vishnevets, meaning that this is what the book deals with. But since Jewish settlement originally began in Old Vishnevets, we need to see the two of them as having one successive demography. Their stages of historical change also included certain geographical changes in that the settlement moved from a hill to a valley, or vice versa, in the same location. This is not unique in the history of Jewish and non-Jewish towns.

The Polish sources available are very lean in the Jewish details that are the main focus of our review. All we can do is rely on chronological facts by comparing dates in order to draw Jewish information out of them. However, each historical research project is a large foundation of theories and estimations built by comparing and combining occurrences, and there is no history without such research.

History and Sources

According to Universal Encyclopedia, "the [fortress] was built in 1395," but "the town itself and its daughters are mentioned for the first time in 1494."

Also, Guide to Volin sees the end of the 14th century as the year that "the town of New Vishnevets was established near the village of Old Vishnevets."

Volin is mentioned in history as the main section of Belorussia (see Schiffer), settled by Jews organized into communities. The most prominent was the community of Ludmir, which existed next to the oldest community, Kiev, from the 10th century on.

Two prominent dates that brought changes in the Jewish settlement in Volin also formed the character of the Jews who lived there. The first date is 1113, the year of Prince Monomakh of Kiev's riot, which caused the exile of Kiev's Jews. In the second year, 1169, the kingdom of Kuzaria was destroyed, causing a panicked migration of Jews from the kingdom's boundaries into the liberal Polish principality's lap, which opposed the Catholic Church and brought Jews from Germany to serve as agents to develop agriculture.

While the stream of migration from Kiev brought Jews who were expert in finance and agriculture, the Kuzari stream brought farmers who worked the land and land tenants.

As we know, both groups enriched the Polish principalities of Mazovia, Koivia, and Little Poland. They became a desirable element in all the developing principalities, mostly the Polish principalities in Ukraine, where they served as tax collectors and estate agents on the farms of the Polish princes, who regarded them as a link and gateway between themselves and the oppressed Ukrainians, who outnumbered them.

[Page 12]

Therefore, we can assume that persecuted Jews also arrived in Vishnevets and laid the foundation for an urban settlement, which in many cases was the only form of Jewish municipality in Polish Ukraine (Belorussia). Both sources mentioned above talk about "the town and its daughters" and the "town next to the village," hinting at a Jewish settlement next to the village and its daughters, etc.

There is no written history for the abovementioned years, because, as we know, there is no written history for that part of the world, only historical facts mentioned here and there. These facts enable researchers to peek inside the events of those days in those countries, and their time period overlaps the period of this review.

Therefore, one can assume that Jewish Vishnevets put down roots in the area at the end of the 11th or 12th century, just as all of Volin's Jewry did. As Dr. Y. Schiffer notes, "Jewish migration from Kuzaria streamed here [to Polish Ukraine-Ch. R.] during the Kuzri kingdom era and its destruction. Jewish settlements began to grow during the 11th or 12th centuries at the latest" (The Jewish Economy 218/50).

In any case, Jewish Vishnevets is already mentioned in 1597 as a town that left a great impression on contemporaneous Jewish life (I am referring to Register of the Council of Four Lands). The fact that "the meeting" of the "leaders of the four holy communities in the Volin district"-that is to say, Ludmir, Kremenets, Lutsk, and Ostra-took place here (Register of the Council of Four Lands) proves two important, relevant facts: (1) Vishnevets was an important market town, and the meetings of the Council of the Four Lands took place only during a fair and only in the venues of large fairs (Lublin, Krakow, Lutsk, and so on). (2) There was a structure in Vishnevets fit to house such a meeting, meaning a respected rabbinate's community hall. Neither of these conditions for such a meeting blossoms overnight. We must understand that they are the result of the longstanding existence of a Jewish community. They are evidence that the market town-with an organized community, a respected rabbinate, and a site for an extensive interdistrict meeting- was not built overnight.

A very interesting incident took place in 1781, when the town's rabbi welcomed King Stanislaw August with an excited speech in Latin. What is interesting is that there was a rabbi in Vishnevets who could give a speech in Latin in that year and a community that employed such a rabbi. But the most interesting point is that Polish sources repeatedly mention it in the Polish Encyclopedia, which was under Catholic influence and financed by the church. This rabbi had authority, from their point of view, and if he held the rabbinical chair in Vishnevets, it was a sign that the town deserved him.

According to a Jewish census conducted 1765, "the community registered 475 Jews in Old Vishnevets, 26 in New Vishnevets, and 163 in the surrounding villages." In addition, in the spring, 1,653 Vishnevets Jews were slaughtered, and their homes were destroyed with the Tatars' return from Berestechko (Jewish Encyclopedia).

[Page 13]

We can therefore say for sure that an established, rooted Jewish community existed in Vishnevets in the 17th century. That was also the location of the Tatars' hostile acts after their defeat in Berestechko, and the numbers mentioned above are not only a sign that the place and its name attracted Jews to return and settle there.

In 1847, "the Jewish community of Vishnevets" [emphasis added-Ch. R.] numbered 3,178 persons. This community was equal in importance and size to communities of 300 or 400 during the 13th and 14th centuries (Rupin, History of Jewish Sociology), which were then considered "large communities."

Vishnevets in Sefer Vishnevets

This book is actually the last record of the town, and it seals her existence with one of grief. From this book alone one can learn about this community from the last trustworthy source. Since the editors of this book made sure to examine the material brought to them-even on descriptive, emotional, and spiritual matters-and test its accuracy, we can use the facts scattered in this material as a foundation for writing about the history of Vishnevets before its destruction.

The great majority of those who participated in writing this book are imbued with love, trust, passion, and honesty, and one can say that the grace of the place and its people is evident in all its Jewish residents' deeds. Its special landscape, the great Horyn River, the forest, and the palace, all of which are "gentile," so to speak, added a special character to its Jewry.

Here stood a Jewry with a faith like that of all others, as the saying goes, "How lovely is this tree, etc., and it is bound in his soul," but it can't ignore the scenery, and it absorbs moisture from it. The light and trees stimulate its soul's senses and take hold of its spiritual being. This palace illustrates a man's need of to reach his summit, and its loftiness, splendor, and power accompanied each Jew in Vishnevets from early childhood.

This Jewry could not remain wrung out and dehydrated from the entire "world of delusions" when the good landscape and its loftiness took hold of their senses and formed a different Jewish conception of heavenly devotion.

The only thing that could have happened here is a Jewry composed of Jews who, though devoted to their Judaism, had a childhood imbued with beauty and scenery, which allowed them to avoid everything belonging to today's world. And so the problems of the Jews, in regard to the Jewish world and its future, can reflect only its community's needs.

Therefore, we find here a reverent, integrated Jewry, which reinforces its belief by separating itself from national values, and therefore it has no attachment to extreme separatism and its piety.

[Page 14]

Therefore, an earthy state of mind arises here, a brother to the particular Jewish nature that does not allow extreme Jewish winds to blow here. They share their fate and help each other, but they do not force their opinions on each other, because anyone who harbors warm memories of his childhood in his soul cannot be tied down by the ropes of dry tradition and fossilization of the senses. A new kind of Judaism of friendship and unity characterized by the earthliness mentioned above is created here.

Therefore, the young people here also love their childhood landscape. They are powerless and angry because the landscape and palace were taken away from them and given over to the control of others. This same palace and its gardens are theirs in their soul, and when they find them suddenly locked, they rebel, and drama storms their soul. They are bound on one hand by their love of the place, where they can live if allowed to do so, and on the other by the need to live without it. It fathers the longing to create places like these that will always be wholly and entirely theirs. The two intertwined, rose, and set in motion hidden forces searching for salvation. And this formed the foundation and background for an active Zionist movement. It is nothing but national stabilization, a connection between man and his maker, and there is no power in the world that can unbind it. And it is in the language of our tangible Zionism, which is the opposite of messianic Zionism.

Every once in a while, and only on rare occasions, we find Hasidic uprisings in Vishnevets, but we do not find a closed piety that brings argument and hatred. We find a rabbi and judge there, but the two men did not gain control of those institutions as a result of division and quarrel between brothers. Also, in their so-called theoretical arguments, practicality takes over, and the calm landscape lowers your stature and silences any desire for conflict and pride; you become well liked when you are kind to the place.

We do not find stormy synagogues, exaggeration of the value of the book, and the need to escape and find refuge in it. Reading it here is within the limits, not above it.

And we find an effervescent generation of young people who tied themselves to the most influential Zionist movement in their town. They are passionate, and they express their passion by participating in organized activities, establishing organizations and movements, collecting money for national foundations, and staging shows, but above all, they nurture their bodies and physical fitness in order to physically wrestle with those who stole their landscape and the fortresses of their childhood, and they wrestle with them at every opportunity. The wrestling is not Jewish morality, and moral victory followed. The young people of Vishnevets express their anger in an almost non-Jewish way, and this is their distinction.

However, the book before us deals with a particular town and particular Jews. The villages extend to the town and its business as one organic existence. There is no wide separation between the two ethnic groups' lifestyles; there are Jews who deal with agriculture, and their attachment to the land and its growth is more natural than that of the area's gentiles. There is no devotion to rabbis, teachers, and judges as people who invade your thoughts, turn your emotions away from you, and drown your energy in a sea of legends and miracles. Also, R' Yosele Radiviler and his life story are discussed here in an earthy, logical way, stripped of all the trappings of wonder and legend that appear in other towns.

[Page 15]

The Vishnevets community was earthy and concrete, her people were people of action, and her public life was saturated with a strong desire for a simple, tangible life.

Circumstances based on racial stupidity and hatred also shocked this Jewry, and she tore herself from her home and looked forward to a national future.

When the great insanity erupted along with the Jewish Holocaust, the destroyer found here a town that was ready to uproot itself of its own will toward a better world and wanted only the time to decide for itself where this world was and what image it would have. There was no need to uproot it, because it would do that itself in time, if allowed to.

And before it wanted to uproot itself from here for her benefit and that of its dark neighbors, he came and uprooted it from her roots, without historical necessity or justification.

So the Nazis' crime grew and increased in the light of Jewish Vishnevets, as in the light of other similar towns, and turned into an abomination that will never be forgiven.

[Page 406 - Yiddish]

Beloved Youth of Vishnevets

[Page 16]

Guide to Volin
By Dr. Mstislav Orlovich

Sources:

Antiquities of Volin, by Dr. Zigmunt Mormits

Art and Antiquities of Volin, by Dr. Yozef Piotrkovski

Originally written in 1923 and published in 1929

...In the wide lowland of the upper Horyn, 22 kilometers from Kremenets, lies the town of Vishnevets, with its 3,500 residents.

...The road from Kremenets to Vishnevets is not very impressive. It passes over the foot of the Podolia highland through wide, fertile fields that are bare of trees or forests. At the midpoint of the road, we pass the village of Horinka, from which flows the Horyn River, the biggest and most beautiful river in Volin.

...You can see Vishnevets only after you reach the last mountain before the town. As we descend deep into the valley, the town that appears is very picturesque, and the Formalitic Church steeple towers over the roofs of the small buildings.

History

Vishnevets is the base of the mighty principality of the Wisniowiecki family, which originated from Prince Dymitr Korybut, son of Algirdas.

At the end of the 14th century, he established the town of New Vishnevets next to the village of Old Vishnevets. The Vishnevets estates belonged to that family until its decline after the death of Vilna district governor Michal Serwacy, who died in 1744. Vishnevets and all property belonging to the Wisniowiecki family passed as a dowry from his granddaughter, Katarzyna, to the Mniszech family. This matter consolidated the families during the second half of the 18th century. The estates remained in the hands of the Mniszech family until the beginning of the 19th century, when they were transferred to the Plater family, and in 1852 Vishnevets and its offshoots were sold by Baron Andrzhei Plater to the Russians.

The Wisniowiecki principality extended to about 900 square kilometers and included a number of towns and 16 villages.

Vishnevets is located on the higher north shore of the Horyn, which created a number of large lakes at the base of the town. Most are marshy and muddy, and twisted water plants grow in them. The town follows the pattern of Kremenets and Pochayev, in that it consists of a row of ancient buildings that are typical of 18th- and 19th-century residential buildings in Volin. These buildings were built in the Classical or Imperial style. They are made of wood and covered with bricks on the outside. Their roofs are high, and their magnificent façades have balconies and railings. The cottages that encircle the market and extend to its side alleyways are among the most beautiful in Volin.

The Palace

The most expensive antiquity in Vishnevets is the palace. It was built by Michal Serwacy Wisniowiecki in 1720 on the ruins of Jeremi Wisniowiecki's old defensive castle. At first, the structure was built in late Baroque style.

[Page 17]

In the Mniszech era, the palace was extended and rebuilt in the rococo style. As indicated by the memorial tablet in the main vestibule, the expansion of the palace was finished in 1781 and was financed by Michal Wandalin Mniszech and his wife, Urszula, of the Zamoyski family. At that time, the halls were redone with impressive decorations and furnishings in the traditional style of the Stanislaw August period. The Mniszech family also held a famous painting exhibit there.

The entry hall, staircase, and upper ballroom were decorated with 4,500 Dutch Delft porcelain tiles. In one of the halls was a series of portraits of Polish kings and other famous personalities. The mirrored rococo hall, the dining hall, a number of halls in the upper floor, and the library, with cabinets covered with paintings and portraits, were brilliantly appointed. Memorial plates hang the rooms where Stanislaw August and Pawel I once stayed.

Until the second half of the 19th century, when the palace was in the hands of the Poles, it was a substantial royal palace, and few of its style existed in Poland, but under Russian rule it slowly began to decay.

The contents of Marina Mniszech's famous art gallery were sold to Kiev and Moscow, and most of the palace's artistic beauty was removed with it. Most of the remaining art collections were saved by General Demidov, the palace's owner at the beginning of the 20th century. Although he was Russian, he showed respect for the history and art of Vishnevets. During World War I, Baron Grocholski purchased the estates and the palace.

.... In 1920, during the Bolshevik invasion, the palace was completely destroyed, its glory was stolen, and only its naked walls remained. The remaining artistic decorations and expensive collections were looted, and the Dutch porcelain tiles on the upper floor were also pulled out.

After the war, the Kremenets District Committee purchased the palace for $40,000, renovated the building, and turned it into a trade school, orphanage, and hospital.

.... The palace garden, which was planted on top of the hill that overlooks the Horyn River and covered around 3,000 dunam, was one of the most beautiful gardens in Volin.

The palace standing on the site of the Wisniowieckis' fortress and its ramparts and dugouts are still there today. The king's father, Prince Jeremi Wisniowiecki, was born in the fortress. In 1640, he created the palace garden on the site of the fortress. The garden was completely destroyed in 1672 by the Turks, who also pulled out the roots of the town's residents.

On the opposite shore of the Horyn River is the town of Old Vishnevets, a village with a population of 1,900 that replaced the old settlement.

[Page 18]

Vishnevets (History and Description)
Encyklopedia Powszechna

Historical Facts

1. *Universal Encyclopedia* (1867 edition)

...a town in the Volin region, Kremenets district, located on the right shore of the Horyn River between two big dams (lakes).... It is famous for its ancient fortress, and its history is tightly connected with the history of the famous Korybut Wisniowiecki principality.

The fortress, next to which the town of Vishnevets was built, was erected in 1395 by Dymitr Korybut, the Sewacy prince who was exiled by Prince Witold. He received agricultural land in Volin from him, and he established his chain of generations there.

Some connect the building of the fortress and the house of Wisniowiecki to his great-grandson, whose name was Soltan.

The town itself and its offshoots appear only in the light of burning wars. It is mentioned for the first time in 1494, when a small Polish unit was defeated by Crimean Tatars.

In 1500, Ivan the Terrible was told that the Tatars had destroyed his towns, including Vishnevets, which they had completely burned, and that they had captured 5,000 people from the surrounding area.

The same chronicles recount that in 1502, 9,000 Tatars under the command of Mengli Girany's sons destroyed the area around Vishnevets with fire and sword, but Vishnevets is not mentioned in the report on the area.

Only on April 28, 1512, did the Poles repay the Tatars for the two defeats: a Polish army of 6,000 under the command of Count Mikolai Koniecpolski penetrated the lines of the Tatars' 24,000-man army, which was camping near Vishnevets, next to Lopuszyna. They killed many and took 16,000 as prisoners.

After that, the enemy did not dare approach Vishnevets's fortified walls for more than 100 years.

In 1672, the fortress was rebuilt by Jeremi Wisniowiecki after it fell into the Turks' hands because of the Jews' betrayal (so to speak).

In 1781, after the death of Michal Serwacy, the last of the Wisniowiecki family, the estate was given to his daughters, Oginska and Zamoyska.

In October-November 1781, King Stanislaw August visited Vishnevets during the months to conduct talks with Prince Pawel of Russia. It is mentioned here that the town's rabbi welcomed him with a passionate speech in Latin.

In 1867, we find Vishnevets described as a town built of wood, rich in trade, and poor in industry. There was one fabric factory and a number of tanneries. Five thousand citizens were registered.

The fortress, which was rebuilt in 1720, contained a very rich collection of paintings and sculptures as well as a library rich in very important manuscripts.

[Page 19]

2. Jewish Encyclopedia, edited by Dr. Katsnelson and published in 1908-1913

.... In 1765, the Jewish community registered 457 Jews in the old city, 26 in the new city, and an additional 163 Jews in nearby villages.

It is said that in 1653 the Jews were slaughtered by Tatars returning from Berestechko and that their homes were totally destroyed.

In 1847, the Jewish community in New Vishnevets registered 3,178 people, and in 1897, 2,980 out of a population of 4,196.

3. Register of the Council of Four Lands, edited by A. Heylperin

1. In Register of the Council of Four Lands, the town is called Vishnitets.- V. Volin

2. In 5717 (1957), one rabbi wrote,

... "and despite this, I did not retreat, with God's help, blessed be He, and at the holy community of Vishnitets in Lutsk province, the leaders of the four holy communities in the Volin subdistrict, which are Ludmir, Kremenets, Lutsk, and Ostra, met. There on 18 Adar, we also appealed and renewed the decrees and requisitions."

He is referring to boycotts of rabbis who buy their seats and rabbis who engage in Kabbalah.

From the Council of Four Lands' 1635 discussion of Volin matters in Vishnevets, we learn that Rabbi Yom Tov Lipman Heler, rabbi of Ludmir, complained bitterly that many had jumped on "rabbinate" positions in various towns and that district leaders and rulers of the provinces negotiated for the purchase of "rabbinate" positions and became rich from it. Yom Tov was authorized by the Volin community council to stand on guard and forbid the purchase of rabbinate positions, which was troubling a number of communities. The meetings of the council of Volin Assembly took place in Kozin, Korets, and Vishnevets. The community leaders' main business was the just distribution of taxes (Volin Treasury 2).

[Page 20]

Vishnevets in Ruins and Her Annihilated Jews
by Meir Or (Averbukh)

[Translation Editor's Note: This section has not been translated.]

[Page 27]

Here is a portrait of Bat-Sheve Chazan, of blessed memory, a beloved daughter of Vishnevets, who on her death commended half of her property and that of her husband, Zalman Chazan, of blessed memory, to our organization.

Her estate, worth thousands of pounds, motivated us and set the publication of the Vishnevets memorial book in motion. Her part in setting up a memorial for our loved ones is significant-please remember her forever.

[Page 29]

Our Town

Cradle of Our Childhood

By Yakov Ayzenberg

In the heart of each one of us, the town awakens wonderful memories, experiences, and longing for the life we had and that no longer exists.

A person's childhood is unique. It is a world of impression and dreams. It is a reality full of imagination and aspirations.

Some passing events are not recognized or activated by the child's soul. In comparison, some events, visions, and impressions are hidden in the depths of that soul. At first contact in a time of need, they float upward and draw the longed-for image from the past.

Before my eyes is the community of Vishnevets, with its homes, streets and synagogue, the town on which the cruel hand of fate fell. My cradle stood there, and I spent my childhood there. I remember the first page: my time in cheder. The town was blessed with various teachers who taught Torah to their students and instilled it in them-with their arms. Each teacher used his cruel strap on his students. A long table stood in the middle of the room, with the students sitting around it and the teacher at the head, leading the class with great authority.

Memories of evening lessons are carved especially deeply into my memory. The children study in the dark, looking forward to the cherished hour that marks the time to go home, each with a flashlight in his hand.

The time I spent studying at the Vishnevets yeshiva speaks clearly to my heart. When the yeshiva opened in our town, it was housed in the study hall of our town's rabbi, of blessed memory. The yeshiva head, teachers, and tutors all came from other towns. The headmaster was the rabbi's son-in-law, R' Aytsikel, of blessed memory, a wise, friendly scholar who represented the Enlightenment: "Be a Jew in your home and a man when you leave." Many yeshiva members came from different locations.

And last, I remember our young people who stormed the different Zionist youth movements, from Pioneer, to Young Pioneer, to Youth Guard, to Betar. In a pioneering fervor, they dreamed about immigrating to Israel to build a new life; they wanted to be among the builders and farmers in her cities and villages. What a pity, what a tragedy for the Jews and young people of Vishnevets. As young people in Volin, they constituted the natural reserve of working manpower from which the revival movement was built.

The heart aches for this Jewish human source, which was destroyed and diminished.

Until the end of our lives, we will fight the human tendency toward amnesia so that we will not forget our parents, brothers, and sisters, who were our flesh and blood.

[Page 30]

When I Remember Vishnevets

Conversation with the children of Binyamina,

who adopted the community of Vishnevets)

by Sonya (Shats) Levanon

I lived in Vishnevets until 1933. I left for pioneer training and returned in 1936. In 1939, when World War II broke out, I left my wretched birthplace and moved to Rovne after the Russian occupation. I was there until 1941.

Vishnevets was a small town of 5,000 people. Life there was happy, her people were lovely, and the teenagers were such good teenagers.

There were active Zionist youth movements in town; everyone hoped to immigrate to Israel.

There were no sidewalks in Vishnevets, and the roads weren't made of asphalt. In the center of the town were many shops and a big market. Every morning, the "gentile women" brought farm products to town-eggs, milk, cheese, vegetables, and chickens-and sat in the market to sell them.

There was a palace in the town, and a magnificent garden surrounded it. On the Sabbath, the Jews strolled there, but only next to the garden; only a few dared to enter it.

The Horyn River divided the town, and a long, wide bridge connected the two sections. A water-powered flourmill stood at the end of the bridge. This mill was owned by a Jew. There were little boats by the mill, and Jewish teenagers sailed in the water and picked beautiful "water lilies." Under the bridge were a waterfall and the town's swimming beach. We used to take turns going into the water: first the men, and when they came out, the women. On the riverbank outside the town was a wide meadow where horses and cows grazed. Beautiful blue wildflowers grew there. In the center of the town stood the Great Synagogue, and around it stood seven more synagogues, one for each social class.

I attended a Polish elementary school and a secondary trade school. But there was also a Tarbut School in town, where my brother went. There was also a Talmud Torah, but only the sons of poor families, which the community supported, studied there. There was also an ORT school, and an agricultural school, but Jews didn't study there.

At the Polish school, 50 Christians and 10 Jews started in the first grade. Ten Jews and 5 Christians graduated. Some teachers treated the Jews fairly, and some hated Jews and harassed us. The Christian students treated us nicely, because they needed us-the good students. The school was far away, outside the town, and the road there was difficult. A Christian woman's property stood in the middle of the route, and we could have saved ourselves some distance if we could have walked through it. But the "gentile woman" was a Jew-hater, and if a Jewish child dared to approach her yard, she urged her dogs to attack him.

We had no contact with Christians outside school.

Today, it's difficult for me to talk about the relationships between the children in town. It was a strange relationship; children who liked each other at school weren't allowed to play together, by order of their parents and the inadequate societal standards. There were different social classes in town.

[Page 31]

The Trade School and the Palace

[Translation Editor's Note: The Polish title on the photo reads, "Grade 3 of the Coeducational Trade School in Vishnevets."]

[Page 32]

Community leaders' and notables' children didn't make friends with workers' children. Each class lived on its own street. Once, a tailor's daughter befriended a merchant's daughter, and the merchant's family opposed it. Also, a marriage had to be made according to pedigree.

For some reason, I remember two prominent incidents from my childhood: when I was a girl, a fire broke out at the flourmill at midnight. All the town's residents, old and young, packed their belongings and got ready to escape. Then, suddenly, the wind changed direction, a heavy rain fell, and the fire went out.

The second incident is connected with the melting of snow .The water overflowed the riverbanks, and all the streets in the lower part of town flooded. Water entered homes and brought chickens, furniture, and other utensils with them. It was a few days until the "flood" stopped. For many years, natural disaster affected the lives of various families.

I escaped from Vishnevets with nothing.

The Poles left town when the war broke out, and for two weeks we lived without a government. We were afraid of the Ukrainians. Rumors circulated that they were planning pogroms against the Jews. Two weeks later, Russian tanks entered, and we were happy. But our happiness was short-lived. Certain Jewish communists grasped the ruling power in their hands and took revenge on the "middle class." For the first time, the community of Vishnevets experienced cruel brotherly revenge. The town was like a cemetery. Work in the trades stopped, and the stores closed after all the merchandise was sold. Zionists were accused of being middle class and were exiled to Siberia. I stayed in town for a short time and later moved to Rovne.

I remained in Rovne until 1941, until the German occupation. I escaped to Russian territory when the first German bombs fell on Rovne. I wandered the roads for days, weeks, and months. Many stayed, and only a few continued to travel east. Once, when I was exhausted, I lay in a ditch; a heavy rain fell, and I slept. My parents had a hard time waking me up. Finally, we arrived at a kolkhoz. We were given a cold, empty room. In the meantime, I gave birth to a son. I didn't have any diapers. I didn't have any clothes for him or bedding to warm his tiny body, and I had no disinfectant or medicine to heal his wounds and the rash on his delicate body. To this day, it's difficult for me to understand how he survived.

Even with all the hardship that befell us on our way to Russia, many Jews survived. It's a pity that there were so few. Our brothers, the residents of Vishnevets, loathed the Russians and their restrictive regime, and during the short time they tasted this regime, they chose to stay in their homes. There were also personal and community reasons. Individuals were afraid of being separated from their places of residence, dining tables, and comfortable beds. In short, it was difficult to be a refugee. The Jews in Volin had seen the sufferings and personal crises of the refugees from Warsaw and didn't want to be like them. In addition, the Jews didn't believe that the cultured German nation would do what it has done.

[Page 33]

Opening Remarks at the Adoption Ceremony
Moshe Kahan   Elementary School Principal, Binyamina

Honored chairman and respected guests,

With awe and compassion, I open the memorial ceremony for the community of Vishnevets, one of the thousands of Jewish communities in the European Diaspora that were destroyed and annihilated by the Nazi oppressors.

Magnificent Jewish communities, centers of Torah and wisdom, where Torah study never stopped within the walls of the synagogues and study halls-

Where your pride was-your geniuses, great souls and knights of the Torah-your ancestry-the rabbinical chair held by many generations of wise scholars, learned in Jewish law and Scripture-

Where your dignitaries-community elders and benefactors, and your community leaders-generously and with self-sacrifice cared for the public's needs-and your glory was-the homes of the Hasidic rabbis, leaders of their generation, the righteous who are the world's foundation -

How the reaper descended on you, the magnificent, holy communities of Israel.

Little communities of Israel, made up of poor, simple, modest, honest Jews in the remote regions of Volin and Polesia, people of Ein Yakov and Psalm readers, honorable, self-respecting Jews, who spun the web of their pure and honest life with humility, embroidered a dream of redemption in secret, and sweetened their painful existence with love and reverence.

[Translation Editor's Note: Ein Yakov is a compilation of stories from the Talmud.]

How the wick of your life was cut short at the hands of the profane.

Lovely children of Zion-

You, who were privileged to hear the steps of redemption, have come here today to witness the memorial ceremony for the community of Vishnevets, to be part of an alliance of heritage and Jewish fate-the fate of suffering and hardship, a heritage of courage and pride.

Please carry this double trust as a cherished gift and an order from above, in the spirit of "from one generation to the next."

Dear students,

You walked-in your imagination-down the grieving alleyways of the community of Vishnevets, saw the Jewish homes, viewed their synagogues cloaked with bereavement and grief, peeked into a Jewish child's sad eyes-and his hot tears mixed with your blood, and his silent cry now beats in your heart-hide it in a secret place in your soul so you will deliver his last will to the next generation: to remember and not to forget!

May their souls be bound up in the bond of renewed life in Zion-the destination that their souls longed for but could not reach.

[Page 34]

Vishnevets as We Saw It
Children of Binyamina

Editors' Note:

Binyamina's elementary school children adopted the community of Vishnevets, of blessed memory. They studied its way of life; they were impressed by its Jewish life, they were shocked by its destruction, and they enjoyed its legends. They collected details in order to reconstruct it in their imagination and their hearts, and they expressed their emotions in words and poems.

We present their works as they wrote them, without the need for explanation.

From the Children

We, the students of the seventh- and eighth-grade classes of the Binyamina elementary school, took on the campaign of commemorating the community of Vishnevets in the Volin region. With our teacher's help, we contacted a number of former residents. They accepted our request willingly, dedicated their time to us, and brought memories from their destroyed homes.

We were divided into small groups, eight students in each group. We set goals for ourselves, prepared questions, and sent a delegate from each group to Afula, Givatayim, Hadera, and Haifa. The delegates returned with experiences and notes that they shared with the group.

We learned a lot, we discovered a distant world that no longer exists, and we created a bridge that connected us to a culture that we nurture even today... .

History of the Town

According to the dates on the graves in the old cemetery, Vishnevets was founded 600 years ago.

Until World War I, Vishnevets was under the rule of the Russian czar. Life was peaceful in those days, jobs were available, and bribes enabled you to live in peace. To be sure, every once in a while the town experienced some trouble, such as the blood libel of Rabbi Yosele and the abduction of children to work for the army. But those troublesome days were short, and ordinary Jews lived in sadness. After the Russian revolution, the government changed often. In two years, the government changed six times. Each ruler created his own currency and canceled the currency of his predecessor, legislating new laws while canceling the old ones. During that period, the Jews suffered greatly at the hands of the Ukrainians, who tried to grab control. Petliura and the rest of the Jew-haters rioted against the Jews and spilled their blood. It was only after the Polish occupation that the town experienced a period of serenity and prosperity, which lasted until World War II. In 1939, the Russians conquered the town, and the times of horror returned. The town's Jewish Communists took over and retaliated against community leaders and the town's notables. Trade stopped, the Zionists were exiled to Siberia, and sadness fell upon the town.

[Page 35]

In 1941, the Nazis occupied Volin, and Vishnevets became the area's ghetto. Under the command of only three Germans, 6,000 Jews were destroyed by their Ukrainian neighbors.

Today only one Jewish family, which has taken on the duty of protecting the Jewish graves, lives there.

The Town's Appearance

It was a small, beautiful town with a spectacular, varied appearance-a mountain, a river, and a wide meadow. It was a town that was full of life and 3,000 simple, kindhearted Jews. Vishnevets was named after Prince Wisniowiecki, who built himself a magnificent summer palace in the area.

The palace was the pride of the town. It was said to have 365 rooms, one for each day of the year. A beautiful garden and forest surrounded the palace. Jews were not allowed to enter the garden or the forest, and those who dared to do so walked in groups out of fear of the guards. The Jews walked around the wall on the Sabbath, enjoyed the smell of the flowers, sat under the trees, and drank kvas, which they bought on credit until the Sabbath ended. The Horyn River split the town into the Old City and the New City. In the center of the New City stood a group of stores, and around them were a market and a small public garden. The main street running on both sides of the stores was where important people's homes stood. Workers lived on the side streets, and fishermen's families lived by the riverbank. There were no asphalt roads or sidewalks, but a bustling, peaceful life prevailed in the town.

[Translation Editor's Note: Kvas is a fermented beverage made from black rye or rye bread.]

Livelihood in Vishnevets

Economically, Vishnevets was connected to the 60 Christian-owned farms in the area. The Jews traded with the farmers, and they earned their living from each other.

Town Jews worked in six trades:

Wheat merchants: The black, fertile Ukrainian soil yielded a vast quantity of grain. Vishnevets was located in an area that was the "wholesaler" of wheat. Jews would buy the year's crop and export it to all the European countries. By doing so, they served as mediators between the villages and the outside world.

Leather merchants: The "gentiles" in Volin wore tall boots. The Jews supplied Christian shoemakers with leather that was cut and ready for sewing, and in return they received ready-to-wear boots that they sold throughout the country.

Basket merchants: A special reed grew in the Horyn River. The gentiles would harvest it, dry it, and weave baskets out of it. These baskets were in demand in Poland, and the Vishnevets Jews supplied this merchandise to those who asked.

Fish merchants: The fish merchants had a special status that was lower than any other. They lived by the riverbank, caught their own fish, and bought more from the "gentile" fishermen. They also sold their catch to other countries.

Grocers: there were grocery stores and an iron industry in the town.

[Page 36] Some grocers succeeded and had plenty of income, and other small grocers had difficulty earning a living.

6. Craftsmen: tailors, cobblers, milliners, and carpenters. These were good people who held a special position in town. Most were very poor, and few had enough bread to eat.

Children's Education

The stories about education differed by age group.

The oldest man in the group told us this: In my day, the children in Vishnevets studied in cheder, which was divided into four levels according to the students' achievement. A three-year-old child entered the young children's class and studied "how to be Jewish." At the age of five, he advanced to the second level and studied the Pentateuch with Rashi. At the age of 10, he entered the third level and studied the Gemara.

A year or two later, he advanced to the "older boys' cheder" and studied in a study hall or yeshiva.

It was possible to learn the language of the educated, meaning Russian, at the two-year Russian school, but only children from rich families went there because the tuition was very expensive.

If a man wanted to give his son a general education, he had to send him to a school in the district seat.

A woman told us this: In my day, the Poles ruled the town. There were cheders where most of the Jewish children studied, but there was also a government elementary school. We studied Polish there and received a general education. Most of the teachers were anti-Semitic and discriminated against the Jewish children. Nevertheless, 60 of us, 10 Jews and 50 Christians, started in first grade. Fifteen students finished school: 10 Jews and 5 Christians.

And another told us: I studied at the Tarbut School. Sure, there was a Polish elementary school in town where you could study for almost nothing, but the town's intellectuals and important people preferred to pay and send their children to the Tarbut School. The language of instruction was Hebrew.

There was also a Talmud Torah in the town, which in a way inherited the role of the cheder, which began to disappear. There were also other educational institutions in town, such as a three-year trade school that only Jewish students attended, an agricultural school, and ORT, where Jewish student were not accepted.

A nursery school teacher's aide told us this: The Jewish nursery school was the pride of the educators and Zionists in town. A nursery school in a town was rare, and a Jewish nursery school all the more so. The Vishnevets Zionists searched for and found a nursery school teacher and gave her an aide, and the first Jewish nursery school in the whole area opened in Vishnevets.

Yearning for a Homeland

As spring rain along with a thunderstorm raged outside, seven-year-old students sat in their classroom, and in their imagination they traveled with Rabbi Akiva and his students to the small forests in Israel, holding a bow and arrow in their hands and aspirations of freedom in their hearts. I sat among the students and saw myself hiding between the thick oak trees. My bow is ready, and I am waiting for a Roman... .

[Page 37]

Two days later, Tarbut School students gathered in the courtyard of the Great Synagogue, ready to parade out of town to celebrate the holiday of Lag BaOmer.

I was asked to lead the procession. They dressed me in a big blue and white box, as big as my body, with an opening for money chiseled on it. They put a blue and white hat on my head inscribed with "Tel Aviv," and we left.

For me, the ringing of the coins sounded like arrows sent into the hearts of the Romans. I felt that we would win and that our homeland would be free forever.

Youth Movements

There were many different youth movements in town: Young Pioneer, Youth Guard, Zionist Youth, Betar, Pioneer, Zionist Worker, Freedom, Jewish Legion, Freiheit, and the Communists. As usual, peace didn't prevail between the movements. Each one fought to acquire members for their branch, and all methods were kosher ... but all the Zionist movements had one thing in common-they worked for the Jewish National Fund. The Jewish National Fund Central Committee was located in town, and representatives from all the different movements met there. The youth movement members delivered blue boxes to each home and emptied them each month. The teens visited all weddings, circumcisions, and other celebrations and collected donations for the Jewish National Fund from the guests. Also, on the Sabbath, they collected money for the Jewish National Fund from the men who were called to the Torah, and organized a Hanukkah bazaar, donating all proceeds to the Jewish National Fund. A competition took place between the movements, and the group that collected the most money won a citation.

The members of the movements met every evening, each movement in its own "nest." They studied the history of Zionism, sang Hebrew songs, danced the hora, and prepared for their departure for the training that was a bridge to Israel. An additional target that stood before the movements was the spread of the Hebrew language. From the beginning of the 1930s, the sound of the Hebrew language rang in the streets of Vishnevets.

Training Kibbutz

When a member of a Zionist youth movement reached the age of 18, he or she was eligible to go to a training kibbutz. The purpose of the training was to prepare pioneers for working life in Israel. For that purpose, the young people lived together, worked at manual labor, and waited for the moment when they would receive their certificate-their license to immigrate to Israel. The pioneers didn't receive financial help from their parents, and at times they were hungry for bread. They stuck to their goal: to strengthen their bodies and souls for the hard life in Israel. The pioneer groups' financial situation was different in each town.

A pioneer woman tells us: I trained for two and a half years, and during that time we suffered from hunger and cold. The young men in our group worked at the sawmill, and the young women tried to get domestic work. The people who provided the work, even if they were good Jews, did not trust the physical strength of Jewish children, and of 60 people, only 10 were able to find a job. We obtained government health insurance to help those who became sick. Yes, we were hungry for bread, but we were happy because we were looking forward to our future.

[Page 38]

A pioneer man tells us: I was a member of the Youth Guard. At the age of 18, all the members of my level and I joined Pioneer, only because Pioneer received certificates. My training kibbutz happened to be in my town, and the community took care of its income. The rabbi's wife was our benefactor and provided for our needs. We worked in factories, had government health insurance, and our situation was good.

A pioneer woman from a training kibbutz in Vishnevets tells us: The training kibbutz in Vishnevets was a chapter of a kibbutz from another town. When I belonged to it, there were five members-three young men and two young women. The men worked as woodcutters and water drawers, and the young women worked as domestic help. Later on, I received a special task: I got a job as a helper to a nursery school teacher. There was only a sandbox in the nursery school, and the two of us built games with our own hands.

The town's residents were enthusiastic Zionists and cared a lot about the livelihood of the kibbutz, but the sources of income in town were limited. And here's an interesting episode: we were unemployed for many days, and we were waiting for even a day of work. One night, around midnight, we heard a loud knock on the door. We all jumped in fear. And then we heard someone calling: Friends, wake up, I've found work for you. We wondered, Work at midnight? And then we heard the answer: There's a dead man in town, and we need you to stay with him. Come and work.

Activities for Israel

The main activity for Israel was to collect money for the Jewish National Fund and United Israel Appeal. The town's Zionists recognized the value of learning the Hebrew language and introducing the aspiration to immigrate to Israel. To that end, they founded the Tarbut School, opened a nursery school, and organized parties whose income was dedicated to the Jewish National Fund. They collected large donations to United Israel Appeal from the town's residents. During Simchat Torah, when every Jew was called to the Torah, the Zionists collected a lot of money from the community. That day they had a special minyan, sold "places," and gave the money to the Jewish National Fund.

The town organized a party for each Jew who was granted permission to immigrate to Israel and accompanied him or her with the singing of Hatikva, hoping to follow his or her footsteps to reach the homeland.

Synagogues

All the town's synagogues were concentrated in one courtyard. In the center stood the Great Synagogue, where the cantor and the poets sang. Around it stood seven other synagogues. Each social class had its own synagogue, and no tailor or merchant ever prayed in the Great Synagogue.

Homeowners used to place their sons' canopy in the Great Synagogue courtyard, and during the Sabbath the courtyard bustled with activity. But in the evening, in the dark, the Jews avoided walking near the synagogue. They believed in their hearts that ghosts lurked in the women's gallery at night.

During the Holocaust, the Germans rounded up all the town's Jews, put them in the Great Synagogue, and murdered them. Only a young woman and a small child escaped through a small window, and we learned about the murder from them.

[Page 39]

The Hole in the Synagogue

(From tales of Vishnevets)

By Avraham Rozenberg

Yakov, the rabbi's son, had disappeared. The news passed from mouth to ear very quickly and spread throughout the town. The rabbi's wife fainted, and Rabbi Yitschak had difficulty standing up. An extensive search began. We looked all over; there was no place that we did not inspect, and the child was nowhere to be found.

The rabbi and his wife didn't know what to do. They no longer had a child, but what has been taken cannot be returned: "God has given, and God has taken away. May God's name be blessed."

Many years passed; we grew older and had children. Our parents passed away, as did rabbi and his wife. One day, I took my grandson for a walk. The child pressed me to tell him something. After many pleas, I agreed to do so. I said, let's sit under a tree at the entrance to the town, and I'll tell you a story.

We sat down, and I began to tell the story:

One day, when I was still a young boy sitting in cheder, a man suddenly came in and spoke to the rabbi who was teaching us at that hour. We saw that the rabbi's face was somber, and he quickly said to us, "We're done for the day; you're free." We went home, and very soon we learned the reason. The rabbi's son had disappeared.

We looked everywhere, and we couldn't find him. Even today, no one knows why he disappeared.

I finished my story, and we were about to get up and return, when a bearded man walked toward the town and in our direction. We greeted him, and he asked, "Where is the Tailors' Synagogue?" We answered him, and I asked, "Why are you looking for that particular synagogue?" He turned and told me, "My name is Hans. I work in a coalmine in Russia, but I don't know my identity. I know that I was born in a Christian woman's home. At the age of 20 I was taken into the czar's army, I served for 25 years, and later I was taken to work in the mines. I escaped from there and wandered around the world to search for my parents and my identity."

When I reached the home of the Christian woman who had raised me, she told me I wasn't her son. I remembered that I'd been taken from a synagogue with a hole behind the Holy Ark. After clarification, I found out that this was the place.

I was glad to hear his words, and I knew that the rabbi's son had returned to our town, thanks to the hole behind the Holy Ark.

[Page 40]

In Memory of Vishnevets

By Chayim Elyovich

A little town, quiet and beautiful
was ruined, destroyed without a trace.
But the name of that lovely corner
will remain in our memory forever.
Here! From there the street continues
from here-to the left is the big market,
and on this side is the synagogue, for the great and rich,
and here the poor and small will pray.
The tranquility of the town, its silence, is
all that will not be removed from the heart of the community.
Suddenly, as in a windstorm,
the small, beautiful town was destroyed.
The villains did it, the foreigners
who hoped to erase the memory of the Jews
therefore we vow not to forget
and to always remember.

[Page 41]

It Happened Not Long Ago

By Nurit Sheyner

Not long ago, it is not difficult
to remember,
our beloved brothers were slain
for nothing,
slain just like that.
By enemies, murderers, who
destroyed and slaughtered
without reason,
just like that.
A mother whispers to her son and
pours out her heart,
where do the trains that never
return travel to?
Your father and many others left
and did not return.
It was not long ago, it is not
difficult to remember,
our good brothers who were slain
for nothing,
slain just like that.

[Page 41]

Oy, Mama!

By Nitse Biv

A pretty girl cried, where did the town disappear to?
Where is my father, and what happened to my brother?
Why did they all disappear, why was life silenced here?
Vishnevets through Its Institutions

[Page 42]

Vishnevets through Its Institutions

Tarbut

[Page 43]

Artistry

[Page 44]

Reading

[The main caption within the photo reads

"Founders and Administrators of the Vishnevets Municipal Library, 5687 [1926-

1927]-5692 [1931-1932]."]

[Page 45]

Prayer …

Financial Activities

[Page 46]

Youth Guard Exhibit at the Jewish National Fund Bazaar in Vishnevets

[Page 47]

Organization and Immigration

Organization and Immigration

[Page 48]

In the meantime:

Orphan Care

Worker Protection

[Page 49]

In the Tempest of the Holocaust

(Survivors' Testimonies)

Rabbi Meir Nachum Yingerleyb,
Last Rabbi of Vishnevets

[Page 51]

History Will Not Repeat Itself

by Edna Yafe

Translated by Sara Mages

In the presence of the picture of the rabbi of Vishnevets.
Don't look at me like that, Rabbi,
don't look with your wonderful eyes.
Your penetrating glance enters me,
your face reflects your kind heart.
I will not forget, Rabbi, I will not forget
how you crawled on your knees and your beard was made up
like a cross.
On your last day,
how they exploited you over there.
Rabbi, light has already come to our nation,
and once more David's capital is whole;
Rabbi, history will never repeat itself,
and so the voice reaches high places.

[Page 52 - Hebrew] [Page 298 - Yiddish]

The Vishnevets Ghetto

by Zev Sobol

Translated by Sara Mages

I'm not from Vishnevets. I lived nearby, in a village near Vishnevets. I had a grocery store there and also traded in wheat. I had a very good relationship with the village farmers. There was a sort of social capacity to my life in the village. They came to seek my advice, and they received interest-free loans and my help with their public needs.

My ties with Vishnevets were through my business connections. I traveled there to purchase merchandise for my store, and I had family and religious ties to the town, too.

When the Nazis arrived in our area, my Ukrainian friends volunteered to help the Germans with their work. They collected all Jewish males from the families in Svinyoche, and they also brought Menashe Brimer and his father-in-law to our village from the village of Ostitsek. They took us to the village council room and hit us with murderous blows, with the excuse that we knew where Communist survivors were hiding. When we couldn't tell them, since we didn't know a thing about Communists, they had us stand facing the wall with our arms raised, and they beat us. From behind our backs, they demanded answers. Otherwise, they would kill us.

Our wives came screaming and crying to the council building, begging for our release. The Ukrainians rounded them up and beat them, too.

After a long time, we were released with the promise that they would take care of us. We returned to our homes beaten, ashamed, miserable, and wounded, hoping for a merciful end.

We didn't have any food. Secretly and in great fear, we went to our neighbors, giving them our clothing and valuables in exchange for bread, and that's how we lived for several months.

***

At the beginning of March 1943, a gentile friend, the council head, came to me and told me that the next morning I would have to leave the village with my family and move to Vishnevets, where a ghetto would be set up for all the Jews. The following day we bought, at full price, a winter wagon, loaded it with food bundles we had "purchased" in exchange for our clothes, furniture, and bedding, and set off for the Vishnevets ghetto.

When we left the village, our neighbors accompanied us, booing and expressing their exaggerated joy.

Before we could leave home, a mob of old people, women, and children stormed us and robbed us of everything they could put their hands on, in front of my family and me.

I arrived in the town. The ghetto was being planned. I settled in at Yisrael Derbarimdiker's, my brother's in-law. By chance, this house was included in the ghetto that was later established, and I stayed there until the end.

A week later, all the men were taken to set up the ghetto.

For many years, I had lived among gentiles. Suddenly, I was among my beloved and miserable Jewish brothers. In a way, it was something to think about. I walked among them as a newcomer and stranger, but I felt good. We all wore two yellow patches, one on the chest over the heart and the second on the back.

[Page 53]

When the ghetto was set up, all the Jews were moved there, and a Jewish Council (Judenrat) was elected. The first order communicated through them was that in a few hours a work siren would be sounded from the big mill, indicating that from that moment on, Jews would not be allowed to leave the ghetto, roam the streets, or be seen outside it.

The world closed in on us.

***

Before the ghetto was established, the Germans took away more than 200 men. Among them were Dr. Yosef Tsinberg and the town's rabbi, a beloved elderly, gracious Jew. They were taken to Pochayev and murdered on the way.

Before they took them on the road, they rounded up all 200 on the Boulevard. They laid them on the ground face up, with their hands on their backs. The Ukrainians ran on top of their backs like children running over a soft carpet. They danced with their heavy shoes and hit them with their clubs. Among the stretched-out, beaten men was my older brother, Motel Sobol. I saw him suffering, and I couldn't help him.

Before the murderous march, they stood Dr. Tsinberg and the rabbi on the side of the Boulevard. They put Dr. Tsinberg's hat on the rabbi's head, over his eyes, and put the rabbi's hat on the doctor's head and stretched it all the way down to his neck. Then they tied cables around their necks, making them look like giants. A short distance from them stood a Ukrainian playing an accordion, and both of them were forced to dance to the beat of the accordion.

Also among the 200 who were tortured was Barukh Tenenboym, Sender the carriage driver's son. The father stood next to the home of Moshe Tenenboym, who owned a leather store. When he saw his son suffering, he walked over and asked for his son to be returned to him. The German agreed to his request and told him to come back and wait for his son by the wall next to Tenenboym's store. As the old man stood there, full of hope, the German shot him between the eyes and killed him on the spot.

The show was organized by the Ukrainians, but it was directed by their masters, the Germans, from quite a distance.

East of the Boulevard was a tavern and hotel owned by Yisrael Gnip. The Germans sat there by the tavern gate, stretched out on armchairs, and gave orders to the Ukrainians.

After two and a half hours, the men were lifted from the ground. Armed with submachine guns, the Ukrainians surrounded them and began chasing them toward Pochayev.

The rabbi trailed behind the walkers. Two Ukrainians approached him, tied a rope under his arms and around his neck, and then tied the rope to a cart. The horses started running, and the old rabbi fell and was dragged behind the cart. His blood dripped slowly until he died.

When the rabbi's wife realized the rabbi hadn't returned home, she ran from person to person begging for an answer: "Where's my husband? Where's the rabbi?"

[Page 54]

When they tried to comfort her, telling her he had been taken to work and would be back in a few days, she wept and said, "What will happen? He didn't take his prayer shawl and phylacteries."

Dr. Tsinberg, who was bleeding, struggled behind the walkers. They pushed him with their rifle butts. He was killed later, along with the others, on the way to Pochayev.

***

Two weeks before the ghetto was established, when I was still in my village, I traveled to the town every once in a while to bring food to my brother's family and my parents. I spent the night there since I was afraid to travel after dark. One night while I was sleeping in their house in town, we heard the loud noise of sticks banging on metal cans. The drumming was extremely loud, and we didn't know what it meant.

We experienced a frightful night. We didn't sleep. We expected trouble at any moment. In the morning, when we woke up from our short naps, which we took either standing or sitting, we went outside into the street, where we found out that the previous night all the Jews from the Old City had been taken outside the town limits, where they were killed. So that the victim's screams and cries for help wouldn't be heard, they positioned a large number of evil youths on the metal roofs of several buildings and asked them to make noise to drown out the sound of weeping.

That night, the Old City of Vishnevets was completely annihilated. I can't remember the exact date, but the event is engraved deeply on my heart, and my blood is full of its horrors.

***

They took us out to work every day. They walked us in a tight formation, so tight that we rubbed and pushed against each other. We walked on the road. We weren't allowed to step onto the sidewalk, and when a horse cart passed by, we had to move aside. They walked us the same way a shepherd signals his herd to move fast.

If a Ukrainian policeman happened to walk toward us, we had to greet him from a distance of six meters before he reached us by lowering our heads and taking our hats off-all of us as one, as we were ordered.

Once when we were on our way to work, a Ukrainian policeman ran toward us. Full of rage, he approached one of our escorts, also a policeman, and started yelling at him, "Why did you hit my Jew yesterday?" When the other one didn't understand, he apologized. Then the angry Ukrainian grabbed a Jew from the line. Everyone in Vishnevets knew him. He was a chicken merchant known by the nickname "Kovila." The policeman began hitting him with a rubber club. He hit him until he swelled up and turned blue and his face looked like chopped meat. We couldn't see his eyes anymore. In their place were two cracks sealed with dried blood.

***

Once when Meir Derbarimdiker was returning from work, he passed by the guards posted by the gate. A Ukrainian policeman by the name of Yakub Ostrovski approached him and said to him, "Tell me, my friend, what did you do in the Soviet regime?"

Meir told him where he had worked. He had nothing to hide from him. Meanwhile, two policemen hit him with their rubber clubs. They tore and cut his flesh, and his blood spattered around him. His clothes ripped from the force of the blows. They tore his shirt and undershirt until they were stuck to the cuts on his skin and flesh.

[Page 55]

His entire body turned into a mass of flesh and blood and rags mixed with human skin and flesh.

***

When the ghetto opened, Jews we didn't know were brought there. We found out that Jews from Vyshgorodok had joined the Jews from Vishnevets and the surrounding villages. So more than 4,000 people lived in this narrow ghetto.

We crowded into rooms, dozens and dozens of souls in one room.

Filth accumulated, lice multiplied, and hunger increased. There was no way to get food from other places. Women's and children's bodies swelled up from lack of food and were covered with open wounds and bleeding abscesses. Deaths increased from day to day.

Many died of hunger. Every day there were four to six funerals. We became immune to the situation, and our only worry was whether we would be allowed to bury our dead.

We carried our dead to the cemetery. Only a few of us accompanied the pallbearers. A police escort guarded us, following us and supervising the unfortunate ceremony with seven eyes, afraid we would escape.

Funerals endangered our lives, we all knew. Since we didn't have any physical strength, it was very difficult for us to carry the swollen bodies. But we performed the deed with extreme dedication.

Fear of living with the dead, fear of epidemics, and worry about our miserable lives made us forget that we were human beings.

***

Liquidation of the Ghetto

At the beginning of Elul 1943, about 10 SS men arrived from Kremenets. They gathered a large number of armed Ukrainian policemen from the surrounding area and stationed them in the shade. One SS man stood next to the great master, Mr. Shtayger, the destroyer of Vishnevets Jewry. He stood up and gave a short speech that I heard in full and still can't forget.

He said, "Today we're going to liquidate all the Jews in the ghetto. Go knock on each window, open it, and tell the Jews, 'Leave your homes, you traitors, you Jewish Communists.' Beat the Jews who refuse to leave their homes with the butts of your guns. Pay attention: you can strike to kill, but make sure you don't kill them inside the ghetto. Take them outside town, to the designated area, and kill them there."

I still don't understand why he didn't want to exterminate us inside the ghetto.

***

During the walk from the ghetto, people were beaten to the point of insanity. In some cases, people had hysterical fits while walking in rows next to the others.

[Page 56]

They started to pull their hair out and pinch their flesh. Some tore their clothing, with heartrending screams. Yente Klayn tore her clothes, and by the time she arrived at the pit, she was completely naked.

Young women screamed and wept. One stood up, faced them, and gave a terrible, mad speech: "Why can't we get married? Why won't we have the chance to satisfy men's wishes? Why don't they let us prove it? Why did they choose to kill us before we'd known our husbands?"

A big truck drove around the walkers. The Ukrainians loaded it with the elderly, the blind, the frail, and babies. Those who trailed behind the procession were thrown into the truck: the wounded, the sick, and those whose legs had swelled from hunger.

Piles and piles were thrown into the truck. The Ukrainians riding on top sat on the growing stacks of bodies as if they were bundles of wood or straw.

It's very hard to think about the look of importance on the murderers' faces as they sat on top of innocent people who didn't resist.

I walked next to my wife, holding my Rivkele, who was 21 months old, in my arms. My wife held Henele, who was four and a half. Suddenly, several policemen approached us, extracted our children from our arms, and threw them on the truck as if they were bundles of rags. When they separated us, I wanted to give them a last look to tell them I would love them for eternity. The policeman realized it, and I received a blow from a rifle butt. I was pushed from the place where I was standing and forced to follow the procession.

Yudke Shag was walking with his four-year-old son. The boy pushed himself between his knees, screaming wildly and begging, "Father, don't walk, where are we going? Let's go back!" Yudke picked him up, held him in his arms, and kept walking. At that moment, a Ukrainian tore him from his arms and threw him on the truck, separating them.

From the beginning, we were marched in groups of two or three hundred. After I slowed down to take a last look at my children, I got pushed, fell into another group, and was separated from my wife. I never saw her again. By chance, my brother was in this group, and I continued walking with him.

***

As we walked over the bridge between the new and the old cities, German military trucks approached us, and we were forced to clear the road for them. I was pushed to the side.

I felt lightheaded. I tripped and fell into the river. At that moment, I recovered and felt refreshed. I crawled to the side and took cover. Since I didn't hear gunfire and noticed that nobody realized I was missing, I blessed the incident and stayed hidden.

Hiding next to me was a Jewish doctor from Warsaw-a refugee from the Nazis who escaped to Vishnevets after Warsaw was captured by the Nazis. My brother also jumped in after me.

We separated. If they looked for us, they wouldn't find us together.

I stayed hidden until evening. I didn't say a word. I didn't talk to my brother, but from time to time I sent signals to him.

I got up when it was dark, and my brother and the doctor from Warsaw got up with me.

[Page 57]

We left, and with great caution we approached Dmitro's house. I had known Dmitro for many years. He lived in Melinovits, and his house was next to the forest. I had given this gentile my cow just before I left for Vishnevets, and in exchange, he had promised to bring food to me in the ghetto. I didn't see him in the ghetto once. Nevertheless, I wanted to believe in our friendship.

I knocked on his window. He came out with his wife. He let us into his house and expressed his great sorrow. Our situation touched his heart, but what could he do when he didn't have the ability to do anything? With a generous hand, they fed us and gave us something to drink. At long last, our friendship hadn't let me down.

They told us to lie down, get some rest, and sleep. They understood that we were tired and exhausted. We fell into a deep sleep. At dawn, this same gentile went out and informed the authorities that Jews were staying with him.

We didn't have enough time to wake up from our deep sleep. Two Ukrainians armed with submachine guns arrived. They kicked us while we were still lying on the ground, screaming and shouting at us. They woke us up and ordered us to move quickly. They took us to the Great Synagogue in town. We had returned to Vishnevets. The town was empty, with no sign of life, but I heard a strange sound in my ears: screaming, groaning, and moaning that were swallowed by the horrible silence.

In the synagogue, we were placed next to two young men whom we didn't know. Talking to them, we found out that they were from Vyshgorodok and lived in our ghetto. They had seen all the horrors: how the people had been divided into groups and murdered in large numbers. They were in the last group, and when their group's turn came, Shtayger approached and asked if there were any craftsmen among them and for shoemakers and tailors to raise their hands. They raised their hands, and by doing so, they survived for a few more days. That was how we found out the fate of the last few from Vishnevets.

At the other end of the synagogue was another group of people, around 70. They were Jews who had been taken from their bunkers. When the ghetto was emptied, they went in search of Jews who were hiding. They took them out of their bunkers with all kinds of temptations and threats, and now they were facing their fate.

We stayed in the synagogue together for a whole day. They shut the doors and windows on us. It was unbearably suffocating inside, and in front of us, the bunker people, who were starving for bread and air, began to die, including our old doctor.

At night we could talk, and we asked the two young men from Vyshgorodok to tell us what had happened. And the two young men from Vyshgorodok told me what they had seen with their own eyes-how Vishnevets Jewry had been destroyed-and here is their story.

All the people were brought to a ravine behind the Old City on the road leading to Zbarazh. The ravine served as a readymade grave, with a capacity that met the Nazis' needs. The ravine had been prepared by Ukrainian farmers. They stood with their tools, clearing the surface of the ravine. They leveled it, removed small mounds, scraped the stones from the sides, and dug the walls. They covered the bottom with the stones and soil they had removed from the walls in order to create a kind of crushed-soil foundation for the victims.

Once the foundation had been prepared, the first group of Jews was led to their burial place.

Two policemen ordered them to take their clothes off and remain in their underwear. They undressed, piled up their clothes on the side, and were then ordered to lie down in a row in the ravine, face down.

[Page 58]

When they were all lying face down, the policemen ran over them with their submachine guns in their hands, shooting bullets into the heads of the people who were lying down.

Afterward, they inspected. They walked from person to person and with a handgun killed those who didn't die immediately, using the gun butt or a bullet shot into the center of the skull.

When they were done with one group, they brought the second, and so on.

The Ukrainians walked over the bodies inside the ravine with horrifying skill. They lifted the bodies that were not level and laid them straight. The Germans sat on the walls of the ravine and supervised the work. They gave the orders, and the Ukrainians executed them.

The farmers took over after the Ukrainian policemen were done inspecting and leveling the layer after the last round of shooting. They covered the layer of bodies with soil in order to place another layer on top. They used shovels to do this. They covered it with a thin layer of soil, and the area was ready for another row of bodies. The clothes piled up on the side were given as a gift to the farmers in exchange for their work. Immediately, they collected the victims' clothes and loaded them onto their carts, and while the others were busy with their work of killing and taking care of the bodies, they set off to sell their booty.

That was what the two young men from Vyshgorodok told me, and it is the utmost truth, because while they told us their story, they were very detailed and corrected each other so as not to distort what their eyes had seen.

***

At night, they forgot about us, and nobody came to check on us. Tired from their experience and the killing, they also wanted to rest. Armed guards stood around the synagogue; they weren't afraid we would escape.

I couldn't rest; the brothers' story simultaneously depressed and energized me. I decided to escape no matter what. And from here.

We felt trapped, but we believed there was an opening in the trap and if there was none, that we could create one.

We looked for a way to escape. We climbed on top of each other's backs to see if there was an opening and thus liberation in the windows above us.

Meanwhile, one of us found a nail, walked over to the iron bars encased in the building's old wooden frame, and started scraping away the rotten wood little by little. The wood was soft. A crack opened around the base of the iron bars, and one fell out of the window frame. Then we bent it upward, tied a belt to it, and climbed down.

I was the first to climb down. I found the Ukrainian guard leaning on his gun and covered with his big coat, snoring and fast asleep. I tore a sleeve from my shirt and, with Hershel Duvid Feldman's brother, shoved the rag down his throat. We removed his gun and killed him with the butt.

He fell over, and his brains spilled out. Then we knew we had an opening to escape. Little by little, we took everyone out and told them to run. We ran separately, each going his own way.

I escaped to Svinyoche, my village; I forgave the village residents for what they had done to me and to the Jews in their village.

[Page 59]

I played with the hope that now, after the final liquidation, they might feel sorry for me. I went to the home of Yevdokim Shvedki, my acquaintance and friend for many years. I didn't go into his house or wake him up. I climbed up to the attic.

It was full of straw being stored for the winter, and I found shelter for the night there. My brother probably followed me there. He also arrived at Yevdokim's, and together we climbed up to the attic.

We stayed there for two weeks without anyone knowing we were there. During the day, one of us climbed down to milk the cow. We lived, and we ate. It was warm for both of us inside the packed straw. To my surprise, when I climbed down to milk the cow, I found Yevdokim standing and waiting for me. He probably knew someone was milking his cow. He expressed his anguish, gave me food, and begged me to leave. It was too dangerous, a real crime to hide a Jew. People will know, they'll hate me, they'll tell. He begged and explained for a long time and persuaded me to leave.

I left at dark. We took over another attic. We hid and again used the same method: cow's milk and pig food. No one noticed us for quite a while. But then a bad case of lice infestation broke out. Fat, cruel lice sank deep into our bodies and sucked our bone marrow. It was extremely strange; this was the worst of all blows. We would get down from our beds, find a stone, and use it to scratch. The pain from the wounds was a lot more pleasant than the tickling of the lice. We scratched until we bled. Our clothes stuck to the dried blood on our bodies. They dried out like tarpaulins and caused additional pain, but this pain was much better than the pain of itching.

So we sat in secret until summer arrived. In the summer, we hid in the corn and grass. At night, we quenched our thirst by sucking dew from the leaves, and we satisfied our hunger by eating ground wheat grains.

So 1944 came upon us.

One night we heard a rumor that Russian partisans were roaming the area and that the Germans were getting ready to flee.

My brother couldn't endure our living conditions. The lice depressed him. He longed for a shower, a change of clothes. Our clothes stank and spread the stench of death around our bodies. He didn't want to suffer anymore and decided to join the partisans. I tried to talk him out of it. I talked to his heart, telling him he would live for a while longer and it was a question of just a few more days. I asked him to be patient. I explained to him that things were going our way and that we were on the threshold of salvation.

He couldn't have listened to my advice even if he'd wanted to. The lice infestation had taken over his mind. At night he left. To his horrible luck, a trained German guard dog smelled and caught him. The dog kept hold of him, not letting him move. In the morning, the Germans arrived and killed him.

This happened on the outskirts of Vishnevets, on the Bolonya; gentiles told me about it.

When the Russians entered the village, I walked over to them and gave myself up.

For a month, I stayed with the partisans; they didn't dare enter the town or be seen during the day.

[Page 60]

I washed my wounded body. My wounds healed, and I ate until I was full. I blessed those days even though we were still in danger. I had a feeling I was on the way to salvation- this time I would survive.

***

In 1945, I entered Vishnevets with the Russians, and I stayed there until 1959.

Moshe Goldshub and Tsvi Yuger were with me. Our holy mission was to catch the ones who had killed not only our families but also the survivors and all the Vishnevets Jews. We caught the two killers: Ostrovski and Poslevski. We hit them with murderous blows and tortured them until they gave up on their own lives. Then we handed them to the authorities.

They were tried along with 15 additional killers we found. They were sentenced to 25 years in prison based on our testimony.

When Khrushchev came to power, they enjoyed a full pardon.

[Page 61 - Hebrew] [Page 311 - Yiddish]

Nazi Atrocities in Vishnevets

by a survivor

Translated by Sara Mages

When the Russians arrived in Vishnevets, they "found out" that I had once been a businessman. I was arrested, sentenced, and sent to their prison in Berdichev.

After they retreated to the depths of Russia, I escaped from prison and returned to my town and my home on July 14, 1941.

For the two previous weeks, the town had been occupied by the Germans. I knew that. I knew they had entered Vishnevets on July 2, 1941. But I couldn't do anything else. The town and my father's home tugged at my heartstrings. My whole family-my loving wife and my children, the love of my life for eternity-lived in the town.

I thought that someone would be glad to see me, that someone would be happy and hope for different days, but except for my family, no one smiled at me. The town was under a deep depression. The events of the past two weeks had indicated what was to come, and they already had facts on which to base their fears.

A few days after my return, 36 men were taken hostage and locked up in R' Issakher Sofer's cellar. Unluckily for me, 35 of them were murdered the day I returned home.

Those prisoners weren't murdered with the usual tools of murder or in the usual way. It was strange, but the fact is that the way they were murdered added more misery to the whole event.

The Ukrainians received permission and orders from the Germans to kill them. They stormed the cellar, with the two Ostrovskis in the lead. Full of blood lust and the desire to kill, they tore down the entry door and threw heavy rocks and other heavy objects into the narrow room, pushing and shoving the prisoners into a corner and suffocating them little by little.

The men died while watching death approaching them, step by step, centimeter by centimeter, with each stone thrown at them and with no means of escape.

Alter, Makhtsi Ruach's son, was the only prisoner to survive. He was saved in a horrifying and amazing way. He was a small, skinny man. When the prisoners were pushed into the corner, he was covered up by a pile of human bodies twisting in the last moments of their lives and slowly dying in agonizing spasms. Underneath the bodies, he succeeded in digging himself a hole, where he hid his head and survived.

In the evening, the Ukrainians left the murder site only after they had checked and found not a single sound of life coming from the bodies. Only then was Alter able to release himself from the pile of humans. He left his hiding place and found shelter in my house.

He told me what had happened and described the way the murder was carried out and the suffering of the people who died. His story made my hair stand on end, and it will remain in my memory for eternity.

I knew many Ukrainians who participated in this horrifying murder. I knew the Ostrovskis, and I couldn't understand how they could do such a thing and enjoy it.

[Page 62]

Later, they didn't surprise me. I saw them day after day, invading and killing, invading and robbing without any control, conscience, or respect. I saw them standing by the Germans' door early in the morning waiting to receive their terrifying orders. Like puppies waiting for scraps from a good meal, they waited for an assignment they'd be happy to carry out.

The interesting thing is that they didn't take money. They didn't believe in it; they didn't believe the current regime would last. They knew things would change and they should enjoy the lunacy. They just took valuables, jewelry, and clothing.

***

July 23, 1941

Early in the morning, we saw the Ukrainians running wildly. Suddenly, I saw them stop and pick up every person they came across in the Jewish streets. Shouting and laughing, they pulled them violently to one location. In all, they picked up 65 people. Later, they were all led to an unknown location. None of them came back. For many days, we tried to find out their fate and burial place, but all our inquiries came to nothing. Even now, nobody knows their fate.

A week passed without any special incidents. The Ukrainians and their German commanders were somewhat shaken by their own doings; they were frightened and tired.

July 30, 1941

The Ukrainians executed the same operation again, but on a larger scale. This time, they developed a new method for their killing. They collected almost 400 Jews, gathered them on the Boulevard in the center of town, and laid each one facing the ground. Then they walked over their backs with their spiky boots, holding heavy clubs in their hands. When a person raised his head to see what was happening or to see if it was over, a Ukrainian would jump on his back and beat him badly with the club he held. The Jews remained on the ground, wounded and bleeding, for a very long time, waiting for their fate or for the time when the Ukrainian animals would be satisfied with the groans and blood and let them go.

When they had the correct number of people ordered by the Germans, including my oldest brother, R' Yosef Erlikh, the town's rabbi, and others, they were led on foot out of town. Their fate is still unknown.

The Ukrainians kept their superior secrets for many years. Even now there are no witnesses to or hints of where the 400 were murdered or how they disappeared.

After each operation, the number of widows, orphans, and bereaved parents, whose world darkened, increased. Their lives entered a passage where everyone was thirsty to know the fate of their loved ones, who had been taken away from them to an unknown location.

[Page 63]

Then the Ukrainian women appeared. Who said farmers were harmless?! They were naked as snakes, and so were their wives. They would approach a woman and talk to her emotionally, with pain, sadness, and understanding, telling her that her loved ones were alive.

They would say that their son or husband was guarding them in the place where they were imprisoned and had sent the following message: "Don't worry" (meaning that her loved ones were still alive) and had asked her to send clothes and food.

The poor, unfortunate ones swallowed the imaginary good news as if it were really good news, the news their hearts wanted to believe. With tears of happiness and worry in their eyes, they thanked the messengers from the bottom of their hearts and gladly gave the righteous Ukrainian women everything they asked for.

Every day the Ukrainians repeated their ploy, and every day there were enough victims holding onto the thin edge of hope. They took the last piece of bread from their mouths, tore the clothes from their bodies, and sent them to their loved ones far away.

It was not enough that they'd lost their loved ones at the Ukrainian murderers' hands. They also lost what was left of their food and clothing to the wives' false claims, the "crazy mothers."

The ploy took its toll. Several days later, the wives and mothers were left without food for their young children, who died of hunger. Their small bellies swelled up from lack of food, and many died. The streets were full of children's bodies, victims of the worthless women's fraud. There is nothing more terrifying than seeing a small, skinny child swollen to twice his size and watching him die.

The tragedy of the Jewish men, who were heads of families, husbands, and masters of their own lives, began with the Russians' arrival. Suddenly, they were unnecessary. The breadwinners, who had been proud of their work and the substance of their labor and only wanted to sustain their families, became useless creatures.

Even during the regime that preceded the Nazi tragedy, the heads of families looked like weak members of society. The framework of their lives came apart, and their families weakened. The social structure cracked, and Jewish conscience crumbled.

Without any intention on the part of the Soviets, the structure of Jewish society in Vishnevets, which was based on family values, was shaken.

But what happened to them during the short Nazi occupation had no relation to past horrors. Husbands became worthless shadows, and fathers stopped being the center of their families. Everyone knew their father was not the one they used to have.

People avoided each other. The depression was way too deep, and the anguish of many deepened the shame and brought pain and helplessness.

As a result, the streets of Vishnevets were empty of people and men.

[Page 64]

The physical and emotional torture forced on people and the fear of what was still to come forced proud and honest Vishnevets men to hide.

A few days later, figures moved here and there. Shamed eyelids were raised, glancing and saying hello with their expressions, and then a sigh would escape, which was answered with a sigh and a begging look; maybe the Jewish nation's troubles were coming to an end.

And then a strange thing happened. Jews began to believe that those who had been taken from the town were still alive. They proved it the way Jews analyze a thought: "everything is simple." They said something like this: if they'd wanted to kill them, they could have done it right here. What was stopping them? If they took them away from here, they probably needed them somewhere else, so it's a sign that they're working there. Another logical thing is that however you look at it, if they're not alive, it means they're afraid to kill us here. Let's suppose someone is keeping an eye on them. If so, we're immune... . And they ended it with a joke. "Look, they outnumber us. They're afraid, and they walk around armed with guns. There are just a few of us. We're not afraid, and we're walking without guns. Therefore, we need to hold on. Those who can cope with the situation will shame them, and the most important thing is to be strong."

September 4, 1941

At dawn, Rachel Sendler, the 28-year-old daughter of a minor wheat merchant from the Old City, came to us soaking wet in her underclothes. She had escaped from the Old City through the river. She told us the Ukrainian `police had collected all the Jews at night and taken them somewhere outside town, and no one knew where... the town was empty, without a living soul or a sign of life... a few had been shot on the threshold of their homes and buried where they were shot... she had escaped through the river, the only place she could cross, which was not guarded by Ukrainian police....

In the Old City, there was a tannery owned by Avraham Shimkovits. Duvid Feldman, Avraham's son-in-law, worked there. That same night, the Ukrainians came to him and told him, "Go hide, and save your life. Don't tell anyone that all the Jews are going to be caught and taken outside the town tonight." He told me that at first he didn't believe them, but he realized they were telling the truth, knowing that they still needed him since they were short of tanned leather. Nevertheless, he hid in a corner of his tannery, whose main gate faced the hostel belonging to Yone Tsimbler (Zimbel) and his brother Moti. While he was hiding, the reptile Vasye, a Vishnevets resident who lived near the Jewish homes, came armed with a gun and leading Avraham Shimkovits's daughter, the one who was married to Motye Grinberg, Shimon the Soldier's son.

[Page 65]

He was leading her as if he were escorting a prisoner on trial. The woman was in the last months of pregnancy and carried a baby in her arms. The baby cried and twisted in her arms out of fear and nervousness. The woman was very tired; she faced Vaske, her neighbor of many days and years, and spoke.

"Vasye," she said. "Look, Vasinke, look at my condition. I've never harmed you. Have mercy on me and my baby, have mercy, Vasinke."

The reptile didn't answer. He moved back as if he wanted to measure her with his eyes, and with unusual calm, he aimed the gun at the baby's mouth, shot him, and quieted him. The boy convulsed, collapsed, and fell from her arms... she passed out and went into labor. When the killer saw the newborn coming into the world, he aimed his gun and killed him the minute he was born... him and his mother.

***

When we heard the news, we wanted to go to the Old City to see the unbelievable sight with our own eyes-to see how a town could be emptied of its residents in such a short time.

We arrived at the Grabliye. It was blocked. The entrance to the town was closed off by a wall of Ukrainian policemen. We returned.

A couple of days later, after the murderers had calmed down from the shock and fear of their own deeds, we returned to the Old City. We found a dead town. The streets were empty, and the homes broken into. Inside the homes, the beds were made, and the pillows and blankets of those who had been taken while they were asleep were stained and sprayed with human blood. Next to one of the homes, we saw a mound covered with fresh soil, and we knew... this was a freshly dug grave.

One of the women, whose name I forget-a widow of many years who was known for her modesty and culture-the murderers didn't have the time to bury her in a deep grave. The thin layer of soil that covered her had blown off in the wind. Her face was clearly seen outside her grave, and her eyes stared with a deadly gaze at a world of human insanity.

A town was murdered and buried overnight in the few hours between evening and night. Strenuous work was done here: the slaughter of innocent people in the name of holy idealism.

Shock hit all of us. This was a general massacre. No longer were men being taken and their families left alive. This time, men, women, and children had been killed. The murder was general and final.

All our illusions dissolved. It was clear to us that the murderers' agenda was undoubtedly a final liquidation. No one was watching over them or frightening them.

We went to Dr. Landesberg in Kremenets to seek his opinion and ask his advice. Maybe there was something else we could do. He was very quiet, so to speak, and he answered simply, as if he were analyzing a situation that didn't concern him.

"Go home. Our end is near, and there is nothing we can do."

[Page 66]

We returned.

Darkness settled in our souls. All the chambers of our hearts were filled with desperation.

***

One day, a farmer came to town and stopped his cart in an alley. Two women, one Aba Klinman's wife, saw the gentile and innocently thought that maybe he'd brought something to sell. They approached him with items they wanted to trade, hopeful for a moment that maybe a miracle had happened and their luck had changed. They'd have something to eat. Meanwhile, two Ukrainian policemen passed by, arrested the gentile and the women, and took them to the police station.

We don't know what happened to the gentile, but an hour and a half later, the women left the police station, bleeding and crawling on their stomachs. They were exhausted, beaten, and wounded. They couldn't stand upright. Their elbows were broken. They knelt down and crawled on all fours.

Who can forget such a heartbreaking sight: women beaten so badly by men who were sworn to respect the weaker sex.

October 1942

Winter came early. The chilly fall brought the fear of winter-maybe because it was dark and cold in our homes, or maybe because it was unusually cold for that season.

We were busy with funerals almost every day. People died of epidemics; typhus ran its deadly course. There was not a home without a sick person. Starvation also claimed many lives.

Escorting the dead was the only occupation for the living; we brought them to their burial place and we left. We had nothing to comfort the mourners with. We all mourned. We felt that taking care of the dead was the center of our activities and the existence of Judaism, Jewish unity, and respect for the Jew.

The Ukrainians escorted us, the coffin bearers, with great joy. For some reason, we felt that by fulfilling our religious duty, we were united and shared the same fate.

From October to March, there were no murders or victims. With that came a reprieve from our fears and the depression that had often struck us.

The brutalities continued. "Contributions" were forced on us. We had to collect clothing, money, and jewelry for our oppressors. Two or three Germans would suddenly appear, receive our contributions, and leave.

Those breaks put us to sleep. At times we imagined that our suffering was ending. For the fear of God, how can a man, an entire human race, run wild and live only on evil and murder? People who were known to be wise and experienced were suddenly led astray by false idealism and encouraged to follow worthless visions. Enough with God's will.

[Page 67]

Resourceful people became useless while waiting for miracles. It was easy for us to think the end of our troubles was coming. Without thinking at all, we couldn't do anything.

Once the Germans came and demanded 100 men for work. They would be sent-they said-"first to Kremenets and from there to their place of work," and so on. We knew from the past that they weren't talking about work. Each of us knew the purpose of that transport, but hunger weakened our judgment, and people came and volunteered to work, to be included in the "workers" quota. Maybe they could live a while longer; maybe they'd be given bread in their place of work.

The 100 got together. The "quota" left on foot for Kremenets. On the way, an idea crossed our minds. We said, "Maybe this is a death trap that we had forgotten about over the winter. Is there is something we can do to save them?"

We took the initiative, Yosef Shapiro and I. We approached Veloshin, the Ukrainian police commander, and offered to pay him a lot of money to give the order not to accelerate the walkers' pace and to aim their arrival in Kremenets for after the train had left. We explained to him that if he gave the order, we wouldn't complain about him. For some unknown reason, he agreed to our request.

And the people arrived late for their train.

That one day, and from that one "action," they survived.

They all scattered and went to stay with their families in Kremenets, and from there, they returned unharmed to Vishnevets.

Anyone who hasn't seen the happiness of the condemned being returned to the arms of their homes and their town has never seen happiness. There was joy at home and joy in the streets. People danced and blessed each other with the blessing of the One who bestows, frees the fettered, and gives life to the dead. They kissed and hugged. It was a sign and a signal; everything would pass... the miracles weren't over... we have the right to... and we'd live....

March 16, 1943

On that date, which was a Tuesday, the order was given to set up a ghetto. The buildings to be included in the ghetto were marked. According to the order, the ghetto had to be constructed in three days. The Jews were assigned to build the ghetto with their own hands and with materials they had to supply.

To make sure the order would be carried out in full, two hostages were taken: Yakov Markhbeyn and the writer of these lines. Any diversion from the details of the order would jeopardize their lives.

They also wanted to add Avraham Tsimbler to the two of us, but we asked them to release him. We knew he was the only person who could negotiate with the Ukrainians, and the community needed him that day. It was better for him to remain free and save others than to become a person in need of saving.

The Jews were worried about the hostages' fate and desperately tried to obey the orders down to the last detail. The ghetto was built in two days. The residents worked hard, took fences apart, connected sections of walls, and the work was done. Everything was carried out by volunteers, with unity and exceptional organization.

[Page 68]

The Ghetto

The ghetto encircled a narrow part of the town and the length of one long street. It extended from Alter Layter's house to Beni Mazur's house and from the road leading to Lanovits to the entrance to the Old City.

The fence reached nearly the height of the buildings. In some places the fence was connected to the buildings, and the outside walls were used as part of the fence. To do so, windows and doors had to be sealed with wood. Since we didn't have enough wood, we requested that small spaces be allowed between the boards. For some unknown reason, they agreed to our request, so air and sun could enter the crowded rooms.

***

Every day, the Judenrat received an order to send 50-70 men to work. People went to work willingly. They didn't get paid for their work, but the fact that they could spend time in the fresh air and the hope that they might be able to provide food for their families bewitched all of them.

People who went out to work "smuggled" food into the ghetto when they returned. This was forbidden.

The Ukrainian policemen who guarded the ghetto gate searched for hidden food, "inspecting" and beating with the butts of their guns. Woe to anyone who got caught. At times, people who were beaten suffered broken ribs and permanently collapsed lungs. The Ukrainian sadists' greatest joy was to find eggs in people's bags; they beat the egg white and the yolk together, and the man would be left bleeding with broken, mixed eggs.

The Judenrat

After the Jews were transferred to the ghetto, a Judenrat was appointed. Its members included Shlome Ayzenberg, who served as the treasurer, collecting the fines enforced on the Jews; Hershel Margaliot, who drafted people for work according to demand; and Yakov Markhbeyn, who was in charge of the bakery with me. Elected Judenrat leader was Koylenberner, who had come from Lodz and found shelter in Vishnevets after escaping from his birthplace when it was captured by the Germans in 1939. He was a warm Jew who loved Israel and was ready to sacrifice his life to save each Jew in the town. He was the central figure in the town during those tragic days. He was everything to us. Each us was ready to do anything for him, way beyond our ability and willpower.

Koylenberner spoke fluent German and was liked by the Germans. At times it looked to us as if they wouldn't kill him. He was murdered after the ghetto was liquidated.

Avraham Tsimbler was also added to the Judenrat as a negotiator with the Ukrainians.

[Page 69]

The Judenrat was not appointed right away. At the beginning, the Jews were ordered to choose their representatives, but no one agreed to this. In the end, candidates were nominated by a group of Jews. When they refused, the Jews begged them to accept the nomination. They were afraid riots would break out in the town if they didn't have a committee to represent them. The list was given to the Germans, who approved the nominations.

Food

When the ghetto had been set up, the Germans knew they had created a prison where a free labor force was concentrated. To benefit from their prisoners, they had to maintain them-sustain them with almost nothing. They gave each of us 140 grams of flour a day. From that, we baked the bread that saved the lives of the ghetto's residents. Later the portion was lowered to 100 grams and, finally, to only 60 grams.

The Ghetto's Population

More than 4,000 people were concentrated in the Vishnevets ghetto. Of them, close to 3,000 were residents of Vishnevets and the surrounding area, and around 1,000 Jews were from Vyshgorodok.

The news of the Vyshgorodok Jews' arrival reached us in the evening. We knew they would arrive early in the morning, after a night of strenuous walking, cold and frozen from the rain of a difficult winter. We stayed up all night and boiled tea, and prepared tea and bread for them. We didn't have anything else.

They arrived early in the morning, tired and frozen, hungry and beaten. We welcomed then with a piece of bread and some tea, and we revived them.

Before the ghetto, there were 4,600 Jewish residents in both parts of Vishnevets. On July 23, 1941, 65 people were murdered; on July 30, 1941, 400 souls; 60-70 died of starvation; and 146 were murdered in the Old City.

Entering and exiting the ghetto was totally forbidden, but we were allowed to walk freely inside it. People didn't "move around"; they didn't want to see or be seen. Victims of hunger were lying in the streets, swollen-until they died.

Homes were always dark and overcrowded with people. Each was a ball of fear, desperation, and depression.

Some sat on their doorsteps staring at the darkened world and waiting for the worst to come. When the street turned dark, they entered their homes, took their clothes off or not, and went to sleep.

They woke up in the morning without purpose. They were indifferent to their surroundings and completely hopeless; even a spark of light or a glimmer of hope seemed impossible to them. They received no news from the outside. Rumors stopped, and connections ceased. They were cut off, and there was nothing to look for in the street or from its inhabitants. Nothing was there to revive their souls.

Actually, they'd all reached their limits. One more step, and everything would be over, and it was good that the end was near! But the step wasn't taken, and it lasted too long.

[Page 70]

The situation was the same for all age groups. Family members, from infants to the elderly, lived together with no separation. The same world united them and wrapped them in a mystery that neither the elderly nor the young could solve. They were equal in their lack of hope and solutions. No cry or laugh, no argument or quarrel. A dead town whose sounds had all died and that no longer existed; a desolate place without color or voice. No prayer or plea. No music or song. Their power was removed. No one needed them to ease their lives, to deceive themselves and live with false hope. Even the deception was missing and was no longer there.

Death in the Ghetto

When May arrived, the sun warmed us, and its light unveiled a terrible picture: people who were useless to themselves and their families lay in the streets. They warmed up in a sun whose rays tried in vain to penetrate their swollen bodies and revive those who were starving to death. And if you passed by someone swollen from hunger and waiting to die and he stretched a hand toward you, it wasn't for help, assistance in getting up, or charity. All he wanted was to say a word of parting: farewell, I'll die tomorrow. And the next day, he'd actually die.

From the windows, I saw children swollen from hunger whose mothers took them out into the generous sun, and they walked toward it, apathetically and without a care, and died in the light of its rays.

Once on a Friday, Idel Kovilis, who sewed patches on clothes, came to me and entered my room to drink tea. He enjoyed the tea but complained about his ailing health, and he said to me, "I'm not swollen, but the hunger is showing its signs." I tried to comfort him and said to him, "Be strong, my brother. Salvation will come very soon, and you'll have a chance to enjoy this world."

My words didn't reach him, and he said, "Even if salvation comes the day after tomorrow, meaning on Sunday, I won't enjoy it."

And indeed, he passed away on Sunday.

I cried very hard when I escorted him to the cemetery. For many days I hadn't cried; the source of my tears had dried up. But now for some reason, their source opened up. In normal times, I wouldn't even know Idel Kovilis had died, and if I knew, I wouldn't pay attention or react to it. Now he was the source of a deep cry. His image, drinking tea and talking about salvation and death, followed me for many hours like an awful sign and a measure of the depth of the tragedy that took revenge on man and could hit him at any time.

***

It was good that we were allowed to bury our dead in the cemetery; it brought hope back to our souls, and we paid our respects to the person and buried him in the designated location.

Yisrael Feygeles, the town judge, died suddenly of natural causes-old age and fragility-and his death was a source of jealousy among the people, who said, "This is how we want to die."

[Page 71]

It also added value to his personality when they said, "If he died that way, it's a sign that he was a righteous man."

During a strange period of unnatural death, a normal death was something to talk about.

One day I stood by the window looking through a crack and saw a young man around the age of17 returning from work. He left the group, approached the fence, and threw a package over into the ghetto.

A Ukrainian saw it and grabbed the youth-the boy. And the boy didn't realize that he had seen him. I knew the Ukrainian; he was a reptile but not one of the worst. I called him. He came to me, and I said to him, "Vaske, what are your intentions?"

And he said to me, "He's done something that deserves punishment by death."

I asked him to give him a fine. Punish him with money and let him go, strongly warn him, and in this way, he would satisfy his "conscience" as keeper of the law. But he held on his own and explained to me in a beautiful way:

"You have to understand, he doesn't have any money. If I punish him with a fine, he'll have difficulty paying it. Why should I enforce something that will make his life more difficult and cause him trouble with the Germans? It's better for me to kill him. It'll be a lot better for him."

[Page 72 - Hebrew] [Page 336 - Yiddish]

In the Sea of Human Madness

by Sore Kitaykesher (Kirshenboym)

Translated by Sara Mages

(A candle to Yohana Venshitska-Kreshitska)

When the war broke out, I was on my way to Israel. We weren't allowed to cross the Rumanian border. Even though we had passports and legal documents, we weren't given permission to move "until things clear up," and the war put an end to everything.

I was ashamed to go back to Vishnevets. I went back to my brothers in Zaloshtsy and stayed there from Rosh Hashanah until Purim. I couldn't help myself; I wanted to see my loved ones-my family and my town.

I went back to Vishnevets on Purim. The Soviet regime had left a strange situation; some people-the worthless and irresponsible ones-were happy with the change. Most people were depressed. My parents and brothers, who were merchants, suddenly found themselves outside "worthy" society, and we didn't have bread at home. Hearts were heavy; depression ate us alive.

I, who wanted to work, was worthless because I was the daughter of a merchant of worthless origin.

Meanwhile, my father died of depression and hopelessness.

On June 22, 1941, when war broke out between Russia and Germany, I wasn't in Vishnevets. My brothers had left the town, my father was dead, and I couldn't find a place for myself there. I left and traveled to Ternopol, where my brothers worked. I overcame my troubles. I knew I needed to build a life. I ordered furniture for myself. My boyfriend, whom I had dated for a year, wanted to get engaged. I was ready to get married. On June 24, I received a telegram from my future husband telling me we needed to move to my brother's in Zaloshtsy. My sister and I were left alone, and the situation in Vishnevets was what it was; most of the young men had been taken into the Russian army. The town had been deserted to its elderly, who were panic-stricken and without prospects. We didn't have a place or a means of support in the town. Naked and poor, we left on foot for Zaloshtsy.

On the way to Zaloshtsy, the Ukrainians caught us and wanted to kill us, but when we told them we were Hershko's sisters, they let us go, but added, "It doesn't matter. The Germans will do it better than we can. Once and for all, we'll cleanse our country of Jewish filth."

We walked 28 kilometers with our bundles on our backs. Our knapsacks were made from sheets we'd taken from home, tied like crosses. The road was full of danger. The Ukrainians swarmed the roads: it was a holiday for them, the holiday of sacrificing Jewish blood, and they celebrated it with great joy. They also celebrated their bloody holiday in Vishnevets. They ridiculed us and laughed at our distress. A woman-our neighbor of many years-who followed us from our home, which we had left forever, said, "This is God's punishment because you crucified Jesus. How long will you be a stubborn nation? When will you understand your suffering?"

After three months in Zaloshtsy, when the month of Elul arrived, we decided to go to Vishnevets to lay stones on our parents' graves, a Jewish tradition, and to see our two brothers, who were living there with their families.

[Page 73]

It was before the establishment of the ghetto. But the Jews were already imprisoned and chained.

A few days before it was established, the Ukrainians went to the Old City and massacred all the Jews. Not a single soul was left there. Only Fride Yakira was left alive, but not for too long. I saw her while visiting my sister-in-law. She was at home with her young son. Both women were alive, and both were widows. On the first night of the German occupation, my brother, my sister-in-law's husband, had been taken by the Ukrainians to an unknown location. We still have no details about his fate. Fride's husband, Shike Grinboym, had been sent to Siberia by the Russians when they first arrived. So their tragedy united them and made them one. They sat depressed and wrapped in an indescribable gloom. Fride's face reflected memories of the overnight massacre in the Old City. She told us, "For many days, we felt we were imprisoned in a cage. The freedom to move around had been taken away from us." One evening, she was sitting at home with her child. She heard the strange sound of drumming and gunfire around her, but she didn't pay any attention to it. Suddenly the door burst open, and two Ukrainians she knew entered and informed her, "We've come to kill you."

She thought it was a practical joke and started to wonder and beg them, "How, Mikhilo, Ivan, how could you kill us? What wrong have we done to you?" And more questions of that order.

They were a little embarrassed, but she saw the desire to kill in their eyes and knew they would carry out their mission. She took advantage of the few moments of confusion, broke through the door, and ran away with the baby in her arms.

The night was dark. She ran downhill from her home to the river. She submerged herself in the water with her infant son. The boy cried and fell asleep in her arms. She stayed in the water, letting her son sleep.

Loud screams and heartbreaking shouts reached her ears. The sound of gunfire rose and fell, and murder was carried out around her. She could tell what was happening, minute by minute, and to whom. Doors were broken down, shouts were heard, and then they were silenced. The sound of gunfire silenced the sound of nature.

Shocked and shaken, she stayed in the water for many hours, until it was quiet. Then she understood that the massacre was over. The murderers went to sleep, and the whole town and all of her Jews also fell asleep, for eternity.

I knew that the fate of Vishnevets Jews had been cast. I didn't believe it would affect all of us.

We slept together that night. I woke up in the morning and left for Zaloshtsy to see my brothers and husband. I left my sister-in-law, who was caring for her small children and elderly mother. She didn't dare leave on the long walk with me.

We also left Fride; she saw my sister-in-law as her only family, the only one left.

[Page 74]

Many years later, we found out Fride had been saved from the first massacre, but when the ghetto opened, she died with her infant son and my two brothers' sons and widows.

***

In May 1942, they came to pick up my husband on the pretext that Mikolski, the workers' commander, wanted to see him. A Jewish policeman moved back and whispered in my ear, telling me my husband was going to be sent to a concentration camp. I told my husband. He thought for a moment about how to escape, and then he said to them, "If a Ukrainian or German comes and tells me the same thing, I'll go with them." When they turned, I opened the back window; my husband jumped out and ran into the fields.

I escaped, too.

In the evening, I returned home. I didn't see my husband. In the morning, while working in the yard, I heard someone calling my name and asking in German, "Are you Mrs. Kirshenboym?"

I knew I couldn't escape. I approached him as I'd been ordered. He started to shower me with questions about my husband, his whereabouts, and why I'd helped him escape. He took me to the commander. It was a long walk to the commander's office, more than a kilometer. He didn't pay attention to the fact that I was very weak and had difficulty walking. All the way, he asked me questions, trying to get information about the location of my husband's hiding place. The truth is that I really didn't know. Then he started to beat me. I arrived at the commander's office wounded and in pain. He threw me into the cellar and let me stay in the dark for a short time. Then he came down and continued to torment me for my sin-saving my husband's life. Fortunately, I fainted. I fell and seriously hurt my head. When I came to my senses, they came to take me to the central command office in Zborov.

Upstairs, a coal truck was being unloaded. The truck was covered with soot and coal dust. They put me in the back, and we drove off. The German sat next to the driver. Two other Jews sat in the back with me.

I wanted to escape on the way. They realized it and shouted at me, "Mrs. Kirshenboym, we know your intentions, and we'd advise you not to do it. You'd do better to travel with us to Mr. Kraus, and we'll clear up the matter of your husband. You'd be smart to listen to our advice."

So I arrived at the Zborov labor camp.

He handed me over to the commander and explained the extent of my crime.

Kraus, the camp commander, said to me, "I'll give you 24 hours. If you don't produce your husband, we'll shoot you like a dog. Yesterday we hanged a Jewish woman who hid her son from us. The same fate is waiting for you."

While I stood there in the commander's office, which also served as the camp office, I saw the people.

[Page 75]

My intestines turned inside me from fright, anger, pity, and weakness. Dead, human shadows, transparent bags of bones were walking around. Their empty eyes were wide open, staring from their holes, vacant and indifferent to the world around them.

I knew my husband was in Zborov, working as a leather worker in a tannery, but I couldn't get in touch with him. Somehow, my arrest, and the danger I was in, reached him. He asked the tannery manager to do something. His name was Yenkevits, a gentile with a Jewish heart. He and his mother had done a lot to save Jews. He said to my husband, "There's no other choice. You must go; if you do, you'll save her."

My husband took his advice as if it had come from a friend and came to the commander's office. For some reason, they were satisfied and locked him up in the camp. That was his punishment after they found him. They released me. We separated. We divided a loaf of bread, half a loaf for him and half for me.

We told each other we would meet again. But doubt ate at our hearts. We almost didn't believe it.

Yenkevits came to take me to his house and told me, "I'll rescue your husband from the camp. We love him. Meanwhile, you can recover here."

The house was like a palace. They were extremely rich. There were a lot of lights and shiny, valuable objects, and I was gloomy, barefoot, dirty, and covered with coal dust from the truck. They put me in a bathroom. A woman came in and washed me with her own hands. She gave me food, calmed me down, and gave me hope. I didn't forget that evening for many years. She was an angel in the form of a woman. Sometime later, I was told she had risked her life to bring baskets of food to the Jews in the camp. Everyone called her "mother of the Jews." I still haven't been able to find any information about her. Maybe her name brought her death. This is how the Yenkevits family was.

I returned to my home in Zaloshtsy, and my husband remained in the Zborov camp.

For three months, until the end of August of the same year, I walked to Zborov, a distance of 29 kilometers, to bring him food. Through a secret corner we had agreed on between us, I handed him the food.

We risked our lives the moment I gave him the food. I risked my life each time I walked alone among the bloodthirsty gentiles to revive my depressed husband's soul.

At the end of August, we had found a way to release him. We paid Kraus $350, some fox leather for his wife, and a fine leather collar and trousers for Mr. Kraus, the representative of German culture.

Yenkevits executed the release. When he took my husband out of the camp, he put him on his bicycle and brought him to us, a strenuous, 29-kilometer bicycle ride.

How we can forget Yenkevits, a dear man with a beautiful soul, and not just him and his wife? His sister took part, too. She was a beautiful woman, and numerous times each week she walked to the camp to bring food, risking her life and taking the chance that she might be caught and tortured.

[Page 76]

On September 15, 1942, Zaloshtsy's drummer, a gentile by the name of Yanko, walked around announcing that in two weeks Zaloshtsy was to be cleansed of its Jews. All the Jews had to leave and move to Zborov, where a ghetto would be established. All the Jews from the surrounding area had to move to the ghetto and be locked in.

My brother, his family, and my sister decided to go to Zborov. I knew what would be waiting for us. I tried to persuade them not to go, but I didn't succeed. They said, "What happens to everyone will also happen to us."

And in Zaloshtsy, the killings continued, and the Jews wanted to run away.

I decided to stay.

We lived with a gentile woman by the name of Yohana Venshitska-Kreshitska, a Polish widow who was married to a Ukrainian and living with her 80-year-old mother. She was poor and hungry for bread. She had one cow on her farm, and her land couldn't support the two of them. She had been forced to work as a cleaning lady at other farms even though she was an aristocrat's daughter. Her brothers were doctors and teachers. They were alive and lived nearby, but she didn't need their help.

She accepted our offer, and in doing so she risked her life. We dug a hole under the stall and put beds and bedding there. We lived in our shelter under the stall for almost two years.

Her home was raided many times, and from time to time we were forced to run and hide separately in a large marsh located outside town. The marsh served as a hay barn for the entire community and the local farmers. I dug tunnels in the piles of hay by tearing the hay. I hid there while my husband looked for someplace else to hide.

This gentile woman supported us constantly. When we left her house-the bunker we were hiding in-she brought hot tea to us at a designated location. Every once in a while, my husband and I went to her house. Four times, we were caught after the neighbors reported us. She bought our release from the Germans with the last of her money. Once she gave them her only cow, the source of her milk, as ransom. Another time she gave them a box containing the last of the food she had in her house. I owe my life, and my husband's life, to this righteous woman, Yohana Venshitska-Kreshitska; I'll remember this spark of radiant humanity for the rest of my life.

***

Meanwhile, my brother and his family returned to Zaloshtsy, his town. We tried to find a way to see him, but we couldn't. My husband had to find himself a hiding place apart from me. After wandering around, I returned to my benefactor, Yohana. In order not to endanger her life, I didn't let her know I was there. I didn't enter the deserted barn but hid in a bunker I prepared for myself in a pile of garbage outside. Someone suspected I was there and reported me. The Germans came; their leader was a bloodthirsty man. When he arrived at the bunker, he took me out. I was dirty, my hair was uncombed, I was skinny, and I stank.

[Page 77]

He said to his men and the group of Ukrainians who were waiting for the killing feast, "This is a woman who is fighting for her life. We need to keep her alive. Don't touch or harm her." They left, but I had to run away. The Germans were hunting down the last of the Jews. I came across a cellar; a frightened gentile woman stood there, demanding that I leave immediately. I told her I wasn't leaving.

I asked her to go and see my family. I promised her I would leave if she brought me news. She came back an hour later and told me all of them had died, adding, "Get away from me. You have nothing to do with me!"

I ran.

The next day, Mikolski came, following his dog to my hiding place. They didn't find me. I was saved. But I didn't care. I had had enough. I wanted to go to the commander and give myself up. I was tired of my life. The last few weeks had been too difficult. I had failed and reached the end of end of my suffering.

I ran to their office. On the way I ran into Yohana. I hadn't seen her for some days. I said to her, "I've lost my husband, and my family is dead, so why should I live?"

She calmed me down and said, "Your Henik is very skillful. I'm sure he escaped and saved himself. Don't do it. Stay strong, and stay alive for him.

Her words gave me strength.

***

I saw Henik in January 1944. Both of us had been persecuted up to our necks; we were poor, frozen, and starving. But in our hearts, we had decided to live.

In February 1944, Yohana came and told us that Russian partisans had arrived at the village entrance. We decided to go to them. That same night, the Russians got drunk and passed out. The surviving Germans slaughtered all of them.

The area returned to German anarchy.

We found shelter in a cellar in a building. In the morning, we discovered that a German outpost was stationed there. Our situation was desperate.

We waited for two days. On Saturday, we separated and ran in opposite directions. I went into a Polish woman's house. She thought I was Polish and arranged a job for me as a cook for the village priest. One evening, she told me that a young Jewish man, who wanted to become a Christian, told her he knew that I was Jewish and that I was related to him. She kicked me out, saying, "I have a heavy heart for the Jews. All their lives they've used us. Loaned us money at high interest and didn't think about the fate of others."

I begged her. The young man's story was correct. I knew who he was, but I denied it.

At night she changed her mind; her heart felt sorry for me, and she let me stay, but this time she took me to the cellar.

[Page 78]

On Friday morning, March 26, 1944, she came down to the cellar and happily informed me, "We have visitors. The Russians have arrived."

Immediately, she fell at my feet, begging and asking for forgiveness. She only wanted to know why I had lied to her.

I answered her, "I wanted to live."

I went to look for my husband. He had left messages for me in various locations.

On March 27, 1944, we met, this time to wander together in Russia.

I left Poland, the sea of human madness; I left it forever.

[Page 325 - Yiddish]

The Old City ! Wiped Out in One Night

[Page 326 - Yiddish]

[No caption]

[Page 331 - Yiddish]

On the Boulevard ...

[Page 79 - Hebrew] [Page 326 - Yiddish]

I Was a Girl in the Vishnevets Ghetto
by Rachel (Sobol) Fuks (Vyshgorodok)
Translated by Sara Mages

Vishnevets Welcomes Its Brothers

I was 14 years old when they took us to the Vishnevets ghetto.

It was the beginning of January 1941. A fierce snowstorm was blowing outside. Our homes were covered with frost inside and out. Life was frozen, and families were hiding in their homes waiting for the worst to come. We were told that very soon we'd be taken to the Vishnevets ghetto. We spent all day with all our clothes on, freezing in a house that had been without heat for many weeks. That day, Ukrainians decorated with German police badges came knocking on our door, shouting that we were each allowed to take a bundle weighing 20 kilograms with us. They told us to go to the town center and be ready to leave the town for Vishnevets in a few hours.

We arrived in Vishnevets exhausted, hungry, and frozen from the long walk. The people in Vishnevets knew we were coming. They waited for us all night and welcomed us with brotherly warmth, warm soup, and a piece of bread they'd saved from their own mouths. I'll never forget that meeting; it's a shame so few have survived to remember it.

All the houses in the ghetto were occupied, and a large number of families lived in each one. The Judenrat moved the Vishnevetsers to the already overcrowded houses to provide housing for us. We lived like the Vishnevetsers, 10 families per house, with only one bathroom for all of us.

The morning after our arrival in the ghetto, we were told that each day we needed to provide a quota of men for work. There were three men and three "women" in our family. My 11-year-old sister and I went to work in the men's place. We were informed that men were being tortured, and we wanted to prevent our father and brothers from suffering.

We worked at cleaning the snow that accumulated in the streets after storms. We worked in the fields collecting frozen potatoes and repairing torn and moldy potato sacks. Every once in a while, we brought food with us when we returned home: two or three frozen potatoes and a handful of kernels we'd found here or there.

They searched us at the entrance gate to the ghetto. They beat us up if our "smuggled loot" was discovered. But the worry that our loved ones would die of hunger was worse than the fear of being beaten. Often we found the bodies of people who had died of starvation lying in the streets, and the substance of our existence centered on the search for food.

Once I saw Chayke Shapiro, the Vyshgorodok ritual slaughterer's daughter, in the ghetto. She walked by me, rubbed against me, and didn't see me. I tried to talk to her, but she didn't respond. Her vacant look and wide-open eyes staring into the distance indicated that she had lost her mind. Why didn't anyone take her home? Why didn't anyone, including the members of her family, take care of her? I'll never know. She ended her life in front of everyone as a madwoman in the ghetto streets.

Zioma Vays, my friend from school, also went crazy. Other people who had lost their minds also wandered in the streets, but I didn't know them.

[Page 80]

Of all the many horrors of the ghetto, the one that is carved deepest in my mind is the memory of my friends' insanity. The humiliation and suffering terrified me. God Almighty! Anything but that. I decided I wouldn't go crazy, as if it were up to me, and I also decided I wanted to live, and I felt it really was up to me.

The Liquidation and the Judenrat

One day, the Germans ordered the Jews to give them a certain quota of gold and valuables. If not, a certain number of Jews would be killed. And the quota was found. Everyone gave what was left, just enough to save other Jews from death. The order was repeated over and over until the supply ended, and Jews were taken and never returned.

And so it lasted until the beginning of August 1943.

In August there was a pervasive rumor about an upcoming action. We knew our end was near.

Before the final liquidation, the Germans informed the Judenrat that Jews were allowed to leave the ghetto, go home, and bring their hidden treasures. Some would be given to the authorities, some would be left for them, and those who obeyed the order would stay alive. The more they gave to the Germans, the better their situation would be. Jews left for home, near and far. Each one was escorted by a policeman. The Vyshgorodok Jews went to Vyshgorodok, and policemen escorted them all the way there. The Jews were tempted, left, and brought back their treasures. They didn't survive.

The ghetto was closed for three days after the Jews came back with the last of their treasures. The buildings inside the ghetto were also closed. Those who walked from building to building were shot and killed in the street. We knew what was waiting for us: death lived in each cell of our consciousness. We were frightened.

When the days of the liquidation arrived, we saw the Vishnevets Judenrat in its full, shining tragedy.

Pure-hearted Jews with generous souls gave their lives for the smallest cause, for the fate of the members of their community.

For many years I wondered: from where had they drawn the courage and the spirit to support others when their fate was no different?

I was mature and independent for my age. I saw their dedication and heard the conversations of people older than I. Opinions were united-the messengers who carry the orders are the most tragic ones.

The most distinguished of them was Koylenberner, the head of the Judenrat. He was a refugee from Katovits or Shlonsk. He had escaped from the German border to the Russian border and had been captured here. While the action was going on, he was given the privilege of staying alive. The Germans offered it to him, but he joined the death march with everyone else. He took advantage of their mercy, asking to take the first bullet so he wouldn't witness the death of his beloved flock. They agreed to his request. So it has been told.

The Judenrat members were the first to die. I was later told that one had survived the same way others did: at the mercy of the situation, with the agility and willpower to escape death. There was no other way to survive.

Shredded Memories

From my life in the ghetto and my terrifying memories, a few horrifying events stand out in my brain. They are registered so deeply that it's difficult for me to return to them.

[Page 81]

Few they are, and many were the wounds in my heart when they happened. They shred my frightful soul. They terrify me, and more than that, the horrors storm in me all over again; they grab me and don't let me go. I live in the shadow of new fears, waiting for something horrible to happen, something whose horrors are known to me in their full details, from which that I can't escape.

I'll tell you about a few of them here:

It was Passover eve. Families gathered together to observe the Passover seder according to "tradition." Mother had collected the last of the flour and baked pitiful miniature matzos. We were sitting at the table; mother asked my brother to read the Haggadah. My brother was religious and loved tradition, but this time he refused: "If this 'seder' is appeasing God, I won't read the Haggadah to Him."

Mother was consumed with worry about us. Her day was full of worries; she was always looking for ways to sustain us. Every day was the same. Every day she came up with new inventions. On some days, she tore up the spring crop of tall grass growing around our home, mixed it with something, and baked thin cakes for us, and the cakes had 77 different flavors to them. I tremble when I remember my mother, who was extremely serious and the center of our lives, bending to collect the meager sprouts, like an animal, a goat in a barren country. My mother was grasping them. To me, she resembled an animal in a desolated land.

We were staying in Alter Layter's house. In this spacious house, we discovered a large cellar running under the length of the whole house. We kept its existence to ourselves as protection from future troubles. The day came; we climbed down to its depths and discovered that it was half-full of water-maybe clean water or maybe melted frozen water, because it hadn't been used for many years. We didn't have a choice; maybe there was a way to survive and live for a few more days. Maybe we could hide in the cellar, and no one would see us when they came to take us and kill us. The third day, the last day of our lives, arrived. All the families gathered in the cellar, and the men built rafts out of wood. I don't know if they floated on the water, but we all sat on them. The killers came, and they didn't find what they were looking for. They couldn't see us. We hid the entrance to the cellar with a heavy wardrobe, and they didn't notice us. In the afternoon, a second group arrived, but they weren't satisfied with a quick look, and they started making loud noises. It was a terrible sound. The babies among us got scared and started to cry, one wail after another. A child joined a child, and they all cried loudly together. At the same moment, we heard a noise, and father said, "We're finished. We've been found because of the crying babies."

And so it was.

They found the entrance and shouted, "Come out peacefully. If you don't, we'll toss hand grenades into your cave, and we'll shred you to pieces in there."

That convinced us.

For some reason, they didn't want to be shredded to pieces and die in the cellar. Even though they knew death was certain, they went out and gave themselves up.

I decided to live no matter what. I dove into the water, holding to a board with the tips of my fingers. Another girl, named Ester Frenkel, stayed with me.

[Page 82]

Father collected his family and went out. I stayed with Ester. He wanted us to be together until the end. Suddenly I heard him asking mother, "Otye (my nickname) is missing. Where's Otye?"

Mother hushed him. "Maybe she'll be saved separately from us. Leave her there.

He stopped talking.

Suddenly I head my mother utter a painful cry. Apparently, she was being separated from the rest of her loving family.

Everything was over. The world had been silenced, and we were submerged in water up to our necks. We were wet and frozen on a hot August day. For a moment, we forgot what we were waiting for. The knowledge somehow escaped us. Suddenly we heard steps. The murderers had returned. They were afraid to enter the cellar; they just shouted into it: "If anyone is hiding there, get out right away. We're going to drop a bomb into it." We didn't get out. It was quiet. We heard only faint knocking, like the ticking of the hours, and my teeth started to chatter. To quiet myself, I pushed my fist between my teeth and separated them until I punctured holes in my fist and blood started to trickle out.

After many hours, we left and climbed onto the roof. On top was a gutter made of stone chips, maybe two meters high. We decided to climb inside the gutter. It looked like a good hiding place, but we couldn't, we were too heavy. But somehow we managed to climb in. When we reached the gutter, we found a space wide enough for both of us to sleep in. We also found a bottle of water and a jar of jam. The heavens had prepared them for us. Every once in a while, we heard the sound of gunfire. We said to each other after each shot, "Now they've killed our fathers, now our mothers, and now it's my sister they've killed." Maybe we knew; who knows. It was clear then that they were being shot.

We sat there for three days, sustaining ourselves with bottled water and the jar of jam. We decided to climb down. Ester said we should leave at night. She knew a friend of her father's, a farm owner by the name of Lifishuv. We'll go there, she said, he'll save us when he finds out who I am. He owes my father a lot of favors. Under cover of darkness, we climbed down. Meanwhile, a group of people walked by. They weren't policemen or killers. They shined their flashlights on the entrances to Jewish homes trying to find valuables, and they discovered us. Immediately, we hid behind the two heavy wardrobes standing there. They lost us even though they'd seen us clearly. They came in, saw the locks on the heavy wardrobes, and said to each other, "They're on the roof. We need to kill them. The locks are heavy, which shows that there's treasure behind them. We can't leave witnesses: it's too dangerous. First we should climb on the roof and grab them; we'll open the wardrobes later, but first we must get rid of the Jews." When they climbed up, we escaped. We wanted to jump through a window. A cornfield was behind it, and the tall cornstalks were a good hiding place. But we were afraid to jump from such a height. In the end, I overcame my fears and jumped. I hid and waited for her to come. [Page 83] She didn't come out. I decided to wait and wait. She was the only one left for me. She was the only one who had survived with me, and I.... waited.

I heard the "guards" walking around the ghetto, searching and listening. Maybe they'd find more Jews. And then the steps stopped. The night passed. Dawn began to break. I had to run. I was afraid the morning light would give me away, and she hadn't come. The fence was high, and the boards were tight against each other. I pushed myself through a narrow opening between two boards and left. It was a miracle. It's difficult for me to believe even now that a human being could pass through such a narrow opening. I didn't know Vishnevets; I only knew the way from the ghetto to work and back. I ran in that direction and, unfortunately, I arrived at the commissioner's home. Dogs barked in his yard, but no one came out. I crossed the forest and hid in a potato pile. I chewed the dirty potatoes and fell asleep.

A few days later, on a Friday, I ran down the main street. I was discovered. Two Ukrainians caught me and dragged me to the river, wanting to drown me there. But meanwhile, an elderly Ukrainian passed by and said to them, "You'll throw her into the river, and we'll all suffer. Her blood won't give you peace or rest." "Don't do it."

[1] That convinced them. They left me and ordered me to run. I ran. They shot many bullets after me. Running frantically, I fell into a pit. I disappeared, and the shooting stopped. When night came, I climbed out.

I arrived in Chichinits after a whole night of running and was shocked to see a "Police" sign in front of me. A gentile with a cart approached me and said, "You're Jewish. Get out of here. It's dangerous, they'll kill you."

I asked him to show me the way to Verbovits.

An elderly farmer stood in the field cutting wheat. He was shocked when he saw me!

"Child, where are you running to?"

I told him, to Holanda Honerchuk, who had been our friend for many years. I assumed her family would save me.

He blessed me, wishing me long life, and showed me the way to her house.

This family saved me. The Germans came to their home to confiscate things. They risked their lives and didn't give me up.

They transferred me from family to family and between their friends. Each one fulfilled the commandment of saving a small, persecuted soul. They risked their lives. They lived in fear of sudden raids for many days, knowing they'd be sentenced to death if their great crime were discovered. Nevertheless, they did it.

Thanks to them, I reached the end of the Holocaust and what followed it.

There are more stories about my life away from Vishnevets, but they don't belong in a book.

[Page 84]

The Destruction of Vishnevets, Volin

(As told by Shaul Shvarts)

by Mendel Zinger

Translated by Sara Mages

(From a booklet)

During the intermediate days of Passover, I traveled to the religious youth village to talk to one of the teenagers who had arrived in Israel from Vishnevets in Volin. When I met with the teenagers near the border with Syria just after their arrival in Israel, they pointed out that this teenager had endured a lot of suffering. I looked at his pale face and frightened black eyes, and I decided that it wasn't the right time to talk to him. A few weeks later, the teenager had calmed down, and his face looked better. When I walked through the village with him, I realized he'd adjusted to his new life even with his minimal knowledge of Hebrew. But it was still difficult to talk to him.

The teenager's name was Shaul, and he was 15 years old. His body was well developed, and the marks of the many beatings he had received were still visible on his face. Like all teenage refugees from the Nazi inferno, he was wise for his age, and the details of his terrible memories were carved deep into his mind. He even remembered exact dates by associating them with certain events. For example, this and that happened exactly a month before my father died. This happened about two weeks before they killed this and that. Shaul was quiet by nature but became extremely excited when he brought up memories of his past. It made our conversation more difficult, so every once in a while I found an excuse to stop for a short time.

According to Shaul, around 4,500 Jews, and 500 gentiles, mostly Ukrainians, lived in Vishnevets near Kremenets in the Dubno district.

The Soviet army stayed in Vishnevets for almost two years. This period was not easy on the local Jews. Vishnevets Jews earned their living mostly by trading with local farmers, but under Russian rule, trading had been cut considerably. It was difficult for the Jews to get used to the new conditions, but there were some Jews, mostly the young ones, who could endure physical labor and earn a living.

Not a single Jew was arrested by the Russians. Most of the rich Jews moved to bigger cities in the district. Several kolkhozes were established, but their numbers were few because the Russians were careful not to force them on farmers. Out of goodwill, a small percentage of farmers agreed to the kolkhoz lifestyle.

When the Russians retreated from the advancing Nazi army, they took Jews and Ukrainian men between the ages of 25 to 35 with them in order to draft them into the army. Shaul couldn't estimate the number, but he knew that the Ukrainians escaped and later returned to Vishnevets. The Jews remained with the Russians, except for one Jew who escaped and returned to Vishnevets. Later, he was murdered by the Nazis.

Before they left, the Russians executed three Ukrainian nationalists and one Jew, a German refugee. The Jew was buried in the Jewish cemetery.

[Page 85]

The teenager talked quietly about the Russian occupation. He took his time, wanting to remember every detail, holding onto the events as if he were remembering good times.

The Germans Arrive

However... a sigh escaped from the depth of his heart. Immediately after the arrival of the German army, riots against the Jews began. Local Ukrainians and farmers who came to Vishnevets instructed the soldiers, and together they stole everything they could put their hands on. Jews who came across Nazis or Ukrainians were beaten and injured. There were no murders.

This situation lasted for almost two weeks. Meanwhile, the German army was probably moving east or encountering heavy battles.

The Ukrainian farmers and locals quickly got closer to the Nazi invaders. Most of the Ukrainians, who served as a militia for the Russian army, joined the Nazis and served an auxiliary police force to aid the German army and the Gestapo. A small number of Ukrainians who refused to serve the Nazis were executed.

The First Murders

After the first two weeks, a Gestapo unit-numbering around 30 men-settled in the area, and murderous attacks began. The first action was to "avenge" the murder of the four men executed by the Russians before they left. For each one-three Ukrainians and a Jewish a refugee from Germany-they decided to kill 10 Jews. The Ukrainian police abducted the victims, and 40 Jews were murdered in a cellar in a town building.

Later, they started abducting men for forced labor, which always included physical and emotional torture. And men went into hiding. One day, hundreds of Jews were abducted, mostly women and teenagers. They were taken about 5 kilometers outside town to the fields of an estate owned by Romel, a Polish farm owner exiled to Siberia by the Russians. They were ordered to dig a ditch 2 meters wide and 100 meters long and were told they'd be buried in it. The digging was done with heartbreaking wailing and crying.

The Jews were kept under threat of execution by gunfire until late at night, and then they were allowed to go home.

The Slaughter Begins

A few days later, Ukrainian policemen and the Gestapo conducted a house-to-house search and abducted around 300 Jewish men. The women were told they were taking the men to work. The kidnapped group included three Community Council members (Shaul knew the names of two of them: Shike Yakira and Lifshits). They were all brought to the ditch next to Romel's estate, where they were shot to death and buried.

[Page 86]

The murderous attacks lasted around four months. Every day, a large number of Jews were abducted, taken outside town, killed, and buried there. The number of murdered Jews had already reached 1,000.

A Break in the Murders-More Looting

The Gestapo unit left the area in the direction of Proskurov. For a time, it was quiet in Vishnevets. Trusted local Ukrainians, who had come to Vishnevets from the Russian sector, told us that all the Jews, down to the last one, had been murdered there. Russians who were married to Jews had also been killed.

During the break in the murders, Gestapo agents frequently visited Vishnevets. Using the threat of murder and with the help of Ukrainian policemen, they extorted silver, gold, merchandise (even pins and needles were demanded), clothes, and furs. One day, three German soldiers walked from home to home with Ukrainian policemen, taking whatever their hearts desired.

One day, they announced that all silver, gold, and jewelry owned by Jews had to be given to the Nazis. A Jew found with those items would immediately be shot.

The Jews accepted the robberies, hoping their looted possessions would serve as ransom.

Establishment of the Ghetto

When Passover arrived (the Jews ate leavened bread during that Passover), a ghetto was set up within the boundaries of the poor neighborhoods next to the Horyn River. Five thousand Jews were moved into the ghetto. These included Jews who had escaped to Vishnevets from the nearby farms or had been evicted from them.

The Jews' transfer to the ghetto gave the Nazis and the Ukrainians another chance to steal furniture and household items from the Jews. They extorted and stole everything they could use.

A Nazi "order" was organized in the ghetto. A Jewish Council was established, with Avraham Tsimbler, a leather merchant, and Mr. Kolmbren, a refugee from Germany, as leaders. A Jewish police force was elected. They were armed with clubs and served mostly as negotiators and inspectors. At the beginning, every Jew received 15 dekagrams of bread a day, but later only 7 dekagrams of bread and 2.5 dekagrams of barley. The Jews earned their living as forced laborers in agriculture and the orchards. The daily income was enough to purchase 7 dekagrams of bread.

During the first five or six months, 1,500 Jews died of starvation and disease. Most of the victims were poor, since those with financial means could bring valuables into the ghetto and exchange them for food with the Ukrainian policemen guarding the ghetto.

The Jewish Council's duty during those months was mostly to provide Jews for forced labor.

[Page 87]

It was always done under the threat of death and with the help of the Jewish police, who used their clubs to chase Jews from their homes to their workplace. In addition, the negotiations of buying and selling jewelry and collecting the money needed as ransom for Jewish souls never stopped. In the end, the Germans came up with demands the Jews couldn't fulfill.

At the head of the operation was a Nazi by the name of Miler, who resided in Kremenets.

One night, the ghetto's Jews were frightened by the sound of gunfire at a short distance. There were different guesses. Some were hoping the partisans were getting closer, but after some time, we found out that the Jews who worked as forced laborers for the Ukrainians had been murdered. Among them were young men and women who had been shepherds. The slaughter site was not far from the ghetto, near Stefanski's farm. The victims were buried the same night in a nearby marsh.

The next day, the killers lay in waiting around the homes in the ghetto. Those who left their homes or looked through the windows were shot. I need to emphasize here that we didn't receive any written or spoken order forbidding us to leave our homes.

The slaughter lasted two days, and the number of victims was around 150.

Under German leadership, the Ukrainian police ordered us to bury the victims. We weren't allowed to bury them in the Jewish cemetery. We were forced to bury them next to the river. (By the way, in Kremenets they didn't allow victims to be brought to the Jewish cemetery. The victims were buried inside the ghetto.)

Bitter News

Day after day, we received reliable news that Jews were being exterminated in several cities in Volin. In Dubno, half the Jewish population had been murdered in the past eight months. Desperation increased day by day. Everyone knew there was no way to escape from this prison. Apathy took over the ghetto, but there were Jews who saw what was coming and looked for ways to escape from the killers' hands.

Renewal of Mass Murder

A new unit of around 15 Gestapo men arrived in Vishnevets. With the group's arrival, the situation in the ghetto immediately worsened.

Almost 1,000 Jews were abducted during the first days of the change in power, including members of the Jewish Council. Only Mr. Kolmbren, a refugee from Germany, wasn't taken. The kidnapped Jews were taken to an unknown location near Kniazshe, and no one ever heard from them again. Local farmers told us that they were all shot to death. Kolmbren was kidnapped by a Ukrainian police force, which cracked his skull and killed him.

The "operation" lasted close to a month. Jews were kidnapped daily and taken to the synagogue. From there, they were taken by a Ukrainian police force to be killed.

[Page 88]

The Ukrainians were helped by Jewish policemen, around 30 of them. Their chief duty was to collect the property of those who had been murdered. In exchange for their work, the Jewish policemen were promised that their lives would be spared. Property that the Ukrainian or German robbers weren't interested in was sold to local farmers, who came to Vishnevets and loaded the Jewish articles on their carts.

Mothers Sacrifice Their Babies

The Jews trapped in the ghetto were trying to find hiding places in their homes, mostly in closed cellars or attics without light or air. Some dug pits under the floors and covered them with wooden planks.

Sometimes they stayed in hiding for many days without food or a drop of water because their killers were waiting for them, day and night, inside or outside their homes. Hiding caused terrible family tragedies and brought mothers to the point of madness.

Sick children died in the arms of mothers who couldn't give them a drop of water. Three-year-old children were trained to be quiet and tolerate their suffering in silence. But little babies cried when they were feeling bad. So that the killers wouldn't discover the hiding place, their mothers suffocated them with their own hands. Most of the time, the mothers lost their minds after doing so.

The Killers at Shaul's Parents' Home

There were 17 people in Shaul's house, and 15 were in hiding. Only Shaul and his brother, who was two years younger than he was, remained. A Gestapo man broke into the house and asked him, "Where's the rest of your family?" "There's no one but us," Shaul answered. "My little brother wanted to hide, but I didn't let him. I calmed him down and told him nothing would happen to us." Shaul assumed that the Nazi had seen movement inside the house before he entered and wanted to divert his mind from the thought that people were hiding there.

The Nazi took out his handgun and threatened to kill the two if they didn't tell him where the rest of the family was hiding. When the Nazi realized he couldn't get anything out of the two children, he took them and handed them over to the Ukrainian police.

When the boys arrived at the Ukrainian police station, the commander began slapping their faces and demanding that they tell him the location of the hiding place in their parents' home. It was discovered later that the chief of police had helped them out. When the Nazi commander asked him how many slaps each child had received, he told him he'd given each of them 50 slaps, when he'd slapped them only a few times.

After a short discussion about their fate, it was decided to bring them back to the ghetto.

[Page 89]

Ghetto Reduction...

The number of Jews had decreased so much that the size of the ghetto could be reduced by half. Berstovski and Chinik, both refugees from Germany who worked as mechanics for the Nazis, were chosen as community leaders.

The abductions continued. One day, Shaul's father was also abducted. His mother, who was left alone with three children, was able to hide.

Every morning for the next six days, a roll call was conducted. Everyone was rounded up and counted. Only the sick were allowed to stay home. During those days, Shaul's father and one of his brothers were sick with typhus.

On the fourth day, Shaul's mother and two brothers were included in the roll call. Suddenly, the Jews found themselves surrounded by armed Ukrainian police. The sight terrified the Jews: they felt that something terrible was going to happen to them. When the Gestapo men saw the frightened look on the Jews' faces, they laughed and ridiculed them.

An order was given to remove 32 tradesmen needed for work from the roll call, including the two community leaders, Berstovski and Chinik. Shaul was also included in the group. He assumes that the Germans thought he was a tradesman's apprentice. The rest, around 600 people, were taken to the synagogue. Shaul was separated from his mother and brothers. Everyone saw the approaching danger, but Shaul never thought he wouldn't ever see them again.

For one night, the Vishnevets Jews slept in the synagogue. The following morning, they were taken to a field near Vishnevets. When the Jews who remained in the ghetto woke up in the morning, they heard the sound of gunfire mixed with the terrible sound of men, women, and children screaming and yelling. They now knew that the fate of their brothers, parents and friends, whom they had said goodbye to only yesterday, was cast.

The Survivors

Three of the hundreds of Jews who were murdered were lucky enough to escape, and they returned to the ghetto. They told us about the shocking sight and the physical and emotional torture endured by the hundreds of Jews until they died. The killers were Ukrainians. Only a few Gestapo men, who gave instructions to the Ukrainians, took part in the killing.

In addition to the 32 tradesmen who had been saved from slaughter, close to 100 Jews with typhus remained in the ghetto, including Shaul's father and brother. Shaul also got sick with typhus. His fever was over 40 (he had a thermometer in his pocket), but he wasn't lying in bed. When I asked him how could do that, Shaul answered me, "Yes. Now, when I have a little wound on my finger, I suffer and I can't work, but then you didn't feel pain as long as your legs could carry your body."

Three days later, Shaul's father died in his bed next to his 18-year-old son. He was buried in the Jewish cemetery.

About two weeks passed without any special events. And then the kidnappers came to collect the remaining Jews. Shaul and his sick brother went into hiding. His brother climbed into the attic and was separated from Shaul, who hid in another part of the building.

[Page 90]

The sick brother fell into the hands of the killers, and Shaul saw them load him onto a cart. The kidnapped people were taken out of the ghetto, never to be seen again.

At midnight, Shaul and another 15-year-old teenager, a relative, escaped from the ghetto. Only 50 Jews remained inside.

Shaul's Wanderings and Adventures

After the teenagers left the ghetto, they entered the home of a Ukrainian whom they both knew, hoping they could stay there for a week. The Ukrainian refused to let them stay. The next day, Shaul separated from his friend and left in the direction of Dubno.

That was the start of a long period of roaming and adventure in Shaul's life.

Around 10 kilometers from Kremenets, he was caught by a Ukrainian policeman. Shaul managed to escape but was later caught by several Ukrainian youths who were helping the police. Twice, he tried to escape but was caught and locked up in a cellar. With the help of an elderly farmer (a kindhearted man), Shaul was let go. The old man announced that the Jewish teenager should be taken back to the ghetto, and he ordered a farmer to take him to back to Vishnevets, but the farmer abandoned him on the way. The teenager tried to find shelter with an old Polish peasant woman in the area, but she chased him away. Shaul returned to the ghetto.

It was impossible to stay in the ghetto. The place was desolate and empty. The next day, he left with another teenager. On the way to Galicia, they crossed the fields where the last hundreds of kidnapped Jews were killed and buried.

The teenagers managed to reach Zbarazh in Galicia, where Shaul's aunt lived. A terrible gloom prevailed in Zbarazh. A killing unit had visited the place the previous day, and the signs of its "operation" were visible in every corner. Shaul's friend went out to buy something and didn't come back. Shaul felt that danger was near. The next day, he left Zbarazh, severely depressed over the loss of his friend, who had become like a brother to him during their travels together.

Shaul was afraid to waste time and decided to continue on his own. He was extremely happy when he met up with the friend from whom he'd been separated. His friend told him how he'd escaped from the killers who ambushed him. Together, they kept going, but everywhere they went, they came across Ukrainian policemen and Gestapo killing units. They were forced to return to Zbarazh. Shaul's friend decided to stay, but Shaul left him the next day. He decided to go to Hungary after discovering that you could reach Israel from there.

Shaul left in the direction of Ternopol, avoiding the town and stopping only at farms. On the way, he met Jews who advised him not to continue. But the teenager didn't listen to them. In a town in Galicia, he was caught when Jews were abducted in the area, but he managed to survive. In most places where he stopped later, Jews were afraid to give shelter to the wandering boy. On a farm, a young, kindhearted Ukrainian farmer gave him shelter. According to Shaul, he was a Communist.

[Page 91]

The teenager asked the farmer for advice on how to proceed. The farmer directed him to Lvov via Chodorov-Stary-Lovechne. He and the farmer parted as friends.

The teenager continued on his way. Near Sokola, he was caught by a Ukrainian policeman who decided to hand him over to the Gestapo, but Shaul escaped. Walking through forests and mountains in the pouring rain, he managed to arrive in Sokola to find that all the Jewish homes had been robbed and deserted. He spent the night in a home, and the next day he met a number of Jews. All of them hardened his heart and advised him to stop, telling him he wouldn't be able to cross the border into Hungary.

Meeting with Another Jewish Teenager Lost in the Forest

As he continued on his way to the Hungarian border, crossing mountains and forests, he met a teenager from Warsaw who was orphaned, abandoned, and lonely like him. The teenager from Warsaw was dressed like a Christian and was an expert in the area. Shaul was happy to meet him, and the two very quickly became friends. They separated after a short time, since the teenager from Warsaw was afraid Shaul's typical Jewish looks would jeopardize his plan to cross the border disguised as a Christian.

Shaul told me that he wasn't angry and that he understood his friend's need to follow his plan to save his own life. Shaul showed me a picture of the teenager from Warsaw, which he was keeping as a great treasure. He mentioned the teenager from Warsaw's good sides and told me he had left him with deep sorrow and great fear.

To the Border!

Shaul had learned a lesson from his friend from Warsaw. He thought of a way to disguise himself, too. He purchased a handmade cloth blanket used by Ukrainians in the mountains, covered himself with it, and disguised himself as a poor Ukrainian teenager. The disguise worked, and he was able to reach Lovechne.

Shaul became very weak from his wanderings. He went into an old peasant woman's home and asked for a place to rest. He received food and a place to sleep. The next day, the old woman instructed him on how to cross the border. Shaul realized that his accent might jeopardize his plan, so he decided to pretend he was mute. The old woman's directions were not enough for Shaul, and he lost his way. By dusk, he saw the Hungarian border markings, crossed the border, and reached the vicinity of Subcarpathian Ruthenia.

In Hungary

For a few days, he worked for a Hungarian farmer, until a priest warned the farmer not to keep the young man. Shaul went on his way and arrived in Munkachivo, where he was unhappy with how he was received by the local Jews. He slept in a cellar belonging to a Jew for one night. The next day, the Jews gave him money for a train ticket to Budapest. He spoke Ukrainian on the train, knowing that no one there would identify his Ukrainian accent.

When he arrived at the train station in Budapest, he walked in the wrong direction and entered an area reserved for soldiers. He was caught and arrested. Shaul claimed he was a Ukrainian boy from a farm near Munkachivo. They took him to a Ukrainian-speaking policeman, who accepted Shaul's story that he had come to Budapest to visit his uncle and ask for his help. They sent Shaul with the policeman so he could help him find his uncle's house, since he didn't have his address... on the way, Shaul told the policeman he didn't need his help and could find his way to his uncle's alone. The policeman agreed, and Shaul was left alone in the busy Hungarian capital.

He saw a mezuzah in the doorway of a building and realized it was a Jewish home. He entered and asked for a place to sleep. He was refused and was taken to the Jewish community center. From there, he was taken to a place where he could sleep.

The Jewish community in Budapest didn't take care of him, but transferred him to a refugee labor camp.

He stayed in the camp for about a month.

With all the disappointments Shaul experienced with the Hungarian Jews, all the suffering he endured until he went to the labor camp, and the difficult conditions there, Shaul remembers those days as ones of comfort and relaxation....

The Savior and the Survivor

One day, a Jewish man came to visit the camp. His face and clothes indicated that he was rich. He was interested in Shaul and informed him that he wanted to adopt him as a son so he could leave the camp. Shaul talked about the man with anxiety and joy (he also keeps his picture as a prized souvenir). A few days after the conversation with the unknown Jew, Shaul was released from the camp.

When he arrived at his rescuer's home, Shaul found out that a youth group was being organized for immigration to Israel. He got in touch with them and was added to the group.

Shaul talks about his immigration to Israel, his visit to Tel Aviv, and his life in the village only with tears of joy. His most exciting experience was meeting his friend, the teenager from Warsaw, on the way from Hungary to Israel.

[Page 93 - Hebrew] [Page 346 - Yiddish]

A 12-Year-Old under Nazi Rule

by Gdalye Rozenberg (Zbarazh)

Translated by Sara Mages

Gdalye, the son of Mendel Rozenberg of Vitkovits, now lives in Zbarazh under a different name. His story was given to us by his cousin.-Editorial Board

On the day they arrived, the Nazis took Yakov Chazan, a known basket seller in town, put him on a truck, and took him out of town. His nine-year-old son started running after the truck, crying, weeping, and shouting, "Father, I don't want you to go. I'm afraid we'll never see each other again."

When the Germans heard this, they stopped and put the little one on the truck so he would be close to his father. They killed both of them on the way to Pochayev.

The same day, the mother lost her mind.

***

And thus I observed the Holocaust regime from the start. The incident chased me as a child. I couldn't forget it during the Holocaust. I suddenly realized that a child wouldn't be protected unless he protected himself, and in my heart I decided to do it myself. I felt sorry for my parents. I realized suddenly that even with all my love for them, I was an independent 12-year-old who was responsible for himself.

***

My father, Mendel, worked for the Russians collecting the wheat quota that the gentiles were forced to give to the government.

When the Germans arrived in 1941, they stopped in the village of Zvinatsh. My father escaped in a cart to Kolodne. He also wanted to take us, his family, but when he didn't find us at home, and because he was short on time, he escaped alone.

My mother was left with three children. My brother, the firstborn, was drafted and served in the Red Army. Along with everyone else, we were locked up in the Vishnevets ghetto the day it was set up. At the age of 12, I would leave the ghetto at night, walk to our village 15 kilometers away, and return to the ghetto with food for my family. Each time I walked and came back a different way.

I kept doing this for several months. In August 1942, when I went to our village, I returned to the ghetto using the road leading to Zbarazh. Suddenly, I looked to my left and saw a group of sad, depressed people. I hid and waited. I saw that they were being shot and that they were naked. I saw them fall and drop dead. This wasn't during the liquidation of the ghetto; it was an extra action.

A farmer's wife was walking her cow not far from me. I walked up to the woman and asked her what the event meant. She answered me with great fear, while making the sign of the cross in pity, "They're killing Jews over there, and if you're Jewish, you'd better escape right now."

[Page 94]

I ran. I was also afraid of her. I hid in a cornfield, and in the evening, I returned to the ghetto. I found my mother and my two sisters, gathered other Jews, and told them what I'd seen, and I, the little one, a 12-year-old, advised them to escape.

"Jews, escape as long as you're still alive!" I begged them excitedly.

My family gathered all the food I'd brought, and we decided to escape that same night.

We escaped by running on the dirt road (the Bolonya). We children were able to cross the river at the end of the dirt road before we were spotted by Ukrainian policemen. But our mother trailed behind us and was not fast enough. As we stood waiting for her, we heard a shot and a sigh.

Mother didn't join us. To save our lives, we children-the oldest was 14-year-old Manya, and the youngest was 10-walked alone toward the village where we'd been born.

In the village, we saw policemen walking around, rounding up Jews, and gathering them in one place.

We understood that we had to leave the village. The same night, weary from our long walk, we continued to Zbarazh, where our father's sister lived.

On the road between Kolodne and Zbarazh is a thick forest called the "Black Forest." That forest served as the border between what used to be Austria and Volin. Both areas were under German occupation. In the forest, we were caught by two

Germans who ran into us by chance. One said, "Let's hand them to the Gestapo." The other one asked us, "Where are you going alone?"

When we told him our destination, he said to the other one, "Poor children, we should let them go. No matter what, they'll never get very far."

He warned us, the little ones, not to reveal our conversation. "It would be harmful for us and you."

We continued and reached Zbarazh.

A couple of Jews, members of the Judenrat in Zbarazh, met us by the church at the entrance to the town. We recognized them by their famous sleeves. One caught us and said to the other, we need to hand them to the Gestapo. The other one was interested in our origin and wanted to know where we had come from. We told him we were Mendel's children, and he answered, Mendel was a good Jew, a loyal Communist, but a good Jew. He smiled at us and let us go.

A few days later, we found out that the Gestapo had announced that anyone who gave them 50 Jewish heads would save his soul and stay alive. They showed us the way to our aunt's so we wouldn't have to look for it for long. We went to her house immediately.

Our aunt received us with kindness, gave us food, and later said, "My dear ones, I don't mind if you stay here, but you have to know that our lives are in danger, and if you've survived so far, maybe your luck will play out later. You'd better continue on your way; maybe you'll survive."

We returned to our village, and one of the neighbors, a kindhearted gentile, hid us. He dug a deep pit in the cowshed that housed the pigs, and there the two of us, the little ones, hid.

[Page 95]

My older sister, Manya, was transferred to a relative in Horinka to reduce the risk. My youngest sister died after a few weeks. She passed away in my arms. She suddenly became ill when we were alone in the cowshed. A shiver went through me, and I didn't know what to do. I took her in my arms, and she died.

At night, I went into the garden next to our house in the village and dug a grave under a tree. I carved a memorial on the tree and buried her with my own hands. I left the mound of dirt and went back to my hiding place.

In the morning, when the gentiles saw the fresh grave, they understood that Mendel's children were hiding there.

They started to investigate and found us. My benefactor was also in danger, so I took his advice and left.

At night, I left and hid in the old cemetery next to the village. I had known the cemetery for many years. There were sorts of crypts for Polish nobles in the cemetery. I choose one and hid. At night I went to my benefactor, got food from him, and returned to my cave.

And so I remained alive, lonely and banished until the Russians arrived.

Then I met my sister, and the two of us, lonely and neglected, decided to live and look for our father.

***

When the Russians arrived, Ukrainian outlaws began rioting and killing their opponents to cover up their cooperation with the Nazis. They mostly wanted to get rid of Jews. They searched and found every Jew who had survived the German-Ukrainian killing fields and killed them. They also started to follow us, but a gentile prevented this by converting us. Manya returned to Horinka, and I stayed in Vitkovits. A pair of good little Christians.

The outlaws let us go. We survived.

***

Meanwhile, the girl turned 16, and her caretaker decided to marry her off to a gentile. When the news reached me, I was shocked. Even though I accepted my Christianity, I didn't accept the marriage since it was clear to me that it was against our father's wishes. I traveled to Horinka, kidnapped her from her benefactor's house, and took her to my place.

Meanwhile, a neighbor received a letter from my father, Mendel Rozenberg (who came from Vitkovits). Father wrote that he'd survived the Russians and wanted to know his family's fate. They told him about his misfortunes and said that only Gdalye and Manya were alive. A neighbor, our benefactor's wife, advised him to come and collect us because of the danger presented by the outlaws.

He answered their letter, saying, "If we could decapitate Hitler, we can also decapitate the criminal outlaws' rotten heads."

The letter fell into the outlaws' hands.

[Page 96]

Meanwhile, I moved to Zbarazh, and my sister remained with her Ukrainian school friend. They came, took the friends, and threw them into a well. They searched for me, but they couldn't find me.

When I returned home in the evening, I was told about the incident. The Ukrainian parents took their daughter out of the well and buried her. They left my sister inside. One of the neighbors sent a telegram to Mendel, my father, saying that his daughter had been murdered. My father came to Horinka immediately and began looking for the criminals. He took his daughter's body out of the well and buried her temporarily.

Later, I showed my father the location of my little sister's grave. Father gave her a royal funeral. He took my sisters' bodies and buried them together in the Zbarazh cemetery, where the heroes of the Soviet Union were buried.

After he had transferred me to a safe place in Zbarazh and arranged a school for me, he dedicated himself to distracting the criminal outlaws and Ukrainian police.

He took two armed army units and returned with them to the area around Vishnevets. He was able to find the criminals and destroy them one by one. After he was done, he dedicated his time to doing the same in nearby villages, and with that he fulfilled his vow to cut off the heads of the hated insects.

I live with my father in Zbarazh and hope to immigrate to Israel with him.

[Page 97 - Hebrew] [Page 363 - Yiddish]

From Inferno to Inferno

by Moshe (Son of Hersh Matis) Segal

Translated by Sara Mages

September 1, 1939, the day the war between Poland and Germany broke out, finds me at my father's house in Vishnevets, where I'm spending my summer vacation. The notices plastered outside call the conscripts to join the draft and report to the nearby town of Kremenets. But Poland can't stand up against the Germans' crushing attack, and the government falls in a very short time.

The Polish government escapes to Romania, stopping on its way at the high school in Kremenets. Joining the invasion are the diplomatic corps, senior officers, and others. The road leading to Ternopol is noisy with cars driving quickly toward the southern border. A small number of Jewish refugees, along with several famous journalists, stop for a short break at the Talmud Torah building located at Leybke Chatski's home. A few of the town's activists, who had heard the news of the refugees' arrival, welcome them for their short visit.

The news of the German bombing of Kremenets and the first Jewish victims increases the reality of the upcoming danger and despair. The gloomy music broadcast by the Polish radio service and the call to the soldiers to "aim well" add to the feeling of sadness and grief.

Finally, the radio is also silent.

The town is covered in gloom, looking lonely and orphaned. The police and local authorities disappear. The local farmers roam around town with folded sacks under their arms, sniffing for the smell of unclaimed property.

When darkness falls, families gather together in silence by their doorways. Everyone wants to be together, to hear, listen, and exchange whispered opinions with their neighbors; the atmosphere is saturated with fears of what is to come.

The sudden news that the Russians are coming changes the situation. The first to arrive at the post office are two Russian officers. One stands on top of the roof of his car, preaching to the large crowd around him about comradeship between nations. He points out that a period of freedom is coming to all oppressed nations and talks about the "brotherly hand" offered to the Ukrainians and the Belarusians, and about their liberation from Polish suppression. Shouts of hooray and applause accompany his speech.

Lights return to the streets and homes. A sympathy demonstration organized by the Ukrainian population is marching toward Zamek Square. Local Jews, who have experienced similar bitter situations in the past, stay away from the festive demonstration. The patriotic songs sung by the Ukrainian demonstrators bring back the gloomy sounds of the recent past and the memory of Petliura and his friends.

The disorder starts to get organized. The high school building is filling up with Jewish clerks who sit and do nothing behind their desks. Loyalists to the new regime, who have come out of hiding, are using all their power.

[Page 98]

A Communist Union of Youth chapter is being organized with the best of Jewish youth. Jewish girls look for their Ukrainian girlfriends, and loud gentile language is heard in the streets. The brotherhood between nations is extraordinary.

Military power and its heavy equipment arrive nonstop from Ternopol. Some of it is stationed in the town's suburbs. Armed soldiers sit in their trucks, parked on street corners. The soldiers talk heartily and politely to the people crowding around them. In the town center, a Russian soldier tells the crowd standing next to him about the wonderful life in his country under the leadership of Stalin, "the father of all nations" and "the genius of mankind." In a circle nearby, an accordion plays, and a couple of soldiers dancing the Kozatchok mesmerize the crowd with their acrobatics.

Great rejoicing.

Meanwhile, soldiers raid the shops, buying everything they can get their hands on. Everything is being sold. Dvosi Binyamin, who owns a fancy goods shop, is very excited about the politeness of her new shoppers, who don't argue about the price and pay everything she asks. But soon she realizes that this is an enforced liquidation sale, and she wants to save whatever she can.

A stockpiling panic takes over. The stores are empty. The leaders of the new regime organize a war against "hoarders" who hide merchandise. Searches and arrests take place.

In the midst of these days, I leave my father's home. I obey the authority's order that each person must live in his place of work and leave for the town of Horodok, near Vilna, where I'm a teacher. I sit on the bus, and through the window I see the image of my father, of blessed memory, framed in his white beard. Old age has leaped onto him before his time. He puts a few copper coins in my hand, pressing them between my fingers, blessing them with a silent father's prayer and asking the heavens for mercy. Father's heart predicts that this will be our last farewell... when the bus moves, he wipes a tear from his eye, and his lips murmur quietly, "May the Lord bless you and keep you; may the Lord show you favor and be gracious to you," etc.

**

I arrive in Horodok after the long, difficult trip of those days. I work at school, keeping my thoughts to myself, as I did under the Soviet regime. But I'll skip this period, since I want to tell you about the Holocaust that the Nazis and their helpers brought to us. I dedicate this story to the memory of the thousands from my hometown of Vishnevets who, like me, were uprooted and stuck in a foreign land. In their struggle to survive, a struggle of emotional and physical torture, bound by the hands of their destroyer, they perished in the human crematoriums, and the location of their ashes is unknown.

The town of Horodok is no different from many other towns in eastern Poland. The ghetto and life there are no different than they are in any other ghetto. The Nazi extermination machine works according to a well-planned system whose tactics are based on fraud and deception, and its goal is extermination and uprooting.

[Page 99]

The same frightful atrocities that take place in the Rakov ghetto are also inflicted on the Jews in the nearby city of Radishkovits. Here in Rakov, Jews are forced to wrap themselves in their prayer shawls and phylacteries and stand and watch their wives, naked as the day they were born, dancing around a fire of Torah scrolls until hand grenades and machine gunfire stop the dancing women's movements, sealing the night of horrors.

A 16-year-old boy manages to escape from the fire and arrives in our ghetto. According to a police order, housing a stranger in the ghetto area isn't allowed, so we have to hide him in a pit dug in a cowshed. He escapes barefoot in the middle of winter. All of his toes are frozen, swollen, and bleeding. He sits in the pit crying and begging for someone to take care of his legs. Secretly, without anyone noticing, I bring him rags, warm water, and a little bit of food.

In the nearby city of Radishkovits, men women, children, and infants march to open ditches. Alive, they are thrown in and shot to death.

News of horrifying atrocities reaches the ghetto residents from towns near and far. For some unknown reason, the destroyer has not arrived here yet. Physical and emotional tortures continue nonstop. Here, for example, today the town's pranksters put the cantor and two of his singers on a balcony in the town center to entertain the residents, who are enjoying a leisurely Sunday stroll, with their prayers. The sound of the prayers enters the ghetto through closed shutters, pinching our hearts and shocking our souls.

And here the ghetto's residents are taken to the town square, and 30 men are shot on the spot. An order is given to go back home and return with articles of silver and gold, coins and precious stones, and fill an empty truck to the rim. Horrified and scared, people run here and there. The sound of children crying and adults shrieking reaches the center of the heavens: "Jews, save yourselves, rescue, and bring."

And the Jews save themselves... and bring... and the truck fills up with silver and gold and precious stones. Family heirlooms.

On the long winter evenings, the ghetto is saturated with gloom that wants to swallow its own shadow. The homes are extremely crowded. In the room's four corners, five families stretch out on their bundles, using them as a mattress. In the dark of night, the shadow of the angel of death hovers. No one knows what tomorrow will bring.

A young couple with a two-year-old baby sits in a dark corner behind the oven. They also want to be swallowed by their own shadows. To be invisible. They shrivel and shrink, knowing the baby will be exterminated first, and they want him to live. The baby absorbs his mother's pain and sighs from his heart, and he doesn't cry. From the day they came to stay with us, no one has seen him. They never take him out of the dark corner. His mother doesn't want anyone to know of his existence. She stands very close to him, bending down, hovering over him, hour upon hour, day and night.

In the dark nights, all your senses listen. You're afraid of the echo of your own steps and grumble when someone gets up from his place. You need to listen to what's happening outside behind the barbed-wire fence.

[Page 100]

A noise reaches your ears, the sound of a truck stopping. The engine is turned off, and along with it, your breathing stops. Your blood freezes, you stay down. Have the destructive angels arrived? Is this the end?

Also in this ghetto, a Judenrat is being held captive by the Gestapo, grasping the deception of "maybe" and "perhaps," turning nights into days to supply the twice-weekly quota enforced on the ghetto. Two council members travel around the area buying the items on the imposing list at imaginary and exorbitant prices.

And here the two deliver the "order" to the Gestapo, which is stationed in the district seat, and return with a new list. And the list is long: 100 women's furs, 200 men's leather furs, 1,000 pairs of warm gloves, and much more. The ghetto is fearful and worried. Where would they purchase all of that? The Judenrat collects silver and gold with a calm word and a tyrant's hand.

And one August day, after the ghetto is completely looted and its people have been turned into skeletons, the Gestapo kill their helpers. Close to 700 students, young children, and babies are forcefully loaded onto death trucks and taken to the valley. With their own eyes, mothers and fathers watch as hand grenades and machine guns shred and kill them. Old people and others are locked in the cellar of the Great Synagogue, where they are tortured through starvation to prolong their dying. The young, who are fit to work, are sent to a labor camp in a nearby town.

***

When the ghetto's surviving residents arrive at the labor camp, I'm already a veteran there. I was brought there with the first group of laborers when the Judenrat received the demand to supply manpower. I work on the roofs of the large, tall buildings being constructed in the camp area. I sleep on a hard wooden board in the large sleeping hut and work around an hour from the camp. My clothes are also my covers at night. The metal can I brought with me from the ghetto, in which I receive my daily share of soup, is still in my possession.

When the workers return from work to their sleeping huts, a long line of hundreds of human shadows snake around the kitchen to receive a piece of moldy bread and the daily watery soup with small pieces of meat floating in it. Waiting in line is tiring and exhausting. The Ukrainian guards use their clubs to control the line, making sure we're standing upright.

The person standing in front of me fails when he hands his metal cup to the soup distributor. He misjudges the distance from his hand. The long metal soup ladle hits his head. He drops to the ground, convulsing and dying in agony. No one helps him. It isn't wise to look in his direction and feel sorry for him.... It's a matter of so what? A routine: tomorrow they'll bring a new worker in his place.

The soup distributor's mood isn't good today. He, his helper, or one of his friends is playing a game. The soup kettle is poured onto the ground so they can watch a creature with little resemblance to a human crawl on his stomach, licking and collecting pieces of foul food. The sight amuses them.

During the warm summer months, I sit on top of the weak structure, immersed in daydreams about food. The young man sitting next to me talks a lot about food: about the stew his mother used to make on Friday and the cakes she used to bake with her own hands.

[Page 101]

Here he dips a piece of fresh challah in the garlic-seasoned soup, puts it in his mouth, chewing and chewing with pleasure, eating and swallowing...

I feel the smell of the soup, the garlic, and the fresh challah, and I swallow my saliva. I'm carried on the wings of my imagination. I eat and eat... I put a finger deep inside the corner of my pants pocket: maybe a lost breadcrumb will stick to it. I take my finger out, bring it to my tongue, and return to reality.

On those days, the remaining ghetto inhabitants arrive at the camp. They are the mothers who have watched their children's execution, fathers without wives and children, young men without parents, abandoned orphans, creatures with little human resemblance. They don't have the energy to die, and they live against their will. A sense of survival forces them to go to work, stand in line for soup, and go to sleep so they can get up the next day and go to work, to suffering and torture, until the end of their endurance and until the end. This is the sense of survival.

One of the new arrivals from the ghetto settles next to my sleeping space in the hut. It's Ayzik the blacksmith, a kindhearted, quiet Jew. He's not starving like me; otherwise he wouldn't leave his piece of bread on the windowsill, saving it for morning. He's new, and he doesn't know that you don't leave bread until morning.

The slice of bread winks at me from the windowsill and doesn't let me fall asleep. I move closer to the edge of my bed to be closer to it, smell it, and enjoy the shining piece of bread in the gloom of night. I twist in hunger, turning from side to side, get down from my bed, and climb up and down again. The slice of bread bothers my soul, and I can't pass the test.

And just before dawn, when the hut is in deep sleep, sunk in the mud of physical and emotional pain, when only deep sighs emit from the mouths of the sleeping, I slowly climb down from my bed, walk to the window, and stretch my hand toward the slice....

The next morning, no one pays attention to Ayzik the blacksmith's screaming and swearing.

I have a small, ornamented leather coin purse, a gift from my childhood friend, and in it is a reminder of tenderness and love, yearning and memories of days not long gone. A gentile, a laborer in the camp, sees the purse and brings me a little flour in exchange. I cook the flour with water behind the hut. Salt is nowhere to be found. I taste it and leave a little of the solution for tomorrow.

From the height of the roof, not far from the camp, on a tall hill, I can see a large concentration of thousands of Russian war prisoners, all of them young. They were brought here by the thousands, and the earth is swallowing them. Each morning hundreds of bodies-the night's crop-are taken for burial by their comrades-in-arms.

Here, it isn't cheated, starving Jews who are buried in silence, but young men, heroes of the Russian war....

From where I sit, I can see an armed German leading a group of Russian prisoners. They look very young but starved and weak. One leans over, pulls a wildflower, and puts it in his mouth. The armed German shoots him.

[Page 102]

On my left, underneath me, two Jews saw wood. A German collaborator, a Jew from Shavel, Lithuania, beats one of them for no reason, just like that, without cause. Who will say to him, why are you doing this? The collaborator doesn't stop; he hits him until he turns blue, loses consciousness, and dies.

Day after day, we bury the bodies of typhus victims. Every once in a while, dead Jews are replaced with new Jews brought from a distance to take their place.

On one of these days, I make up my mind to escape.

To run to the forest and try a new way of life, the way wild animals live. It's an innocent delusion, but it awakens in me the will to think, make decisions, act, and find ways to save myself.

This occupation lasts days and nights. It causes me tension and exhaustion. But it also takes my mind off the bitter reality and awakens my hope. And indeed, after many months of conversation with friends and after many secret meetings, the decision forms skin and veins.

One day, when the convoy makes its way from the camp to the sleeping hut, passing the locksmith's workshop located outside the camp, a group of Jewish laborers comes out and joins the convoy, as they always do. From the hands of one, I receive a bundle of the small pieces of wood that we're allowed to bring to our hut. The bundle contains two pieces of wood pressed together, and between them is the barrel of a Russian gun. That night is a sleepless one for me. In secrecy and care, I hide the barrel in a hollow space in one of the boards I sleep on. Later, we take the gun barrel and other gun parts to a deserted stable near the hut, where those with typhus hide from the Germans. Over there, we put the gun together and hide it until it's time to escape.

***

On a frosty, clear night in February 1943, the fence is broken. Equipped with a gun that has not yet been fired, a few bullets, and a handgun, eight of us break out of camp. By the time they start shooting at us, we're already across the road at our meeting point in the Jewish cemetery. Afraid of an encounter with the partisans, the Germans don't chase us. We walk slowly, in zigzags, to erase our tracks.

Walking in the deep snow exhausts us. We're forced to stop so we can rest and dry off. After crossing the river, we knock at a farmer's door. We walk inside and stand in front of him, this time not to ask for mercy. The rifle and handgun are impressive. We take our shoes off and dry off our clothes and the wrappings from our feet. After we eat our fill, we leave for the meeting point, where the representatives of a partisan unit are waiting for us.

Three partisans are waiting for us to arrive. They're disappointed when they see the poor weapons and the eight Jews. Only the strongest among us, the one who holds the gun, is accepted and taken wherever he's taken. Our handgun is also taken from us. It's clear to us that without weapons, there's nothing we can do. They can't understand our situation, and the expression on their faces indicates that they're not fond of Jews.

[Page 103]

The meeting is short, and the partisans retrace their steps. We're left alone, and again we lack protection and hope; we're depressed and desperate. We spend three days in the forest. Each time we leave in search of food, we put ourselves in danger of falling into the hands of all kinds of killers who swarm the roads and the villages in search of Jews.

The depression and desperation and the inability to endure how we're living bring four of us to decide to return to the camp and take a chance on our lives. Two others decide to embark on a long walk to an area familiar to them. I'm left alone in the forest.

It's quiet around me. The forest is still and mute. The tall, thick trees stand erect and quiet. The autumn leaves are covered with a layer of snow. The world around me is frozen and cruel. Above me, leaden clouds cover the sky and lock the gates of mercy and prayer, and underneath me is a vast field of glaring snow.

Again I walk backward and forward in the deep snow to let my blood flow so I won't fall victim to the cruel freeze. By evening, when it gets colder, I walk closer to the edge of the forest. From a distance, I notice shining lights burning in the farmhouses. I walk toward the light and approach the first house. I open the door, stick my head inside, and in Russian ask for water, a little water.

A woman's voice answers me from the dim room: "Enter, my son, enter," she says. It's the voice of the farmer's wife. She understands who would be asking for water on a freezing cold night.

The word "my son" casts warmth and love into my bones. Tears of happiness choke my throat. The woman gives me a glass of milk and a large slice of bread, and after I hungrily swallow it, she gives me another slice and says, "Don't stay here in the village. The people are bad. Ukrainians and Lithuanians visit the village at night. Go to 'Punya,' where the farmers dried their hay today. It'll be warm there tonight, so go sleep there."

A small, lonely structure stands 200 meters away. I walk toward it and open the small door, which swings on its hinges. A stray dog beats me to it. He raises his ears and doesn't respond. I enter slowly and lie on one of the steps next to him, half-awake, half-asleep. At dawn, when I open my eyes, the dog is no longer there.

I return to the forest for the second day of my march. In the evening, I repeat the previous night's exercise. This time a wicked woman welcomes me and, yelling and screaming, throws me out her door. I run away from her. Under the cover of darkness, I slip into the barn, dive into a pile of hay, and spend the night sleeping next to the cow's warm body.

Before dawn, I return to the forest. My energy has left me. Hunger oppresses me. Desperation chews at me, and bad thoughts come to mind. I sit on a tree trunk, helpless and clueless.

[Page 104]

Suddenly, I hear a thin, metallic sound coming from the forest. I recognize it. It's the sound of a saw in action.

Certainly, those are local farmers working in the forest, I think.

And if they catch me, they'll kill me. If they hand me over to the Germans to be tortured, they'll get a monetary reward.

This is my only choice, I say to myself. I get up and walk in that direction. When I arrive, two Jews who are standing and sawing raise their heads, turning white from fright. They're worried that their hiding place has been discovered and the end has arrived. But after a short conversation and after they recover, they take me to the cabin where they're staying.

The cabin was built in a deep ditch inside the forest's shrubbery, covered with branches and well hidden. Four families, which numbered 20 men, women, and children, live in the cabin. They are residents of the village who get donations of food from their neighbors. No one knows the location of their hiding place. Night after night, one goes out to get a little of the flour or potatoes they needed to sustain themselves. And so they've lived that way for a long time, and they're planning to continue living in the darkness of their secret place. They stand around me, listening in silence to my stories about the Jews and the killings, and great sadness prevails in the cabin. They give me a little hot barley soup, which warms and revives my soul. After a short time, it's clear to me that I can't stay there because of the crowded living conditions, and mostly because of the shortage of food. I get up and, on their advice, go in search of a similar cabin where a woman whose son I know is hiding. Her son is a member of a partisan unit, and maybe thanks to him, I'll be saved, and maybe I can join the partisans.

And again I'm marching in the deep snow, walking around farms, crossing walkways and roads, and my new search is accompanied by false hopes alternating with new hopes.

The day is getting darker, and I'm walking toward the unknown. Unexpectedly, walking toward me from the depths of the forest is the young brother of the partisan I'm searching for. The young man is on his way to a farmer in the nearby village who is serving as a contact between his partisan brother and the rest of the family, which is sitting in the cabin.

He brings me to the farmer's house, making arrangements for me to spend the night there. But he returns to the cabin since it's too dangerous to stay on the farm, as every once in a while, partisans and Germans show up there. He also expresses his sorrow that he can't take me to the cabin, since he and his mother are staying there as a favor, and a guest doesn't bring a guest.

I lie on the hay mattress the farmer prepares for me that night. My boots by my head, I feel better, since I haven't been able to take them off for the past two weeks. I lie there and make a decision: if the Germans or the Lithuanians visit the farmhouse tonight, I'll jump through the window in front of them so the bullet will hit me in the back, and I won't fall into their hands alive.

It's midnight, and someone is knocking at the door. I stay frozen; I can't get up. My legs don't listen to me. The farmer walks over to open the door, and the following conversation reaches my ears:

"Are there any strangers here?"

"Yes."

"Who?"

[Page 105]

"A Jew!"

"A Jew? From where?"

"From Krasne."

I feel a little better. Listening to the stranger, I recognize the familiar singsong voice of a typical Jew. In a matter of seconds, three Jewish partisans dressed in white clothes-a perfect camouflage in the sea of snow-are standing in front of me. I know two of them from Horodok. They traveled a long distance to take the rest of their families out of the ghetto to the forest. The third is from Minsk. He's looking for his 12-year-old daughter, who escaped during the action. According to a rumor, she found shelter in a farmer's house working as farm help in his yard.

The four of us move in a winter cart harnessed to two horses, moving slowly in search of the girl.

Before dawn we find the place.

It's difficult to describe the meeting between the father and his daughter. It's a heartbreaking sight. The farmer, who has just learned of her origin, is shaking from the knowledge that he's saved a Jew's life. But he is promised help with food and is informed that it's his responsibility to protect her. He gets the message when he sees our determination.

The two go on their way. The man from Minsk and I stay in the farmer's house to wait for them to return. By evening, we find out that, on their way, they ran into a battle between partisans and a Lithuanian unit. Two Lithuanians have deserted from their unit and fallen into their hands. They find out that they are two young Jewish men from Vilnius who have been living with Christian papers. As Christians, they were drafted into the Lithuanian army to fight against the partisans and liquidate the ghettos.

The two young men take advantage of the situation, desert, and surround themselves.

The partisan commander, who in the past has acted with forgiveness toward gentiles who desert and join the unit, acts cruelly toward the Jews. The following day, both are executed for collaborating with the Germans.

Because of the delay on their way, my two friends can't get in touch with their families and are forced to return to their units.

Before their departure, they approach the cabin's occupants, asking them not to abandon a young Jewish man who is wandering in the forests, anticipating annihilation. The same evening, I sleep in the cabin as a member of the group.

But I stay in that cabin for only a few weeks. When spring arrives, German attacks on the partisans and actions against the remaining Jews in the ghetto increase. A few refugees, survivors of the burning fires who have escaped from the killing pits lose their way in the vast forest in search of refuge. Many are caught, tortured, and murdered on the roads. Only a few find refuge in the forest.

Meanwhile, the Germans increase their war against the partisans, who have gotten stronger. Thousands of German soldiers and their Lithuanian and Ukrainian helpers raid the forest in order to destroy the partisans' strongholds.

The ground starts to burn under our feet. We're forced to uproot and leave, not knowing where to go. The wandering of the cabin residents begins. Other Jews, persecuted and frightened, without clothes or food, join us. We make our way to the vast swamp of Byelorussia. Many of us fall; only a few survive.

Our only ambition is to obtain weapons so we can join a partisan unit. The unit commander, a sensitive Jewish engineer from Minsk with a warm, kind Jewish heart, comes to my aid. He's been forced to hide his Judaism because of the murderous anti-Semitic feelings in his subordinates' hearts. Helping to keep his secret is Vanka the redhead, a young man from Pinsk who has also been forced to hide his Judaism. The few Jewish members of the unit suffer a lot at the hands of the anti-Semitic Russians. Each time the unit returns from a sabotage mission, they report that a Jewish comrade-in-arms has been killed in action. It's impossible to know whose hands killed him, but the fact is that it happens over and over, only to Jews.

Many facts have proved that Jewish partisans were murdered by their Christian comrades-in-arms whenever they had the opportunity to do so, and they had the opportunity each time they exchanged gunfire with the Germans.

With all the goodwill of the Jewish commander, he can't accept me into his brigade. But he doesn't abandon us. We hide and we wait.

One day, Vanka the redhead secretly brings a couple of guns to our hiding place, one for me and one for my friend. We take the guns, say our goodbyes, and leave. We go far away to another unit, and then a new chapter of my horrible life begins.

[Page 107 - Hebrew] [Page 382 - Yiddish]

Jewish Communism in Vishnevets

by Yehuda Margalit

Translated by Sara Mages

When the Russians entered Vishnevets, I continued to work with my horse and cart in the steam mill belonging to Shag-Lifshits-Bisker. I thought that under this regime, which I hated so much, things would be better for me because I was a laborer. That's what I told my wife. But this wasn't what the local Communists wanted; it was Jewish brothers from our town.

Avraham Guber rose to power and was nominated immediately as the town's commissioner, and Kalman Choish was nominated as chief of police. The two started to "purify" in the Stalinist style and to distribute power and its benefits among their family members, relatives, and brothers in ideology, providing them with a secure income on the backs of the people they evicted from their jobs.

I was also among their victims.

Shmuel Guber, Avraham's brother, was given the management of the mill, and the day after he sat on Shimon Lifshits' big chair, he informed me that I was fired, meaning that I didn't have permission to come and work there, where I had worked for many years, where I had labored and exerted myself. I came to him and tried to say to him: how is it possible when I've worked at physical labor every day of my life, and this is my place? I earned it with my hard labor and my sweat, and I have a clean past.

He didn't let me finish and said, "If you talk too much, I'll send you to Siberia. You should thank us that you're still here."

I left.

I couldn't understand the measure of their justice. They disposed of me and evicted the Jewish mill owner, but Grozinov the Russian, who was well to do, a rich man who owned fields, forests, and a flourmill, they allowed to stay. I wondered how they could do it. Meanwhile, I was left without a slice of bread, and my family was hungry. I went to Grozinov, the Russian gentile, and told him, "I have a wife and four children. I've been thrown out of the place where I worked for many years, and we're starving."

The elderly gentile didn't let me finish. He nearly cried.

"Leave them," he said. "Take your harness, and come to me in the village. You'll work for a few weeks. You won't lack for bread. Later, we'll see. Their lives aren't finished yet."

My wife didn't want me to travel to the village each morning. She said she would go to Kalman Choish, talk to him, and soften him up.

He threw her out and also threatened to exile us to Siberia. The oppressor worked according to one formula.

She came back from seeing him degraded and depressed. I ran to the police. I stood in front of Choish, the commander, and said to him, "I've come. Send me to Siberia right away."

On Sunday, Grozinov's agent came to me and said, "The master wants you to come to work. Take the horses and cart, and come to work. There's enough work for a hundred devils."

[Page 108]

That man's gesture, the gentile's, warmed my heart. I went to Grozinov's. They hadn't touched him yet, and he was allowed to keep his farm and forest.

His crippled brother said to me, "Here, they're your brothers, and these are the good days someone prayed for."

At the end of the day, they gave me potatoes, flour, and other staples. It was a holiday at home. For many days, we hadn't had enough to eat.

At midnight, exactly at 12:00, there was a knock on the door. The children were frightened; my wife was shocked. I calmed them and went to the door, and when I asked, "Who's knocking?" he answered, "Kalman himself," saying that he was the one knocking on my door.

I opened the door. Kalman stood by the door with two policemen. He said, "Get dressed, and come with us."

I asked, "With my wife and children?"

He answered, "No, just you. Get dressed now!"

I said, "Do you hear me, my great commander, I'm not moving without them, and secondly, what's burning? Where's the fire?"

He pulled his gun and said, "I'm going to kill you right here."

And he pulled his gun in front of my eyes.

I told him, "You're such a hero. I didn't know you were like that. You need to know that I'm tired of living under your rule. You can do whatever you want with me, but I'm not moving without my family, that's it."

He insisted and tried to get closer to me. My wife approached him and gave him a ringing slap on the face. Blood started to pour from his nose.

That helped. Angry, he ordered his policemen to take her to Siberia, too.

The children began to cry, the four of them crying in unison like a choir. I said to them, "My dear children, don't be afraid; let it be. You have nothing here. Get dressed and we'll go. We have to obey the commander's order. Come, we won't enjoy the rest of our lives."

Meanwhile, the dripping from his nose increased, and he became angrier. He was mad and screamed, "Hurry up! Get dressed so you can go."

We left-me, my wife, and our children. The four lambs were shaking, crying emotionally the way children cry when they are awakened from sleep. And the moon was bright, and the picture was very emotional.

Kalman Choish stood there embarrassed, not moving from his place and bleeding from his brain. I said, "So what's going on? Why are we standing here? You ordered-we obliged. We're going," I shouted. "Friends! We're going, move."

[Page 109]

Then a surprising thing happened. Kalman faced his Ukrainian policemen (I forgot to mention the policemen were Ukrainians) and said, "Wait here. I'll be right back."

He left and didn't return.

We waited for him for an hour, two hours, the chill eating our flesh, and the policemen were stuck with us. I said to them, "Friends, what are we going to do without the commander?"

They answered, "Take your wife and children, put them inside, and you stay and wait with us."

I took them inside, and when I came out, the two reptiles were also gone.

I found out later that during our conversation and the slap the commander received from my wife, a crowd had started to gather in the distance. Kalman was embarrassed and disappeared, and the policemen who saw his disgrace also took off. In the morning, I went to work for Grozinov, and nothing happened. He waited for me.

He had been informed of the previous night's events; he was serious and angry and asked, "What happened to you last night? Tell me, tell me everything."

I tried to cover it up, but he said to me, "It's nice that you don't want to embarrass your brother, but I know everything. Your wife deserves a medal."

From that day on, I stayed with him, and I lived.

One day, the two Guber brothers entered, called me over to the side, and asked me questions about my situation, about my life, whether I had any difficulties, any complaints. I answered them, "You two, along with all the Communists, can go to hell. I'll hear about your failure in Siberia. You're burying yourselves."

They begged, asking me to go with them. They promised to give me proper work, asked why I wanted to work for a bourgeois, and so on. They didn't say "with gentiles," nor did they explain why a gentile could remain a bourgeois.

I refused, telling them, "You don't deserve to say his name; I won't replace the dust on his feet and shoes with you. We studied together in cheder. Remember who you are. Aren't you ashamed of yourselves? Who are you?

For some reason, they begged and threatened me, telling me I wouldn't continue working there for too long.

A month later, they also evicted my benefactor, Grozinov, and again I was left without a way to earn my bread.

I stayed in Vishnevets, but I didn't go back to them.

I went to Kalman Fishman, the Gubers' uncle. He was a porter, and we had a common interest. I said to him, "What should I do?"

He answered, "You talk too much. That's it."

[Page 110]

Ignoring what had happened, I went to the mill to ask for work. The manager went to Shmuel Guber and asked him to forgive me, and he refused. Kalman said to him, "You're acting like children; you don't know what you're doing."

I heard the conversation from behind the door. Finally, someone told Shmuel, "Give him work."

Yakov Krigsehver, Mitye's father, worked there. He was the storekeeper; he gave me a note and said, "You have 16 sacks over here. Get to work, and try not to talk too much."

Even though Shmuel never stopped bothering me, Yakov took a chance and gave me work notes, like everyone else.

In the general meeting, Shmuel was not reelected as manager. His brother Avraham took over the position his master had abandoned.

The decline of the estranged Jews began.

Meanwhile, the Germans arrived. They separated me from my family and sent me to Dubno, and from there I escaped alone to Russia.

I've forgotten everything, but I won't forget my brothers' betrayal, which remained in my heart like a wound.

[Page 111- Hebrew] [Page 379 - Yiddish]

Jewish Communism in Vishnevets
by G. Nudel

Translated by Sara Mages

When the Poles left, chaos controlled the town. The Ukrainians, as they always do during times of uncertainty, joined the ruling power with the intention of pillaging and killing. We saw them waiting in different corners of the town, holding sacks in their hands.

Immediately, the local Jews organized as one to guard the gate. But when the news of the Russians' arrival reached the town, the Jewish Communists withdrew and organized a ruling body with T. Tsinberg and Avraham Guber as leaders, preparing themselves and trembling in great anticipation of their great day-the day the regime they hoped for would arrive.

The Russians entered through "Mount" Kremenets and camped for a day or two near the Zamek, seizing the homes belonging to the Lifshits and Gnip families to house the important ones among them. Meanwhile, several commissars in army uniforms were seen moving toward the town.

The Russians were welcomed by the local Communist group, and a surprising cooperation emerged between them. Young Vishnevets men jumped out of their skins not only to show their new masters signs of loyalty but also to award themselves with Jewish property, even if they had to slander their own brothers. As a result, the lives of many good Jewish people shriveled and ended in Siberia and local prisons.

We had never imagined the blackest of the black: that in Vishnevets brothers would betray their own brothers. We had never imagined how sick those young men were and how consumed they were by jealousy and greed.

In reality, there were only a few traitors, but their many shocking actions resulted in physical, emotional, and property damage.

At first, several of them, with Matis, Rivke the fish seller's son, the leader of the National Communists' Vishnevets Division, arrested Nachum Beren, Yosef Shapiro, and other loving sons of the Jewish community and the best of that generation. They transferred them to a dark prison cell in Kremenets, with Avraham Gruber and Chana Gruber conducting the arrest and selection of prisoners.

Those fresh Communists committed to testifying at their trial, and they kept their promise.

After the "Zionist" purification, they began cleansing the town of its "capitalists." They took over property belonging to the Lifshits family, Shpiglman, Todros, and all the owners of large and small stores in town. Anyone who had dared to be a bourgeois in Poland, they sent to Siberia.

I remember that the Lifshits brothers, Shpiglman, and Gnip were among the first to be sent into exile. Their sin was their wealth, and their crime was their success in life and their failure to anticipate Stalin's rule of Poland.

The Jews were sent to Siberia at the end of December 1939.

When they were done with them, they collected their allies and the Polish discharged officers, also sending them into exile. The banishment was carried out with torture and brutality.

[Page 112]

They did it in haste at all hours of the day without trial or judgment. They entered the home of the person selected for exile anytime they wanted, telling him to get dressed for the road. The sleds were waiting for the painful journey, and mounted commissars were waiting to escort them so they wouldn't escape during the journey.

Few of those who were exiled survived. The Lifshits brothers died, Gnip died in exile, and no echo has yet been heard from the others.

The deportation was carried out by the Communists-Matis and the Gruber brothers-with great enthusiasm and dedication. Their behavior depressed us: how could a Vishnevets man fall so far after years of togetherness and brotherhood? Where did the estrangement and cruelty come from?

Later, we discovered what drove them to behave like that. We found out that it was greed that had lived in them for a very long time, and now it was satisfied.

The Grubers took over the big flourmill belonging to Shag and his partners and enjoyed its profits. Yehoshue took over the bakeries, and Miler, the town's factories.

Yehoshue introduced norms and lines for bread and other food items. Our bakery was considered a middle-class operation because our whole family worked there and did all the hard labor. The gentiles understood, and we were able to keep our business and earn our living. But the Jewish Communists couldn't digest it, and when they couldn't stand up to the gentiles' amusement, they transferred us to Sofer's bakery, and they were sent to ours.

The norms they set weren't logical. For every 100 kilograms of flour, we were supposed to provide 140 kilograms of bread. Once when we weren't careful and baked 143 kilograms, Yehoshue got mad and started to talk like a "big boss," and at the end of a torrent of cynicism and cursing, he said: "You've eaten enough challah: you've fattened yourselves all your lives, you've gorged yourselves all your lives."

I couldn't help myself and said, "Don't forget, your mother also gorged herself on challah and fish, and you ate with her."

Finally, I slapped him several times. The next day I had to run away. I escaped to Rovne.

I also escaped because at that time they started to harass Youth Guard members. Zionist activities were forbidden, since they regarded the new Youth Guard leaders as a dangerous threat to Communist rule.

All of us decided to escape and enlist in the Red Army.

In Rovne, I was able to enlist in the Red Army. I no longer heard about the actions of the "local," fresh Communists in our town, our brothers and our flesh and blood. But something strange happened to me far from my town, and I remember it in all its terror.

It was 1942. I was at the Shepetovka front. I fell asleep in the trench and began to dream that I was visiting Vishnevets. I was walking on the road by the stream next to the Horyn. It was around Passover. I arrived home, entering quietly through the back door. I walked to my father's bedroom, passed through the other rooms, and saw my whole family, but my father was missing.

[Page 113]

I looked for him, but he wasn't there. I asked my brother and mother, "Where's father?" And they told me he'd been executed earlier that day.

The matter came true later. I found out that the Communists had taken the town elders outside town and killed them. That was the first public execution in the town before the Germans' arrival. It was Communist Nazism.

The gentiles Ostrovski, Storozh, and Vilinski, who hated Jews, carried out the murder, but the Jewish Communists fully supported them.

[Page 114]

Years of Senseless Horror

by Chayim Korin

Translated by Sara Mages

In September 1939, I was staying in a rest house in Yuzefuv. The long pioneer training in Klosov had weakened me. We were hungry for bread in the kibbutz and suffered from malnutrition. The work was tiring, and there was no escaping the workload. The kibbutz sent me to recover and rest. With me were members of other pioneer groups, who, like me, had come to recover. The rest house closed after the first German attack. We scattered all over. There was no reason or way to return to Klosov. We ran home. I ran to Vishnevets.

Vishnevets was then in Russian hands. They were looking for qualified workers, people who were passionate about their cause and from the pure lower class. Being considered a "farmhand," I enjoyed their trust and was given a job as a storekeeper at town hall. Their trust was not complete because they didn't dare give me a public job. Someone hinted that my lower-class status had been contaminated because of my pioneering.

I went to work for Avraham Gruber, a veteran Communist who had been elected general manager of all the Polish farms that had been confiscated after their owners left.

After a couple of months, Gruber was also dismissed, and a Russian Jew, who had grown up on the knees of the Communist regime, was nominated as general manager. After a month, we became very good friends. He trusted me and allowed himself to talk to me in the way a Jew talks to a Jew. One evening he said to me:

"Vishnevets is swarming with 'informers,' your former friends included. They're tarnishing each other's reputations. Listen to me, Chayim, they're also gossiping about you because of your Zionist past. Very shortly you'll be fired, and if that's not enough, you'll be sent to Siberia or another hell. I'd advise you to leave without delay, and don't remember only the worst of me. You don't bother me."

I knew my secret had been discovered, and I didn't have too many choices. I left the town at night to hide in the nearby villages, hoping to return to the town at the first opportunity.

Our area was bombed in June 1941. The Russians retreated, but I couldn't return to Vishnevets since I was considered to be a Communist worker. Nor did I want to return. I had read too much about the Nazis to want to taste their regime. My heart predicted only the worst.

I came to Vishnevets for only one night to say good-bye to my dear family and leave.

My heart was heavy. I was tired from my wandering and depressed about my inability to reach Israel. But I had made up my mind-to leave.

For a long time, I had wanted to keep a distance from Vishnevets, my "birthplace." The "glorious" Polish regime prevented me from leaving Vishnevets, but I decided to do it now.

[Page 115]

That night, seven friends, including Leyb and Motil Sofer and Geler Moshe Yosef, came to the same conclusion and decided to enlist in the Red Army. In doing so, we were hoping to clear our names and smuggle ourselves into Russia.

In the morning, we went to enlist, but all the government offices were deserted. The officers had escaped that same night. There was no one who knew how to direct us or tell us where to go; there was no one to approach. We couldn't enlist in the usual way, the official way, so we decided to enlist in a different way, to break into Russia and live.

We went to the front lines; maybe someone would want our sacrifice. We caught up with the Russians on the way to Starykonstantin. They were tense and frightened, they suffered from a lack of self-confidence, and they were suspicious. They caught us and beat us hard trying to find out if we were German spies. We didn't tell them anything; we had nothing to tell; we begged them to enlist us, and we told them the whole truth. But it didn't help, and we were judged in our absence as spies. The next day, they would finish us off. We knew what was coming to us even though we didn't want to believe it; something good was predicted in our souls. Luckily for us, the unit's highest-ranking artillery officer was Jewish, and he let us go. He also implied that we should run away.

We were scared. We were afraid the Russians wouldn't give up on killing us, and we told him so. He sent us with an armed guard and advised us to run to Konstantin and mix with the local Jews. And so we did. When they left, we continued to run.

A few weeks later, we arrived in Stalingrad. All the Jews from the surrounding area went there. The rumors about the fate of the Jews in German-occupied territories were shocking. We dragged on and also went there.

We were drafted to work in a kolkhoz, since as Polish citizens we were not trusted to serve as soldiers on the front lines. They were worried that our intention was to liberate our "homeland" with the help of the Germans and that we would betray the Russians in favor of the Poles.

We worked at the Malogolovsk kolkhoz. Until winter arrived, we sustained ourselves with whatever the field and the farm provided, but with the arrival of winter, our food source ceased, and we were not given clothes. In addition, the "hired workers'" field kitchen was closed. The kolkhoz was very rich, but our condition, the hired help's condition, worsened while the members of the kolkhoz lived in prosperity.

We deliberated and decided to move to the nearby town. The place was cut off, and the only mode of transportation was groaning and moaning wooden carts harnessed to bulls. There weren't any roads, and it took us 16 hours to reach our destination. I registered to work legally. We were planning to stay there for a short while, eat well, warm our frozen bodies, and decide what to do next. But news arrived from all sides saying that the Germans were advancing, and we decided to escape, even without permission. We wanted to be as far away from there as we could travel, even if we had to walk.

We disappeared at night. The rumors that the residents of the areas occupied by the Nazis cooperated with them in the name of holy anti-Semitism sent shivers through our bones. Tired and weak, we walked, covering hundreds of kilometers on foot, in freight cars, by hitchhiking on bull carts, and again on foot until we reached Central Asia.

That's where we separated, each going his own way. The train stations were crowded, the noise level was great, and hunger was even greater.

[Page 116]

Committees were organized immediately to help the refugees. Able workers were sent to a kolkhoz far from the main roads. I arrived at a kolkhoz named after Stalin, a desolate place that was cut off from the world. I realized that it was better for me to enlist in the army: I was worried about "civilian locations." Maybe they would "invite" the Nazis; who knew the great power of hatred of the Jews?

I succeeded. I was drafted into the army without anyone investigating the fringes of my past.

I was sent to an accelerated training camp in Ashkhabad, Turkistan, and four months later, I was sent to the Ukrainian front lines in Debaltsova, in the Donbas, and again, not as a soldier fighting on the front lines, but as a soldier's servant.

Our conditions were unbearable. Our job was to stay at the rear of the retreating army-and it retreated and retreated-and sabotage vital installations so they wouldn't fall into enemy hands.

The retreat always happened at the last moment, and we were abandoned to the advancing enemy. We sabotaged trains and power and telephone lines. We lived the life of laborers, but we acted within the jaws of danger, taking the same risks as the soldiers on the front lines. The best part was that we were always near trains, and we were able to slip away at the last minute. Most of us were Jews, and we all had the same idea. We sabotaged the installations before the army retreated, and we ran off.

Once when the Germans caught us with their tanks, we were hiding in a ditch covered by a roof made of branches and railroad tiles. The heavy roof fell in on us with its ton of weight. Those who were crushed by its weight were killed and buried there. Three others and I, who were lying on the side, were wounded and survived.

I gave up on my own life. Too many miracles had happened to me, and a strange fear settled within me. Maybe the miracles had ended. But my will to live got stronger as my fear got stronger.

The last miracle happened that day. The Germans were driven out of that location by a Russian counterattack. I was "discovered" by them and taken in serious condition to a hospital in the city of Kagan. When I recovered, I was given 70% disability and released from the army.

At the hospital, we were taught different skills for our recovery in civilian life. I finished a full course in general storekeeping. I studied finance, economics, and food distribution.

I enjoyed my new occupation, but the distance from the front lines and my civilian life in the Asian city, whose name I have forgotten, created a strong longing for my home, Vishnevets, and for my parents, family, and friends, and my heart pulled me there.

***

In 1945, we returned to our hometown.

Finally, I arrived in Vishnevets. I was there for a few days, but I couldn't take more than that. The town had been destroyed, life had been pulled from its roots, Jewish life had disappeared, and our loved ones were gone. All that pushed me to run away. Our former Ukrainian neighbors influenced me to escape.

[Page 117]

Their talk was full of too many clear lies, "they had helped the Jews," "smuggled food into the ghetto," and "risked their lives," each conversation canceling out the preceding one. Their cynicism mixed with hidden joy made me fearful and nauseous. With all the pretend help they had given my friends who were no longer with us, they didn't let me sleep in their homes, not even for one night. I knew that, for me, Vishnevets was dead.

There were a few Jews in town. I remember that they included Moshe Yosef Geler, Moshe Fishman, and Avraham (?). I spent the night with them. Avraham still lives in Vishnevets. He was a veteran Polish Communist, and the current regime is his ideal regime. He works in a Russian clothing store.

How I Found My Town

There was nothing left of the whole town. Niuni Roytkoytel traveled with me on the train from Lvov to Vishnevets. This was his second visit to the town. He said to me, "I'll cover your eyes, bring you to the town center, and leave you in the street. Then you'll open your eyes and see if you recognize the place." I did as he asked. I took my handkerchief off, and I really didn't know where I was standing. I turned around, shocked and confused, until I saw the flourmill still standing in its place. Only then did I know I was in my hometown, the town that no longer existed.

Only a few buildings remained standing in Vishnevets. The Great Synagogue remained and was being used as the district prison. They didn't touch the synagogue at all. Inside, I found the ancient stone about which many legends were told. It was said that it was 800 years old and came from a holy place.

Remaining of All of Vishnevets...

[Page 118]

It had been brought as a protective shield when the synagogue was built, and the saying "You will be blessed when you enter, and you will be blessed when you leave" was carved on it.

For a synagogue-prison, only the end of the saying is accurate, but no one paid attention to the text's meaning or value.

In the yard next to the building, the small cemetery, the Kvaresil, remained. Deadly silence and desolation hovered above it, and the atmosphere was extremely gloomy. Standing next to the gentiles' flowing life in the new town, the Kvaresil illuminates how it was and is a witness to what happened: one chain of pogroms against the Jews since the Kvaresil was created.

[Page 119 - Hebrew] [Page 335 - Yiddish]

With the Soviets in Vishnevets and Afterward

by Y. Mazur

Translated by Sara Mages

On the Sabbath before Rosh Hashanah 1939, rumors arrived that the Russians were getting closer. They had been seen in Zbarazh and Lanevits, and they were ready to take Vishnevets into their hands.

Out of fear of the Ukrainians, the guards of the collapsing Polish regime left for their homes to hide. And the Ukrainians, who understood the message, gathered by the monastery. They took the keys from the monks who were concentrated inside and wanted to beat them up. I don't know why, but a group of Jews, Shike Shteyn and I in the lead, approached the rioting Ukrainians and told them, "Friends, what are you doing? We've lived together for many years. Why are you taking advantage of the disaster that has come to them? Give them the keys and leave; they haven't done you any harm.

Strangely, they listened to us, let the Polish monks go, gave them the keys, and left.

I was a teenager then, but suddenly it was clear to me that the foundation of humanity was weakening. The relationship between different nations was starting to collapse, and the world wasn't what it used to be. Something trembled inside me, and I made up my mind to be resourceful. Even at my young age, I was aware of what was happening around me.

Three days later, on Monday, the weekly market day in Vishnevets, which also served as a fair for the whole area, I saw the Ukrainians rushing around. Suddenly, the Ukrainians began to organize themselves outside town. It looked like they were getting ready to start a pogrom. The town was shocked. The storekeepers took measures and closed their shops. Some of the Ukrainians started to bother storekeepers who stood next to their closed stores, demanding that they open them. The Jews understood that they were planning to rob them even though they were shouting mercifully, "Open up, today is market day, we want to buy. Why did we bother to come to the market when they won't let us shop?"

The Jews didn't open up. Immediately, a defense group was organized by young men from the town, who had always been known for their bravery. They grabbed rifles that they'd collected from Polish soldiers who had deserted the front lines (I must mention that when the Ukrainian soldiers began to leave for home and let the Poles go, a Soviet representative immediately appeared and organized the young men as a unit. Their duty was to strip them of their weapons, search their wagons, and bring the hidden weapons to one location.) When I looked around me, I suddenly saw that everything was organized and in order. Rifles were everywhere, and young Jewish men were standing next to them. I can't forget the resourcefulness and bravery shown by the young men of my town during worldwide confusion.

The rioting Ukrainians were confused and asked each other what to do.

In order to make them quickly decide to leave, a group of young men walked over to them and said, "You see, we're ready, and you have nothing to gain. You'd better disperse quietly. If not, we'll use our weapons."

[Page 120]

The rioters kept up their loud consultation and decided not to leave empty-handed. Since they had decided to riot, they would riot. But when no brave volunteers willing to resist the Jews were found among them, they folded with embarrassment and left.

Immediately following this incident, the town's Young Communist group organized "self-defense" units. I was a teenager, and I couldn't investigate the matter, so I can't tell you how the group was organized or whether they were given an order from a high-ranking official or whether it was a personal initiative. But owing to them, the town was saved from pogroms for a short time.

We all took turns guarding the defense posts until the Russians arrived. We created an intermediate regime, and for a short time, the Communists forgot our Zionist background. Jews collaborated with Jews.

We stood firm from Rosh Hashanah until Yom Kippur, and at the termination of the Days of Awe, the Russians arrived.

***

In 1940, two young men from our town were drafted into the Red Army. I still can't understand why only Yitschak (Leyzer the barber's brother) and I were drafted.

We were away from the town for many years.

I served in the Red Army until 1942 and took part in many battles. Later, when they remembered our Polish citizenship, they declared us unfit, and we were sent to a working battalion. It was very dangerous work at the rear of the battles. I escaped from there to a different workplace, where I worked for many months with beets and sugar.

The end of the war was near, and I decided to return to Poland. I found a talented gypsy painter who was an expert a "useful" painting. He counterfeited Polish citizenship documents for the six of us: me, Kardash from Rovne, Losgos Yehoshue of Krasna (both of died of hunger next to me), Holtser Rozye (who lives in Holon, Israel), our public health nurse Goldshteyn from Stanislavov, a doctor from Kolomiya, a certified lawyer whose name I can't remember, and another person whose name we can't mention because he's being investigated by the Israeli Secret Service after it was discovered that he had been the one who informed on us to the Russians. Because of him, we were arrested and sent to Siberia for many years.

Meanwhile, Polish military troops were transferred to different battlefields in Poland.

We planned to leave Russia legally before it was too late. For some reason, I had the feeling that we wouldn't be able to build a personal or social life here. This feeling was based on the authorities' attitude toward us and on that of other citizens, who treated us as enemies that they should dispose of.

Our aspiration was to cross into Poland with the Polish troops and emigrate from there to Israel.

[Page 121]

As we were planning our legal departure, we were detained without explanation.

We were arrested on April 21, 1943, and I was sent to Alma Ata in Kazakhstan. From there, I was sent to Tashkent.

In Tashkent, I ran into Dzhigen and Shumakher, and together we moved to a camp in Aktyubinsk, Kazakhstan. Twelve thousand people lived in the camp, which was divided into three sections: men, women, and the sick. People died like flies in that camp from starvation and humiliation.

I was there for eight months waiting to be judged in court for my Zionist past. My trial took place in Moscow, and I was transferred there.

On November 13, my friends, who had allegedly cooperated with me, and I were judged and sentenced. I was given 10 years, and each of the others received 8 years. We knew someone had betrayed us.

My official charge was antirevolutionary activities as a "Zionist political activist" who endangers the existence of the international labor regime.

I was sent immediately to the Northern Urals. For a month, we traveled under inhuman conditions, using all modes of transportation, until we arrived at our place of punishment. On the way, we spent two weeks in Chelyabinsk prison so we could get an idea of what was waiting for us in Siberia.

We were put in prison so we could recover from the malnutrition inflicted on us on the road. From there, I was transferred to a prison in Sverdlovsk, where a large transport was leaving for a place in the Urals located 100 kilometers from the tundra.

During our trip, people fell and died from lack of food and lack of suitable clothing for the harsh, freezing weather. A third of the 200 died on the journey. After we arrived at our destination and were divided into groups, more people died as a result of the month-long, difficult journey. From my group of 26 people, 24 died, and only two of us were left.

***

At first, we worked in the carpentry shop that provided us with occupational therapy-so we could recover. Later, I was transferred to work as a barber in the camp barbershop.

When I arrived at the camp, I was swollen from malnutrition. Those responsible for feeding the camp inhabitants stole the food supply, and we had nothing to eat. I became weak, and I couldn't carry myself. I couldn't even move a little in order to climb the few stairs to the hospital. I crawled on all fours each time I had to climb up or down. At the hospital, I also contracted pellagra and dysentery. According to the camp's statistics and the doctors' opinion, I was supposed to die. I also knew my condition, and I was ready to die. But a miracle happened, and somehow I recovered.

Recovering from pellagra weakens you for a long time and brings you terrible physical pain, but you feel your life is improving.

When I had completely recovered, I was put in front of a medical board, which gave me an excellent bill of health.

[Page 122]

Although I wasn't feeling well, I was sent to a camp whose inhabitants were cutting down trees in the forest. For a month, I worked under difficult, unbearable conditions. I cut down trees during the day and loaded wagons at night. We didn't have food, only bread that we soaked in water. All the good food was stolen and sold by the commissars. While they ate greedily until they were full, their "working kinsmen," their brothers in unity and idealism, were starving to death.

Again I was exhausted, and I realized my end was near. Depressed, I loathed my life, and I wanted to commit suicide. I did this in a particular way. As I rolled heavy tree trunks upward into the wagon, I grabbed one of the trunks, which weighed around 500 kilograms, pulled it upward to the height of the wagon with what was left of my energy, and stood it up in the air. I hesitated and hesitated, and finally, when my energy had left me, my hands started to tremble, my knees buckled, and I weakened my hold. I decided to release the rope, slide the heavy trunk, and let it fall and crush my body underneath it, ending my suffering and the difficult life waiting for me. Luckily, I hit my head on a railroad tile, lost consciousness, and rolled under the wagon. When the huge tree trunk fell, it rolled downward with a thunderous sound. One end got stuck in the ground. It remained upright, and I was saved.

I was sent to the hospital to heal my head and recover my strength. My head was extremely swollen, the bruise was large, and I was twisting in pain. They gave me five days off to recover, and after that I had to go back to work.

My pain didn't stop after my time off. My ability to think had been taken from me, my nerves were frail, my brain was clouded, and I was confused. I started to change my behavior, realizing they wouldn't send me to hard labor again. I felt my energy leaving me, my health was deteriorating, and I couldn't endure one more day in the forest.

They got scared of the way they were treating me and sent me to work in the camp laundry washing underwear.

Two weeks later, I was taken to the location where the mental patients were being held, and I was constantly supervised by the doctors. When I had recovered a little, I went through another medical board, and I was sent to the forests again.

Meanwhile, the war ended, life returned to normal, and I continued to serve my sentence.

In 1949, I recovered fully and was sent to another forest managed by a Polish gentile, a native of Dnipropetrovs'k who treated Jews very well. People hinted that he was Jewish or of Jewish origin.

He took me home, and I recovered under his care. There was plenty of food there, and my condition improved.

In December 1949, an order was given to separate the political prisoners and send them to a special camp in Karagander. It was a concentration camp for "political" prisoners. According to the camp's orders, we were dressed in prison uniforms, and our heads were shaved. We worked in construction during the day, and at 10:00 at night, they locked us in our homes. It was a Russian invention; we weren't prisoners in a prison, we were under house arrest.

We were locked up and sealed into our houses until 7:00 a.m. From 7:00 until 10:00 at night, we weren't allowed to roam the streets.

[Page 123]

This was to prevent us from creating a faction that was dangerous to the regime. Except for that, our living conditions weren't difficult. After experiencing life in the land of "freedom," we began to think that our situation wasn't too bad. We ate until we were full, and the food influenced our minds, sending them in the right direction.

Ukrainian outlaws who had collaborated with the Nazis were concentrated in this camp. They were also considered political prisoners. In reality, they were bands of robbers who formed a gang inside the camp. They left their homes in separate groups and roamed the streets from 7:00 to 10:00, when they were empty, killing people who felt not right to them.

In that way, they killed Ingel, the Jewish author, in front of me. They murdered him with an ax, struck him, and left him dead where he fell.

With me in the camp were famous Jews who had been charged according to the famous section 58. These included Professor Emden, grandson of R' Yakov Emden, who had been a genius educator in Leningrad, and Shmuel Kantor, a university history lecturer, also from Leningrad. He had been arrested because he raised his glass on Yom Kippur with two of his friends and said, "Next year in Jerusalem." One of his friends was an informer, and the lecturer paid dearly for his crime. I also remember the author Hirsh Osherovits from Vilna, the Jewish poet Motel Grubian from Minsk, and Ochitel, a profound Jewish scholar from Bessarabia and a famous Hebrew teacher whose crime was his connection to the language he was famous for: Hebrew.

***

In 1942, I was transferred from the camp in Karagander to exile in Akmolinsk. It was a famous camp for those who had been given "life sentences." It was established in a desolate place near the Vishnyovsk district in southern Siberia. My trial never took place, and I still don't know why they worsened my punishment. I was asked to sign an order for that transport. I read the order. It said that it was my idea and was being done with my knowledge.

I signed it since I had no other choice. I was indifferent to my fate and depressed. At times, I was sorry my suicide attempts hadn't succeeded.

In 1956, I was pardoned by an amnesty order given by Khrushchev. I stayed in the camp and lived there as a free citizen. I was able to travel from there to visit Vishnevets.

I traveled to Dubno by train and from there by taxi to Kremenets, to the intersection leading to Vishnevets. I stood in the street for almost an hour and didn't see a single Jew pass by. I couldn't find anyone to ask anything. I was shocked. I knew about the Holocaust, but I couldn't accept the fact that there weren't any Jews left in the world. I couldn't believe that I wouldn't be able to find one of us from Vishnevets in Kremenets.

Suddenly, a woman walked by. I recognized her from the way she walked. She was different from the others who were passing by. I assumed she was Jewish, and I started talking to her. I found out that she was from Katerburg and was living in Kremenets with her husband, who also came from her town.

[Page 124]

They had always dreamed of living in the city of Kremenets, and now they could realize their dream. They didn't long for more than that.

I heard from her that not a single Jew was left in Vishnevets except for Tsvi Miler, who lived in Kremenets, according to her. I didn't know whom she was talking about. I sat with them for a few hours, and then I traveled to Vishnevets.

In the evening hours, I took the bus to Vishnevets, and half an hour later, I arrived in my town.

I'm not someone who gets emotional very quickly, but this trip was an emotional one.

When it was announced that our bus had arrived in Vishnevets, I didn't know where I was. I saw that our town was gone; not a trace was left of her.

There is no Vishnevets. Nothing.

I discovered that a few buildings were left, and Avraham Rozenboym lived in one of them. I spent the night there, and in the morning I went to see Vishnevets.

I went to the street where the synagogue was. All the buildings had disappeared. Only the holy house was left. That year, our house of prayer was used as a prison, and later it was converted to an apartment building. It was divided into three floors of apartments. It was explained to me that the district institutions had moved to a different town and that the prison had also been closed.

Also, the Tarbut building that we all knew was still there, as were Y. Kamtsan's and Gun's (Idil Hun's) homes on Zbarazh Street, those of Mazur and Berele, Moshe Aron's son, Moshe Yosl Geler's mother-in-law, and Shmuel Reyzels' sons.

I stayed in Vishnevets to file a claim in court for the release of our home and for the return of my right as its only heir.

Nothing Remained of Vishnevets but Mass Graves

[Page 125]

After three months, I won the case. I sold the house and went to Zbarazh.

Before I immigrated to Israel, I visited Vishnevets again. This time, I found changes. The palace has been restored, and now it looks like its sparkling past. Tall buildings are being built now, and the town is overpopulated. The monastery was bombed, and there is no trace of it. After being cleansed of its Jews, Vishnevets is being "cleansed" of all of its Polish roots. The palace was restored because they considered it Russian property.

Something about Soviet Mankind

In 1946, it was February, and it was cold, only 40 degrees outside. They collected us and wanted to send us to work. We didn't want to go because we were hungry and weak. Suddenly, the commander, a major by rank, who was known for his cruelty and extreme anti-Semitism, walked in. He started to harass me, telling his secretary to write up a report that I had destroyed government property, like a blanket or a mattress. It wasn't true, but he did it. He wanted to provide an excuse for my arrest and the punishment he was going to give me. I took my clothes off, threw them at his face, and said, take them and give them to your children as a gift.

That angered him even more. He gave an order to take me outside, naked as the day I was born. Two Russians were standing there, and they chased me for hundreds on meters, back and forth in the freezing cold and the deep snow. Later, they put me in a prison cell and locked me in for the night. It was cold in the cell, and wind blew in all directions. There was only a small stove whose fire had been put out a long time ago. I held onto the bars of the warm stove, which were created to keep prisoners away from it. I hung on the bars the whole night without any clothes on, warming my frozen body with the remaining heat that blew from it and the metal frame around it.

***

One evening, on February 15, 1951, I was playing chess with a Jew from Tshernovits. Suddenly, the camp commander came in. His name was Anotova, and he was a great anti-Semite. He was angry, claiming that we were disturbing the peace, and put us in a prison cell with a cement floor. My friend was dressed and wore felt shoes on his feet. I had come back from my job at the washhouse, and I was lightly dressed and wore lightweight shoes on my feet. Half an hour later, my legs began to freeze, and I felt as if I were going to lose them. I collected what was left of my energy and started to run around the cell, which was only six meters long, to warm up my legs.

And so I ran from 9:00 in the evening until 6:00 in the morning, when they came to call me for work.

If I had not been needed as a laborer, they would have forgotten me, and I would have ended my life innocently in the cell.

[Page 126 - Hebrew] [Page 393 - Yiddish]

The Victims We Sacrificed...

by Sonye Shats

Translated by Sara Mages

In 1936 I built a home in Lodz. In July 1939, a month before I was supposed to immigrate to Israel, I decided to travel to Vishnevets and say goodbye to my parents and to everyone in that town who was dear to me.

August came, and my parents, who were having a hard time being separated from me, asked me to stay with them for another month. I stayed, and the war caught me. Vishnevets fell into the hands of the Russians, and I was stuck there.

I lived under the Soviets for three months. There was no way to escape them and immigrate to Israel. Later, we found out that we could save ourselves if we could reach Lithuania. The border there wasn't completely closed, and we'd be able to emigrate from there.

When I left my parents, we knew we'd be traveling to Lida, the last Lithuanian city in Soviet hands. From there, we'd be "smuggled" to Eyshishuk-Vilna, and the road was open.

My brother Eliezer, who had never left the bosom of our parents, decided to go to Yampol, which was originally a Soviet town, and build a life there. He was a member of the Youth Guard movement and saw Communist life as his ideal.

In Yampol, he sobered very fast when he saw the regime and its results: standing in line for every food item and the living conditions. He returned home having decided to immigrate to Israel.

He told our parents he'd go with us to Lida and come home. And so we left for Lida with my little brother.

In Lida, Israeli political party delegates only took care of their own members. The Youth Guard people didn't want to take care of us and told us to approach our own people. But they took responsibility for Eliezer and promised to organize his immigration.

I left my little brother, young and tender in years, with tears choking me. In my heart, I thought that at least we'd meet again in the near future, but the tears fell on their own.

**

A strong snowstorm was blowing the night we left Lida. The roads were covered with layers of snow, and the tracks were blurry. Our guides-smugglers got lost, and we couldn't find our way out. The night was dim, the chill was strong, and no one knew where we were. We kept on walking because we felt that if we stopped, we'd turn into pillars of ice. Suddenly, we heard shouting in Russian: Stop! And we fell into the Russians' hands.

They kept us for eight days in a place that is still unknown to me. They interrogated us as if we were spies, deserters, or traitors and brought us back to Lida.

The first thing that worried me was my little brother's fate. I looked for him in the town and couldn't find him. I asked the members of his party, and they told me he'd crossed the border and was on his way to Israel.

[Page 127]

I calmed down and decided to go back to Vishnevets.

On the way, we decided it was too dangerous. Maybe they knew there that we'd "fled." We turned and went to Rovne. We let our parents know we'd come back, and they joined us. A former family friend, who had joined the new regime, informed my father that it was known that his son had run away and that the authorities suspected our family. It was better that he'd left.

We spent two years in Rovne, and in 1941, the war between Russia and Germany erupted. Rovne was bombed, and we were forced to move away. The Russians asked my father to join them in their escape, but father insisted that we return to Vishnevets. He believed he'd be able to live through the Nazi regime. He was unfit in the eyes of the Russians-he said-and we'd certainly appease them. We couldn't convince him. His answer was final: "I saw the refugees in our town. I don't have the energy or the will to be a refugee, wandering in the streets and living at the mercy of others."

***

He was drawn home to Vishnevets.

We were forced to oblige him.

We couldn't reach Vishnevets. The road had been bombed, and many villages had been captured by the Germans.

We were swept up in the stream of refugees. We traveled 200 kilometers on foot until we reached Novograd Velinsk. Those were five days of hell. Enemy airplanes flew low, spraying death on our area. The wounded and the dead fell around us, and a shower of bullets and bombs spewed above us.

Before we left Rovne, a message arrived saying that Eliezer was living in a Youth Guard kibbutz in Yanove, near Kovne. According to the message, he'd arrived safely and would continue to Israel with everyone. Thank God.

The news eased our journey. We played with that hope. We told ourselves that Eliezer would come and take us with him.

Days later, we came to the conclusion, and we had a basis for it, that he'd died in Yanove. He was so young and innocent; it was the first journey of his life, and he died taking it.

From Novograd, we continued our journey, alternating between walking and freight cars, until we reached Charkov through Kyuv and Dnepropetrovsk, with me in the final months of pregnancy.

**

Our suffering increased on the way to Kuybishev. We were transferred there along with other pitiful, poor suspects. We traveled standing in cattle cars, squeezed together with 90 people, for three weeks. We stood for 20 days without food or water. We slept standing, and we urinated were we stood. When we stopped, we took a chance and jumped into the frozen fields to dig into the frozen earth and pull carrots, beets, and other roots left in the fields to fill our stomachs and satisfy our appetite.

[Page 128]

Every once in a while, I felt painful cramps. A fear came over me: maybe I'd deliver my baby standing in the middle of an overcrowded car. It depressed me more than anything else. Meanwhile, we arrived in Penza, and the management informed us that we'd be staying there for three days. I went to the doctor to ask his advice.

The doctor informed me that I was fit to travel for two more weeks. We scattered between the lines to receive our bread allotment, and we were ready to continue our exhausting journey, which was difficult and dangerous for me.

At night, I felt sick. Pains overtook me. At one after midnight, I delivered my firstborn son.

A few days later, we were sent to a kolkhoz in the village of Lunina. We didn't have any clothes, not even for the baby. It was a dangerous journey. It was unbearably cold. It's beyond my comprehension how the baby coped with the extreme cold. We felt better and said, in a couple of days we'll reach the kolkhoz, and we'll have walls and a roof over our heads; we'll have bread and warmth.

We reached a poor kolkhoz. Its inhabitances were hungry and needy. We received four kilograms of flour a month per person. We didn't have our own house. They housed us in an unheated clay hut, and the cold air leaked through the cracks.

Somehow we coped with the hunger, but the chill weakened us. We wanted to live. We stayed alive only because we were worried about the boy.

My father couldn't cope with our difficult situation. He died of hunger shortly after we arrived at the kolkhoz.

We couldn't leave the hut, since it was sunk in deep snow. My dead father stayed with us for three days without being buried.

On the fourth day, we gathered our courage, pushed the door open, and went out. We informed the authorities about the dead person, but they were not excited. There were many more like that. Digging a grave was impossible. They had an open grave that they'd prepared weeks before, and several frozen bodies were already in it. They threw father into that open grave.

Father is still buried with 10 gentiles of many religions. Father was not brought to a Jewish grave. I'm not strict in religious matters, but I'd pay the highest price to liberate my dead father from this "brothers" grave and bring him to a Jewish grave, as he'd wished and longed for all of his life.

I don't know if and when I'll have the opportunity to do so.

Many are the Jewish victims that we've planted all over the world. If only we could provide a logical explanation for their death and bring them to a Jewish grave.

[Page 129]

Under Justice-Perverted Regimes

by Yerachmiel Servetnik

Translated by Sara Mages

During the Russian occupation, our town's reprobates came to power. Kalman Choish became the chief of police and later the public prosecutor, and Avraham Gruber became the mayor.

We moved to our farm in Horenka, and every Sunday we came to town to hear the latest news.

Those two extorted money from the Jews and retaliated against those who were rich and earned a respectable salary.

Provincial feelings of jealousy, which were aided by the new gentiles' ideological approval, enabled the town's weaklings to sustain the envy and inferiority that had nested in their souls for many years.

Jews closed their stores in fear of looting or requisition and tried to empty them of merchandise in secret, but their Jewish employees informed the authorities. An order was given to open the stores and sell the merchandise, and every zloty would be counted as a ruble.

Jews emptied their stores at night in order to save whatever they could. Yakov Tenenboym asked me to hide some of his leather and complained about the cold weather.

I brought him firewood and saved his leather. I looked like a gentile when I rode my sled, and no one investigated me.

When the war erupted on June 21, 1941, I was drafted into the Red Army. At 5:00 on the same day, they lined us up in rows and transferred us to Yampoli. Fearful of bombing, we slept in a Polish cemetery, and the night predicted injury and wandering. In the morning, they transferred us to Lanovits by rail. We disembarked at Kornochevka train station, where they stripped us of our civilian clothes and dressed us in old uniforms, and we became soldiers. They transferred us to Ternopol, and from there we were directed to Lvov to "protect Lvov." Immediately after we arrived, enemy planes bombed the whole area.

When the bombing stopped, we escaped and returned to Ternopol.

The Ternopol train station had been completely destroyed. We returned to Proskurov in vehicles and later on foot. We were bombed at night. I lay hiding in a potato field.

We were collected in the morning, and we walked toward the Dnieper until we reached Tshernigov. On the way, we saw that Bilotserkov was burning. They distributed us among the homes. A gentile said he wouldn't allow us to enter his home, only his barn. We slept in the straw, itching from lice. We were tired and dejected, and we heard our "benefactor" say to the Ukrainians among us, "Why are you dragging behind the lice-infected Reds? You sleep here tonight, and tomorrow the Germans will arrive and liberate us, all the Ukrainians. We've been trampled by the cursed Russians for too long."

[Page 130]

In the morning, the gentile woke up, announcing, "Tomorrow the Germans will arrive, and I'll send the Jews and Russians to take my pigs to the meadow."

We knew we had to hurry and leave the Ukrainian trap, since they were waiting for the Nazis to arrive.

I was in Vinitse, it was August, and it was very hot. I lay down to rest along with hundreds of depressed and tired men like me. Suddenly, I heard someone shouting, Yerachmiel! I looked around to see who was calling my name and saw a group of young men from Vishnevets sitting together and resting in a ditch by the road, including Motil Sofer, Noske Layter the watchmaker's son, and others who had been drafted into the Red Army after me. I then understood that Vishnevets had been emptied of her youth.

They called me, pretending to ask my advice, but all they wanted was to tell me how depressed they were. They wanted to return "home" and tried to convince me to join them, but I didn't agree. I told them that according to my prognosis, a Nazi holocaust awaited the Jews, but they didn't agree. I left them in the ditch and went away. Later, I found out that most of them had returned and died.

I reached Poltava on foot. We stopped there and waited for orders. We didn't know what was happening around us. We rested for a week, and then it was "decided" to take hold there and stop the Germans from entering Russia.

An order was given to disarm all the "Westerners" and transfer them to Siberia. I now knew that the Jews were not wanted by the Russians.

In Priluk, they loaded us onto a train, and we traveled toward Siberia.

We traveled for two weeks until we arrived in the northern Urals.

On August 15, 1941, we arrived in a town by the name of Myed (copper) in the Urals, near the new city of Novaya Uralsk, the city of copper, tin, and gold.

The gold was mined from a mine 300 meters deep, but there were also open mines and rivers where water pressure had washed the sand out and the gold was left lying on the sand.

One day, they started to build factories, but we didn't know what kind of factories they were. Later, we found out that ammunition for missile launchers would be manufactured in those factories.

Three thousand people worked in construction. Most of them were Estonians, Moldovans, and "Westerners." We lived in different camps and were taken to work in groups, but we lived separate lives. Each group was escorted by a political agent who supervised our political opinions. They also served as taskmasters who supervised us to make sure we supplied our daily quotas. When we complained about the lack of food, the political agent answered: thousands of our people die every day, and the world isn't shocked. What will happen if you die?

One day, our political agent passed among us and announced, "Anyone who is a craftsman, step forward."

They were looking for construction laborers. When he approached me, I answered, "I'm a carpenter," and I was taken away.

We repaired a burned-down factory .We cleaned it and turned it into a carpentry workshop. The work was long, and I was a supervisor.

[Page 131]

Twelve people (a brigade) worked under my supervision. The director of all the brigades, who was in charge of all the tasks, was a Jewish engineer from Krakow. He was a good Jew, but he didn't know how to write reports to his supervisors. He didn't know Russian, and he didn't know "how" to report. He heard me speaking Russian and asked me to work in the office as his personal assistant. I started to write began writing his reports in Russian. As a result, our food was delivered to us, we ate well, and the crew was happy. In time, I understood the small details, learned the craft, and went to work as an assistant to the engineer.

One evening, the engineer told me to deliver the report to the office. A young Jewish man sat there and gave an order for me to be appointed as official report writer. Two weeks later, a high-ranking political agent called me and appointed me as a storekeeper. I didn't enjoy it, but I took the job and worked there until March 1946.

The Russians worked indoors under good conditions. The hard, difficult labor was done by the Uzbeks. They worked like slaves, like second-rate citizens, and didn't dare lift their heads. I was a clerk, which everyone needed. I was a storekeeper with unlimited possibilities, and I was in charge of my own time. I observed the regime and its citizens' lives. Desperation ate at me; was this a righteous regime? How could I live among them?

With the first repatriation, I left everything. I moved to Poland and immigrated to Israel.

I immigrated on the boat Exodus and went through everything involved with that, but I don't think the story is important for Sefer Vishnevets, so I'll skip it.

Finally, I only want to say this:

I agreed to write something in Sefer Vishnevets because I think the book is a memorial book, and the memory will serve as a historical lesson. Let's learn the lesson that no regime is part of our national identity. For us Jews, the Holocaust and the disaster were concealed from the beginning.

[Page 132]

Russia, Which Was My Undoing

by Menashe Tsvik

Translated by Sara Mages

In 1941, the day before the war started, I was drafted into the Red Army as a gunner. I was transferred to Kremenets in order to approach the front lines. There we were informed that the road to Lvov had been blocked by the Germans. We were forced to travel to Ternopol via Vishnevets.

So we returned to Vishnevets. Six kilometers outside Vishnevets, we were told that there was no way to reach Ternopol. We turned and walked to the Lanovits train station, where we stayed. We couldn't board the train because German fighter planes were flying over our heads in wave after wave. We lay without moving. Three days later, we boarded the train and went to Shepetovka, but we couldn't advance. We retreated and moved interchangeably until we arrived in Novograd-Volinsk.

There they turned me into a medic, and I was attached to a medical unit. We didn't know what our duties would be. When we arrived at the train, we were engaged in removing dead soldiers' bodies from the cars. We dragged bodies out for three days in a row. We emptied the rail cars for new people heading for a new, scorching journey.

We constantly had to take care of piles of bodies. The train moved. We remained, and we were forced to escape on foot. We walked at night, resting during the day, until we reached Zhitomir, a 180-kilometer hike. We stopped, and the front moved toward us. We fortified ourselves in trenches full of water, without food or rest at night. After a long day's hard labor, we received only dry bread.

***

We arrived in Priluk after a two-month hike. Once there, an order was received from Stalin to transfer all western Ukrainians suspected of being hostile to the homeland to labor camps.

They disarmed us and rounded us up by the thousands, Jews and gentiles together. There were several young men from Vishnevets with me, but I remember only Mikhael Valdman. We were loaded onto cattle cars, 70-80 people to a car, in a long train pulled by two huge engines, one in the front and one in the back. We traveled for 11 days with the doors locked until we arrived in the Urals.

People died in the crowded cars from thirst and suffocation, and there was no time to bury them.

When we reached the Urals, we stopped in the city of Rizh (Shchut in Hebrew) in the Sverdlovsk district. When the doors opened, thousands of bodies were taken out. Only around 16,000 people were left from a caravan of cars thousands of meters long that carried thousands of people.

We were taken into a forest. Once there, we were promised that we'd be taken to a place where the food we were longing for would be found. They walked us the whole day until the depth of night, without the food they'd promised us.

The next day, after we woke up, the camp commanders ran a strict inspection, asking for our parents' names, place of birth, and place of origin.

The forest was 12 kilometers away from a source of water.

[Page 133]

Once more, many died from thirst, and again we spent a second night in the forest without food or shelter from the cold. It was August 9, 1941, the first day of early autumn in that area.

On the third day, we were ordered to gather twigs and make ourselves permanent huts to live in. Each evening we received two pieces of hard bread to sustain our souls. Thirty to 40 people lived in each hut.

On the fourth day, we went through a roll call, and everyone was asked for his occupation. I told them I'd been a carpenter from birth. They gave me an ax, paired me up with another young man like me, and ordered us to cut down 40 trees a day. We had to cut them and sort them into stacks of cubic meters. Each pair had to create nine cubic meters to earn 600 grams of bread.

And so we worked until September 15, which was the middle of autumn. Then they took me to dig trenches. Every day, we each had to dig a trench 8 meters long, 80 centimeters wide, and 4 meters deep to receive the amount of bread mentioned above.

People were frail and fell asleep from fatigue and chill when they dug deep into the earth, sometimes forever. The supervisors pulled them out with ropes, piled up the bodies, and at the end of the day, a tractor came and "removed" them.

I also got sick at that time. Exhausted and frail, I was transferred to a rest house. Fortunately, the doctor who examined me was Jewish, and he said to me, "If my mother's situation was no worse than yours, I'd be happy."

His words shocked and angered me. I answered him, "If you, a doctor, talk like this, I don't trust you. You're not my doctor." I turned my face to the wall and away from him.

The political agent, a short Jewish man by the name of Shvayke, came in to find out what was going on and who the man resisting the doctor was. I told him. He asked my name, and I told him my name was Moshe, son of Avraham (Moisey Abramovits). He was startled and asked, "Where are you from?"

When I told him I was from Vishnevets, he started and said, "My father's relatives live there, and my Jewish name is Tsvik, not Shvayke." He was happy to see me:

"Maybe you're related to me. Shvayke is a Ukrainian name that I took for convenience. I'm Tsvik."

Immediately, he requested that I be allowed to rest for five days, and gave an order that I be allowed to rest.

I was treated with Epsom salts. I had diarrhea day and night. I looked like a shadow, and I could only lie down.

Five days later, the nurse told me, "You must leave; we need the space. We have others who need rest." I left even though I couldn't get up. With difficulty, I got up and slowly dragged myself to my unit.

I entered the commander's office and was directed to my former hut. When I arrived there, I found out that I hadn't been registered, and I didn't receive my share of food for that night.

[Page 134]

Meanwhile, the first snow had spread throughout the forest, and I was stationed in a unit whose duty was to cut down trees and peel off their bark. We used the stumps to build ground-level cabins (zemlyanka). When the cabins were finished, 500 people were stuffed inside each one. We slept in levels, and each level was as crowded as the others. With the completion of the cabins, we were stationed at the quarry. For a full year, we worked at the stone quarry.

Again, I got sick from malnutrition and extreme fatigue. I lay unnoticed; no one paid attention to me; no one there paid attention to sick people. One day they found me and told me to leave the cabin. They were afraid I would infect the rest of the people with my disease. I found a place in the pantry where they peeled potatoes. I lay in a dark corner in that pantry, running a 39-degree fever without covers, bleeding and dying. People who came in and recognized me felt sorry for me and brought me slices of bread and a little soup made from frozen cabbage leaves.

As the days of my illness progressed, I was forgotten, and so was the place where I was lying.

I was inflicted with diarrhea, a high fever, and lice; my hair was dirty and uncombed. One day when I came out to go the bathroom, the camp inspector entered the pantry and saw me. He panicked when he saw me.

He thought he had seen the devil or a scary evil spirit and asked, "Who is this spirit, who is this devil, this filthy ghost?"

I answered, "I'm a living human being, not a spirit and not the devil."

He called people over and they told him this was impossible. If this is the man, he was registered as dead a long time ago. What happened here?

He called the cook and asked him if he knew me. He recognized me and said I was a laborer who had worked too hard and become weak. That convinced him I was not a devil, and he said, "If you know him, Vanya, it's all right. Take him, fatten him up a little, and bring him up to working condition."

I recovered a little, and they sent me to work in shifts at the sawmill. Week after week, I fulfilled large and difficult quotas. One week the day shift, and one week the night shift.

The supervisor over there liked me and promised to regard me as a "non-Jew." It was kind of an advanced Russian compliment after many years of brotherhood.

I was put into the hands of a Jewish forester, and he promised me that if I filled my quota and more, he would give me additional bread. I worked hard for him for two and a half years. According to the card, we were supposed to receive 1,500 grams of grits, 600 grams of fat, 15 kilograms of meat, and 200 grams of sugar a month. We didn't get any sugar, and instead of meat, we received small amounts of salty fish. I lived like this for 30 weeks that seemed like jubilees.

***

During repatriation, we were loaded onto a train and transferred to our place of origin. I didn't go to Vishnevets because we were told the Ukrainians would finish us off.

[Page 135]

Instead, we traveled to Strigum, in the Sudetenland, and from there we went to Valbezhikh.

We spent only five days there. Someone hung a boy on a tree, and we were blamed. It was a blood libel directed at us by our comrades-in-arms. We escaped, and after a lot of suffering and hardship, we arrived in Vienna. It hurt us that after so many years of misery, all the hardship that had befallen the Jews was yet not over. We returned to Poland as if we were returning to our homeland, assuming that during this difficult period, we might be rewarded with a warm welcome. We assumed that the Poles would see our return as an expression of brotherhood, but we were disappointed. The Poles stood in the middle of their dream of a total liquidation of the Jews, and with that dream, they healed their wounds. We left them.

In Vienna, we were put into the hands of Bericha[1]. I was sent to Italy with immigration papers for Paraguay in my hands. When I arrived there, I found out that my wife and my son had perished in the Holocaust. I married for the second time and waited for the journey.

One day, it was May 26, 1948, as I was passing by Grugliasco Street near Turin, I found the city roaring and busy. I understood from the news that Israel was in great danger. The Arabs had attacked the Jews, Israel was surrounded, and excitement was high.

My heart was wrenched. My wife was pregnant, but my decision was clear. I approached Gur Arye, the Israeli delegate, and told him, "I have 30 dollars. Buy me a weapon and send me to Israel. My wife will wait for me here." She heard our conversation and agreed. But Gur Arye answered me, "You've come from Soviet Russia. First travel to your destination, and if you want, you'll reach Israel from there."

I arrived in Israel without any favors from the Israeli delegate.

Translator's Footnotes

Bericha (escape) was an organized effort to help Jewish Holocaust survivors, mainly from Eastern Europe, reach new homes, mostly in Palestine.

[Page 136]

An Answer to a Grandson (Poem)

by Meir Or

Translated by Sara Mages

..."And you have united yourself with sorrow, and your heart will be filled with it for the rest of your life." -Ch. N. Bialik

Don't say it's already enough, enough of that,
to cry over the destruction of communities and man;
don't say God decided;
the dead are already dead, and the living must live.
Not God the Almighty, because there is humanity in Him;
He spilled their blood, destroyed their homes;
therefore we will cry, we will cover our heads in shame
because man is cruel, and his heart brings pain.
For they were all precious to me,
and I will not forget until I reach my grave
how they set the dogs after them
and their ashes scattered in all directions.
I will mourn all my life
for my pure souls,
who innocently exulted in the
gentiles' culture in the Diaspora.
We will remember for the sake of the future
our simple past,
we will light a perpetual memorial candle,
we will learn a lesson and respect their memory.

[Page 137]

My Trip to Vishnevets in 1956

by M. Meliv (Frayer)

Translated by Sara Mages

When I was in Valbezhikh after the Holocaust, ready to immigrate to Israel, I decided to visit our town before leaving Poland forever.

I also wanted to visit my poor sister.

I got a tourist passport. I arrived in Kremenets in the afternoon, but I didn't go directly to Vishnevets. I stopped there to calculate my next steps. I acted with extreme caution because the area was swarming with Bandera's people, and getting to Vishnevets was dangerous.

I was in the area for almost three months, and I couldn't reach my hometown fast enough. I spent only three days in Vishnevets, and I dared to spend only one night there.

Our house and Yakov Chachkis's house, which were next to the rabbi's, were gone. All the ghetto streets were destroyed, and their buildings completely leveled.

I found three families in town: those of Avraham Rozenberg, Duvid Gnip, and Zev Sobol. The first two are still there.

The town center had been completely plowed under, and a town park had been planted there.

Several buildings that were still standing were occupied by Ukrainians who had collaborated with the Germans. In the space where Shapiro's home once stood, Ostrovski, the well-known piglet, built a mansion using bricks he collected from destroyed Jewish homes. The Lerners' house had completely sunk into the ground. I don't have any idea how it happened. Its windows were shattered and covered with wooden planks. It's not habitable, but a Ukrainian from the area lives there.

The Tarbut School building that belonged to Shmuel Balch is still standing and is used as a government-run hotel.

The Great Synagogue was left standing. It was converted into an apartment and office building, and it's full of partitions and doors. It's difficult to recognize that it used to be a place where Jews met to share their souls and beliefs.

The purpose of my trip was to visit my unfortunate brothers' graves. I was afraid to go alone. Zev Sobol joined me, and together we went the holiest place in our hearts.

The grave I arrived at was located in a ravine on the road to Zbarazh. When I walked into the ravine, I stumbled on human bones lying in the full view of day. Dismantled skeletons, disconnected bones, hipbones, parts of skulls, pieces of skeletons, and ribs from what at one time were our loved ones were scattered in the wind. I wanted to cover them up with earth, but I didn't have a tool in my hand, and there were so many bones. I could only cover a few with loose red earth, and my heart trembled inside me. Who knows whose bones I pushed into this contaminated earth? Who knows what body they belonged to? How had this body been shaped? For a moment, I imagined they were the bones of my father, whom everyone loved, maybe my good mother, my brothers, my sisters, and maybe my friends from school.

[Page 138]

I broke into hysterics and continued walking and crying, bending over and collecting bone after bone, and each bone lacerated my heart.

The valley of scattered bones stretched for more than a kilometer.

It was explained to me that different visitors cover the bones, but the water flowing in the ravine uncovers them every so often, hurling them from place to place without giving them rest, bringing them shame and pain. The grave itself, the deepest one, is open and exposed. The murderers didn't bother to cover it, and all that is dear to us is piled up, one body on top of another, exposed to the day, fierce storms, and beasts of prey, without shelter or shade. And now there's nothing at all, the skeletons are piled on top of each other in an eternal tight hug. The sight is shocking and bloodcurdling.

Zev showed me the hill on the other side. The marksmen stood on top, firing burst after burst of bullets onto the poor victims, killing them in large quantities. According to him, my soul's loved ones stood on the bank of the ravine, and the bullets rolled them directly into the depths of the open-mouthed mass grave.

On the way, I recognized the faces of several Ukrainian friends and neighbors. I had to ignore them, since I saw the joy of our demise in their eyes.

In the Valley of Skeletons (Photographed by Tsvi Yugur)

[Page 139]

Institutions and Movements

[Page 141]

Tarbut and Culture

by Chayim Tsvi Mazur (Baltimore)

Here in the United States, I sit and think that whatever so-called culture I possess came to me from the Tarbut School in Vishnevets.

The fact that I'm writing in Hebrew, my knowledge of my nation's history from ancient times, my actively patriotic thoughts, and my connection to my brothers, wherever they are, are all thanks to the education I received at that school.

That's why I write fondly about my memories of the school's development and establishment.

***

There was a Russian school in Vishnevets whose entire staff consisted of one man named Ternikov. He was the principal and the sole "teacher." I remember Ternikov with kindness. He was a kindhearted, fattish man with a neat mustache and a smile that never left his face.

This institution taught the Russian language, Russian history, and a little mathematics. The emphasis in the school was on beautiful handwriting, meaning that the letters had to be rounded, symmetric, and beautiful. This was the objective; what you wanted to do with those letters was up to you.

He had only a few students. Only those who wanted to learn to write letters and "petitions" in Russian studied there. In fact, the number of Jewish students was restricted, and the few who could study there had to pay a high price as well as a bribe.

The school closed after the Russian Revolution and all the small revolutions that shook our area. Other schools were established, and there was even a Ukrainian school, where we were taught about "glorious" Ukrainian history, including Mazepa, Skoropadsky, and Chmielnitski.

With the stabilization of the Polish regime, the zealous Ukrainian nationals changed their skin, became Polish patriots, and studied at the Polish school.

Meanwhile, the two Chezkelyovna sisters showed up in Vishnevets and, in the empty Roynik building, established a school where they taught both Russian and

Yiddish. I can't remember how and why this Russian institution was established, but its existence brings back memories of the lack of direction that prevailed in education in the town. By the way, Tsvi Roynik was hired as a teacher in that school. He taught Hebrew and a few Hebrew songs and organized Chanukah and Purim plays in Hebrew.

At that time, Froyke the Teacher began his excellent educational program. In his lessons, he dared to include Judges, that is to say, the Prophets and Writings, which were then banned by traditional Jewish education. He also dared to teach Jewish history in his cheder. The Hasidim in the town opposed him, and the Derbarimdiker family, which was descended from Rabbi Levi Yitschak of Berdichiv, amazed us with their war against Froyke. But Froyke paid no attention to them. His students clung to him, and every child begged his parents to send him to Froyke's cheder.

[Page 142]

Froyke continued with his revolutionary teaching methods. He taught us Graetz[1] rom the German text, which he himself translated into Yiddish, adding his own interpretation.

At Froyke's, we tasted the flavor of Jewish culture. We felt that it really existed and was an important part of our education as sons of the same nation and human beings. We adored and loved him. When Froyke left Vishnevets, our world – the world of children who, with his help, had tried to peek inside our nation's perplexing world – was empty.

It felt as if the world had turned dark for us, but meanwhile I learned that the situation wasn't hopeless. A group of dignified, respectable men from Vishnevets got together to turn on the light of Jewish culture and plan a cultural future for the younger generation.

Of the group, I remember Dudi Lerer, Avraham Leyb Katz, Idel Shapiro of the older generation, and Kopel Dobrovitker, Duvid Der Osterers (Rotenberg), Korin, Nachum Beren, Kornfeld, Chachki, and others of the younger generation.

In a short time, a yeshiva and a number of cheders opened, and the Tarbut School was established.

The most outstanding school was Tarbut, where the power of Jewish renewal was uncovered and a different kind of human ability was developed. This was the ability to witness history and politics and make the right choice in the marketplace of choices flooding the Jewish street, where every Jew – not knowing what was really good for the Jews – adopted his own opinion and viewpoint. The Tarbut School developed the ability to make individual decisions, and most students suddenly found themselves completely different. They rebelled against the authorities and discovered that they were standing on firm ground as members of the same healthy cultural nation, with a unified language and a clear personal and national destiny. How did that happen?

At the same time, a man named Volk and his wife arrived. These two were unique, differing from all of us in their dress, their speech, their manners, and everything else. They spoke to each other only in Hebrew, not Yiddish, and they were very serious. Their seriousness was different; it was based on security and belief, not the usual sadness and despair.

Duvid Lerer, a respected and well-educated man who read a lot and knew English, immediately supported Volk and increased his prestige. Avraham Leyb Katz, who later immigrated to Israel with his entire family, and Idel Shapiro also supported him. They rented an apartment for the school in the Vitels building in the center of the market, and the school was founded.

Volk added Nachum Beren, Kopel Dobrovitker, and Leyb Korin as teachers. With certainty, he knew whom to choose as educators of the younger generation. The atmosphere and academic standards at the Tarbut School were high. Volk was powerful. He understood that by adding Yosef Erlikh as a history and Bible teacher, he had established a treasure within Vishnevets.

A short time later, most of the town's children were studying at the Tarbut School. They all ran willingly to their classes, and they had all already begun speaking Hebrew. They were interested in Jewish literature and deliberated vital topics, such as the community, the nation, and their place in society.

[Page 143]

It's worth mentioning that it was the kind and sweet Yosef Erlikh who formed our "modern" Jewish identity, which, I must say, we needed then. He presented the Bible to us as a historical subject and described the prophet as a common man with a vision who felt his nation's pain, rebelled against tradition, and sought the best for the simple man. Using the Bible as a backdrop, he embroidered a large web of geographical subjects and much more. I'll always remember Yosef Erlikh with kindness and admiration. How did a man with such a broad vision get to our town?

And the Poles were hopping with anger. Their government school was empty, and without Jewish students, the academic standards dropped. Tarbut burdened them and was a thorn in their plan to enforce Polish culture. They began to increase their demands, declared the building unfit, and demanded a license when one wasn't required.

The struggle was difficult. Idel Shapiro emerged as a proud and unyielding fighter. He fought like a lion for our national right, but nothing helped. We had to leave the Vitels building, and the school closed, so to speak.

The Poles were happy with their victory, but the Tarbut School continued to operate in secret.

How was it done? How could they do this underground? It was very simple. We returned to the place of assembly and study. We went to the street where the synagogues were and housed the classes in various synagogues. Children supposedly went to pray there, and no one had the power to stop us.

Board of Directors of Tarbut in Vishnevets, with I. Shapiro in the Center

[Page 144]

Tarbut in Vishnevets was not only a school. It was a place where a new order and new identities were formed.

Therefore, I remember it for its great teachers. It's dear for me here in my new foreign land, and the language it provided me is my language even today.

Addendum by the Editorial Board:

Mr. S. Rozenhek, chief supervisor of Tarbut and later central office director, didn't agree to our request to write about his contributions to our school so as not to discriminate between cities, but he asked us to mention the following in his name:

It was the only school whose establishment was not opposed by the town's residents, not even fanatical observant Jews.

Sympathy toward the school was active and not just "sympathetic."

In Vishnevets, the center experienced no financial difficulties, delays in paying teachers' salaries, or inability to purchase school supplies – all thanks to community leaders' enthusiasm and resourcefulness.

At one time, the institution and its standards were in danger. The Poles insisted that one of the teachers (probably Erlikh) wasn't qualified to teach there since he wasn't certified. The Vishnevets rabbi rose to the occasion and provided him with the required document. It was an extremely rare act of "sanctification of the Holy Name" when an observant rabbi sided with secular culture.

Translator's Footnotes

Heinrich Graetz was among the first Jewish historians to write a comprehensive history of the Jewish people (in 1853).

[Page 145]

A Hebrew Kindergarten in Vishnevets
by Tsipora (Shlayen) Kornfeld

The town's Hebrew kindergarten opened at Shlome Ayzenberg's home. Several wooden steps led to the ground floor, where the kindergarten resided in one room. Next to it was a small yard with a sandbox for the children to play in.

For me, it was rare thing. In our town, we didn't know that an institution like that could exist.

Parents hurried to send their children to study in the cheder at a very young age so that a Jewish education could be implanted in them before they strayed to foreign fields. I saw the kindergarten in Vishnevets as part of the ideological changes taking place in our community, and working there integrated nicely with my pioneer training.

The local Zionists and town intellectuals created the kindergarten. They weren't wealthy, but as Zionists, they wanted to raise their children in the environment of the songs, words, and sounds of their future language, Hebrew. Some also wanted to make it easier for their children to adjust to Hebrew school.

The kindergarten teacher was Dora Mofshit, of blessed memory. She came from the town of Rovne, which as then Volin's Hebrew cultural center, where she received her professional training. She was a good-looking young woman, noble and calm. Later it was discovered that she was then already suffering from a terminal illness, and she died young. Nevertheless, she was dedicated to the children, she met their needs with her heart and soul, and her illness didn't affect her work.

Ozer Mofshit, her life's companion, helped her with her work and dedicated himself to the institution's development. I was hired as a teacher's assistant. I then belonged to a local training kibbutz detachment. I knew Hebrew, and it looked to me as if they were planning to help our detachment with its meager existence.

The kindergarten wasn't supported by any public organization. All expenses were the responsibility of the parents, who couldn't always fully support the organization but maintained it with love and dedication. Little by little, the school became the Pioneer-Zionist community's responsibility, and the kindergarten became an important component of the Hebrew environment in our town. It was surrounded by love and admiration, which helped it to endure.

For our part, we donated items to our beloved institution. With our own hands, we built tools, teaching aids, and various games and toys.

The people of Vishnevets were happy with the institution and proud of their children, who spent their innocent days immersed in a world of games and childhood, expressing themselves in Hebrew.

When we walked in the streets with our kindergarten youngsters singing Hebrew songs with their little mouths, the town's residents stood by their doors and proudly watched their beloved children, whose future would probably be in the land of their patriarchs.

We had the feeling that, with our work, we contributed directly and indirectly to increasing the value of Zionism in the town.

[Page 146]

I don't know what happened to the kindergarten after I left Vishnevets and after Dora, its dedicated, noble teacher, died. But during its short existence, it was a respected institution on its own and a glorious testimony to Vishnevets Zionists.

May these lines be a memorial to the souls of Vishnevets Zionists and a memorial candle to dear Dora.

First Kindergarten in Vishnevets

[Page 147]

General Zionist and General Zionist Pioneer
Representatives in Vishnevets
by Y. Ron

The General Zionists were the most prominent Zionist party in Vishnevets. Its members were the wealthiest and most highly respected people in our town. Since it was a general party, it didn't take a stand on the matter of denying the Diaspora and didn't require its members to fulfill their Zionist duty. Its members could interact moderately with other Zionist parties and show them sympathy and mutual respect. More than once, they helped other parties reach their goals even if they stood on opposite platforms. Everyone favored and respected them. They were responsible for collecting donations for the Jewish National Fund, the Foundation Fund, and other charitable organizations. With the cooperation of other parties, they kept busy collecting money, and they had a decisive influence in this area. They were responsible for the Tarbut School's establishment and upkeep.

The most prominent party member was the chairman, Yehuda Shapiro, of blessed memory. There was no organization for which he didn't act as chairman at some point, and for that reason he was called "seven times chairman." He helped everyone who asked, and his home was a meeting place for the best and most active members of various Zionist parties.

More than once, he donated or loaned his own money to failing institutions during their crises. Although the General Zionist party didn't force its members to immigrate, Yehuda Shapiro came to his own decision and immigrated with his wife, who was always by his side helping him. He immigrated with his family and helped other families from Vishnevets to immigrate.

Yehuda died in Hadera, weary of his many activities and hardships in the Land.

***

Yehuda Shapiro created a generation that continued to follow the General Zionist tradition and fulfill its Zionist duty. The most prominent member was Chayim Zev Brik, whose delicate soul and unlimited dedication to Zionism served as a personal example and gave the party and its members a good name.

He came to our town from Pochayev and very shortly became one of us. He was privileged to immigrate to the Land with his family and fulfilled his dream when his sons settled in the Land and built a reputable name for themselves. Chayim Zev Brik died in Hadera, the village-town he helped build and was proud of.

Simche Zak, of blessed memory, was also considered one of the most active members of the General Zionists in our town. He added his own personal touch to the Zionist party's work in Vishnevets. Like the other two, he latched onto Zionism as his generation's duty and saw his work as personal fulfillment.

Simche Zak was one of our first immigrants. He purposely settled in the holy city of Jerusalem when it was still a mixed city and never moved away from there, waiting for its reunification until the day he died.

Yakov Fishman, of blessed memory, who was famous for his exceptionally powerful memory, was a founder of the General Zionists.

[Page 148]

Each conversation with him left a great impression on anyone who took part. Thanks to his hobby, Yakov Fishman got a job at the Israel Electric Corp. In his miniature letters, he wrote the history of the construction of the Rotenberg power station on postcards. The Israel Electric Corp.'s management was interested in the man, and when they realized that he had an exceptional memory and was a certified accountant, they gave him a job with special benefits. He lived and died in Tel Aviv.

Yosef Erlikh also made an impression on the party. He didn't immigrate, and he perished with all the other martyrs of Vishnevets. We remember his many educational activities with kindness. Thanks to him, the Hebrew language was implanted among young people and served as a main driver of their immigration.

The list of active Zionists in our town is long. Each one had his own qualities and personal interpretation of his political work. We will remember them for eternity in our memorial book; may these lines be a memorial to them and their blessed work.

***

General Zionist Pioneer was considered to be the young guard of Al HaMishmar[1], founded by Grinboym and Kleynboym (now Sana), who lent a helping hand to the Zionists in their various public activities. For a while, the writer of these lines served as Pioneer chairman and was honored to be elected to various district party offices after our chapter excelled in social and public works.

General Zionist Activists

At the top right is the author of this article; seated on the right is E. Tsinberg.

[Page 149]

To our regret, our activities began too late. Although we were able to organize a small group of middle-class young people, we couldn't increase the pace of immigration in the short term. Only four of us were lucky enough to immigrate to the Land, in many different ways: Yitschak Rozental, Lusik Tsimberg, Elkane Senders, and me. Those who remained were destroyed and murdered with the rest of Vishnevets while they were still young, full of life, and active on behalf of the nation and the Land.

May their holy memory remain with us for eternity.

Translator's Footnotes

Al HaMishmar (On Guard) was a newspaper.

[Page 150]

A Treasured Memory of Vishnevets

by Hentsye Zak (Zeyger)

Our town was extremely picturesque, with a fantastic view. The two parts of the town – the new and the old – were connected by a bridge over the river. Above it was a big park with a sprawling palace, which the town's residents strolled around, mostly on the Sabbath.

During World War I, Vishnevets was close to the Austrian-Russian front and was full of soldiers and weapons. We lived in fear. Some soldiers escaped a number of times and returned. We knew what we needed to do to protect and save ourselves, and we knew how to be careful, so the number of victims wasn't high. After the war, many people immigrated to the United States.

Close to 4,000 Jews lived in our town. A few were rich, and the rest were needy and had a difficult time earning a living by trading with gentiles. Every Monday, a market took place. The gentiles hurried to town with horse carts full of farm products. The money they earned selling their products was spent in the Jewish stalls and stores for all kind of commodities, mostly for excessive drinking. On market days, it was dangerous to go outside, since they were rolling drunk in the streets.

We were connected to the town, and all our young interests were dedicated to it.

Freedom Movement in Vishnevets during the 1920s[1]

***

[Page 151]

Everything changed after World War I. The young people grew older, developed, and began to study. Many of us studied in the town's high school and in the nearby city of Kremenets. Delegates and lecturers began to appear in our town and encourage us to fulfill our Zionist duty, and excitement grew, mostly among young people. Most joined different movements than did the veterans, who were either General Zionists or Zionist contributors. The new movements called on their members to do more than just raise money – that is, to get up and immigrate.

Our movement, Zionist-Socialist Liberty, had a large concentration of talented members. We studied Hebrew and met now and then to engage in ideological discussions and exchange ideas. We took on various national assignments. Our lives changed direction, and we concentrated our thoughts on creating a new society in the Land.

At that time, the Tarbut elementary school opened in town. Its academic standards were high, and Hebrew was taught as a living language.

In 1922, a number of people left town and immigrated to the Land. In addition, a number of established families closed their business, sold their property, and immigrated. This was a daring and impressive move on their part, and, no doubt, it made a big impression and added excitement to the Zionist concept. My brother, Mordekhay Zeyger, who was very active in the Zionist movement in Odessa, and his wife immigrated. He was one of the first 10 lawyers to receive a work permit from the Mandate government. A short time later, he brought me, my parents, my two brothers, and my sister, along with our families. Thanks to him, we were saved.

Translator's Footnotes

In Hebrew, the Liberty movement was called Dror.

[Page 152]

Young People in Vishnevets

by Moshe Shteynberg

The substance of life in our town was similar to that in many other Jewish towns in Polish Volin. Its economy was based on minor trade and light industry.

The town's special character was the result of its distance from large Jewish and cultural/educational centers. A sense of separation and distance prevailed.

The closing of the immigration gates to countries on the other side of the ocean and the Polish masters' narrowing of income sources impoverished the Jewish population. The struggle for survival was difficult, and the Polish authorities' animosity took the form of legal anti-Semitism during the 1930s, the second decade of independent rule.

The Jews in town were mainly traditional and nationalistic. A longing for Zion beat in their hearts in spite of their objection to Zionism, and they kept their affection for the Land of Israel a deep secret. The road from there to feasible Zionism was long. The Pioneer movement, established in the 1920s, united the best young people in its ranks. The concept of immigration was like a breath of fresh air. Young people pulled out of town, and some immigrated to the Land. For various reasons, activities stopped, conservatism grew, and the public continued to be narrow-minded.

Zionism in Poland began to gather momentum in the 1930s.

Youth, Nature, and Relaxation
The text inside the photo reads "District Meeting of Young Pioneer in Vishnevets,
5/4-5/6, 1934."

[Page 153]

Jewish centers revived the concept of the nation's rebirth. Young people prepared to immigrate, and large-scale immigration to the Land of Israel began. Vishnevets was also swept up by this energy, although a little late. Youth organizations were established in the town: Young Pioneer, Pioneer, Youth Guard, Betar[1], Religious Zionist Youth, and others. We met young people from other cities in summer camps, meetings, and conventions that awakened new ideas in us – ideas that shook the foundation of our remote province.

***

Subsequently, a Youth Guard chapter was established in our town. A number of Young Pioneer and Pioneer members, with Yakov K. in the lead, left and established this branch. This group of young people, who were emotionally restless and agitated, rebelled against tradition as if an invisible hand were pushing them, forcing them to mutiny and rebel. They deliberated many different issues, such as life in the Diaspora, human relations, social problems, and the war against discrimination, that overwhelmed our world. We were thirsty for knowledge, action, and new horizons.

Youth Guard and its doctrine quenched our thirst. We filled our lungs with its idealism and teachings. The Tarbut School was a great pearl of our town, and every movement was blessed to include within its ranks the young people who studied there, who were among the best in our town. The Youth Guard chapter succeeded in capturing the hearts of most of the young people at the school.

The first Tarbut graduating class joined our branch. A group of girls who shared the dilemma of "how" and "where" integrated quickly into our activities and took over some responsibilities. Our chapter became our second home. It bubbled as we did and fully understood of the needs of a young soul. We were taught how to fill the gap between our needs and the fulfillment of our pioneering. We were ready to break out of our tradition and our family's thresholds and row toward a new life.

We didn't gain much sympathy from the locals and our parents, even though they respected our obsession and actions. Local Zionists didn't agree with our deep socialism, and parents saw us as the cause of their children's rebellious behavior.

The parents claimed that we "stole" their children, and at times they prevented them from coming to our meetings. But that also passed, and attitudes changed. The branch's graduates, who had left for training, came home to get ready for their immigration. The second group left for training, and relationships with their parents improved when they realized their children were serious. They also hoped that maybe one day their "rebellious" children would help them.

This is the history of the branch as it was being established, and this is the story of its young people. Only some members of any movement had the chance to immigrate to the Land. A portion of the members who were ready to immigrate were stopped on the way because of the Mandate government's restrictions and weren't able to immigrate.

The beloved young people of Vishnevets who had been preparing to immigrate were forced to stay home, and they fell victim to the sudden Holocaust. My heart aches, and their memory will always follow me.

Translator's Footnotes

Betar, which stands for Brit (covenant of) Yosef Trumpeldor, is the educational youth movement of the Revisionist Zionist Organization.

[Page 154]

The Founding of Young Pioneer in Our Town
by Yakov Chatski (Givat Hashlosha)

The bloody riots of 5689 (1929) in the Land of Israel shocked the Zionists and also awakened patriotic feelings among non-Zionist Jews. We found out about the riots from the newspapers, and a deep fear took over the town's residents. During that time, we gathered in groups and talked loudly and with concern about events in the Land. The news from the Land was frightening, and each day brought more victims. We believed from the bottom of our hearts that the Yishuv[1] in the Land knew how to protect the people, but doubt ate at a corner of our hearts: could they?

The population's firm stand attacked our souls and inspired young people from various trends and factions. As one, they were ready on a moment's notice to go and lend a helping hand to the Yishuv. Longing for Zion increased. The Pioneer movement, along with the rest of the Zionist organizations in town, organized a meeting (I think the meeting took place in the Great Synagogue). Numerous Jews from all walks of life and of all ages rushed to the meeting, and the space was soon too small to accommodate them. We listened to the speakers' words with fear and with trembling hearts. I remember the words of Moti Goldberg, of blessed memory, which shook his listeners' hearts and brought them to tears. After the speeches, a spontaneous collection of money, jewelry and other valuable items took place. The young people were ready to give their lives, immigrate, and help the nation in Zion. But... the gates to the Land were bolted.

Meanwhile, a small group of 16- to 18-year-olds joined us. With the help of Pioneer member Aharon Goldman, of blessed memory, a Young Pioneer branch was established in the town.

At the same time, the kibbutz movement in the Land saw the need to educate its members from a young age about the duties facing them, but how could we attract the town's young people to the movement when we didn't have instructors? The same year, the Young Pioneer central office organized a month-long district meeting in Klevan, near Rovne, and one agenda item was to create a pool of instructors. It was decided to send two young people from our branch, but the meeting cost 45 zehovim, required the loss of workdays, and didn't meet with parents' approval. I managed to convince my parents and Nisan Servetnik's parents, and, paying our own expenses, the two of us left for the camp. Many young people from the district gathered there. The best delegates arrived from the Land of Israel. Among them were Tabenkin and Lyoyita, who spread the spirit of the Land and taught us from morning to evening. We absorbed that spirit and returned home "burning" with youthful excitement, and we dedicated ourselves to working for the movement.

Very soon, we captured many hearts and attracted young people of all ages and lifestyles to our branch. Our membership reached 180-220 young men and women. As a result of our growth, we had to leave the temporary home Pioneer had given us.

[Page 155]

We rented a home and decorated it well, and the young people spent most of their evenings there singing, playing, and dancing until midnight.

To the chapter's council, we elected Shalom Kornfeld; Leybel Vilsker (from Shumsk); Tova Chatski; Azriel Blinder; Duvid Ba'almelakhe, of blessed memory; and (may they live long) Verdi Yitschak (Reyzels), Koler Tsvi, P. Markhbeyn, and the writer of these lines. The council's duty was to organize and plan the branch's activities. Pioneer members, such as Aharon Goldman, of blessed memory; Nachum Beren; Shvats (a teacher in Tarbut School), of blessed memory; and (may they live long) Meir Averbukh and Yakov Yeshurun (Ketaykisher) helped us with cultural activities. Reading material came from the Pioneer and Young Pioneer centers. We received newspapers such as Davar, He-Atid, and Das Vort[2]. The Davar newspaper arrived from the Land and was grabbed, passed from hand to hand, and read in groups. There was a great thirst to know what was happening in the Land, so a political review and Hebrew classes at different levels took place every week.

Trouble also came from other sources: the "homeowners" (the rich) weren't pleased that their sons were mixing with the lower class. Fathers and sons had many arguments on that subject. For organizational reasons, the branch was divided into three age groups. Each group was divided into subgroups according to the number of instructors available and by education level. Each group had its own name, such as Ein Harod, Trumpeldor, and so on.

Young Pioneer graduates in the Land remember how the different groups of our branch met every Sabbath dressed in uniform.

Pioneer and Young Pioneer Federation in Vishnevets

[Page 156]

We marched down the town streets holding our group's flag and singing Israeli marching songs in powerful voices. On the way to the Kremenets Mountain, we spread out, and each group turned to its own corner for games and dancing. I remember well the look on the faces of the town's Jews when we passed them in the street. Many shook their heads as if to say, "They have time for this nonsense?" but a small number understood that something new was happening there. Who can forget how we went out to the palace garden on Saturday evening, and you could hear our singing from far away?

Once, when we wanted to go on an extended long-distance trip (such as to Dubno), but not all of us had the money to pay for it, we decided to go out to work as a group. By doing so, we accomplished three goals: we strengthened our bodies for hard labor, helped each other, and earned the money we needed for the trip. Day after day, a group of our young men went out to get construction jobs. The Jews looked around in astonishment: young men, sons of well-to-do fathers, doing unskilled labor? How?

Young Pioneer had a special duty. It collected money for various foundations, such as the Jewish National Fund, the Palestine Workers' Fund, the Pioneer Fund, and others. In groups of two, we went out into the street, walking from home to home, door to door, and with excitement and great awe, we brought back the money needed to redeem the Land of Israel and protect the settlements. Who can forget the Chanukah "bazaar" we arranged year after year, the hot potato latkes, the games, and most important of all – the money we collected and dedicated to the Jewish National Fund! Young Pioneer presented itself in an amazingly decorated corner. Its presentation included diagrams about the Federation's resources and branches, newspapers from the Land of Israel, and pictures of kibbutzim.

Year after year, Young Pioneer members and graduates left for training detachments throughout Poland, most of the time disobeying their parents' wishes. One clear day, an article appeared in the Vishnevets newspaper (I think the paper's name was Der Tag) under the headline "And the boy is missing." The article told the story of Avraham Geler, of blessed memory, who ran away to a training detachment without his parents' permission and how they forcefully brought him back home.

In 1933-1935, thousands of young men from all over Poland, many of whom were far away from Zionism, joined Pioneer. They established Pioneer detachments in cities and towns. The "conquest detachment" also entered Vishnevets then, and we helped its members with arrangements and helped them find jobs to support themselves. Morning after morning, the members left armed with saws and axes and worked as lumberjacks, as water drawers, at various household chores, or at any other available jobs.

Today, Young Pioneer members from Vishnevets are scattered all over the Land in kibbutzim, villages, and cities. But most young people couldn't reach the Land of Israel because they were murdered by the Nazi beast.

Translator's Footnotes

Yishuv (settlement) refers the body of Jewish residents in Palestine before the establishment of the State of Israel.

Davar means Word; He-Atid, the future; and Das Vort, the word.

[Page 157]

How I Came to Immigrate
by Chayim Verdi

Mother registered us – my brother Yitschak and me – for the Polish elementary school. She rightfully thought we should know Polish, the national language, and all that was involved in it... and that was where it started.

Vishnevets, our beloved birthplace, suddenly turned into hell for us. The students at school beat us up, saying we came from "that place." That place was a sort of permission to beat someone up, and the beatings came with insults that ended with "Jews, go to Israel."

I didn't know why they hated us so much. What pushed our enemies and friends to unite against us? But when we complained to our teacher, he was of the same opinion: that it was our fault. Why? We couldn't understand. We stopped complaining.

And so it continued, day after day. We suffered, and there was nothing we could do. Once I stood in class thinking about our situation and the troubles our mother's good intentions had brought us. Suddenly, I saw Yitschak surrounded by a group of gentiles, as if he were trapped, and one walked up to him and smeared pork on his mouth. When Yitschak asked him why he had done this, the other boy began beating him up. This time I couldn't control myself. I pulled out a weaving spoke that I kept inside my boot and hit the boy until he bled. Yitschak did the same. We always kept the spokes with us so we could be ready for trouble. We beat them well, a commotion began, and the gentiles ran off to return with reinforcements. They also wanted to arm themselves with an efficient weapon. The principal showed up, and the turmoil stopped.

The principal investigated the situation and pulled our ears, and then it became "clear" to him that it was our fault. He didn't do anything to the boys who had attacked us. We were expelled from school and told to send our father to see the principal the next day. When I asked him why he was only sending us home, he said that, in his opinion, we were the guilty ones.

The next day, our father took us to the principal, who, to our surprise, welcomed father and talked about the incident as if nothing had happened.

Here we learned another fact. The principal was a regular customer at our father's store and owed him money, so he didn't dare insult him, and all his anti-Semitism evaporated. We also learned that a Jew's safety depends on money and bribes. All this was carved into my memory for many years. We also discovered that the Poles and Ukrainians were cowardly and bloodthirsty by nature. After that incident, attitudes toward us completely changed.

***

When I graduated from school, I was already a "big boy," and I needed to find a "purpose." At the age of 16, I took a chance and opened a fancy goods store.

[Page 158]

The wholesalers treated their young customer kindly and gave me merchandise on credit... for one day. I picked up the merchandise in the morning and paid for it in the evening. Little by little, I began to succeed, and my business grew. I settled down. I had my own money and even loaned some to my father. I became an independent man, free to do whatever I wanted.

With all that, the memories of my Polish schoolmates still ate at my heart. They had left a deposit of bitterness and the taste of degradation. I had saved money, and I was free to do what I wanted, but my thoughts centered on memories from my days at the Polish school.

One day, a couple of friends came to me, saying that a man from the Pioneer central office in Warsaw was in town and wanted to see them. They suggested that I go with them.

The man was pleasant. He was convincing and knew how to explain things. His words brought me new possibilities for my future and showed me that my situation could be different in a new world.

That same week, I was one of the founders of Young Pioneer in our town. We rented a room and met in our free time. The group grew, words became actions, we matured and transferred to Pioneer and... I was still a merchant.

Little by little, our branch experienced separations. My friends left for training, and to me it seemed as if the town was emptying out. It looked as if everyone else was stepping forward and I was stuck. My progress in business didn't thrill me anymore.

That evening, when I brought my father the news that I was liquidating my business and planning my immigration, was the darkest day of his life. He rebelled against the idea of being separated from me and threatened to hit me and take any other measures available to him.

[Page 159]

But I felt that it wasn't up to me. On my first day at the Polish school, I realized that I had to escape from here, and I escaped.

If anyone said that immigration wasn't an escape, I would say to that person:

I wish my father, my friends, and the friends of my friends had run away and immigrated.

And so I immigrated.

Dreaming of Immigration in Vishnevets

[Page 160]

Youth Guard and More in Vishnevets

by Moshe Leshed (Markhbeyn)

To write about the Youth Guard movement in our town, we need to mention the geographical, economic, and social aspects of this remote town.

It was "remote" because of its geographical location; it was cut off from communication with the world around it. It was also cut off from the only mode of transportation in our area, the train.

I remember well the innocent and sincere Jews – wagon drivers – who earned their meager income transporting travelers to the train station in the nearby town (24 kilometers away). On scorching summer days, they used their open carts, and they used their sleighs during the winter. The trip to the district seat during the harsh, snowy winter days was a "mission," but the real adventure took place during the spring, when the snow melted and the ground turned into sinking mud. At times, travelers got stuck for hours on the road, unable to continue or turn back.

This isolation also affected the town's economy. The only source of income was trade and light industry, and there wasn't any primary source of income, industry, or agriculture. A few Jewish families earned a living from fishing. Those Jews were healthy in body and soul and earned their living honestly from the labor of their hands. Most of the Jewish population earned their income by trading with the Ukrainians who surrounded the town from all sides and supplied the town's food. Jews traded in wheat, fruit, and baskets they wove out of reeds, and their merchandise was exported all over the country.

The town Jews' social life was peaceful. Each child started life and development in the cheder, later in a yeshiva, and at times with higher-level private teachers who taught Talmud and Gemara. I remember those beloved people well: cheder teachers Avrumche and Livushke, and my yeshiva teachers and educators: R' Aytsikel the rabbi's son-in-law, Moshe Aharon, and the "Kazaner," who was appointed to oversee our "morals" even though we had matured during those years. We can't ignore the strict ethics they embedded in us, ethics that stay with us even today. May their memory be blessed.

***

During the 1920s and the beginning of the 1930s, after the war, the revolution, the civil war in Russia, and the periods of occupation, when our district passed from the Russians' hands to the Whites and from the Reds to the Poles, a change took place in the general attitude among Jewish young people in our town. They realized that the foundation of Jewish life in the Diaspora was crumbling and felt that they were suffocating socially and spiritually in this small, isolated town. Their awakening took different directions. A few leaned toward social revolution in the Russian revolutionary style. Most realized that their future lay in Zionism, and from there, the lion's share turned toward socialist Zionism.

[Page 161]

For the first time, nonpolitical youth organizations were established, such as the Legion of Hebrew Language Defenders during the late 1920s.

News arrived about the establishment of the first training kibbutzim, such as the one in Klosova and others. Young people worked toward one target – immigration to the Land of Israel. And so for the first time, delegations from Pioneer and Young Pioneer arrived, and their influence was enormous. Meanwhile, the youth organization Trumpeldor Guard Scouts was established, but later it fell apart, and its few members joined Young Pioneer.

At the beginning of the 1930s, when the international Youth Guard movement was established as an advanced revolutionary movement within the Zionist Organization, young people, mostly students in the Tarbut School, which opened then because of an increase in anti-Semitism in Polish elementary schools, embraced a more serious movement.

On 15 Shevat 1932, the branch opened legally under the leadership of a few "older" members. The most creative and most dedicated to the cause was our friend Yakov Ben Yeshurun. We began our activities under very difficult conditions.

Our main problem was ideological wars with the leftist and rightist movements. Our slogan, "Don't listen" (Don't listen, my son, to your father's ethics or your mother's teaching, but turn your ear to..., a song written by Shimonovits), which influenced children to rebel, had a negative influence on parents, mostly the few Orthodox who belonged to the Mizrachi[1] movement.

Youth Guard in Vishnevets

Standing fourth from the right, in full uniform, is the writer of this article.

[Page 162]

They declared a boycott against us, and we had to fight hard for each child. At the same time, other competing organizations took advantage of the war for their own benefit.

Our war for survival was very difficult, but we had the upper hand. We believed in the sincerity of our ways, and we were sure we would win. We didn't withdraw from any Zionist activities even though they tried to kick us out. We were always the first to collect donations for organizations like the Jewish National Fund and Foundation Fund.

Education was our first priority. We knew how to teach and enrich the children's knowledge. We established a place in the Jewish street through the power of our innocent belief and our dedication to the cause.

The first of us to realize our Zionism and leave for training increased the movement's status.

The greatest blow to our movement came during the 1930s, when the immigration quota for the Land was cut. Youth Guard graduates waited (after they had returned from training happy and ready to immigrate) for many years. A portion managed to immigrate illegally in the last year before World War II broke out.

In the Land, members of our branch have continued their loyalty to our movement by putting down roots in the country, belonging to the Haganah or Palmach, living in the cities, giving their best to the establishment of the country, and continuing to live there as loyal citizens.

A large, strong group of dear young people from our branch was left without a way out. Your heart always contracts when you look at the pictures of groups or individuals. The vision of the best of our brothers and sisters, who desperately waited to immigrate, passes before your eyes, and with them, the life of the entire town. Street after street, home after home, family after family – and with all our brothers, you cry for the loss of what was once dear to you.

Translator's Footnotes

Mizrachi is a religious Zionist movement.

[Page 163]

Betar in Vishnevets

by Sore Kitaykisher (Kirshenboym)

In 1930, Zeyde Geler established a Betar branch in our town. I don't know anything about the first few years. I joined Betar in 1932 and stayed with it until 1939.

During my time in Betar, our branch had around 30 members – 30 in the young age group and an additional 20 older members who were loyal to the Alliance of Revisionists-Zionists.

Zeyde invested his best efforts in the branch. Attitudes toward our movement in Vishnevets were unfavorable, and we needed great courage to swim against the current and gain supporters for the vision of Zev Jabotinsky, of blessed memory.

When Zeyde Geler left, Asher Sofer, of blessed memory, took over the leadership of Betar. He also showed great courage and enthusiasm for the cause.

Betar's activities centered mostly on deepening the conception that a total change was needed in Jewish community life: the need for peace and tranquility, the ability to debate and express opinions on all matters, and the need to take a firm stand. We educated the public on defense issues and taught them how to take and execute an order.

For us, Jabotinsky's articles were thought provoking, and we dedicated many evenings to reading and analyzing them. We taught the young people premilitary exercises and prepared them for discipline and self-sacrifice. We weren't given many opportunities to participate in ordinary public events, and we felt a little isolated. We did the best we could to integrate ourselves into the Zionist system that was accepted in many towns at that time. This provoked feelings of jealousy and enthusiasm, which turned into the substance of our activities.

I remember how we, the girls, walked from home to home on Sukkot eve and on Hoshana Rabbah to sell willow branches in order to collect a little money for our fund. I know for sure that our dedication was seen as a model and was a target of jealousy on the part of other movements in Vishnevets.

My cousin, Yakov Kitaykisher, a founder of Youth Guard, once said he could take care of everything for us, but not for seven Orthodox girls who were clueless to what was happening around them.

I was planning to immigrate through the Betar movement. I left in a convoy of immigrants – blockade runners. My movement didn't help me, and I got stuck on the way. I will always remember my branch house as a place where my uncompromised national attitude was formed – the attitude that gave me the strength to cope with all the hardship I later encountered.

[Page 164]

In a Training Detachment in Vishnevets
by Tsipora (Shlayen) Kornfeld

In 1933, a training kibbutz detachment was established in our town. We served as a branch of the Klosov kibbutz, but we didn't get much help from it because we were supported by our friends in the town.

Our group was small, eight men and women. At first we lived in a rented apartment in Makhovits, which was very close to Vishnevets, but when our numbers increased, we replaced our apartment with a larger one.

Our economic situation was difficult, and as was the case in other towns, there weren't many sources of income.

The town's Zionists and its simple people treated us well and tried to help us out.

Pioneer Training in Vishnevets, 1934

[Page 165]

Our presence in the town provided an additional layer in the construction of a good Zionist program. But it was difficult to live on admiration alone, and everyone was looking for jobs for us. At that time, many good young people in Vishnevets (as in other towns) were unemployed, and we began to work.

Our main income came from chopping wood and drawing water. Moshele, from my town, a diligent and noble man whose employers were pleased with his services, was one of the best water drawers.

The women also worked at cutting wood, mostly doing light chores such as making piles of wood, collecting kindling, and more.

There were many homeowners whose hearts didn't allow them to hire Jewish children for difficult outdoor jobs in the freezing cold, which were fit only for gentiles. They didn't understand that we needed those jobs not just to fulfill our Zionist duty, but also for our survival – for a slice of bread – and this need put a lot of pressure on us. We didn't turn down any job, not only because we needed the income, but also because we wanted to prove that we could pass the test.

Once after midnight, a kind, warm young man who is now in Israel brought good news: I have a "day job" for you! Get up, quick! Get dressed! We need to go, it's urgent!

We soon found out that someone in his family had died and that the family was afraid to stay alone at night with the dead body. They were willing to pay us for a "day's work" if we sat and protected the dead person. I was the victim, and I watched over the dead body.

Little by little, we began to work. We baked matzos, cleaned houses, and ironed linens, and our situation improved.

The Zionist leaders in Vishnevets wanted to hire a minder to help us financially. We refused, since that wasn't our aim, but they outdid themselves trying to find ways to help us.

I remember that one of our friends got sick and needed castor oil, as it was customarily used then. When we arrived at the pharmacy to pick up the oil and told the pharmacist it was for our Feyge, she doubled the amount.

We attached ourselves to that town with the cords of our souls; the place and people were dear to us. I remember that a fire broke out at the Zaltsmans' home, not far from the kindergarten where I worked. We were the first to notice the fire and the first to attempt to put it out. Meanwhile, we had to save what we could. There was a young man from Grodno with us, and the aroma of duck fat reached his nostrils. He ran to the source of the smell, grabbed a fat clay pot with a layer of fat covering its lip, and ran to the kibbutz with it. How disappointed he was when he found out that under the layer of fat, some ordinary Russian borscht was hiding.

We integrated so fully into the life of the movement that we took on assignments we'd never considered doing before.

[Page 166]

It was assumed that we would immigrate shortly, so to test our seriousness, we were given a larger workload than the others were. Every once in a while we were told, "You're on the verge of immigrating, so we're demanding a different attitude from you – dedication to the cause, etc."

We were young then, very young and joyful, but worries ate at the hearts of each one of us, worries that we didn't reveal to the people of Vishnevets. We came from poor homes. We were worried about the expense of our approaching immigration and about leaving our old parents behind without someone to support them in their old age, and our future was cloudy.

But Beren didn't know that. To him, we were a successful, personal Zionist experiment. He didn't feel our distress at our lack of money even to buy a stamp for a letter home. He was a dear young man, and we forgave him. We had to be strong in order to forgive because we were young and because Vishnevets was dear to us.

I will remember Vishnevets, a pleasant corridor to my dream parlor.

[Page 167]

Drama Circles in Vishnevets

by Yone Ron

The first emergence of theater in our town was tightly connected to the personality of Avraham Fayerman, of blessed memory, its founder and director.

His interest in theater began when he was young and living in Kishinyuv, where he learned the art of acting, which he transferred to us. He was a talented director, a superior actor, and a comedian. In our town, he always excelled in acting, and the audience and actors appreciated him. His sister (who now lives in the Land) helped him a lot. She supported him at their father's home and whispered the lines in his first shows.

Fayerman was the heart and soul of our town's drama circles. He directed and acted in the shows staged by troupes of all ages (except for the school plays, which I'll write about later). They say that at that time, Ester-Rachel Kaminska[1] heard about him and invited him to come and talk to her in Warsaw. If not for his parents' firm objections, which caused him to cancel his trip to Warsaw, he might have become a professional actor in her troupe.

Fayerman raised the curtain on the stage in Vishnevets, and with his tragic death alongside our townspeople, the curtain lowered on him and his work.

Fayerman and his friends, who created the theater in Vishnevets, did so only as a public service and not for profit. Their idea was to establish an amateur stage, provide quality entertainment to the townspeople, and earn money for social and cultural programs.

The shows were performed only in Yiddish.

I remember some of the first actors: Avraham Fayerman, Malke Layter, Yente Beker, Rivke Fefer, Mishe Korin, and Avraham Leyb Katz, who performed only once – in the show "The Essence of a Jew" – to prove that older people must also participate in shows for the benefit of public needs. Kopel Dobrovitker, Leybtsi Fefer, Nachum Beren, Reyzi Kagan, Avraham Leyb Korin, and others joined later. In time, Feyge Shulder, Gitel Kitaykesher, Rozi Shapiro, Levi Beren, Yisrael Mofshit, Chayim Hirsh Mazur, and the writer of this article also participated.

The first shows took place in Grozinov's flourmill. Later, the theater moved to a large and well-equipped hall in the palace (Zamek), and a number of shows took place at Tirnikov's school.

The repertoire was mixed. I remember the shows but not the order in which they were staged: (1) "Mirele Efrat," (2) "Two Kuni Lemel," which Fayerman and Dobromdiker excelled in, (3) "The Brothers Ashkenazi," (4) "The Jewish Spark," (5) "Sore Sheyndel the Rabbi's Wife," (6) "Chinke Pinke," (7) "Malkele the Soldier," (8) "The Witch" (or "Koldunye"), (9) "God, Man, and Devil," (10) "The Penitent," with Leybtsi Fefer in the lead role, (11) "The Blind Painter," and others.

[Page 168]

In addition, the Yiddish play "Purim Play" was also performed at the flourmill. Chana Hirsh Lekales played the part of King Ahashueros with great talent. The Tarbut schoolchildren put on the Yiddish operetta "King Saul" under the direction of Volk, the school principal. Yerachmiel Servetnik portrayed King Saul, with Yakov Tenenboym as King David, Yisrael Mofshit as the prophet Samuel, Chayim Tsvi Mazur as the court jester, and many others.

In addition to plays staged in Yiddish, cultural "images and songs" evenings in Yiddish and in Hebrew took place under Duvid Mendelboym's direction. The most remarkable performances were given by Yakov Yakira, as Herzl, and Chayke Mofshit and Yehuda Zinger, with their pleasant and grand voices.

In 1933-34, the Workers' Union established an amateur troupe and staged one or two shows. I can't remember the names of the plays, but I remember that the most outstanding actress was Feyge Sheynker.

The first Hebrew play was "Two Melodies," which the audience welcomed with great enthusiasm. The principal actors were Tovale Rozental and Hershele Katz. At the end of the play, the actress received flowers, the actor got chocolate, and Leybtsi Fefer walked on stage and enthusiastically talked about the play, which was beautifully performed in the purest Hebrew.

The second play was "Chane and her Seven Sons," directed by Fanye Chaskelovna Zeyger, the elementary school principal, and featuring actors Yisrael Mofshit, Tova Rozental, and others. That play was also very successful.

The third play, "The Sale of Yosef," was performed by the Tarbut schoolchildren at the flourmill. It was directed by school principal Volk, and the main character was played by Berele Barbak.

When I write about the history of drama circles in Vishnevets here and list the members' names, I feel that the details aren't correct or sufficient here and there. I regret that I didn't write these things down when they happened. I've also written what I can remember about Avraham Fayerman, and I hope I'll be forgiven for any missing information.

Translator's Footnotes

Ester Rachel Kaminska (née Heilperin,1870-1925) was called the "mother of Jewish theater." An actress in the Yiddish-language theater, she performed in Poland, Russia, the United States, London, and Paris, and she appeared in Yiddish-language films.

[Page 169]

An Anti-Semitic Judge's Verdict in Vishnevets
by Yehoshue Ron (Shike Geler)

Young people from Vishnevets were known in the area for their great enthusiasm and awareness of various public programs. They assisted in the library, helped with Tarbut School maintenance, and participated in the string orchestra and drama troupe. They also took part in religious, social, and sporting events. I had the honor of being captain of the soccer team.

The team included teenagers from all classes. Only the best, the strongest, and those who could play were chosen. We practiced on a suitable field on a mountain called "the Kremenets Mountain" because you could see it from the road leading to Kremenets.

The palace grounds in our town had a much better place to practice and play matches, but the authorities reserved it solely for the Polish and Russian teams. We played there only when we competed against a prestigious team. This beautiful field was located inside the palace forest, quite far from the town. The entryway was a tall iron gate guarded by a 75-year-old gentile with pink cheeks and a well-groomed long white beard.

Soccer in Vishnevets – Players and Their Proud Supporters

[Page 170]

It happened that before the Polish national holiday on May 3, we received an invitation to play against one of the strongest Polish teams, whose players were students from the palace's trade and agricultural school. We knew they would do their best to win the match in order to demonstrate their supremacy over the Jews in front of the Polish-Russian spectators, at least in the area of sports, because in educational matters they were at a disadvantage.

Winning the match was a matter of prestige for us. We wanted to prove that we could measure up to them in a game involving power and strategy. I gathered the team for intense training and tried to explain to them that our victory would raise the morale of our town's young people. I was extremely excited. I brought up the brave deeds of Judah Maccabee, Samson the Hero, Bar Kochba, and Trumpeldor, and demanded from each one a personal sacrifice for our victory on the soccer field, telling them that the Jewish nation's fate and honor were in their hands.

Most of the spectators were Poles and Russians. The Jews were represented by a small number of teenagers. Luck shined on us from the beginning of the match. The training and our great willpower made their marks. During the first 10 minutes of the match, we scored two goals even though the referee was Polish and far from objective. Throughout the match, the Polish spectators whistled and booed the players on both sides, winners and losers.

I had a very unpleasant incident. My pants split open in the middle of the match, and I was left in an unpleasant situation. Since I didn't have a second pair of pants, I had to continue the match dressed in a spectator's raincoat.

The match's outcome was 5 to 2 in our favor. The hostile crowd, which wasn't willing to forgive us for our victory, began to provoke every Jew on the field. I felt that the situation was beginning to get serious and dangerous, and with two of my friends, I gathered 15 young men to protect the Jews. We pushed the Jewish children and teenagers toward the exit, and we, the team members, created a protective wall around them during their retreat. The Polish teenagers chased us, provoked us, and threw stones at us, but we didn't stop to respond. When I realized that the Jewish group had enough time to reach the other side of the gate, we couldn't hold back anymore, and a serious fistfight started after the Poles assaulted Hershele Senders' brother, who was known in Vishnevets as a fighter. Although they outnumbered us, they received heavy blows from us, and many were injured. We also suffered some injuries, but their morale diminished. We took advantage of the pause in the fight and escaped past the gate to return to the town. The old gatekeeper, who shut the gate in our faces, received a blow in the face from Efraim Yakira's strong hands. Blood started to pour out of his nose, the gate broke open, and we were saved.

A few days later, I was invited to the police station. The officer started to yell at me. He accused me of hitting a large number of people who later needed medical care, the old man included. The officer didn't listen to my claims and demanded the names of the people with me. When I gave him the team members' names, he informed me that he was passing the matter on for judicial clarification.

[Page 171]

For one reason or another, we decided not to hire a lawyer. Betshinsky, the only judge in town, was a well-known anti-Semite. We assumed that his judgment would be severe, so we decided that it was better to save the money so we could pay a lawyer to appeal on our behalf.

The day of the trial arrived, and we were terrified. The prosecutor's words were strong and full of malice and lies, and there were many witnesses for the prosecution. My argument before him was simple. After I had convinced him, with the prosecution witnesses' corroboration, that there were only a few of us, I asked him how it was possible that larger group and not us had been beaten.

I had probably touched a sore spot for the anti-Semitic Polish judge. It angered him that they had degraded his courageous race. Unexpectedly, he reprimanded them for not taking stronger measures, and declared, "I have to acquit the accused for lack of evidence."

We thanked him from the bottom of our hearts and went to celebrate our second victory.

[Page 172]

From Cheder to the Northern Fence

by Yitschak Verdi (Reyzels)

I remember my childhood days at the cheder of R' Moshe, Asher-Yoel's son, a well-known teacher of young children in Vishnevets. He was the typical image of a small-town Jewish teacher, whose duty to provide his cheder children's first education was imposed on him by the heavens. He taught us reading, writing, the Pentateuch, and Rashi.

Later, I studied Gemara at the yeshiva belonging to the town's rabbi, under his son-in-law R' Chayim Aytsikel's directorship and guidance.

At that time, I had already begun to feel an inclination toward the Jewish people's fate. I understood that our nation as it existed in the Diaspora, with me as one of its sons, had once owned its own land – the Land of Israel. In my dreams, I often saw myself as someone who returned to the long-awaited homeland, and that was my obvious intention. My longing was strengthened by the reality of my time in the Polish elementary school, where the Christian teachers showed animosity toward Jewish children. The Christian children followed their teachers' example and expressed their hostility with violence inside and outside the school walls. We also experienced their hatred of Jewish children on the way to school. When Jewish children passed a Christian home, they were welcomed with warm greetings that included abusive language, barking dogs, and stones hurled at them.

All this made me think how wonderful it would be for the Jewish nation to be free in its homeland, so I joined one of the Zionist youth movements that began to organize in our town – the Young Pioneer movement.

Fence Builders in the North

[Page 173]

Our branch ran a wide variety of activities, such as discussion groups; work to benefit various organizations, such as the Foundation Fund and Jewish National Fund; and activities to promote the Hebrew language. The centerpiece of our activities was to prepare for immigration to the Land of Israel by going to a training kibbutz, leaving our birthplace, extorting approval to leave our mother's and father's table, etc. All that shook us to the depths of our souls and required difficult preparation. Any young person who reached the age of 18 was a candidate for a training kibbutz when he or she received an approval from the central Pioneer office in Warsaw.

When my turn arrived, I was sent with my friend Yakov Chatski to Kibbutz Stolin in the Polesia district.

In Stolin, the members received us with warmth and real friendship, and we were drafted to work immediately. We cut down trees, worked as porters and watchmen, and more. The kibbutz "patrons" were in charge of distributing the jobs. They were a group of Zionist party workers from Stolin who did their jobs out of loyalty and not for a monetary reward. With a number of members, I moved from Stolin five kilometers away to the village of Horin, where we worked at the local sawmill. The mill was operated by gentile workers even though it was under Jewish ownership.

It is important to mention that while we worked with the Christian laborers, we never came across anti-Semitic problems, maybe because the mill owners were Jewish or maybe because they knew we were working there only temporarily.

After a long stay in the training kibbutz, my immigration to Israel was approved by a vote of the general meeting. I returned to Vishnevets and waited to receive the long-awaited certificate. Since it never arrived, the Pioneer central office in Warsaw sent me for additional training, and I left for the Klosov kibbutz.

The kibbutz's main income came from the stone quarry, where I worked for more than a year. For the second time, I was approved for immigration. Since I was required to enlist in the Polish army, the Pioneer central office pushed for my departure, and in January 1937, I left my parents, my friends, and my hometown and immigrated to Israel.

When I arrived at the port of Haifa, my brother Chayim welcomed me with Dov Sofer and Yakov Nudel, of blessed memory, his friends from Vishnevets who had immigrated before me, the same way I did.

It was a time of bloody riots in Israel. When I arrived at Kibbutz Givat Hashlosha, I was drafted into the local Haganah organization.

Belonging to the organization required intense training under difficult clandestine conditions. After a hard day's labor, I had to leave for guard duty and other defense operations.

During the time I mentioned above, the Land of Israel's northern borders were subject to disturbances because they were open to the neighboring countries – Syria and Lebanon – which the ruling British mandate didn't control. Arab gangs smuggled weapons and also engaged in sabotage and murder in Jewish settlements.

[Page 174]

Therefore, it was decided to build a barbed-wire fence along those borders to block the Arab gangs and help guard against them. It wasn't easy to work for many days facing the enemy. The workers had to be protected, and the Haganah took over the responsibility and provided a security force.

One day, a brief notice was posted on the bulletin board in the kibbutz dining hall: "We are asking for four volunteers for a special operation."

The notice spoke to me. I volunteered and was the first to sign up.

The meeting point was a kibbutz in the Jordan Valley. Volunteers – Haganah members – arrived there from cities, villages, and mostly kibbutzim. At that location, our duty was explained to us, and our training for the mission began that day.

The fence was built quickly, and the security was excellent. Every once in a while, clashes broke out between the guards and Arab gangs, but we always had the upper hand.

One evening after I finished my guard duty, which lasted from sunrise to sunset, my commanding officer, Yitschak Heker (one of the 23 Palmach members whose boat disappeared on their way to sabotage the refineries in Tripoli, Lebanon), met with me and asked if I wanted to join a special eight-man unit for a nighttime ambush. At 18:30 we left for the ambush. We lay quietly at the ambush location, which was about 400-550 meters from the fence on top of a tall mountain inside Lebanon, and waited. Less than an hour later, we heard a rustle and saw some shadows, which began to run away after one of us called out to them.

We began to fire, and we were answered with intense power. When the gunfire ended, we were left with a number of donkeys loaded with weapons and ammunition that the escaping Arabs had left behind. Only then did I reveal to my comrades that I'd been wounded in both legs. Immediately, rockets were shot from our side to summon first aid. With difficulty, my comrades carried me down the mountain on a makeshift stretcher made of guns tied together. An ambulance was already waiting at the bottom.

I was taken to the camp. It was clear that my condition was serious.

That same night, I was taken to Schweitzer Hospital in Tiberias. About a week later, I was transferred to Beilinson Hospital in Petach Tikva, where my medical care was completed. Thanks to the doctors' and nurses' dedication, I survived. It was they who helped me stand up on both legs.

One chain of days leads from the cheder to fence building in the north. It started hundreds of cheders before my cheder, and it doesn't end at the northern fence; it ends far away from there. But when I review the changes that took place during our lives and the changes that will take place in the future, it seems to me that our power comes from them and that the changes flow from each person from Vishnevets, and that's why this article belongs in Sefer Vishnevets.

[Page 175]

How Yitschak Reyzels (Verdi) Was Wounded

(From the Givat Hashlosha Journal – the Northern Fences)

"...There were a few cases of robbery in the north by Arabs who lived on the other side of the Syrian border. That same day, our friends found a pile of iron posts and barbed wire under some bushes in the field, which the thieves had left behind the day before and didn't have time to take with them. For that reason, a group of guards was sent to ambush them at that location. Yitschak was included in that group.

And when the guards approached the place, the Arabs noticed them right away. The group of guards, which was trapped between two groups of Arabs, began to shoot to their left using their rifles and machine guns. Yitschak, who was left alone in front of the Arabs on the right, shot only once before being wounded in both legs. Immediately he was given first aid, which, by the way, was very well organized. At first, they assumed that he wasn't seriously wounded. He was transferred to a hospital in Tiberias, where his condition worsened. I visited him a number of times, but I don't know if I'll be able to do so again in the near future since we're planning to leave our location and move farther inside the mountains next week."

[Page 175]

The Northern Fence Builders

by B. Chabas

The following evening, the guard Reyzels, a member of Givat Hashlosha, was wounded. In the clinic hut, a young doctor with a volunteer sparkle in his eye, who was dressed like a laborer and spoke with a pioneer accent, showed us the operating room, which had been dedicated the day before. Stories of the heroism of that time were circulating in the camp. It isn't true that they broke through the fence – they said with excitement – only to bundles of barbed wire and fence-building materials left in the field. And more was said about the wounded Yitschak Reyzels, who was brought to camp on one of the captured donkeys, and about the fact that he never emitted a moan during the long ride. And of the British policeman, one of two who lived in the camp, they said he hugged and kissed the wounded man because he'd suffered silently and bravely.

[Page 177]

Notes and Letters

English Translation by Sara Mages

[Page 179]

Letter from Kopel Dobrovitker

Kibbutz Vohlin Trumpeldor

Klosova-Rokitna Detachment

To the Vohlin United Kibbutz Detachment in Hadera

Ch. Y.

The subject of this letter is interesting, and it has some charm, even with its errors.—**Editorial Board**

You apparently predicted that the well-known proverb "Don't judge" would be appropriate for my reply. You brought up complicated matters that also exist in our lives, ones that we don't take lightly. Honestly, you sensed the facts, but you haven't looked for the problems they've caused and are causing right now. We don't blame you, although you should have known what was happening to us—so I want to offer some explanations to prove how wrong you are with your help. First, you need to know the movement's current state. This is one factor that has pushed us to find a way to fix the distortion in the direction our lifestyle is taking in Diaspora kibbutzim. The period of stability is over. The Pioneer movement took off its romantic coat a long time ago, and the rumors say that the sky in the Land isn't blue and that there are mountains and valleys there. There are also swamps to be drained, roads to be paved, and weeds to be pulled. All these matters need to be recognized and require our utmost effort. In reality, all this has become a point of emphasis and a main objective of pioneer education. On the other hand, indifference and psychological decline in the Zionist movement is weakening the enthusiasm of Pioneer members in our town, who have left its ranks. Only a few of us are left on the front lines; the few survivors don't demand satisfaction, and the small town or dry city won't satisfy them. They're leaving everything behind and heading for training kibbutzim, and here we have a problem. How can we absorb them, and how can we satisfy them? Maybe with the old song that the kibbutz is just a place for job training and that in a few months they'll leave home and immigrate. Or maybe we should mold them for a lifestyle known to require extensive care and training? The problem has solved itself with the many years of pioneer training and the difficulties of life in the Land of Israel. The never-ending demands there, which required a degree of preparation and education, meant that they underwent the same development in the kibbutz. And happily, we must mention that thanks only to that stabilization, our kibbutz has 100 members, 60 of whom are unemployed during the harsh winter, and there is a shortage of supplies in the kibbutz.

Now for the matters you mention: it isn't true that we've reached the invalid stage. It's true that because of the climate here (the air in Polesia can cause illness) and the difficult working conditions (exploitation is high since each Zionist is a factory owner), and without material aid from the Pioneer central office (the kibbutz paid to build the cow shed and auxiliary farm and to repair some buildings)—the percentage of sick members is high, sometimes as high as 40%. But we're not thinking of sending them to you in the Land, because we understand the demands of our land and our duty here. The issue of medical care has an important place in our kibbutz lifestyle. We heal them and hope they'll immigrate healthy. A hospital has been set up, and new members who have a hard time getting used to hard labor in the quarry recover from their illnesses there and return to work.

[Page 180]

We've also operated on a number of members, who have recovered. So you understand that we're not aiming for invalids but want to create "laborers," which is quite difficult. The saying "They that sow in tears shall reap in joy" is our motto, and we hold it tight.

As for the Ostrog members' departure: only three members left, intending to create a small group. The kibbutz isn't a force that drives people away. If they left, they had to leave. The kibbutz has a magnetic force. I must mention that a few members from Galicia and the far corners of Poland want to come, and what this shows is open to discussion.

We've read member Benari's letter "from the inside," and we're sure you have, too. We're satisfied with the way he describes his longing to immigrate. We just want to add that the halt in pioneer immigration may have negative results. Many of us members have spent three years in the kibbutz and ought to immigrate with our families. The hope that we'll immigrate immediately helps us breathe and hold on.

Your letter arrived late. We haven't had enough time to send any material for your special newsletter, so we're sending a short, heartfelt blessing for the celebration of your second year. We celebrate it not with celebratory words, but with the hope and belief that we're ready to continue your work, which is also our work, and that we'll celebrate along with you a third year that is even stronger.

We still stand behind you.

For the kibbutz

Kopel

[Page 180]

Letter from D. Balmelakhe to Yakov Chachkis

Kremenets, December 19, 1938

Shalom, my dear friend Yakov!

Many thanks to you, my dear friend, for not forgetting me. Your card lifted my spirits and strengthened my feelings. You've tied a courageous knot between our past and our future, and maybe also the future's future...

I thought that immigration, settlement, work, and cells would make you forget and that your friend . . . your most loyal friend . . . would fade from your heart. I thought that no notion of me would enter your head and no form or gratitude would find a place in your heart. I thought you'd stay in touch only with your immediate family and that you wouldn't make the smallest gesture toward your friend across the sea.

Since I see in you the blessing of human and social sensibility...

I want to be in touch with you and, through you, with the land of our patriarchs. Please take an interest in me the way I take an interest in you.

I remember our past friendship . . . we were close, shoulder to shoulder, hand in hand. Together we stood at the center of the association.

[Page 181]

Together we set up the association, asked for money, edited newspapers, and held lectures, parties, trips and meetings, and how lovely those days were. The longings and memories are lovely.

That's when I got to know you... I saw your great energy and your acute sense of responsibility and security. I liked seeing, talking to, and associating with you. I loved you and remained endlessly loyal to you. I hope that there in the Land you'll examine and expand our friendship, and your letters will broaden my heart and give me energy, the will to work . . . and to dream.

Write me a long letter. How was your journey to the Land of Israel? How did you find your place in Kibbutz Givat Hashlosha? How many members does the kibbutz have? What's the kibbutz like? How's morale? What are security and defense like? What's the settlement's economic situation?

What kind of influence do Federation members have on the Yishuv?

The Betar people's influence—revisionism? Send me the addresses of a few of our friends from Vishnevets who live not far from you. What is Yitschak Reyzels doing? They say he was wounded; where is he? What is Chayim Reyzels doing? Moshe Rabin, Yitschak Rabin? Maybe you know something about Idel Shapiro, Rozye Shapiro and Sosi Shapiro, Eliezer Shag, Nisan Servetnik, and so on. Write me what's happening in the Hebrew world. Please send me Hebrew newspapers, magazines, and periodicals, and if you can't, please ask your friends to help you.

I'll pay you for the postage from here so you don't have to worry about it. Please tell me how I can send you money so you can write to me often. If I send you Polish money, you won't be able to use it, and I can't mail Israeli currency. Don't delay answering, and send me the items I asked for.

Your friend who wants to see you face to face,

D. Balmelakhe

P.S.

Regards to your girlfriend who immigrated with you, the friends I mentioned in my letter, and friends in Kibbutz Givat Hashlosha. May your hands be strong when you build the land, and may your arm not pull back in defense!

***

My dear friend,

I send you best wishes for the new year, and I hope you settle in the Land of Israel and build it with strength and spirit. May the Lord let you see the Jewish kingdom on the mountains of Zion and Judea with your own eyes.

Shalom, shalom, shalom, and see you in the Land of Israel.

D. Bal-melakhe

N.B. Don't tear up the letters I send you. Hide them, and they'll serve as memories when we meet in person—the meeting mentioned above.

[Page 182]

Letter from Leybtsi Fefer

Munich, June 29, 1947

Shalom to Lintil and Meir, who are dear and close to my heart.

I received your letter. I feel blessed to be able to tell my childhood friends once more that my heart longs to see them face to face, and I hope that soon I'll be able to hug them close to my heart. I was happy to hear that you're in good health and that you're interested in my personal affairs and willing to help me out. I don't know why I was the only one of our friends to come out of the destroyer's lion jaws alive. My town, Vishnevets, stands in its place, its buildings destroyed and its residents killed. In remembrance of the great destruction, only the Great Synagogue's central pillars were left standing, and various names are carved on them in their writers' blood, such as "my life is over". . . "Tomorrow we will die" . . . and the like.

On both sides of the road to the village of Kolodne, thousands of our town's residents were buried, among them our beloved families and friends: Gorenshteyn, Korin, Presman, and Erlikh—all of them died. Kopel and his family were killed in Rovne. When I was in Vishnevets in 1939, Nachum was no longer alive. According to what my friends told me, the Bolsheviks arrested him at the beginning of their occupation. I looked for him all over Russia, but I couldn't find him. He probably died of starvation and agony in a Russian prison. My family and I survived. We lived in Russia for two years and in Poland for four months, and later left for Germany.

Landsberg Camp with L. Fefer as President
Banner inside the photo: May the nation of Israel remember the
6,000 martyrs from the town of Vishnevets, Kremenets district

[Page 183]

We have two daughters: one is seven years old, and the other is two. Both are lovely and delicate. What a pity I can't marry them off to your family, since according to Yentil's message, your sons are already heroes, like those who stand and guard the nation and the homeland, and my daughters are still young and need my help...

I won't say much about life as a survivor. You probably know our situation. It's a pity when people have sunk to a life of charity and can't support themselves with the labor of their hands. Some have given up on life. Demoralization grows from day to day, and the Zionist movement faces a great danger if the question of immigration to the Land isn't solved in the near future. If only there were a Jewish nation... That would bring redemption... I'm glad to hear that the Yishuv is strong. I don't trust the philanthropists, and I'm willing to fight those who want to put stumbling blocks in the way of building the land and redeeming its people. Nor are we sitting with our arms folded. I've been active in the party since the day I returned from Russia, and today I'm a member of the Labor Zionist Central Office. I remain loyal to the Freedom movement's ideology and continue to follow the road of social Zionism. On behalf of the party, I joined the Committee of Liberated Jews in Germany, and I'm the director of the Cultural Department. All this is not worth a penny because my heart aches with longing for the Land. I'm 44 years old today, and as you know, my health isn't the best, so when will I be able to see the Land? Why have I worked so hard all my life . . . my financial situation isn't bad. We get enough food, and we sometimes receive some rags from the Joint, but all this is nothing, because I detest living among the murderers in their contaminated, cursed land. I want to immigrate in the summer, but the party won't allow it and has postponed it until the spring. I'll try to immigrate at the beginning of May or June. I need five certificates. If the party doesn't hold me back, I'll definitely immigrate. Why haven't you written about the details of your life? What's your apartment like? (They say that it's as difficult to get an apartment as it was to part the Red Sea.) How are your sons doing? What about your job? Why haven't you told me how Hentsi Zeyger and her husband are? What are the prospects for a man like me? Will I be able to settle there? My wife is an excellent seamstress. Is it possible to get an apartment in your town, and what's the price? What items are you short of, and what should we bring from Germany? We don't have any money, but we can ask the Americans to send you some. Please write again. Be well. Many greetings and warm kisses from my wife, my daughters, and me. Answer me right away because we're waiting impatiently for your answer.

Yours,

L. Fefer

[Page 184]

Leybtsi (Arye Leyb) Fefer,
of Blessed Memory

Leybtsi (Arye Leyb) Fefer,
of Blessed Memory

We knew Leybtsi well as a child and as he was growing up. He was always moving, applying himself, and searching for one aim—more knowledge. He was knowledgeable about a wide variety of subjects, and he therefore knew how to arouse the enthusiasm of listeners for his explanations by using glowing expressions and direct definitions, mostly on the theoretical side.

When he was young, he roamed through foreign countries and earned a living by teaching in order to increase his knowledge.

He was an outstanding civic worker from the time he was in the Freedom movement. When he later immigrated to the Land, he continued his political work. He was soon elected United Workers Party representative to the municipal organizations, and he was a member of the board of directors of Yazur's municipal council.

Teaching was his heart's desire and the substance of his personality. He worked as a teacher in the Land as long as his strength held out. He was an excellent educator and was steeped in a deep-rooted sense of Hebrew culture. As a youngster, he did much to promote Hebrew as a spoken language. He walked from home to home, asking people to start speaking in Hebrew.

When he was young, he willingly took on the pain of travel in order to increase his knowledge. Later, bad luck overtook him, and he was sentenced to roam during the emergencies and madnesses of the various regimes.

After the "flood," when he was in a refugee camp, he kept in touch with his friend in the Land, and his letters were saturated with longing and yearning to immigrate (the letter published in this book is a witness to that).

His restless personality didn't let him relax. In the camp, he gathered a group of refugees together—people from Vishnevets and their friends—and organized a social group. The group separated when some of the members immigrated.

He had strong organizational skills and enjoyed his friends. When he arrived in the Land, he was an initiator and founder of the Organization of Vishnevets Emigrants.

[Page 185]

Anyone who hasn't seen Leybtsi shining with the flame of satisfaction during the first meeting of the Organization of Vishnevets Emigrants in the Land has never seen a happy man.

We are sad that Leybtsi is no longer with us as our organization extends its activities in general and particularly as it establishes a charitable fund.

Leybtsi certainly would have taken an active part in Sefer Vishnevets, but the dangerous state of his health prevented him from doing so.

May his memory be blessed!

Meir

[Page 187]

People We Remember

English Translation by Sara Mages

[Page 189]

Grandma Chane-Malke

by Yone Ron

Chane Malke was an amazing person whose lively personality could have unified Vishnevets.

At a young age, she lost her husband, Yankel-Barukh, a learned man who was associated with the rabbinate and studied Torah all his life. As his wife Chane-Malke supported him, and through her work, she assisted the needy and helped the weak. After marrying off her children, she moved in with her son, Yisrael Rozental, and her daughter in-law, Ester Di Zbarizher, and continued with her blessed activities to help those in need. She had a well-developed extra sensibility that enabled her to detect and find homes that appeared well to do on the outside but where poverty prevailed inside. When they were left without even a penny to buy bread and needed a secret gift, Chane-Malke appeared like the angel of mercy, without letting anyone know how she had found out.

Grandmother Chane-Malke with Her Husband,
Yakov Barukh, a Torah Master

[Page 190]

I remember Thursdays and Fridays well, when grandmother wore her big, wide apron and hurried around to collect challahs from homes she knew of and deliver them to the destitute so they could observe the Sabbath commandments. She also had a contact at the town's Jewish bank, from whom she received loans. She divided the money among those who needed a dowry, assistance for the sick, and help rehabilitating themselves so they could earn their own living. To pay off bank loans, she formed a group of women donors. She visited them once a week to get their donations, and she was able to pay back her loans like clockwork.

She visited neglected sick people and always had a kind, encouraging word to say to them. In town, she was seen as an exemplary human being, and they would say that if there were 36 righteous people in the world, one of them was made in a woman's image.

When we youngsters began studying Hebrew at the Tarbut School, we spoke Hebrew among ourselves for practice. She enjoyed watching us children as we did this, and when we saw her, she didn't wait until we said good morning to her in Hebrew. She went ahead and said a broad "Shalom" to us, as if she wanted to identify with us.

She knew not only the solemnity and burden of good deeds, but also happiness and high spirits. She was the head "dancer" at weddings, and demonstrated with her body "how to dance before the bride." We, the younger generation, paid the band generously for her dances. We enjoyed seeing her dance with grace and style even at her advanced age. She was still dancing at age 80 and beyond.

Often when we spent time together and wanted to know whom she had supported, she always answered with pleasure, "Giving in secret is giving in secret."

She never failed, and nothing could stop her from running to do her work. In the cruel, freezing winter weather, she woke up early to go to the women's study hall so she could listen to the sacred words and fulfill the commandment of public prayer.

And that's how she caught a cold that turned into pneumonia and returned her pure soul to God. Many people attended her funeral. It was a rainy day, and it looked like the sky was identifying with our townspeople by crying over Grandma Chane-Malke's death.

[Page 191]

Azriel (Son of Moshe Aharon) Kubrik
by A. Barak

Azriel Kubrik

Azriel Kubrik, son of Moshe Aharon and Miryam Leye (née Shatski), was born in Vishnevets in 1873, the youngest of five children. Until age four, he ran around his father's lumberyard. His father earned a respectable living by purchasing parcels of forest from local landowners and clearing, chopping down, and sawing trees.

At age four, he went to cheder, where he immediately asserted himself as a deep thinker and a quick learner, and his teachers predicted a great future for him. As a child, young Azriel was pulled as if by a magic power to the centers of education. At age 14, he journeyed to the big city of Poltava, where he joined other children his age to study at the municipal high school.

Little by little, he began visiting Jewish homes in the town, and very shortly, he was as welcome as a family member at Tsvi Shimshelevits's home and became a good friend of his son Yitschak. This same Yitschak became Israel's second president under the name Yitschak Ben-Tsvi. He was also welcomed at the Fridland family's home, which served as a cultural and Zionist center in Poltava.

Azriel, who excelled in deep analysis and proper discretion, quickly became the coordinator of Poltava's Jewish youth. During the pogroms against the town's Jews, he led the local Jewish youth defense force that guarded Jewish homes and stores. Once when he was out of town, he learned that the rioters had surrounded the Jewish quarter. Worried that the Jewish defense group wouldn't be able to operate without him, he immediately obtained Cossack clothing and a horse, broke through a group of rioters into the Jewish quarter, and led the defense.

During the Enlightenment, Kubrik became familiar with gentiles and applied to fulfill his Zionist duty through immigration. In 1905, he arrived at the port of Jaffa.

His first destination in the Land was the lower Galilee, where he worked as a farmer and laborer in a number of Baron Rothschild's cooperative settlements.

[Page 192]

At the same time, a decision was made to go up into the foothills of Givat Hamoreh and lay the foundations of Kibbutz Merhavia. Azriel helped found the kibbutz but couldn't fit in with that group. It appeared to him that the time wasn't right for rest and security, so he joined a commune in the famous K'han in Hadera. That group faced the challenge of conquering the labor that had to be done in the fields and Hadera's Jewish farmers' orange groves. Morning after morning, they left before sunrise, carrying their hoes, ready for hard labor in the fields so they wouldn't fall behind the Arab workers, who were used to it. Azriel came down with malaria, and after three difficult attacks, Dr. Yafe forced him to leave Hadera and move back to Jaffa, the "city."

Azriel lived in Jaffa briefly and then moved to Atlit, where he accepted a job at Aharon Aharonson's experimental farm. That work caused a rift in the relationship between Azriel and his friends. Aharonson was considered a middle-class farmer, and Azriel, who was a Labor Zionist founder and the first to preach radical social ideas, had changed his skin, so to speak, and had become the "middle-class" Aharonson's "henchman."

During World War I, Aharon Aharonson and his friends established Nili [1]. The matter widened the gap between the Land of Israel's laborers and their organization, the Watchman, and the established farmers in the Baron's settlements.

Azriel, who had neither a part nor a lot in the Nili organization, decided to leave Atlit. He roamed south to Rishon Letsion and Nes Tsiyona. There he hired himself out to the settlement's committee as a night watchman and worked at this job until the end of World War I. Then he moved to Jaffa, where he got a job in construction as a plasterer's helper. Later, he studied to be a glazier and worked independently on the new buildings being built in Tel Aviv, the new suburb of Jaffa.

Azriel Kubrik was a Federation delegate in Jaffa and an activist in the Labor Zionist Left organization. He carried out many duties for different committees, but he was loyal to his beliefs and decided to be a worker, not a politician.

The same year, he married Sore (Sonye), from the Fridland family in Poltava. With the help of a 400-Egyptian-pound loan, he purchased a building lot and built a three-bedroom home with a big, spacious yard. He planted trees, built a chicken coop, and planted a vegetable garden. The yard on Merkaz Ba'alei-Melakha Street in Tel Aviv became a meeting place for labor leaders. Those who came to Tel Aviv knew they could find their activists there, such as Neta Harpaz, Kitsis, Yitschak Ben-Tsvi, and many others.

After the 1921 riots, Kubrik traveled from Tel Aviv to Rishon Letsion in his horse cart. On the way, he was attacked and stabbed in the chest, and his horse and cart were stolen by the attackers. For many days, he lay wounded at Hadassah Hospital on Nachalat Binyamin Street in Tel Aviv, hovering between life and death. His weak body was ready to give up, but his strong spirit refused to listen to that judgment. He left the hospital very weak. He couldn't return to construction, so he developed a vegetable garden next to his home, extended his chicken coop, and lived in poverty.

[Page 193]

In the meantime, the 1,000-settlement plan was carried out, and Kubrik settled in the Netayim settlement near Nes Tsiyona, where he was given an orange grove and a large yard.

The years in Netayim were difficult, and the members were forced to earn their living outside the settlement, which couldn't support itself. Azriel, who was an agricultural laborer at the Gan Rave orange groves, became weaker and slowly faded. After he was bitten by a snake in one of the orchard's paths, part of his foot was amputated. The couple and their two children were forced to return to Tel Aviv. Sore Kubrik went to work at the tax office in order to help her family. Azriel looked for jobs as a building watchman and other light seasonal work.

His life in Tel Aviv was bitter and difficult. His body started to decay, and his spirit sank when he realized that his friends had deserted him in his time of trouble.

On August 22, 1945, Azriel Kubrik of Vishnevets died. He was among the first to immigrate during the Second Immigration, he fulfilled his Zionist duty, and he was a friend of his country's leaders.

May his memory be blessed among his townspeople.

Translator's Note:

Nili was a small Jewish underground organization that helped the British army liberate Palestine from the Turks. return

[Page 194]

Shimon Ayzenberg
by Lipa Goldberg

Shimon Ayzenberg

Shimon, the oldest in our group, was considered the first pioneer.

In 1920, when the echoes of the world war had subsided, slogans asking for the redemption of the world changed, and the ranks of the Zionist movement did, too. The saying that was pitched was, "During these historic days, we need to help the nation. Not by talking, but by doing."

Shimon had already lost his father, and the duty of being the family head fell to him, as the oldest son. His father had left many thriving businesses, and Shimon, who was active in them, managed to build himself an excellent financial future, but his heart was drawn to a different lifestyle: it was full of longing for Zion and pioneering.

In 1921, at age 30, he severed himself from his business and family duties, uprooted himself from his economic and social roots, and immigrated.

In the Land, he decided that he could be of use by capturing the transport business from the Arabs. In his first days there, he bought a pair of mules and a cart and started to work.

His personal example inspired the people around him, and others joined the profession, which brought a romantic change of status. It was a direct leap from being sons from well- to-do families to being a horse-and- cart drivers of the lowest status.

The late Duvid Remez, who respected him greatly, provided him with dangerous transport jobs held by Arabs in the port of Jaffa. Later, he offered him a position in Jerusalem, a vulnerable point in the war to capture Arab work.

Shimon didn't hesitate for long. He turned his mules toward Jerusalem and went there.

With him were Mordekhay Goldberg from Bielozerka, Gilboa from Merhavia – and the United States – and others.

In Jerusalem, the friends organized a contractual transport business and were the destination for people looking for work.

When Solel Boneh was awarded the contract to build a fence around the cemetery for the fallen Allenby soldiers in Beer Yakov, Shimon and his friends traveled to Beersheba at D. Remez's request.

[Page 195]

For an extended period, Shimon lived there in a nearby tent among the Bedouins.

In the tent camp in Beersheba, Shimon found out that a group was planning to settle in the area. Shimon consulted with his friends, and they decided to join the project.

In 1923, on the evening after Simchat Torah, Simon hitched up his mules, and after a day-and-a-half-long journey through Wade A'ra, he arrived in the Merhavia settlement and set up a mighty tent for himself.

The writer of these lines also joined them.

During our first year in Merhavia, we lived in a different kind of collective settlement. We were inclined toward agricultural success, which gave us social success.

Shimon was in charge of the mules. He took care of them, gave instructions on how to behave with them, and sold and bought mules as needed.

When Shimon started his family and his farm, hidden talents that no one knew about were discovered in him. He was diligent and overcame difficulties. No one could have predicted that any worldly power could stop the momentum of his work, the flame of his dedication, and the extent of his stamina.

Meanwhile, his sons were born. His family grew, but his wife stumbled; the burden was too much for her. The frequent drought and the rats that followed it caused Shimon's business to fail, and he lost his endurance.

Shimon's hidden energy left him. When he was offered the job of coordinator of Hachoresh, the transportation cooperative in Bnei Brak (which he organized before he moving to the settlement), he took the offer and uprooted himself from his home.

Shimon's life in the city was dedicated to helping his friends. He supported, helped, and encouraged them, and his house was open to anyone who needed assistance.

Shimon Ayzenberg died of kidney disease in 1936, when he was 45 years old.

[Page 196]

Something about Shimon Ayzenberg

by Yitschak Kecholy   (Secretary of the Merhavia Settlement)

We remember only a little about Shimon Ayzenberg, but the general impression he left was that he was unique.

He lived with us for 10 years. He came to us with a number of friends, who accompanied him to fulfill their dream of becoming Jewish farmers.

His situation in the city was good. As a cart owner (who had brought a little money with him from abroad), his work was secure, but he wanted to live his life according to his principles and Zionist outlook.

In the settlement, he buried himself in his work and was extremely diligent. He was always willing to help others and was famous as an amazingly kindhearted person.

Conditions in our settlement were very difficult, and only a few could rise to meet them. But Shimon never complained, and he did whatever was thrown at him "with all his soul and all his might."

Shimon was considered a loyal public figure, dedicated and honest. Therefore, he was elected to the settlement's board of directors a number of times. He was recognized not as a lofty man who was seeking honor, but as a man who was willing to take a load on his shoulders and perform any unskilled work given to him.

The friends who accompanied him were attached to him, as if he were the greatest and most important person in society, and they listened to him.

Unfortunately for us, Shimon didn't stay with us long. As a man who understood horses, he dedicated himself to the settlement's animals and neglected his own farm.

Because of his neglect, his condition worsened from day to day. When his sons were born and his wife cracked under the burden of her home and the farm, he couldn't cope with the difficulties and was forced to leave.

We were very sorry when he left.

Many left during the first days of our settlement, but Shimon Ayzenberg's departure cast a feeling of melancholy into the members' hearts. Something had been uprooted from the settlement's human foundation and landscape, and we felt the loss.

[Page 197]

Duvid Roynik

by Lipa Goldberg

Duvid was the son of the rabbi of Krasilov. When he was a child, the rabbi's family moved to Pochayev, where he grew up and became a nice, educated young Orthodox man.

One day, R' Moshe Shniribeker happened to be in Pochayev. He was a respected, well-to-do Jew who was searching through his business connections for a match for his daughter. When he came across Duvid, the rabbi's young son, he "bought" him as her bridegroom.

When R' Moshe got tired of the gentile environment, he decided to spend his old age among Jews and moved himself and his businesses to Vishnevets. He handed the management of his possessions to Duvid Roynik and his brother-in-law.

The two young married men weren't successful in the old man's place, and the business declined more and more. At that time, Roynik was able to convince his old father-in-law to sell his holdings. He liquidated everything and immigrated to the Land.

At the beginning of 1914, the two men left for the Land of Israel. They bought two building lots in Rehovot and 300 dunams for a vineyard in the Menucha Venachala Company, which was managed by Ayzenberg, who later became an activist in the farmer's union.

They stayed in the Land for three months, and in April 1941, they returned to Vishnevets to liquidate their business and immigrate to Israel. Just then, the war broke out.

All the money they had made lost its value. The old man died, and the family was destitute.

At the end of the war, Duvid left his family and immigrated to the Land to settle there and bring his family over.

According to his calculations, his property in the Land was enough for him and his father in-law's extensive family to settle on with respect and prosperity. But when he came to claim his property, his trustee "proved" to him that he'd sold all of his land to pay the taxes on the property.

Duvid left his office almost convinced of the man's veracity, but he was told that the man had sold the land to him and "settled" the price with him. But one plot of land was left, and he was able to claim it for himself. And so that the man wouldn't object, he paid him 400 Israel pounds and forced him to sign a document stating that he didn't have any claims or complaints against him.

Duvid returned to Tel Aviv. There he met Kubrik, one of the first immigrants to the Land from Vishnevets, who was active in the labor union there, and he joined Kubrik's construction company.

People respected him from the start, but Roynik couldn't adapt to the style of work and the workers who made the sign of the cross as part of their prayers, so he left the construction business. He bought cows and established a cow business on Neve Shanan Street in Tel Aviv. He also built a wooden bungalow for his family.

In 1922, his family arrived, and it looked as if Duvid Roynik had reached a state of peace and security.

His bungalow became a community center for immigrants from Vohlin, who came there to take part in "togetherness," share their troubles, and find comfort during difficult times. In time, Zelde, Roynik's wife, became the Vishnevetsers' mother. Between milking her cows and delivering the milk, she always found time to sew a button on a negligent pioneer's shirt or wash his underwear. At his home, they always received a cup of tea with a little "something," and little Tel Aviv recognized the Royniks' home as the Vohlin emigrants' home in Israel.

In 1923, Duvid Roynik decided to be a real farmer. He went to Merhavia with Shimon Ayzenberg and settled there.

[Page 198]

Duvid always made his decisions his own way, without exaggeration or personal promotion. With his calm personality, he always searched inside the issue and saw things that weren't visible. People wondered about his approach; with his income secure, why did he leave it all and move his family to an experimental settlement, following somebody else's idea? Duvid never explained his doings, but he knew in his heart that immigration isn't complete unless a man ascends, settles, and works on his own land.

Duvid stood firm in Merhavia for seven years, but the difficult drought and frequent agricultural plagues exhausted him, and he returned to his former business in Ramat Gan.

After his loyal wife's death, he moved in with his sons in the village of Kfar Yehoshua.

Duvid died in 1953 in Kfar Yehoshua. The whole village cried for the loss of his noble soul, which was crowned with grace and superior manners. He was a distinguished man who was faithful to his own principles.

Duvid Roynik as a Fruit Picker

[Page 199]

The Spirit of Nachum Beren

by Sore Or (Afula)

He was a close friend who sought the best for others. He was respected by many in Vishnevets because of his dedication to and care for his fellow man. Also, the way he looked after his extensive family was evidence of the best in him.

The teenagers in our town who began to mature after World War I, at the beginning of the 1920s, when the world's rebirth brought out the human and Jewish conscience in them, saw Nachum as an active leader who searched for direction and lived a hopeful and tasteful public life.

Nachum, who was a man of fundamentals, started from the bottom. He understood the need to establish the Tarbut School as a foundation for a deep-rooted Jewish culture. He organized it, named it, taught in it, and maintained it until his last day.

He was the first teacher in Vishnevets to teach spoken Hebrew with the Sephardic pronunciation, and he saw it as a spoken language and a communication tool for the forming nation.

Nachum directed the town's teenagers to seek their vision and fulfill their destination without resignation. He was the first to direct his students and his friends toward pioneer training and immigration, and his teachings at the school prepared them for life in Israel.

***

I remember the days after the revolution, when we soaked up the great spirit of freedom for men and nations. The push for education increased to the point where it required us to risk our lives. We journeyed to Kremenets to get a high school education and to Odessa and Kiev. Our parents' finances were extremely limited. We were forced to buy common knowledge with great pain. We traveled in carts in the mud, rain, and storms every Sunday before dawn. Sometimes we got stuck in the mud in the valleys between Vishnevets and Kremenets, with no way to move forward. And so we continued hour after hour, week after week, all to be ready for the great days that were knocking on the world's and the town's doors.

We accepted our suffering with love, as our generation's duty, one that we couldn't escape.

We said that this was our fate, and we were lucky to live through it. But when we came home, entirely home, complete with knowledge and education, we found that our town was behind its time, narrow-minded and weak in substance. It was sunk in a culture that was insufficient to quench our thirst and unable to renew, better, and repair itself.

Dreariness spread. Our present life was boring and tiresome, and our future was covered with fog or quite nonexistent. We were full of worry; we absorbed the misleading lights of a revolution in the life of nations and in people's souls, and the shadow of generations was around us.

We needed a great push to overpower that worry and turn it into a powerful push that would change and organize our Jewish life's order and values.

The worry increased between the two regimes, and the dream of a revolution evaporated.

[Page 200]

Our thoughts began to turn toward Zionism. In it, we wanted to find a solution to all the problems that bothered us as fellow citizens, the current generation, and the future nation. But the road to Zionism led to desolation and an unrealistic destination. It was blocked by hidden idealism of the highest degree. So far, the Zionist movement wasn't organized enough to answer our problems and free us.

There was great dismay in our camp: disappointment in the movement to reform the world let down the Jewishness nesting deep in our souls, and enthusiasm for Zion didn't warm our hearts.

That's when Nachum appeared as a redeemer who removed all the obstacles from our souls. He organized us, creating reading, study, conversation, and discussion groups. With him, we established a library and increased our need to read and study. Instead of a life of idleness and worry, we began to live a full, active life. Our clubs were busy with campaigns for the Foundation Fund and Jewish National Fund, and we did a great deal for workers in the Land of Israel. The town's Freedom branch was resurrected, and Nachum breathed life and activity into it. We felt that our daily life had been healed and that our future was set and getting closer.

With Nachum's initiative, an actual Pioneer group was established. That group saw the need for physical and professional training before immigration to Israel. We leased a large field at the edge of the town, and 20 young men and women went to work there to be trained in agricultural work, and from this physical labor, we left for jobs in the city.

Today, these matters aren't so shocking, but then, we had to have great willpower and fervor to stand up to the objections of our parents, who saw these doings as a deviation from tradition and a lowering of our status, pedigree, and livelihood. Nachum was blessed with this willpower. We sustained ourselves with it, and it gave us the ability to withstand the test of the conflict between fathers and sons.

Thanks to the Pioneer movement's initiative, many people immigrated. Many received the push to immigrate from Nachum, directly and indirectly. But he couldn't immigrate. His weak body was full of energy but eaten up by feebleness. He was afraid that if he immigrated and his body gave out on him, he would be a public burden. He decided to stay behind and didn't immigrate, even though he felt the Holocaust coming more than anyone else did.

***

During the Soviet regime in Vishnevets, vandals of various stripes were permitted to exist. Degenerate young people whose entire dream was to enjoy someone else's labor and who were consumed with hatred for the town's people and Jewish founders of Zionism, came to power and discovered a rare opportunity to fulfill their desires. One of Nachum's students, who had achieved success by flattering the ruling gentiles, allowed himself to denounce the Zionist leaders. He informed the authorities that Nachum was the leader of the Zionist center in town and that he'd led a number of young men toward nationalism. Nachum was put on trial. His student testified against him, saying that Nachum had disgraced Stalin and called him "servant of the nations." Nachum was sentenced to exile.

[Page 201]

Because of the accusation of his former student, who betrayed his teacher, Nachum was exiled to an unknown location, where his pure life ended; his burial place is unknown.

Nachum left a wife, two sons, and many admiring friends who will always carry his blessed name with them.

Nachum was a vessel of strength and blessing for his town, and his many activities motivated that generation.

[Page 202]

In Memory of My Beloved Parents and My Best Friend, Avraham Bisker, of Blessed Memory

by Eliezer Tsinberg (Tel Amal)

Avraham Bisker

I have tried many times to write down my memories of my life with my parents and my friendship with my friend Avraham in Vishnevets, and each time my hand pulls back. I left town long before the horrible Holocaust, and even today, I can't get used to the thought that the busy life in which I also took part no longer exists and will never return.

I lived in Vishnevets for a number of years before immigrating to the Land. My father, a doctor, was director of a hospital in the town of Lanovits and was transferred to Vishnevets to be the district hospital director there. The entire family moved with him to live in a... palace in town.

It was strange to live in a palace that had belonged to a royal prince of Vishnevets.

My father dedicated his heart to his work. It's only from the perspective of time and distance that I can now appreciate my father's work as a doctor. He worked day and night. Many nights, he was awakened to help a sick person in town or a faraway village. More than once, he returned home frozen from being on the road. I remember well when a difficult dysentery epidemic broke out and the whole area was quarantined. We lived next door to the hospital, and the high risk of catching the disease hovered over us. My father worked nonstop without even changing his clothes (he also drafted us to help him). A committee from Warsaw was full of admiration for his work and gave him a medal.

My beloved mother always helped us and managed our home with skill. She dedicated her free time to public works and Zionism. I remember how she helped organize charitable Purim and Chanukah parties for the Jewish National Fund.

My father was also connected to Zionist ideology and donated generously to all Zionist activities. A large number of Pioneers, who did their pioneer training in Vishnevets under difficult conditions, remember my father's help and dedication with kindness. Therefore, I was also able to be active and dedicated myself to my work for the movement.

[Page 203]

I remember that when I decided to leave for a long period of agricultural training, my parents didn't object and helped me with everything, even though they secretly wanted me to continue my studies at the university. They also knew very well that I'd join a kibbutz when I immigrated to the Land.

***

While at the high school in Kremenets, I met Avraham Bisker, who became my best and most loyal friend. We were like twins. It was no surprise that we established a Zionist Youth chapter in town together. We dedicated ourselves to our work with all our young energy, and our work flourished. The chapter grew and gave us a lot of satisfaction, and we lived an active life. We worked together for the Jewish National Fund through the national Pioneer chapter and performed other Zionist and public activities to prove that young people's lives in the Diaspora had substance.

We were helped by two wonderful people: Mr. Y. Shapiro and Mr. Brik, of blessed memory, who immigrated to the Land and built their homes there. I won't forget their dedication to Zionist work, from small, everyday matters to major ones.

Avraham and I dreamed about immigrating, and in our hearts we meant to do so. I knew that Avraham would have trouble with his family, which would hold him back. I immigrated first. I left my friends in the chapter and my friend Avraham, with the hope that we'd meet again in the Land.

I waited for him impatiently.

The war broke out, and the horrifying news began to arrive – destruction, murder, my loved ones among them, my mother and father, and many other family members and friends. My kindhearted father, who had only done good for others, was one of the first to receive payment from the Ukrainian killers that he'd helped more than once; my mother also went after him...

I didn't receive any news about my friend Avraham. I waited for him for a very long time. Maybe he'd arrive the way many others had arrived, but I waited in vain. All I have left is a picture he gave me before I left, with a dedication written on it: "To my beloved brother, from the faithful days we spent together in a warm atmosphere. Very soon, we'll be together in our homeland, the land of our thoughts and longings – be strong. Avraham."

Even today, the image of my town – full of life and activities – remains in my soul. And as in a filmstrip, the images of my loved ones pass before my eyes, and my heart can't comprehend...

[Page 204]

Something about Dad, of Blessed Memory

by Tsvi Katz

Avraham Yehuda Katz

My father, Avraham Yehuda Katz, was one of the most outstanding people in our town. He was loyal and dedicated to his civic work and always in a hurry to help his fellow man. He had an inner balance, he was brave and fearless, and his honorable acts captured the hearts of many. In community life, he came across homeowners who didn't sense the gray future of Polish Jewry, while he was anxious to act on behalf of Zionist ideals.

After World War I, he was among the first to organize the depressed Ukrainian Jews' economic and social life. He served on the City Council in the Kremenets district Jewish community. He acted on behalf of the laborers of our town who lacked work and income. Thanks to his pleading, he was able to get public jobs for Jewish workers in the town from the authorities. He established a carpentry workshop in the Jewish community yard and built furniture for the area government schools. He was also able to get restoration work in the palace. Although the enterprise didn't make money, he was satisfied to be able to provide jobs to the town's Jewish carpenters.

He had a special talent for working with his hands and was a founder of the district's first trade school. He sent his two sons there, and, with difficulty, managed to convince two other teenagers, Mendel Korenfeld and Yehuda Rozin, to attend the school. Nevertheless, the Jews boycotted the trade school. There were only 4 Jewish students among the 300 Christian students. The authorities teased father and showed him how Jews detested manual labor.

He was took part in all Zionist and public fundraisers as a collector and donor.

***

Here are a number of episodes in father's life:

The work ethic was close to father's heart, and he saw in it the terms of the Jewish nation's existence in the Diaspora and the future Jewish homeland.

[Page 205]

He was active among young people in Vishnevets and tried to urge them to change the value of their lives and immigrate to the Land. At a meeting, someone asked father, "Why don't you personally set an example for us?" At that moment, father decided that the young man was right and immigrated to the Land with his four young children.

When the district administrator in Kremenets found out that father was planning to immigrate, he tried to prevent father from taking that step in different ways, saying, "Poland needs Jews like you." Father asked the district administrator in return, "Are there any Jews that Poland doesn't need?"

When the district administrator affirmed his question, Father told him, "This is the reason for my immigration. I'm afraid that sooner or later, it'll be my turn."

We needed to come up with a sum of money, whose amount I can't remember now. The matter was urgent, and father asked the drama club for help. The people agreed under the condition that father take the lead role in the show. They were afraid that, as a respected community leader, he'd be afraid to put his reputation on the line. But father realized the importance of the matter, and took the lead role in the show. He didn't tell my mother and the townspeople about his decision to appear in the show until the last moment, but when the show ended, father was rewarded with extended applause.

When Father reached the Land, he changed his lifestyle, and consistent with his pioneer consciousness, he was one of the first to take on work in the Dead Sea project. He worked there for 17 years. During the War of Independence, he was one of the last employees to be evacuated from Sdom.

By nature, he loved people and saw only the best in them. His home was full of warmth and was always open to those in need.

He was an encouraging figure for young people who worked at the Dead Sea. He was able to overcome his personal and ideological crisis and was always loyal to the party's needs.

My father sacrificed one of his own for the sake of freedom. His dear son, Yosef, was murdered by Arabs in the1936 riots. He mourned him all his life, but he didn't break and was comforted among the mourners of Zion.

The Federation recognized his virtues and allowed him to continue with his fruitful work.

[Page 206]

In Memory of Mr. Avraham Vitels, of Blessed Memory

by Y. N-S

I would like to mention a citizen of our town who wasn't a public figure but whose deeds for his fellow man deserve recognition. I'm talking about Vitels, the lawyer, of blessed memory.

It's true that he didn't study at the university but on his own (according to his daughter, Rachel, who is with us in the Land, he had to hide in a barrel to be able to study). He reached the rank of legal adviser, meaning that he wasn't a certified lawyer.

The area's farmers used his help to settle their boundary arguments.

The Jews also asked his advice, but here he acted according to this principle: a trial can mean a prison sentence for one of the parties, and it's better to postpone it.

Jews asked Mr. Vitels for help in different situations: the Czar's regime hurt a lot of Jews, and legal advice was needed to survive the tyrannical clerks. And this is where Mr. Vitels, of blessed memory, came in.

I remember one incident during World War I. Commander Gomen was acting madly in our town. Many were the Jews that he flogged. I remember that my father, of blessed memory, was one of the candidates for flogging. With Mr. Vitels' intercession, the decree was canceled, and my late father was able to come out of his hiding place. There were many incidents of that order. Mr. Vitels acted quietly, not receiving a reward for his deeds.

May his memory be blessed.

[Page 207]

R' Mordekhay Kechum
by Y. Ron (Shike der Geler)

One of the best-known and best-loved characters in Vishnevets was R' Mordekhay, who limped on one leg and possessed a sharp wisdom. It was said that he had one crooked leg and a straight head. R' Mordekhay was famous for his sharp sayings, and here I'll give a few that I heard him say. By the way, I'll also provide the circumstances in which I heard them.

At that time, we were staying at the home of "Sore Di Osterer," a woman with a personality in which nobility and wealth coexisted. At the end of her, life she willed her store, which stood in the town center, to the synagogue, which was named after her.

Jews went to Sore's home to enjoy the splendor of her homemaking. Mordekhay was one of them. In the evening, he used to come and sit by the big table, where the samovar was ready, and I, a permanent guest in her home, listened to the stories and jokes he told while drinking one cup of tea after another. R' Mordekhay was an expert tea drinker. With no exaggeration, he could drink a dozen cups of tea in one evening. He used to take a piece of sugar, dissect it into 16 miniature grains, suck, and drink tea endlessly.

***

After World War I, it was difficult to find material for suits. One evening, R' Mordekhay walked in, beaming with happiness, and said, "You see, Sore! I'm dressed in royal garments," and he was dressed only in a shirt and coarse, dark khaki pants. We wondered, what's the connection here to royalty? And he explained, "I stitched all that for myself out of a military tent that is the kingdom's property. Therefore, I'm dressed in royal garments."

***

As we know, he had a grocery store. Once a policeman came and wrote him up for a real offense. R' Mordekhay turned to him and said, "Write, write, all this is going to fall on your head." After the policeman folded the report, he took off his hat, which the policemen used as briefcases, put the report in it, put the hat back on his head, and was ready to leave. R' Mordekhay approached him and said, "Wasn't I right when I said that everything you write is going to be on your head?" The policeman, who understood the hint, started to laugh, removed his hat, took the report out, and tore it to pieces.

***

Once during a conversation, R' Mordekhay turned to Sore and asked her, "Tell me, Sore (he was the only one who addressed her, the honorable former rich woman, by her first name), why does almost every woman with a doubtful reputation donate a Torah scroll to the synagogue when she gets old?"

[Page 208]

"I don't know," Sore answered.

R' Mordekhay continued, "It's very simple. She wants everything she did in her youth to be counted as if it had been done before the giving of the law, when she was allowed to do what she wanted."

***

In our time, when Gershon Sirota was one of the greatest cantors in the world and Rozumny was one of the greatest Torah readers, Kopel Zinger was the cantor in Sore Di Osterer's synagogue. He was a handsome Jew who knew how to sing but wasn't rewarded with great wisdom. To Sore, who was related to Kopel, R' Mordekhay said, "Your Kopel is a sirota (orphan in Russian), but rozumny (wise in Russian) he'll never be."

***

When R' Mordekhay argued with someone, he would be the first to attack his opponent, saying, "I have nothing to say to you, since you're a cripple."

By doing so, he used the other person's weapon against him.

***

When we remember Vishnevets, which was full of Jewish hardship and suffering, we remember R' Mordekhay Kechum as our "Hershele Ostropoler [1]," and his image added an interesting color to the bouquet of special people in our town. He was a man who asked for little, overcame his troubles, and turned them into a source of humor.

Translator's Note:

Hershel of Ostropol is a prominent figure in Jewish humor. He is based on a historic figure in Ukraine during the late 18th or early 19th century. return

[Page 209]

Gdalye "Gedoyle"

by Y. Ron

R' Gdalye was a simple Jew. He earned his living from tailoring and lived in poverty all his life. As a tailor, he wasn't one the best. He didn't sew clothes or uniforms; all his work was in mending. His job didn't pay well, and each day he had to work many hours to earn his bread from mending.

Like most people in our town, he had a nickname. I don't know why he was nicknamed Gedoyle; maybe it was because of the wordplay between that and Gdalye, or maybe it was because he emphasized the greatness of the Holy One in his prayers by emphasizing the words "great" and "greatness" in the text and purposely reading in the customary Ashkenazi way. [1]

Among the characters in our town, he was imbued with love and great charm. As a simple and poor man, he saw the spiritual need to do something of his own, bring redemption to the Jewish nation, and increase the Lord's glory through his hard labor.

R' Gdalye-Gedoyle was not a scholar. He found the paths of the prayers in his prayer book not through the correct meaning of the words, but through many years of routine and the arrangement of his prayer book, which had come to him as an inheritance and didn't leave his side for many years.

How could a Jew like R' Gdalye bring complete redemption when his recourses were few? He woke up early on the Sabbath, before the Creator of the world rose, washed his hands, got dressed, and went out into the street to wake the Jews up to worship God. The early morning hour of the Sabbath is an hour of sleep, and as it is known, "It is a joy to sleep on the Sabbath." But it's not a time to sleep when you live in the Diaspora, and Jews should know that, and they'd better wake up and go pray. The Sabbath should be used for something substantial, a redeemer will come to Zion, and we will say amen.

In the stillness of the night, once every seven days, Gdalye's pleasant voice echoed with his extended melody, a melody that was full of sadness about the state of the nation, begging the nation to take its fate in its hands: "Yisrael, Yisrael, holy nation, please get up, please wake up to worship God; you were created for this."

Where did he get the words? Where was the melody from? Nobody knew. But he always used the same version of the same melody. And his voice became stronger and was heard throughout the town streets as he walked around rousing people. And a miracle happened. A number of Jews woke up to the sound of his pleasant melody, listened to Gdalye's begging, came out into the street, and from there went to the synagogue on time.

Suddenly, as if according to a hidden arrangement, doors opened and shadows were seen, starting to make their way to the synagogue, ready for orders.

When Gdalye saw that everyone was awake, he also went into the synagogue. He sat in his corner as they did, because he also complied with his plea and the melody's demand. He "recited" Psalms, chattering "prayers before other prayers" and enjoying the atmosphere this created.

Maybe because of his great confidence in the nation of Israel's deliverance, or maybe because of his great innocence in believing that this was the way to draw it near and that a man must act according to his belief, maybe because of all that, R' Gdalye was great soul, and his nickname came from that.

Translator's Note:

Gedoyle means great.

[Page 211]

On the Nation's Stage

English Translation by Sara Mages

[Page 213]

Betsalel Mishne
by Batye Derbarimdiker (Gosol)

Betsalel Mishne

Betsalel was born in 1914, and like all children in Vishnevets, he studied at cheder, moved on to the Tarbut School, and graduated, but didn't continue his studies.

He lost his father at a young age, and while he was of school age, he had to support himself and his mother. He got a job as a salesman in Moshe Sofer's fabric store. He worked there many hours and found satisfaction in the fact that he could help his mother.

Even so, his soul sought wide-open spaces, and he spent all his free time at the Pioneer branch house in our town.

Later, he left for a training kibbutz in Klosova and immigrated to the Land of Israel. Unluckily for him, 1939 was a year with no immigration certificates, and he had to immigrate illegally on the ship Colorado. After a difficult journey, he arrived in Israel at the end of that year.

He joined Kibbutz Ramat Rachel, and three years later, in 1942, he was drafted into the Jewish Brigade in the name of his kibbutz.

In 1946, he was released from military duty, and he was married on March 18, 1946, just before his discharge.

Mishne didn't return to his kibbutz, which had been dismantled during his service, but stayed in the city. He went to work as a builder, in road construction, or in any available job. Thanks to his diligence and his status as an ex-soldier, he didn't suffer from unemployment. He saved his pennies, and he dreamed of buying a home and starting a family. When he was close to fulfilling his dream, the War of Independence broke out, and as an experienced tank driver, he was one of the first to be drafted into the Israel Defense Forces.

One day, he was able to visit his home and pregnant wife. In another week or a month, he would have become a father, something he wanted so much. But that same night, he was called back to action, and on 3 Tamuz 5709, he fell in the battle of Rosh Pina. No one knew where he died, and for many days, Betsalel was counted among the missing.

With his death, he left a widow, who gave birth five days later to his son, Avitsur, who is now a certified engineer.

We will remember Betsalel Mishne, a man from Vishnevets and a responsible volunteer, as a proud son of our town.

Page 214]

Ben-Tsion (Bentsi) Tsur,
of Blessed Memory

by His Parents

Ben-Tsion (Bentsi) Tsur

Bentsi was born in Haifa on 4 Heshvan 5707, the second son in his family.

At his parents' home and at school, he absorbed a love of his homeland and an unlimited dedication to its values. During his school years, he was active in the Israel Scouts movement and Gadna [1]. He took part in all classes, notably the section commander course, which he finished with distinction.

He was a talented actor and an excellent accordion player.

When he finished his final exams in summer 5725, he asked his parents to sign a document permitting him to leave school immediately, before he turned 18.

At the recruiting center, he volunteered to serve in an elite unite of the Armored Corps and was sent to one of the brigades in the Negev.

For close to a year, he endured difficult training that included courses in navigation, driving, and section and reconnaissance command, and he completed them with great success.

On the completion of his courses, he was appointed the brigade's operations sergeant and carried out his duty loyally.

He was liked by his unit because of his kind heart and his talent for entertainment and music. Bentsi was always the center of graduation parties or even just an evening around the campfire. He organized all the graduation parties.

[Page 215]

When battles broke out, he fought in the armored truck division and took part in the battle in Khan-Yunis and the Rafiah junction. According to his commanding officer, he was a good fighter, and together they cleared fortified posts.

As the battle continued, his armored truck was hit, and during a reorganization, Bentsi asked to join his friends Shaul and Yoram, of blessed memory, in the lead jeep.

In the battle on the El-Jirady post on the road to El-Arish, the jeep was hit by a tank shell, and all three were killed.

In one of his last letters during the preparation period, he wrote to his mother, "Don't worry, Mother, you should be proud to have a son over here."

And indeed, we're trying to find comfort in the fact that he gave his soul for the sake of the nation of Israel, since his only wish was to continue to live in his homeland.

He was nineteen and a half when he fell in battle.

May his memory be blessed.

Translator's Note:

Gadna is premilitary training for teenagers. return

[Page 216]

Neta Hadari
by Yakov Chachkis

Neta Hadari

Neta was born on January 14, 1945, in Givat Hashlosha. During his childhood, he heard the echoes of the Nazi war and absorbed the horrors of the murder of his nation. As a youth, he lived through the War of Independence and our victory in the Sinai operation, when the country's borders expanded and it was liberated from the danger of infiltrators.

Neta Hadari fell in combat at the age of 22-1/2, just before the reunification of Jerusalem and the liberation of the Old City. He was one of the paratroopers killed on Ammunition Hill, and his name is honored and embroidered in the legends of heroes.

At a young age, he lost his father, Izye Hadari. He was educated in Givat Hashlosha and cared for by his mother, who had six sons and daughters. Her family was one of the largest in Israel.

When he reached the age of 18, he joined a Fighting Pioneer Youth corps that was planning to settle in Kibbutz Palmach Tsuba in the Judea Mountains, where he joined the paratroopers.

When he returned home, he met Rachel Rozen of Vishnevets, who became his wife. He got married and fulfilled his dream of building a home and family. As a young father, he was privileged to raise his firstborn son, but not his daughter.

His son and daughter were orphaned, and his wife was widowed at a young age: too young, much too young.

We'll never know how long young people like them will become orphans and join the ranks of the bereaved. But we know that we'll never forget the sacrifice of those who allow us to breathe the air of our liberated, expanded, and strong homeland.

Neta Hadari, a Vishnevets son-in-law, is someone to be proud of from our generation and someone whose name is worth remembering.

Page 217]

Our Dead in the Nation

English Translation by Sara Mages

[Page 219]

Azriel Kubrik

by Yitschak Ben-Tsvi

Second President of the State of Israel

When I returned home from a conference in London, the sad news about the death of my old friend, a friend who had been close to me since childhood – Azriel Kubrik – was waiting for me. Azriel was a beloved friend, a member of the Second Immigration, who escaped and immigrated to the Land holding the workers' flag in his hand long before the name Pioneer was known in the world. He was born in Podolia (or Vohlin) and came to Poltava during his youth. I met him for the first time when he was a soldier in the Russian army. He settled in that town later on, in 5665, and was active in the Zionist movement. Azriel Kubrik was one the first Russian Labor Zionist activists in Poltava, where the party had been established 40 years earlier, and he took an active part in all the party's doings, which were held in secret during the czar's regime. Azriel devoted himself mostly to matters of Jewish defense, to which Poltava's Labor Zionist activists dedicated their best efforts and resources during the October 1905 (5666) riots against the Jews. With Labor Zionist support, a Jewish defense force was established in Poltava (in 1905-1906), gathering under its flag hundreds of young men and women who were party members and a group of Zionist youth who were not. A dedicated and loyal instructor, gifted with courage and valor, who earned the appropriate technical knowledge during his time in the army – this was member A. Kubrik.

I remember the secret meetings in those days that took place at different synagogues in town, obviously illegally. At the meetings, in which Yakov Plotkin, of blessed memory, also took part, we demanded sacrifice from the Jewish community: we asked for financial donations from the adults, and we asked the young people to join the defense force with their bodies and souls. To many, Azriel Kubrik served as a symbol and an example of a man of good deeds and action.

And as a man of deeds and action, he immigrated to the Land during the Second Immigration, and during his life, he was devoted to the words of our Sages, of blessed memory: "Actions speak louder than words." He labored in the city, he labored in the settlement, he worked in agriculture, he was a dear and loyal friend – and so he remained until the day he died: modest and kindhearted, dedicated to his idealism. He left us before his time without a replacement, leaving behind a wife, a soldier son, and a daughter.

May his soul be bound up in the bond of everlasting life, and may his memory not be forgotten by his friends or the next generation as a symbol of a dedicated pioneer who was loyal to our concept until his dying day.

[Page 220]

Duvid Roynik,
of Blessed Memory
by Meir Or

Duvid Roynik

Duvid came from a family of rabbis and Hasidim. He was full of Torah and good virtues, respectful, and well mannered. He was educated in the Dubno maggid's words and the Vilna Gaon's Law passages. He was a true believer in a Zionist future. His virtue was a revolutionary's virtue: from the pillar of the study hall to the ritual of a settlement laborer, from a rabbi's table to working the land, and from a rich man's estate to a settler's tent.

From a wealthy home, he went to desolate Merhavia and conquered its hill. Together with the first settlers, he clung to the desolate, forgotten earth and rejuvenated it.

Without kibbutz pioneer training and without knowing the younger generation's ways, he outlined a way to fulfill his pioneer duty immediately after immigrating. He found his way in the Land of Israel not according to a prearranged plan, but through an inner force, with his healthy mind and pioneer senses.

When he experienced difficult days of great poverty, he plowed on stubbornly with patience and rare tolerance. He sowed, paved the way for his descendants, and left behind him a generation that continued his pioneer work. All his family members settled in working settlements: Beit She'arim, Kfar Yehoshua, Kfar Chagla, and Kfar Vitkin.

The man knew how to direct different lifestyles and combine them into one main road, how to observe his patriarchs' tradition and sing the younger generation's songs, and how to lay foundations by using the old and the new to build his renewed homeland.

Wherever he turned, he gained friends and admirers, and maintained a seriousness of life and action. He blotted out difficult moments with humor and celebration. He carried his pain during bitter times with a Hasidic fervor. He inspired others with his honesty and trust. Like an experienced diver, he dived to the depth of the fountain of life and raised the good out of the bad. In spite of his old age, his body and soul were young and fresh.

May his memory be blessed.

[Page 221]

More about Shimon Ayzenberg

(As Told by the People of His Town and His Era)

...When his father died, Shimon continued with his life's work. He packed small bags of flour and packages of live fish and delivered them to the town's needy.

The people of Vishnevets saw the poor waiting and marking their places in line at the Ayzenbergs' store.

...The material and spiritual help he gave Duvid Roynik in the Land was the most famous of all, and all Vishnevetsers were blessed by it.

...When Shimon was in Beersheba, a Jew by the name of Gordon built a flourmill and became rich. When Gordon found out that Shimon was a great expert in grinding flour from abroad, he asked him to stay with him, with the intention of having him marry his young daughter, who was beautiful and ...spoiled.

Shimon was not tempted and went up to settle in Merhavia.

A while later, Gordon sent his daughter to Merhavia, hoping that she could succeed in what she'd failed to do in Beersheba.

Shimon welcomed her and showed her the marvels of Jewish farming. When the beautiful youngster saw a tender calf after it was born, she told everyone how "the mule gave birth to the little mule." That's when Shimon decided she was not for him.

And so Shimon was saved from a successful "matchmaking."

[Page 222]

A Time to Mourn…

From a Memorial Service Eulogy

by Meir Or

We mourn here this evening a group of friends who were uprooted from us for eternity. Only a few of us were left after Hitler's flood and the terror of his days. When they came from our town, little by little, one family, one soul, and arrived in a safe harbor, we blessed each family, and we were happy with each soul. We hugged the survivors with happiness, respect, and brotherly love, because we saw the remnants of our brothers and our precious families in them, and now we are mourning again.

The heart grieves; in one year we have had to memorialize five of our loving friends. Chaye Marchbeyn, Yitschak Rabin, Yehoshue Zeyger, and the sisters Henye and Sime.

***

Chaye Marchbeyn passed through all the stages of suffering during the conflict between the hostile regimes. When she arrived in our homeland, she immediately poured out her bitter heart during our first conversation and told a horrifying story of how she had struggled for her life under each regime and the foreign regimes' never-ending, humiliating afflictions. More than once, she had to submit herself to the rulers' state of mind during her day-to-day push for survival. In our conversation, she talked about personal acts of heroism by people who lived in hell. Like "pierced-ear" slaves, they were beaten and tortured at the hands of the beasts of prey. She was happy that it was behind her, she was happy for the great blessing of finally being in the Land and for the fact that she could celebrate her freedom and liberty in the Land of Israel every day. But Chaye was not credited with many years of happiness in her homeland.

May her memory be blessed,

***

Yitschak Rabin was a loyal friend. He was full of energy and worked confidently. He always cared for others – with advice and instructions, and with their livelihood. I know at least three incidents when Yitschak helped a number of families settle and get established, caring for them like a dedicated father. It is possible that sometimes we were unkind to him and caused him grief by pointing out his mistakes. But this was his power, the power that forced us to listen to him. He had a sort of active core that stimulated him to think. With the power of his serious, kindhearted personality and his good sense of humor and cheerfulness, he took the sting out of every argument and directed the words to the topic and the essence of the subject. Yitschak knew how to be strong-minded, but at times, without a shadow of ambition, he gave in and accepted the words of those who argued with him, even though he remained firm in his victorious opinion and he had trouble adapting to others' opinions.

The late Yitschak could inspire trust in his fellow man's heart and in the hearts of the desperate and disappointed. He had a maturity of thought and the ability to understand a man in need. He always had a kind approach and always responded to the sufferings of others with charm and a friendly expression.

He worked as a board member in our organization without favoritism, and with sincerity and the naked truth. He was as consistent and firm as a rock.

[Page 223]

He excelled in his work at Hameshakem [1], because his character and virtues were appropriate for a job that required him to understand those who had failed, encourage the elderly, and rehabilitate human beings.

There was a sort of inner strength in the way Yitschak approached a target he had set for himself. I visited him for the first time in Bat Yam right after it was established. He lived in a dilapidated hut. He dug himself in in Bat Yam, grasping the place with his fingernails. He worked harder and harder, brick by brick, with diligence and great dedication, until he had a splendid and well-built home.

Fate was so cruel to him and his family. Just when Yitschak was ready to end the first page of his life and get ready for his son's wedding, standing at the entrance of a new period in his life when he could enjoy the rewards of his hard work, Yitschak was snatched suddenly and shockingly.

Last, Yitschak was dedicated to and responsible toward his family. He was a wonderful father to his children, talking to them like a friend. He knew how to live well in all conditions and situations. He knew how to enjoy life as the offspring of a good family. Happiness flowed in his circle of family and friends.

We honor him, and his loving memory will remain in our hearts.

***

Yehoshue Zeyger. The day before the accident, Yehoshue Zeyger stood before me, strong and clear-minded. It was impossible to think that death was hovering between us and that it would kill him so suddenly, in only 20 hours. Who would think something like this could happen – that the next day, in the middle of a meeting in Tel Aviv, I would receive the sad news about Yehoshue's death?

Yehoshue walked among us without a sound and without a swing, but with peace and tranquility. His words were well measured, actual and not painted. Everything he said was said in simple words with inner weight and mature thought. He didn't push to be in the lead because he didn't like "rowdy" public work. But he had a clear mind when it came to public matters and a clear inner conviction.

When Yehoshue saw himself without a future or purpose in the busy town of Vishnevets, which was immersed in its gray life, he broke out into the big world, got up, and immigrated to America to build a new life. But over there he, like many others, couldn't adjust to a new life in a foreign country that was flooded with materialism. Although the man could live in difficult situations with patience and great tolerance, his soul couldn't cope with a "peddler's" difficult work. With the outbreak of World War I, Yehoshue returned to Vishnevets like a wounded animal returning to its cave. The man was very disappointed until he could overcome his crisis. Thanks to his vigor, peaceful personality, and calm soul, he was able to continue as if nothing had happened.

When he saw an empty void before him in a life full of struggle for honor, a burning love for the Land of Israel and the will to immigrate overtook him. What caused him to immigrate wasn't just his Zionist recognition, but also the new rising culture, the original Jewish culture acquired diligently through dedication to its origin, because Yehoshue was an educated man.

[Page 224]

Ever since he had equipped himself with a "graduation certificate" from the praised Rabbi Simche Ayzik, of blessed memory, Yehoshue had dived to the recesses of human spirit and scientific achievement. By himself, and also with the help of our teacher Mordekhay Blekh-Ben-Tsvi, of blessed memory, he drew knowledge from universal science journals, and with great diligence and a dedication to reading, he accumulated common knowledge.

He was quiet by nature, but he expressed himself powerfully in writing. His beautiful, picturesque articles, in which he wrote about general matters and our town, are loyal testimonies. In his articles, we find lifestyles described as if they're pictures of the local people in words, as well as a review of various organizations and institutions. He was the archivist of various events and historical periods of life in Vishnevets.

His path in the Land of Israel was one of the hardest. He had difficulty putting down roots and adjusting to hard labor. Only his strong will sustained him, helping him overcome these difficult tests. He didn't trust people or donors. He fought with his own fingers, strengthening himself and reaching the age of retirement, prosperity, rest, and tranquility.

Yehoshue was educated according to the Zeyger family tradition, which opposed splendor and self-promotion. They were rich, but they didn't brag about their wealth. Although they were members of the local upper class, they lived simply and modestly, resisting dishonesty.

He reacted logically to public affairs. For many years, he was loyal to his outlook and took a stand without deviation because he was solid and firm in his opinions.

May his image be bound in our memory.

***

The sisters Henye and Sime. Henye kept her distance from the center of our life and our organization. She appeared only every once in a while, and then we saw her as continuing the Chachkis tradition as one of the first immigrants who dared to fulfill their Zionist duty. So she's not a stranger to us, and we remain privileged to have her as one of us. Henye was saturated with Zionist spirit, went through the strengthening melting pot, and endured the pain of absorption. When her situation in the country was uncertain, without the security to survive from day to day, she endured it all through self-sacrifice by giving up her social life, including her friends from Vishnevets.

May her memory be for a blessing and be engraved in the hearts of her family, friends, and loved ones.

Sime. Along with Sime, the image of a dedicated and loyal friend has gone. She was a Jewish mother in all her qualities and a loyal wife to our teacher and rabbi Mordekhay Ben-Tsvi, of blessed memory. With their immigration came the pains of new beginnings, days of financial distress, and hard physical labor. The Ben-Tsvi family experienced difficult times. Mordekhay, of blessed memory, worked at unskilled labor. He had to explain the lyrics to the song "To the Bird" and the mask from "The Talmud Student," by Chayim Nachman Bialik, with the black coal he worked with at the rail yard. He was happy with his lot and rejoiced in the joy of creation. Sime took part in his daily struggle and suffered greatly. Even so, she could listen to others' troubles, and because of that, she aroused respect and admiration.

She was an actress by nature. During a meeting, she would sit in a corner on the side and listen to every sound and whisper; she was far away but so close to us, like a sister.

[Page 225]

She gained a place in our organization with modesty and a deep understanding of her duty. And while she experienced financial difficulties, she possessed a limitless love for her country. Like a good Jewish mother, she spread her wings beyond the boundaries of her family, kept in touch with the organization, and took care of those in need.

It was the time of the riots. Heavy clouds covered the sky in the Land of Israel. The murderers' bullets buzzed and killed. Our young people fell here and there, in each corner of the country. Hatred spread after the Arabs' wild provocation.

Gangs of murderers swarmed the fields, vineyards, and roads, and ambushed the to be a watchman in the most dangerous locations in Samaria. Our young men risked their lives to prevent the riots and protect people and property. During the ceasefire, Azriel came to visit us in Hadera and stayed with us. I visited Sime then to bring her a message from her only son. Who can explain the agony and tears that Sime endured night after night waiting for her son Azriel, wanting to see him alive, making sure the murderers' bullets didn't touch him? But when I spoke to her, she was calm, suffocating her pain and restraining herself silently. With silent pain and great courage, she fortified herself so she could fulfill her civic duty as a Jewish mother in the renewed country. She drew her courage from her love of Zion and was ready with all her existence for physical and emotional pain on behalf of what was dear to all of us.

We appreciated her during her life, we admired her and her simplicity, and we'll also remember her after her death.

Translator's Note:

Hameshakem is an organization that arranges employment for the elderly and the physically challenged. return

[Page 226]

Chayim Zev Barkay
by Meir Or

Chayim Zev Barkay

When it happened that Chayim Volf Brik, of blessed memory, from Pochayev, married Leyeke Shpigelman, may she be set apart for long life, it was said that Vishnevets was blessed with one fine young man.

And so it was.

With his appearance, it was clear to everyone on first impression that a star had stepped down from the sky and promised to sprout. And indeed, he promised, and he didn't let us down.

Barkay volunteered and added to our public life from his great resources as a promoter of cultural projects: the Jewish National Fund, the Foundation Fund, and other cultural fields.

He was dedicated to the Tarbut School, which was the spiritual center of Vishnevets, and helped found it.

When the town was alive with many streams of Zionism, Barkay also belonged to a certain Zionist party. But Barkay wasn't like the others. While Zionist activity occurred within the town's political structure, Barkay always chose a broad line for himself, not like the zealots who enslaved themselves to their narrow limits. He regarded political struggle with disgust; he was kind and showed moderation toward each segment in order to draw the best and most helpful from each fragment of the tribes of Israel, taking the point of view: "pick the best from everywhere." I can't remember seeing Barkay angry, irritated, or annoying others. He was always kind to people and kept away from quarrels and disputes.

My meetings with Barkay always left an impression on me because he knew how to radiate friendship and companionship toward those he encountered. There were contrasts in him that complemented each other: Hasidic enthusiasm, quiet deeds, modesty, the setting of others in motion, inner peace, and storming of crowds.

Barkay's immigration to Israel with his young children was a sort of adventure that came from his spiritual need to fulfill his life's wish.

[Page 227]

He did it with a daring Zionist leap into an unknown future, with a clear decision to disassemble yesterday's chains, no matter what.

When he arrived in the Land of Israel, he settled in a work camp and neglected his former occupation in trade because he saw labor as a way to connect with his nation in his homeland.

He worked at the Israel Electric Company with dedication and cared about the organization's growth. For that reason, he was promoted by his superiors with recognition and respect.

Barkay was blessed with a family of rare quality. With his wife, Leyeke, he turned their home into a cocoon of love that was full of mutual respect and understanding.

The family members were united, holding onto each other with loyalty. It was a pleasure to visit Barkay's home to absorb the calm that prevailed there.

While still in the Diaspora, Barkay cared for his children's Jewish education, training them for good citizenship and loyalty to their nation and homeland.

It isn't by chance that two of his sons serve as generals in the Israel Defense Forces, giving themselves to their country's needs and the demands of the era. We bless his offspring, and we'll remember his glorious name for eternity.

[Page 228]

Simche Zak,
of Blessed Memory
by Meir Or

Simche Zak,
of Blessed Memory

Simche was one of the fine young men of our town who, under the patronage of their teacher and rabbi Mordekhay Blekh (Bentsvi, of blessed memory), dug deep into the Bible to cultivate the Hebrew-in-Hebrew method to teach the language of the past to the nation.

He was modest and dedicated himself to his reading and studies, but no one noticed that in his calm, his active soul was yearning for Zion, action, and fulfillment.

When he got up and immigrated, it was discovered that Simche was also a man of decision and action.

He was a pioneer in everything. To all appearances, he was a publisher, but in fact he was more than that. He published literature for the pleasure of many, and "produced" literature readers. In the course of time, he published books of substance.

I had the opportunity to stay at his home a number of times and watch him proofread. Simche Zak didn't trust other proofreaders, since he wanted to leave his mark on the subject, the language, and the style.

Simche also knew how to respect his masters and show kindness toward a writer, encourage him (to appreciate his literary work), and give him the fair profit he deserved.

It seems to me that there aren't many publishers like him in the nation. He accompanied a book from the time it was in the writers' belly, fathered it with encouragement, and escorted it with his expert eye through all stages until it was printed.

I visited his home after the blockade on Jerusalem was lifted and found him happy with the partial liberation of Jerusalem. He tied his fate to our Jerusalem, escorting his sons with happiness when they left for a battle, and he counted each battle as a battle for Jerusalem, even if it was in the Negev, the North, or the desert.

With his death and during his struggle with death, it was discovered that Simche was a proud member of his generation, and that's how we'll remember him.

[Page 229]

Yitschak Rabin

by Meir Or

We knew him as a boy with curly hair and red cheeks, the oldest of three orphaned brothers who came from the town of Tshan to our town Vishnevets as refugees from Petliura's camps after the riots in Ukraine. Like other refugees from Tshan, they brought an advanced, fresh style to our town's monotonous way of life. According to everyone, he was like a child prodigy, with a splendid face, beauty, and charm. He grew in front of our eyes, attaching himself to the Pioneer movement in our town and setting out on his own road to pioneer training and immigration in order to fulfill his Zionist duty.

I remember when I visited him for the first time in Bat-Yam, being one of its first settlers. The town, which is blooming now, was still in its infancy. He laid in front of me a selection of stories about the struggles of the first days. He spoke with joy about his adventures during the first years, his intermediate stations, and the many different jobs he worked in before he settled there – and all with the special joy he used to influence everyone who came into contact with him, asking for his advice and instructions.

He cared for his brothers in trouble with dedication and without weariness, and assisted new immigrants with their arrangements. It's no wonder that he excelled in his job at Hameshakem, because his qualities and virtues suited that work: a soft heart, the ability to understand those who stumbled with diligence and dedication, and the ability to encourage the elderly and rehabilitate people. He also had the talent to plant confidence in his fellow man's heart and trust in the desperate and disappointed. Because he understood a man in need, he responded to him with warmth, grace, and happiness. He accepted a person's qualities and deficiencies, and because of that, he was willing to carry the suffering of others on his shoulders out of personal responsibility.

He was an active committee member for our organization and performed properly, with sincerity and without bias or compromise. When it was time for him to receive a reward for his work, he was snatched from us at the best time of his life, a few days before his son's wedding.

[Page 230]

Moshe Goldshub,
of Blessed Memory
by Meir Or

Moshe Goldshub,
of Blessed Memory

This man's eyes saw murder and destruction. He carried pain in his soul and scars on his flesh from two periods of destruction that passed through Vishnevets and the people who lived there.

The man was filled with bitterness by two cruel regimes: the Nazi and the Soviet, which left their marks on his body and soul.

It's understandable that he, too, a hero among men, shattered. His death cast sorrow on us.

Moshe was lively in his deeds and emotions. He listened to his fellow man's sufferings, shaking himself like a lion to answer his Jewish brothers.

We had the impression that he kept to himself, but his heart was open to every request for help at any time it came to him.

During the Russian regime in our town, he was appointed administrator of the flourmill. Many received their bread from his hands, and he did this with difficulty and by putting himself in danger.

After the beastly storm that took over the world, when the war ended, he returned to Vishnevets knowing that there was nothing for him there. He went to avenge the blood of our town's Jewish martyrs. Strong and powerful, he took revenge with his own hands on the leaders of those who spilled our blood and killed many of our disloyal neighbors. He took revenge at their homes, sending his holy bullets in front of their family members and bringing honor to our slaughtered nation.

I remember visiting him after he arrived in the Land. We sat for hour after hour, and like a burning torch, he spoke about the misfortune of his community, his friends, his parents, and our parents. He was completely fire with revenge and didn't hold back.

He was a righteous man, and when we met, he never ceased to demand just one favor, an act of true kindness for the martyrs of Vishnevets. He who had taken care of the mass graves day after day was driven to build a memorial for them here in our country. When he found out about the book that was to be published, his wounds healed, and his tension eased.

He was an honest, well-established working man in our country who saw blessing in his work and looked forward to a little satisfaction, but suddenly, he was snatched by death.

May his memory be carved in this book, which he eagerly awaited.

[Page 231]

My Father, Yehuda,
and My Mother, Sore

by Tikve (Rozental) Sklod

I see an obligation, not only as a daughter but also as a partner in the Vishnevets organization and its memorial book, to mention my parents, Yehuda and Sore Rozental, who were among the first immigrants from the town.

They immigrated in 1922, after dreaming for years about returning to Zion and after persistent conversations at home about immigrating to the Land.

Our uncle, Duvid Roynik, who never stopped engaging all members of his family in this thought, planted the concrete will to immigrate in them. In their imagination, they saw themselves settling in the country, sitting under their own vine and fig tree.

Their rich father, who listened to the whispers of his sons' hearts, bought them property in Israel, and the road to fulfilling their dream was open. But when they arrived in the Land, they found out that their property was registered in the name of the "trustworthy" buyer. They were naked and in great poverty, and had no way to support themselves.

My uncle, Duvid Roynik, was not at a loss. He bought mules and cows, and the two of them, he and my father, got jobs as cart drivers while the women took care of the cow shed. Many days later, my father felt that he couldn't cope with the work and opened a grocery store in Tel Aviv. But his practical Zionist conscience bothered him, so he sold his store and went to work as a hired hand.

In Heshvan 1945, my father died, full of bitterness and disappointment that he couldn't fulfill even half of his dream, but he was consoled by the fact that he was one of the first to return to the homeland, a privilege that a man should not dismiss. A few years later, my mother, Sore Rozental, also died.

May their souls and their memory be bound within us.

Yehuda Rozental and Sore Roynik
Roaming the Villages to Earn a Living after World War I

[Page 232]

Sore, Duvid Roynik's Daughter
(Words Said at Her Graveside)
by Mikhael Goldberg

A real friendship existed between us for many years, from the time she arrived in the Land with her family in 1922.

Before she came, I was a friend of her father, R' Duvid, of blessed memory (he immigrated to the Land a year before the family arrived). I greatly admired R' Duvid's loving personality.

He was descended from a family of rabbis and was learned, with a noble soul, and along with that, he was imbued with a pioneer spirit.

We were young pioneers – excited and wild.

And here before us was a dignified, handsome Jew with a long beard who reflected respect and nobility. He also worked with us in construction and public work, full of enthusiasm for building the land. He spoke in pure Hebrew, and his soul sought a laborer's life of honesty and justice.

The family arrived: the mother and children. The oldest daughter, Sore, spoke pure Hebrew and was learned in literature, educated, and clever, with a clear mind.

The period of adjustment was not long, and in a short time, she entered the working life, turned to her studies at a teacher's college, and also carried the load of helping at home.

We were neighbors (we lived in a hut neighborhood) and good friends. We saw our residency in Tel Aviv as temporary. The yearning to settle had followed us from the Diaspora. When I offered to join the group of settlers who were going up to the Merhavia settlement, R' Duvid enthusiastically accepted the offer, and the family moved there.

Sore had to stop her studies at the teacher's college. She accepted the decision willingly. She gave up her career as a teacher and dedicated herself to agriculture and farming.

Conditions were very difficult.

The land was barren, and there was no water (barely enough for drinking). Life was difficult due to lack of experience, dilapidated housing, and a difficult climate.

It was difficult to support a large family in such conditions. The entire family worked diligently, like a community of ants in a field, in the garden and cow shed.

Sore worked hard, as all of us did, quietly, seriously, and without grumbling. She never complained about the difficult situation; she didn't hesitate or despair.

[Page 233]

She loved farming and the village. From her father, she inherited a desire for justice and the dedication to pursue and fulfill an idea.

Some years later, she married her heart's choice, and together they moved to build Kfar Yehoshua.

Here, a difficult life began again, but Sore, who was used to suffering, set about creating a farm with all her energy.

Those were the pangs of creation, and she was greatly satisfied.

Her friends appreciated and liked her. She was active in the community, dedicated, diligent, and enthusiastic – and again without grumbling. A wide smile always covered her face, even if fate brought her bitterness.

Because of a difficult situation, she had to leave her beloved village and move to the Tel Aviv area (Ramat Gan).

I saw sadness and longing on her face, and she was restless, but on the outside she was quite as she had always been.

"How are you? Good, everything is fine!" And the same lovely smile.

She started to recover, found a job, and was also active in public life. During the blood riots before World War II, she dedicated herself to her activities in the Haganah. [1]

I met her at dawn, running through the lanes of the orange groves and instructing a group of young people (even now I don't know what kind of job she held in the Haganah). A secret! She said to me, "Where are you running to, Sore! Is it necessary …yes …necessary."

This was the line of her character: dedication to a social idea and dedication without boundaries.

And everything was done with modesty, with humility, and without the desire to stand out.

She didn't find satisfaction in city life. "I long for Kfar Yehoshua and my friends."

She told me, what meaning is there in this life? It has no foundation or roots…

In the end, she returned to the village and her beloved group of friends, who welcomed her with love and warmth. Again, she dedicated herself to public work and her auxiliary farm.

With love, she nourished each plant and tree in her ornamental garden with talent and knowledge.

In this case, it looked as if the family had reached a state of peace and security. Member Ben-Chayim was working at village institutions, Sore was also working, and their son was growing up and getting an education with the village children. Here he was enlisting in the army, and here there was a wedding for the son. What a blessing! Faces beamed with happiness, a mother's blessing! The wedding party was modest, and friends and relatives met. How pleasant it was to meet after not seeing each other for so many years. What intimacy. We kissed, hugged, and brought up memories of our teenage years.

Sore beamed with happiness.

We didn't want to tire her out. We knew she was suffering from heart disease, but she didn't want to submit to it.

She had great charm and a strong will to live, work, and create.

I remember that when I visited her at the hospital, I witnessed a conversation between her and her family members. She inquired about each detail of her farm, including the chicks in the chicken coop, the trees, and the flowers.

[Page 234]

She gave various instructions on how to run her farm.

Is it true that she didn't know about her serious illness? I asked her, "How are you, Sore?" "All right! I'm in a good mood today. I have a very interesting book, and I completely forgot that I'm in a hospital." She liked books very much. They were like good friends throughout her life.

When we left her, she said (again with the same smile!), "It's going to be all right! Don't worry."

She showed optimism and the will to live even though her life was full of suffering and struggle.

Her loving image will remain engraved on our hearts forever.

Translator's Note:

Haganah (literally, defense) was a paramilitary organization during the British Mandate.

[Page 235]

The Sofer Brothers

English Translation by Sara Mages

[Page 237]

About Yosef Sofer
by Hentsye Zak

Yosef Sofer

In 1921, when he was still young, he immigrated from Vishnevets and was among the first to arrive in the Land.

As a son of a respected, affluent, and well-known family, he was sent to Odessa to get an education. At that time, Zionist idealism entered his heart, and he decided to immigrate here. It was a daring decision, and his parents couldn't prevent him from carrying it out.

In the Land, he settled in Tel Aviv and lived in hardship in a hut with a comrade. It was a dilapidated hut whose roof leaked when it rained. Yosef worked a few days a week in construction and had a hard time earning a living. But he was always in a good mood. Happy and joyful, he visited all the Vishnevetsers in Tel Aviv, and everyone praised him.

A few years before World War II, his parents pressured him to return "home" so they could see him for a short time, but in their hearts, they were hoping he'd agree to stay with them, and he responded. He stayed abroad for a while and married Lola. We were all worried that he wouldn't return to the Land, but how surprised we were when we found out that he was returning to us with his wife.

This time, he didn't go to Tel Aviv. Haifa attracted him, and he settled there. Again, the pangs of absorption faced him, and again he had to adjust to a new location, new connections, and a new society. With great effort, he got a job at Solel Boneh [1]. In this company, he showed great skill at his work and dedication to the company's affairs, and he became one of the senior administrators at Herut, a Solel Boneh subsidiary company.

At that time, his situation improved. He obtained a nice apartment, and he enjoyed life and the rewards of his work. But unexpectedly, Yosef, who was in good health, contracted heart disease, which stayed with him and attacked him, attack after attack. After a number of attacks, his heart was silenced. He died in 1955.

Then we mourned the loss of a good friend, and we kept his memory alive. Now, with the publication of Sefer Vishnevets, we'll write his name before us, and we'll remember him for eternity.

Translator's Note:

Solel Boneh (literally, Paving and Building) is the oldest and one of the largest construction and civil engineering companies in Israel. return

[Page 238]

Yakov Sofer, of Blessed Memory
by Meir Or

Yakov Sofer

I knew Yakov from the time he was a child. We were neighbors. I saw him at all stages of life: as a cheder student, at the secular school, and as a teenager with an appetite for education who exchanged books at the library and swallowed them thirstily. Afterward, I saw him as a young man seeking a brighter future, searching for an outlet and relief from his difficulties, walking like a shadow between us, like us, in our town's gloomy life.

Yakov inherited some rare qualities from his father, R' Issakher Sofer: kindness, patience, forgiveness, forbearance, openness to the sighs of his fellow man, and the will to help him.

His social sense was engraved in him as part of his being. I, who was older than he was by half his age, realized he was unusual. There was kind of warmth in him that enticed anyone who met him. He was a loyal friend who maintained his friendship to perfection, without showing off. His friendship flowed from his personality without any special effort, as an order from his conscience and through knowledge of the person.

In the Land, he passed through the different stages of life that were typical of our generation: pioneer training, living in a kibbutz, and a position in the city at Tnuva [1].

In all the various stages of his life and within his social framework, he was given to helping those who experienced personal difficulties. He assisted those in need with action, advice, and direction, and by taking every possible advantage of all possibilities connected to his role at Tnuva and derived from his connections with various organizations in the country.

I know of one family that was orphaned and abandoned after Yakov's death. A few days after his death, the head of the family came to me and told me that Yakov had been his only savior, the only one who had substantially cared for his existence, and he concluded, "We've passed through various stages of hell in our lives, and we didn't break as we broke when our beloved Yakov died."

Two weeks before his passing, I visited him at his place of work.

I happened to be there exactly on the day when Tnuva's offices were moving to their new home. Yakov, as he always did, took care of each detail of his department's transfer.

[Page 239]

I said to him, "Yankeli, you were ordered to take care of your health. What's this uproar? What's this extra effort, why are you pushing yourself?"

And he answered me, "I know my condition. A disaster could happen any day or any time, so I take my mind off it by continuing to work as if my condition weren't so bad."

Apparently Yakov knew what was coming to him and didn't deny it.

With his death, we lost a man and a dear friend. His loss will be felt in various circles, mostly in the community of our Vishnevets brothers. He cared for their organization and carried its burden since its establishment.

Translator's Note:

Tnuva is a co-op in Israel specializing in dairy products. return

[Page 240]

Asher Sofer
by Ts. R.

Asher Sofer

From the time he was a child, Asher showed us that whatever road he took, he wouldn't turn aside from what appeared right and correct to him, even if his road were exceptional and unlike others.

He was serious in his deeds, loyal to his heart's commands, and righteous and noble in his business dealings. His movement recognized him as an outstanding member and "honorable" graduate, and invited him to work at the Betar center in Warsaw.

At the height of the Holocaust, Asher escaped to the Land and searched for a chance to save his family members.

Asher experienced strange adventures in the Land; even if he planned them himself, he was surprised by the outcome. By chance, Asher joined Anders Polish army to take revenge on the Nazis who had spilled our blood, but he deserted, wounded in his soul and hopeless.

Asher experienced some suffering in his private life in the Land and wandered from job to job, from being a janitor at the municipality building in Tel Aviv to being an office clerk in Netanya. He was cut off from his acquaintances and friends and alone with the worries he had to solve himself, without imposing on others. He carried his suffering silently and with inner tranquility.

When Asher reached the point of building a home and family, he reached the height of his happiness. When the country was at full strength and his family bloomed, he represented his movement at the central employment service office. He was kind to those who approached him and enjoyed his surroundings.

He had a heart attack at the height of his happiness. The great fears of May and June 1967 shook the vision of his growing happiness, and his sensitive heart stopped beating.

Asher the noble, who was pleasant and friendly in his manner, will be missed by Vishnevetsers. He cared for his family and was a dedicated, loyal, loving father and husband.

[Page 241]

Collection

(Contributions Received after Typesetting)

English Translation by Sara Mages

[Page 243]

Those Who Are No Longer
by Y. N.-S.

They pass before my eyes and my soul in a large crowd, the innocent and the pure, whether at school or in the youth movement. In the morning, I was their teacher, and in the afternoon, their friendly instructor.

I have a few pictures from those days, and every once in a while I take the pictures out and look at them. Here's Aharon Gufman from the Old City, vigilant, happy, and smiling. Here's Niume Feldman, intelligent and wise. Here's Furman the little philosopher. Here's Lerer, the serious one, and Lerner, who was full of life. They were all full of love for their nation and their land. With excitement, they took it upon themselves to tramp through the winter swamps to collect small coins for the Jewish National Fund.

You haven't seen youthful rejoicing if you never saw them during song evenings on the mountain by the riverbank.

For a few years, I accompanied them in their youthful way of life...

And again, I take out a picture of the third-grade children – here's Tsizen the graceful one, here's Tenenboym the lovely one, here's Sudman the quiet one, and many more... And I lost them all as a teacher and instructor.

***

Together we learned, played, and dreamed tomorrow's dreams. I remember the trips we took around the area in the summer and winter, scout games, and stormy dances at our branch. We didn't have a permanent home; we wandered from apartment to apartment: at Feldman the carpenter's apartment, by the river bank on the road to the village of Zarudi.

Everywhere we went, we brought the spirit of happiness and youth...

With excitement, we learned about the Land of Israel (from Braslavski's booklets) and Youth Guard kibbutzim established there.

How can I fail to mention my students who in time became instructors? Here's Chave Mofshit, the serious elementary instructor. Here are Pati and Zelde from the Zelber family, who contributed much to the life of our Youth Guard branch.

And I lost them all...

Zalman and Yakov, the Epshteyn Brothers

They came from a poor family, a widow's sons who worked to support her.

They joined our chapter when it was established and became active, even though they were busy with work. They dedicated a lot of energy to chapter life. Zalman asserted himself with his activities. There was no activity in which Zalman didn't participate: collecting money for the Jewish National Fund, decorating the chapter house, instructing, helping with field trips, and much more.

The brothers weren't rewarded with the fulfillment of their dream – immigrating to the Land.

May their memory be for a blessing.

[Page 244]

Among Russian Citizens and on Its Frontiers
by Mikhael Valdman

On June 22, 1941, we left Vishnevets. We traveled for a month. The route was difficult. My departure from Vishnevets was also kind of a mission. I was assigned to bring home a Russian's wife and small children, and my task wasn't easy. Enemy planes escorted us, and every once in a while they dropped bombs.

After Shepetovka, when we were installed in a car that also carried reservists, I ran into Menashe Tsvik, Hirsh Marchbeyn, and others from our town, who were on their way to rescue "mother" Russia.

Since I had left with the members of a Russian family whom I was assigned to transfer to Russia, we had no difficulty joining the other passengers. The car supervisor was a Russian cooperative administrator who knew the family. He let them inside and also let us in, since it was unpleasant for him to leave us outside.

We traveled to Kiev in that car.

In Kiev, notices with mobilization orders had already been posted. They listed the recruits' ages and the exact dates they had report to the flag.

I went to the military commander and asked him what to do. According to my age, I belonged to the group that was required to report for duty. But he told me to stay with the convoy to the end and report for duty when I reached a certain location, and then they'd decide what to do with me.

The family left. We separated, not knowing where to turn.

There was a convoy on the same day. I sat in the open car with my wife and two children, not knowing where we were going. My objective was to travel as far as I could from the Nazis.

We traveled for three weeks, day and night, without stopping. No one cared for us or our needs. We ate what we were given at the stations.

On the way, students and many workers climbed into our ca. They were professional workers who had been transferred with their factories after being evacuated from Leningrad.

We arrived at a station in the village of Zolsk, in the Caucasus.

The world ended there. A barricade indicated the end of the railroad tracks. That place was unique. It was an old Cossack camp that had been turned into a kolkhoz.

The local kolkhoz hadn't received orders to come and welcome the refugees. During those confusing hours, the arrival of so many refugees was a rare event that surprised this small place.

When we entered the village, my wife asked the first farmer she met on the road, "Are there any Jews among you?" She didn't do it with the intention of making anyone angry, but because it was a typical Jewish custom.

[Page 245]

However, he answered her, also without intending anything, "There are only Cossacks here. There's not one Jew among us, and I can't remember a Jew ever living here."

In absolute fact, we were the first Jews in that place.

They brought us to the kolkhoz leader, an 82-year-old Cossack with an amputated leg, and he told me, "I've lived here since I was a child, and I've never seen a Jew here."

We stayed there for two weeks. I realized that I didn't have a place there. I moved to the nearby town of Nalchik in Kabardino-Balkaria SSR. For half a year, I worked there in a factory, and then I was drafted into the army.

My wife and children stayed in Nalchik. Thanks to the fact that she was a seamstress she was able to support herself and the children while I was wandering around for five years, on the frontier and outside it.

She was the only Jew out of 45 refugee families who lived in the hut, and she never experienced any discrimination.

Meanwhile, the Germans entered the town. My son was sick. She couldn't leave the town because of him, and she stayed there. She registered with the Germans as a Jew. Later on, she found out there were other Jews in town who were married to non-Jews. Those were Jewish women who lived under the protection of Christians, and they asked her, "Where are you planning to go? Don't you know how dangerous it is?"

Nevertheless, she wasn't afraid. She went and registered as a Jew.

Luckily for her, the Germans were forced to retreat because their front collapsed near Stalingrad. They left the area, and she was saved.

The Germans who lived among the Russians walked gingerly and didn't act rashly, but this time she was saved by a real miracle.

A Russian prisoner of war who had been brought there by the Germans lived next door to her. He was a shoemaker and helped the local German shoemaker. One evening, the Russian prisoner left his place of detention and spent the night at the Russians' house.

In the morning, when the Germans realized he was missing, they conducted a search for him. The minute they tried to enter my wife's home, a Russian woman who wanted to save her from the "dangerous" visit started to yell at the Germans, "Don't go in there. There's nothing to search for over there. A Jew (Hebrew) lives there."

The Germans may not have understood what a Hebrew was, or they may have been shaken by the woman's hysteria. They skipped her hut and continued the search. That's how she was saved.

Until 1945, I was in the Red Army without knowing if my family was still alive. I approached Nalchik's municipal committee and asked them if they knew of the Valdman family. It was far away, and I wanted to know if I should travel to Nalchik or go in a different direction. They answered me, "There's no family by that name, but a young man named Moshe Mikhelovits Valdman is registered with us. If he's related to you, write to him."

I was confused, and my heart feared the worst. What had happened to my wife? What about my daughter? I knew Moshe was my son, for sure, but I wondered why he was the only one to register.

[Page 246]

Later on, the matter became clear. When the Russians, returned my wife was so excited about liberation that she forgot to register again with them. But my son, who had turned 17, remembered and came to enlist to the army. And so I found my family after great fears.

In 1946, I was discharged from the army at the border with East Germany. I returned to get my family and moved to Poland to build myself a new home.

When I passed Kremenets, I wanted to turn and visit Vishnevets, but the town commander advised me not to do it. He said, "You stayed alive, so stay that way. Vishnevets is swarming with gangs that are hostile toward us and for you. Each Russian soldier was shot and killed by them. Keep on traveling, and wait for another opportunity to see your town. The whole area is a death trap."

I listened to him and traveled to Poland. I was in Valbezhikh and started to establish myself. I worked as a glassblower and earned a good salary. A few months later, after the Kelts pogrom erupted, I didn't wait another day. The day after the pogrom, I packed my belongings, liquidated everything, and went to Italy.

We lived in Italy for three years under the United Nations' care. I worked as a warehouse assistant, and later, I immigrated to the Land.

When I remember the chapter of my life that I spent among the Russians, pleasant memories come to me. I was always the only Jew among the Russians, and I wasn't treated badly or discriminated against. I enjoyed good comradeship. Today, when I see Russia and its treatment of our small and hopeful nation's remnants, it's hard to understand what happened to the good Russian nation – how it has declined and degraded itself so much.

[Page 247]

From a Survivor's Diary
by A. Y. Teyer

After typesetting the sections of the book, we received some chapters from a diary written by A. Teyer, a survivor of the Vishnevets ghetto. We present them literally (not "correctly") so as not to detract from their value. This was how his heart expressed itself, and so we will leave them. It's interesting that at a time of piercing soul-searching, the man needed to return to the Hebrew tongue, because it was the "holy tongue" for him. Therefore, we decided not to change its style or correct the tone of his writing so the words will be read as a plea and a cry of distress. – Editorial Board

The war broke out on June 22, 1941, when the Nazis attacked the USSR, and as it is known, they broke forward at great speed. On July 2, they captured our district, and our town also fell into the murderers' hands. Already on the next day, they caught around 35 Jews, some in the streets and some from their homes, collected them in Issakher Sofer's cellar, and they were killed there through suffocation by our town's Ukrainian residents. A Jew named Alter Ruach, Makhtsi's son, told me about the death of each of them. He was also caught with the unfortunate ones and was miraculously able to escape. He told me about it almost two weeks after the disaster, and the fear hadn't yet left him. Even though 15 days had already passed, it seemed as if he couldn't shake the fear and horror that befell him during those terrible moments. While he told his story, he kept looking around to see if anyone was listening to the details of the horrible murder.

When they finished with them, we don't know how they found out that a few had escaped from the cellar. Immediately, they went out to look for them, intending to leave no witnesses to the cruel murder mentioned above. They said they caught a few of them. One whose name was mentioned as being captured was Kalman Nek (Choish), and even though everyone was almost sure none of them was alive, most of our town's Jewish residents didn't dare or allow anyone to express his opinion about this murder. Most didn't believe something like that was possible, and the rest feared that it would reach the murderers' ears that so and so knew something about the incident.

In those days, I was on the way home from a Soviet prison on the road to Siberia. During the first days after the war broke out, that was where they'd collected the accused whose sentences were already set in order to transport us to the Soviet zone on the fastest direct train, but the Soviets couldn't get us out of the prison in time. The Nazis' military push forced them to leave the town in a hurry.

[Page 248]

They set the prison on fire before they escaped, and we were locked up, but no one on the inside suffered from the fire. It was on Friday, July 4, 1941. The next day, we left for the road. After wandering for nine days, I arrived home, and it was on July 14, 1941.

***

I won't tell here at length about the incidents on my way home. But I'll bring up a few incidents only to describe the Jews' state during those first days. Here's the first: on the road, we passed a well where a few Ukrainian farmers stood drawing water for their homes. We approached them and asked for a little drinking water. To this they answered with eyes full of murder, "What? To give drinking water to the Jews, who cut our women's breasts? We'll give you poison."

I panicked when I heard these words. We had no choice but to leave the well, and we left the well thirsty.

I started my journey in the company of five young Ukrainian men who always stayed together, meaning fellow sufferers, a Jewish man from Chortkov, and me. We were seven in all.

One day, when we passed by the town of Zaslav, where the Gorin river passes, we decided to rest and wash at the same time. After washing, since we didn't have towels, we sat in the sun on the shore to dry off so we could get dressed and continue our journey. Before we were ready for the road, we saw two Nazi soldiers coming toward us. They took handguns out of their pockets and, with his finger, one of them ordered each of us to stand in our place. When five stood in their places, he then said five were enough for him and ordered them to march forward. By chance, the five who were ordered to stand in their places were the Ukrainians, and the two left were we two Jews; so what was our crime? It's clear that we decided to wait for them for a number of reasons. First, it was easier for us to cross the villages in their company, and, secondly they had left the parcels they took with them, not only theirs but also the ones they had stolen from others. We had to watch their parcels, so we sat until sunset. When they returned, it was hard to recognize them. In a few hours, their faces had completely changed because of the hard labor they had to do, and in addition their attitude toward us changed. They openly blamed us for the "Jewish piece of work." We continued on our way with them without saying a word to each other. See how the Ukrainian population was poisoned in a matter of hours.

The road to Vishnevets was long, around 220 kilometers give or take, without a piece of bread or the ability to enter a house and sleep there. In the course of nine days, on July 14, I arrived home. Sometime afterward, he came to me and told me about the terrible death of the 30 and some Jews who suffocated to death, the conqueror's first victims. The panic in our town was at its highest; they didn't know for sure what happened to those people. Fear entered the hearts of each one, and one question passed from mouth to mouth: who knows what the next day will bring? The town's streets were deserted, and all the men stayed home. The murderers started to visit each home with the goal to rob, steal, and pillage.

[Page 249]

They entered and checked house after house with different excuses, such as, for example, a search for weapons or spies. They took everything they found, and it was useless to complain. In the homes where they couldn't find anything, they struck the people who lived there with murderous blows, and everything was done solely by the Ukrainians.

At first, they thought the murderers would take revenge only on those who had worked with the Communist regime, and in time the situation would calm down. The reason for that thought was that from the first day, our town was controlled solely by the Ukrainians. There was only one person representing the conquerors, and his only duty was to ensure that the farmers would bring one tenth of the different kinds of wheat they needed during the war.

Nine days passed from the day I arrived in our town. On July 23, 1941, early in the morning, it was around half past four, I went outside to breathe a little fresh air since it was dangerous for men to walk outdoors during the day. I walked on a narrow street near my home. Various thoughts didn't leave me even for a moment; what's going to happen? Suddenly, I heard a commanding voice behind me: "Stop!" I turned around and found a young Ukrainian man, short in stature, a cobbler's son. I knew his whole family, and he also knew who I was. He started to retreat in order to give himself enough room to pull his gun, which was twice as long as he was, and ordered me to start walking forward, because they were given an order to check the documents of each person they met in the street. At first I was surprised, and I approached him with a friendly remark: "Without documents, you don't know who I am?"

For this he walked closer to me, to the point where his gun was touching my stomach, and said to me in this language, "The days when you can utter your smart talk are over, and if you don't listen to me here, in this place, I'll kill you like a dog!"

After he allowed me to inform him through the window that I was going to the police station. I purposely walked in that direction at extra high speed. When I entered the room where they gathered us, even though it was still very early, I found some Jewish men and a few young men among them. After an hour or an hour and a half, the room was full. Those who arrived barely had enough time to walk in before they started to take the others out, but none of us knew where these people were going. Every few minutes, the door opened, the one who was standing close to the exit was called, and the door closed behind him. Meanwhile, because I was restless all the time, I got close to the door, and from there I suddenly heard horrible cries. It was just after a young man was taken out of the room. I stood close by the door and waited to see if I could hear more screams after the next person was taken out, and here I came to the conclusion that the same screams were heard after they took someone out. I didn't know how to explain it to myself. It was clear that the people who left the room under the Ukrainian murderers' command were beaten very hard. But it was difficult to know what the murderers were really doing with those people, and where were they collecting them? Meanwhile, the time came for my row to come out. At first I didn't know what to do: leave at the first opportunity or wait. Finally, I knew I couldn't avoid it.

[Page 250]

The moment I reported by the door, the policeman showed me that I had to turn left and enter a room where Nadke Badasiuk, the murderers' chief, was sitting. Before we could bless each other with the morning blessing, I started to explain to him that I was afflicted with a stomach ailment after spending 13 months in a Soviet prison, and for that reason I couldn't stay in a room without a toilet for a number of hours. To that he answered, "Go home."

Before I could ask him to inform his policemen who were standing by the exit door that I was going home, he stood in his place and told them to let me pass, and no one dared to raise his hand to strike me. From that incident, I understood that those who weren't allowed to return to their homes were beaten extremely hard.

The streets were empty, simply desolate. Shivers and fear took me over when I couldn't see a living soul on the entire length of the street. While I was walking, screams suddenly reached my ears, and suddenly I saw group of women standing in a corner whispering to each other. They all fainted when they saw me from a distance, and I had to help all by myself. I whispered in their ears that I was among the living until they regained consciousness, and we ran home together leaning on each other, shivering and afraid.

That afternoon, we found out that 60 men had been taken from the town and, even today, no one knows their burial location.

Avraham Tsimbler told me that his brother-in-law was among the people who were captured that day. To save his brother-in-law, he ran to the Vaytsman family with the intention that maybe they could influence the chief of police, Gnadke Badasiuk, to save him. He risked his life walking outdoors in the desolate, empty streets, but it was all for nothing. Out of great fear, they didn't allow him to enter their home, and through a window they informed him that, to their sorrow, they couldn't help anyone. Suddenly, wild screams reached his ears, with the sounds came from the municipal (Gemine) building, which was across from the Vaytsmans' home. So as not to be seen from a distance, he lay on the ground in their garden, and from there he saw how the murderers were taking each of the captured men out of the cellar, striking him on the way with horrible blows until he lost consciousness, and before he could walk halfway, he fell without the energy to continue. Then the two who accompanied him handed him over to the two other murderers, who dragged him on the ground, one by the hands and the other by the legs, to an automobile standing next to the house, and threw him inside the automobile, and they did this to each one. By the time they arrived at the automobile, they were half-dead. Two hours or more passed, and the automobile moved from its place, but he didn't know in what direction.

The next day, early in the morning, the murderers' mothers reported to the homes of all unfortunate families whose husbands or sons had been taken and told those who were left with their children in great secrecy that the rumors in the town that those who'd been taken were no longer among the living weren't true. Therefore, they could help bring their husbands or sons back home, and as payment, they'd take clothing or valuable items and give them to the policemen who guard the concentration camp where they were staying.

[Page 251]

In order to take more from the unfortunate women, they came back two days later and explained to them that the situation wasn't too bad, and meanwhile they took something else from them. It was a complete fabrication; a week passed and no one returned.

Exactly on Wednesday, July 30, 1941, in the morning, they started to visit house after house, taking only men, without letting them know where they were going. Whoever had the time to hide was saved, and many who weren't able to escape from the murderers' claws fell into their hands. The same thing happened to them but with one difference: this time the disaster was seven times larger than the one the week before. In two hours they collected around 400 Jews, and they all disappeared the same way as before. And again, a few Ukrainian mothers came and tried to deceive those who were left. It's understandable that a large number believed their words and gave the murderous women a few items so that maybe the father of the children who were left orphaned would return. In two or two and a half hours, a large number of men disappeared, and also this time only men.

On the same day, the town's Rabbi, Yosef Erlikh, and Shike Yakira were also among the kidnapped. The Jews of our town, Vishnevets, were killed and destroyed solely by the town's Ukrainian residents. Those in the villages didn't take part, not because they objected to the holy mission, but because the Ostrovski, Badasiuk, Shapoval, Kovalski, and other families like them didn't allow the farmers to enter and do anything in order to keep the spoils and plunder only in their hands.

Almost everyone in our town knew Hentsi Feldman. She lived on the corner of Korolka by the road to Kremenets. She had an only son named Moshe. She was so attached to her only son that whispered rumors flew around town that she wouldn't allow him get married until he was at an advanced age out of fear that he'd leave her. The day of the great disaster, her son was among the kidnapped. Not surprisingly, as a mother, she did everything she could to save her son from the murderers, who were all her neighbors. After screaming and crying, she realized there wasn't any solution, and then she asked the murderers to take her, too, so she could stay by his side in each location. At first, they explained to her that they weren't allowed to do such a thing, because they were ordered to collect only men to work behind the front lines (again the same version). After a few moments, when she refused to separate from him, they struck her with such cruelty that she fell and only a pile of bones, flesh, and blood were left.

After that great disaster, panic increased among the town's residents, who really didn't know what to make of everything that was happening around us and the fact that there was no one to help us. On one side, there was the event of Moshe Feldman's mother, and on the other side, there were the rumors that the murderous Ukrainian women were spreading, that those who were taken weren't destroyed. All these together removed from the Jews' imagination the thought that this was the beginning of the end and that they should think of organizing a revolt under the slogan "Let me die with the Philistines" and the bloodshed among them would decrease. They really reached their target when some the town's Jews brought up the Moshe Feldman incident, and the majority came to the conclusion that she was the one to blame, because it was clear that during a war, the sides always need people to work behind the frontline.

[Page 252]

Misery increased along with the panic. Poverty was followed by hunger and death without deliverance, epidemic diseases without medicines, trouble and misfortune without benefit. Days passed, with each day bringing another decree, and they also started to demand laborers to leave early each morning to work for the farmers. At first they were afraid: surely they always say that those who disappear live in some kind of labor camp, but no one saw them. But later, when the demanded quota of workers returned without anyone missing, it's true that they weren't paid any wages, which is unthinkable, but nevertheless, the number of workers increased from day to day, because they were able to smuggle some food for their children and decrease hunger at their homes.

The distress around us increased from day to day. Sighing and groaning, a man asked his friend, "Are we going to be rewarded by seeing the days when we can live a normal life?"

The majority were sure the downfall of the modern Haman of the civilized nation of Central Europe would come, but who would be alive? And who would be rewarded by seeing their downfall with his own eyes? We shall expire before redemption comes! After the murder of July 30, 1941, when almost 400 men were exterminated, the killings stopped. But the fear wasn't lifted. They didn't know what the day would bring, and along with fear, the robbery and cruelty didn't stop. In addition, hunger among the Jews brought different contagious diseases. Not a day passed without some deaths. Each time, we had to ask for permission to take the dead out and bring them to a Jewish grave. When they returned from the cemetery, most expressed their wish that they'd be rewarded with the same death. In their hearts, they were jealous of those who'd already died and been brought to a Jewish grave.

Together with time, the summer also passed, and they started to worry: what are we going to do when the cold weather arrives? How are we going to hold on? On one side there was hunger, different diseases, horrible epidemics, and in addition, the approaching freezing weather would finish those who were still alive. Cold, hunger, sickness, and death were the share of our lives, and there was no help. The only food we officially received in the beginning was 300 grams of flour, and in time they decreased that amount.

***

A month and several days after the great disaster, when hundreds of Jews disappeared, it was on September 5, early in the morning before sunrise, a light knock on our neighbor's door woke us up. We panicked; what was this noise? I got up and walked to my neighbor's house. When they opened the door, we saw a horrible sight. At the door stood a young woman, Rachel Sendler's young sister, who was almost naked. Before we could ask her what had happened, she fainted and couldn't talk. A few minutes later, after she regained consciousness, she started to tell us about an event that froze the blood in our veins.

In summary: the previous night, the Ukrainians from the Old City, along with several Ukrainian policemen from the New City, removed every living soul from the Jewish homes, and in a matter of a few hours exterminated all of them, babies, women, men, and the elderly.

[Page 253]

The only one to survive was the one who escaped from her bed, went into the river that divided the two parts of the town, stayed in it for a several hours, and before sunrise came and brought this horrible news. This was the fourth murder, and there was no one to yell and complain to. And what would happen in the future? What would tomorrow bring? The abandonment of the Jews reached its height, and there was no rescue or relief. We were given over to the beasts' hands.

At one time, we endangered our lives, Avraham Tsimbler and I. We left town, removed the symbol of shame from our chest, and decided to go to Kremenets. We wanted to use this opportunity to tell them about all the incidents and listen to what they said to us, whether there was a spark of hope or not. By chance, we didn't have to wait long. The first car that passed by took us (for sure not knowing we were Jewish), and in an hour or less, full of fear and worries, we arrived in Kremenets. Our first step was toward Dr. Landsberg's home to hear from him: was there a way to defend ourselves? Are we lost? We didn't spend a lot of time with him since he didn't want to frighten us even farther. But to our sorrow, and the sorrow of all Jews who were then under the Nazi regime's control, he couldn't find one word of comfort for us. We understood from his words that it was destruction and total extermination. He advised us not to delay our stay in the city, because here we were in danger of falling into the killers' hands, and if they caught us, no one would be able to save us. We didn't realize how difficult it would be to return home. To leave the city, we had to walk in the back streets so the Vishnevets murderers who visited Kremenets every day wouldn't see us and suspect that we were trying to make a daring move to protect ourselves, meaning, to complain about their actions. With a great deal of luck, at sunset, when darkness fell on our town, we returned home. The answer we brought with us was very easy to understand: that during our long stay in the Diaspora, which was saturated with tears, we hadn't been humiliated in such a frightening way. But how could we express this in front the nation and each community and take away the spark of hope that continued to live within us?

The puzzle that none of us knew how to solve was this: If it was true that we were given such lawlessness to be killed and destroyed, why didn't they finish us off all at once? And each time they took people and killed them, why did they strictly keep it a secret so no one would find out? None of the town's residents could understand it, and all the more so, explain it to somebody else. This "stalemate" made our lives even more difficult. What was clear was that it wouldn't take long, because on one hand, people died day after day from starvation, illnesses, and lack of medicine to cure them, and on the other hand, from the frequent murders. These facts together would bring our end faster. Several days after the fourth murder, as previously, thoughts started to cross their minds: maybe they were really lying when they said those who were taken from us had been killed? Who'd ever think such a thing could happen, that our neighbors, whom we have lived with for hundreds and hundreds of years, suddenly, in such a frightening way, would turn into beasts of prey? It was quiet after every event, and as in other times of trouble and misery, this time, to, they started to compose various jokes.

[Page 254]

For example, when a man asked his friend, "What's going to happen? What will be after all?" the answer was, "What this has to be. Meanwhile they don't bother us, and let's not bother them either."

And so a few more months passed. Autumn ended, the cold weather started to organize a full assault, and thus a complete symphony was created: hunger, epidemics, and contagious diseases without any medicine. In addition to all that was the frigid weather with no ability to get food, since the amount they legally gave us was lowered every month. The calculation was clear; if they continued to keep the situation mentioned above without a change for the better, then in a very short time, not a single soul would remain alive in our town, and we didn't see a sign that it was going to end. The robbery and cruelty didn't stop, and they kept on coming back to the homes in the town and taking everything they wanted. From day to day, our world was getting darker. If we take into account that this situation was taking place in each occupied location, then they, with the help of the Ukrainians in Ukraine, the Poles in Poland, the Lithuanians in Lithuania, the Hungarians in Hungary, the Romanians in Romania, and so on will completely destroy Europe's Jewry.

On one terrible day, a new decree from the day our town was captured was announced. They demanded 150 men to be ready in two days so they could transfer them to labor camps without even telling us where they were going. What they did tell us was that the number of men mentioned above should report on the next day to the train station in the city of Kremenets. I can't measure the great panic that spread in the city from moment to moment. Negotiations started with the chief of police, whose name was Shapoval. At the beginning, they were talking about totally dismantling the entire decree, but he said that it was impossible. And so they started to talk about the possibility of lowering the number, but the main question was, if they lower the number, how to collect the smaller number? Meanwhile, the news spread that they'd reached an agreement that for a certain amount, those who gather would leave on foot with in order to delay their arrival, and when they could, as one man, they'd return home. All that was arranged by one Jew, the Judenrat leader, named Koylenberner. It was clear that not everyone believed these rumors, mostly those who decided to join of their own free will. A suspicion arose that it was all a lie and that the rumors had been started to calm those who were departing, and since they'd decided to leave out of desperation so they'd no longer see how our children, no matter what age they were, drop swollen in the streets and die of cold and starvation in front of their parents, who couldn't help them even for a moment. The departure had to be prepared for the next day. That evening, it was necessary to collect clothing, shoes, and underwear for those who were leaving, and it's worth emphasizing that those who had to collect the items mentioned above didn't show any resistance. With great sorrow and heartbreak, they handed the collectors all they could provide, and with eyes full of tears, they expressed their wishes that they'd leave in peace and return in peace.

Early in the morning on August 10, 1941, instead of 150 laborers, only 50 left. I don't have the power to express here on paper how the Vishnevets Jews felt on that day. As in the previous times, the possibility that they wouldn't return alive was set in each person's heart, but no one thought about himself.

[Page 255]

Maybe in the depths of their hearts they knew there was no hope, and as always in cases like that, to be certain, a man asked his friend's opinion: Are we going to be rewarded with another life? And the answer was, God knows!

After those people left the city, everyone remained worried about their fate, but there was no choice. They almost didn't talk about the subject because they were waiting for the day to pass so they could see the results of the agreement struck in regard to those people's return. During the day, rumors started to spread that they saw some people leaving in the morning for the Kremenets train station. Rumors passed from mouth to mouth, but no one wanted to believe the matter until they could see the few with their own eyes. It's no wonder that there was no end to the happiness. It was a restrained happiness, happiness without noise, and we could say it was a hidden happiness.

I heard the following words from a participant in the transport mentioned above: the treatment during the walk was terrible. When they arrived in Kremenets, they were given an order to go and visit their families, and those without one were told to visit friends, under the condition that each knew where the others were. The reason was known: by the time they started to collect them, they found out they had missed the train. That evening, they were ordered to return home. What happiness during a time of sorrow and misery, hunger, and different methods of death! Who could imagine such a strange situation? Surely, the people who left the city agreed to do so only out of desperation and as an escape from the terrible situation in each home so they'd no longer see their children's suffering. And so whoever didn't see our sorrow in those days, how a town of a few thousand people was dying little by little, and how their number was lowered by hunger and disease from day to day, hasn't see sorrow in his life. However, when we saw the people returning from their way, a spark of hope was awakened, that maybe? Maybe in the future, meaning from that day forward, the attitude toward us would change and in the future we could arrange things the same way. From that they learned that the rumors being spread in the streets of our town about those who were taken but not murdered might be true, and maybe it was true that they exist in labor camps.

It was an autumn day, with the rain and cold starting to merge in the evening little by little, and together it was a very strong attack. It was simply difficult to think about what would happen when the cold days arrived and we couldn't get a small amount of coal or maybe a pile of wood. It's impossible to say who would be able to cope with all that. The strongest enemies of a human life, cold, hunger, and epidemic diseases, merged under a difficult regime whose purpose was one and only one: to destroy and exterminate us. Even a heart of stone would be moved by the sight of the tragedy that took over our miserable town. Poverty and the crowded conditions were over our heads, and no one helped, not brother to a brother or father to his son, and we were all locked up, unable to go out and search for medicine for our dying children. The Jewish quarter was judged and sentenced to death by starvation. Survivors will try in vain to describe the depressed towns that lived under the difficult and striking force of our Ukrainian neighbors under Nazi rule, and there wasn't a pen or enough ink to write about even a small percentage of what happened to us.

[Page 256]

The oppressors and robbers destroyed and took everything from us without mercy, so much so that there wasn't anything left at home to trade for a piece of bread or a drop of milk for our children. Our world was getting darker from day to day. Parents watched their children, no matter what age they were, die of hunger, and there was no salvation. And in addition, the murderers returned to the homes of Jews, who already looked dead, to search for and take furniture, utensils, clothing, and underwear out of their homes. It was like a hidden but clear hint: soon they wouldn't need anything.

We didn't get any messages from the outside or know what was happening in the towns around us or in the entire European zone occupied by the Nazis.

On one of those days, we were told to prepare a place for around 1,000 Jews from the town of Vyshgorodok. We didn't have a choice. One night, when the winter was most aggressive, they started to arrive in loaded carts, almost naked, frozen from the cold, and hungry. We greeted them and could only welcome them with hot water and a corner to stretch out their legs. The next day, we also had to find a corner for them so they could get organized. Our guests' arrival tripled the Jewish quarter's tragedy. They also came naked, hungry, and with nothing. How could we help them when we couldn't help ourselves. The number dying from hunger and various diseases increased every day. Preparation for winter's departure lasted longer in our eyes than in years past. Sometime after we welcomed our guests, a decree came out one that none of us ever imagined.

All the town's residents of the Jewish race had to concentrate on only one street, starting from Alter Layter's and ending at Zise Mazur's house. And from that day on, Jews were forbidden to reside outside or leave the boundaries of that area without special permission from the authorities. We had to create a wooden fence from home to home and block the windows. With that, we'd be separated from the "pure" Christian race that lived around us. To make sure the work was finished by the deadline, they demanded two Jews as a guarantee, and all efforts to disassemble the decree were for nothing. The two Jews who given to them as a guarantee were Yakov Marchbeyn and I. On the same evening, on February 14, 1942, they took the two of us from the Jewish quarter and delivered us to the cellar under the municipal building on the condition that the work be finished on time, and on February 16, 1942, they'd let us return home. If not, they'd send us to a concentration camp. Everyone, like one man, first started to collect material, and exactly two days later, it was done. That same day, the two of us returned home.

However, with the ghetto's establishment, almost all of us remained in our places, meaning that none of us was taken out. A special tremor entered each of our hearts: what was coming now? What was the reason behind the ghetto decree, with the new law that no Jew could leave his homes for even one moment? And also, why weren't

Christians allowed to enter the ghetto? What was the exact intention? But who could give us a clear answer in those days?

[Page 257]

All we could do was wait, full of fear and worry about what was in store for us. We began to get used to the new life. Darkness ruled in most e rooms within the narrow ghetto's boundaries, because they also ordered us to block the windows with boards. The homes were filled with more men, women, and babies, all of them hungry, sad, and sick. A few looked like human shadows.

I simply don't have the words to express my opinion about the situation then in regard to the new decree.

One day, I saw a Ukrainian policeman leading a Jewish young man from a distance. I imagined to myself that he had "broken" one of the new laws – for example, maybe he'd left the ghetto without a permit or, in addition, maybe he'd been able to exchange something for a piece of bread for his sick mother or father. First, I decided to save this young man from the murderers' hands, since they first would strike the people they caught with murderous blows, and second, there was a dangerous possibility that they'd take him to a concentration camp. I called the policeman by his name. I knew them all, since they were Vishnevetsers. The two of them came closer to me, and he started to explain the young man's great and terrible crime: that is to say, he dared to throw a piece of bread from a location outside the ghetto to a family member who was on the inside. After I heard the subject of the crime, I appealed to him to give him a monetary penalty note with a given sum of money as a fine, and before I could take the money out of my pocket, he spoke to me in these words: "What? Are you crazy? Why would I give such a poor young man a fine?" When I gave him the sum of money for the punishment, he let him go. It was simply difficult to understand these people's nature. We were in their hands, and there was no one to save us. They were our neighbors, we'd lived with them for hundreds and hundreds of years, and we didn't recognize them. Who could have imagined that the moment they were given free rein to do as they pleased, they'd storm us like beasts of prey. They not only stole and took everything from us and left us 100% without means to live on, but they, only they, ruined, demolished, and destroyed our lives, from the infant to the old, men and pregnant women.

***

Duvid Feldman told me about this incident:

After each murder, rumors spread that townspeople who'd been taken away were in a labor camp. The main purpose was to deceive the unfortunate families and to take valuable items from them and, secondly, to prevent any kind of opposition under the slogan "Let me die with the Philistines!" That could have caused great bloodshed among them. After each campaign, when rumors started to pass via whispers from person to person, most of the town's residents expressed their opinion: maybe it was true? Maybe they were all alive. Weren't the Nazis in a difficult war, and didn't each side need workers behind the front lines? Fate had fallen on us to do this physical work, and every once in a while it would occur to you: maybe we can hold on until this awful anger passes.

[Page 258]

If so, don't despair! The main question in those days was, would the daily violence and robbery stop? How long are we going to be in our murderous neighbors' hands? And no one replied! And again the days passed, the piercing cold and the lack of heating that was eating our flesh slowly began to withdraw, and clear days began to arrive, with an evening sun that melted the snow accumulating in piles in the area where we lived. It gave us a sort of special hope; the sunlight brought a little happiness to our desperate aching hearts, even though the disaster with all of its horrors didn't decrease even one percent. It was true that with spring's arrival, the situation was a little easier than the previous winter days, but hunger grasped us with all its strength. People who looked like human shadows began to go outside to warm themselves under the sun, and when you walked down the street, you saw relatively young people say farewell to each other, saying they wouldn't live for more than a day or two, and the next day or the day after, they would die of starvation. And so, even if they didn't destroy us with bullets or different kinds of murder, the calculation was clear that in a short time they would finish us off, and if they were using the same methods in each town and city, this was nothing but a total extermination, and the end would arrive for Polish Jews and maybe European Jews. At all times. We were cut from the outside world, and we also didn't hear any news or know anything about what was happening in the political or military fields.

The ghetto became a no-man's land. Officially according to the law, it was an area that a "Christian" wasn't allowed to enter without a special permit, but who was asking? And to whom would you complain?

From the day the ghetto was created, violence and robbery increased sevenfold, and there was no restraint outside the ghetto in the buildings that had been emptied of Jews. Our neighbors came daily with their family members and destroyed house after house to emphasize that they knew they couldn't remove any valuable items, because most of the buildings were already old, and they couldn't even take a piece of wood that was worth something with them. But they did this with special satisfaction and with great enjoyment, solely under the realization that they were not only destroying but also removing all Jewish symbol from the land, and thus nothing would remain.

Amidst all the tragedies we experienced during those days, it was difficult to comprehend what our eyes saw. Even an author with the greatest talent couldn't put down on a sheet of paper or express the smallest percentage of what we really experienced. It was clear that the sword that the murderers held over our heads was coming down, we knew that the process of destruction was worse than the destruction of the body, and there was no rescue. Our children wandered in the ghetto streets, swollen from hunger and from various illnesses, like drunks without the energy to carry their weak bodies, and died like flies. There was no advice or device. Naked, hungry, and thirsty, our fate was sealed in the environment of cruelty and under our sadistic oppressors' rod. How could the Nazis have poisoned the locals in each place they occupied and also bring our downfall in such a short time?

[Page 259]

I want to use this opportunity to describe another incident so the way the Nazis prepared our extermination in cold blood will be understood, although local Christians in many locations executed their work with extreme dedication.

One day, I received a permit to leave the ghetto, and my intention was to exchange items for food for my family members. When I returned, the danger that they wouldn't let me pass hung over me, and when I reached the ghetto entrance, one of the guards who guarded the exit approached me and jokingly said to me, "I am interested to see what the Jew can bring into the ghetto in his bag." I didn't have a chance to say a word, and the other guard told him, "We're not going to check. Let him bring it in this time; it doesn't matter." To that, the first one answered him, "Good. I won't object this time, but if you think that he'll come out to protect you when the regime turns because you let him pass, then you're mistaken." How the matter ended isn't important, but what was interesting from this conversation was that in their view, they had to erase all the Jews so no witness to their deceitful murderous acts would remain. All the locals in those places were against us, and they not only helped them with their murderous work, they also helped them by spreading rumors that those men weren't dead. The food they distributed at first to the Jewish quarter's residents, and later on in the ghetto, was lowered from day to day until there was nothing. Various epidemics and death from starvation reduced day by day the number of men who could do something in that direction. There was no way for news to travel from town to town, so how could sick and hungry people do anything? The murderers, with the help of the locals in each location they conquered, prepared with cold blood and advance planning, and there was no reason to blame. We need to memorialize everything we experienced so generations that come after us will know what the people of civilized Europe were capable of. There was no deeper lamentation or greater tragedy to enter beside the lamentations that have been memorialized ever since.

One April day in 1942, on Monday the 13th, a decree was enforced on us. It wasn't a new type, but it was a lot more terrible from all the decrees enforced on us until that day. They demanded that in two days, 50 women or young women be ready to leave for the landowner Grocholski's farm in Kolodne and stay there for a month. The decree was severe, and all the negotiations to cancel the decree came to nothing. For that reason, it looked a lot more serious in our eyes. Who knew their intentions: if we didn't oblige their demand, would they start to abduct people in the streets and in their homes to send? Who? Who among the young women would willingly agree to go? During conversations held with our killers, they promised at each step that nothing bad would happen to them during that time and that they'd all return to their homes healthy. But who could believe them? Finally, after they promised to allow the parents, husbands, or brothers of those who stayed there to visit the farm each day and bring them food, they slowly started to gather, and on the assigned day, the full number left on their way. Great fear grew among us from moment to moment. The most essential thing was that the day after they left, a few family members went there and returned with the relatively good news that they were working on the farm and that their guards' attitude was sufficiently good.

[Page 260]

This news calmed the young women's families and all the ghetto's residents. And so day after day passed. Family members went there almost every day, but they couldn't bring them food. They only visited them so they could see with their own eyes that nothing bad was happening to them, although they couldn't do anything to help them. But when the people came back, day after day, with the news mentioned above, peace and also satisfaction arrived. The Jews themselves started to explain the murderers' good behavior. Maybe there had been a change for the better? Who knew? A month passed, the young women returned to their homes unharmed and healthy, and as always after such an event, special hope entered each person's heart, and a sort of hidden power was getting stronger, calling quietly, don't despair! This was our fate and our lot all the days of our life in the Diaspora.

Who could ever have imagined what the murderers were preparing for us? Death never stopped ruling with full strength in the ghetto streets. We reached a situation where there was no home without dead people, and there was no help. The number of dead from starvation increased from day to day. Parents lost their minds watching their children die in front of their eyes, and they didn't have the power or ability to slow the Angel of Death's pace. And behold, one day in July, a new kind of decree was enforced on the ghetto, one that nobody could on any account have imagined, that is to say: the ghetto's full capacity, the length and width of the street, must give 120 tons of flour in two days. The screaming and the yelling reached the midst of the heavens, panic increased from moment to moment, and everyone asked in fear, how can we fulfill their demand? It was clear that the end was near, and just to spite us, this time they didn't demand a guarantee. Each person's heart filled with a special fear. Everyone tried to explain it differently. We had the impression that time was running out at full speed, and here the day was passing, and in two days they would enter the ghetto to receive the full amount of the decree. With eyes full of blood and tears, bitterness and desperation, some ghetto residents went to each door asking for mercy, and it's true that long ago flour had been our only food. In a matter of hours, a few ghetto Jews who had long ago prepared themselves brought what they could from their homes to the designated location. It felt as if the ghetto residents' sentiment and the responsibility were united, and they decided to remove the ax swinging above our necks with all their power. The very fact that they'd collected a few hundred kilograms of flour by the designated time when hunger prevailed at full strength showed that each person had taken the last drop out of his home from desperation, and that way they were able to collect a few hundred kilograms of flour. It is difficult to describe the situation, how hungry people, skin and bones, as thin as human shadows that had been suffering from hunger for some time could watch the sight. And here the oppressors came and forced them to give away the only food they had. Many fainted from lack of energy and from hunger.

Everyone as one understood that if they'd enforced this horrible decree on the ghetto's residents, it was clear that the end was getting closer.

[Page 261]

That same day, the murderous Ukrainians entered with their carts and took out what had been collected. It was at the end of July, Tuesday, July 28, 1942. The people, who had gathered when the flour was taken out, started to scatter slowly and go home. It was a terrible sight that had never happened before, and no one knew what tomorrow would bring. What would they give their hungry children, who wandered in the streets and dropped from lack of food, to eat tomorrow? It was clear that the ghetto residents' lives were hanging upon nothing, and a man would ask his friend, can we cope? The carts left loaded with the flour stolen from the Jews, and the hunger that grew from moment to moment never stopped killing children, babies, women, and the elderly. We were all tired. The sights in the ghetto street had drained our energy, and great fear showed on each passerby's face. Anyone who didn't see our sorrow has never seen sorrow in his life. Step by step, we were separated from the world of the living until we reached an unbearable state. Our ancestors were also tortured and suffered great pain, but no one knows the history of our torture. Of all our neighbors, with whom we'd grown up and studied all our lives, there wasn't one who could comfort us or express his feelings about our horrible situation, one who would offer his help – none of the ghetto's residents even dreamed about that. The facts of the three events caused arguments and gave rise to different explanations of our situation. The return of the 50 men when they'd demanded 150 for a transport to a labor camp, the return of the 50 young women from Kolodno with the realization that nothing bad had happened to them, as they told us after they returned home, and at the end, when instead of 120 tons of flour they were given a smaller percentage and didn't say anything – the ghetto population explained all these together by the fact that maybe the waters were calmer. If they didn't stand firm on their demands and it was possible to arrange things with them that way, maybe they'd moved away from their cruel system. And who thought that these signs only predicted trouble? No one in the ghetto thought the murderers had set up these facts for a reason. After the horrible decree of the flour, one day followed the other, and nothing new happened. It was clear that we remained satisfied, but the fear of the unknown settled deep in our hearts, and everyone had the same feeling that we were living out our quiet moments before the storm.

One night, when the ghetto slept its restless sleep, we suddenly heard gunfire. Our hearts filled with great fear. The men woke up first, thinking it would pass. Then they started to wake the children and dress them without thinking about what to dress them in: Where are we going? Does death rule around us? The children were crying, the women screamed in silence, the men bit their lips until they bled, and the situation lasted for an hour and a half. Everyone in every home was simply going crazy, and there was no word. Suddenly the gunfire ended and disappeared. We waited for it to restart, but when it became quiet, everyone fell asleep in their places until dawn entered and the day after it.

[Page 262]

We couldn't leave the ghetto at all, and we were also afraid to leave our homes, but a few risked their lives, went outside, and found that nothing bad had happened to any of the ghetto residents. We couldn't find out the reason for the gunfire because we were cut off from the outside world. We were left without an explanation, and we were satisfied that nothing bad had happened.

It was quiet until one day at the beginning of August. As usual, the known number of people gathered early in the morning to go to work, but they were informed by the ghetto guards that today they wouldn't go. After a short break, the peace was broken again. Other than forbidding us to leave, they didn't say anything else. The storytellers, meaning those who weren't allowed to go to work, said as one that they understood from the expression on the killers' faces that they were preparing something. This was solely a personal feeling, and the whispers stirred up a storm in the ghetto. The first half of the day passed without any special incidents, but calm didn't return. On the contrary, they dreaded the approaching night, and they didn't know why. We wandered around inside, and no one dared to calm his friend's soul. After the ghetto decree, a hiding place had been prepared in each home. We knew for sure that it wouldn't save us from the murderers, but even so, we'd prepared one in order to escape death even for a short time. So were our lives. Surely it was known that in general, particularly in those days, life was a hundred times more difficult than death, but they did all they could to delay the Angel of Death's arrival anyway ...

No one could explain the gunfire on that night or later on the ban on leaving for work, a daily matter we took for granted, which was suddenly cut off. All these together increased the silent panic. What was going to happen? And what would the day bring? And no one could solve it. If the robbers had paid us a visit 10 times a day in the past, the visits stopped in those days. This was something that brought different thoughts, and no one could comfort us. In previous times, when our murderers visited us, we could hear – even if it was a complete fabrication – but now, none of them came in or showed their faces over the ghetto's fence. A few started to express their opinions; maybe it was connected with the Nazis' downfall? Who knew? Surely we were cut off from the whole world, and news couldn't reach us, so what was the sudden change?

We had the impression that the sword had been given to our oppressors only to frighten us, and now there was no one to control them, no one to stop their murderous acts. How bad and bitter was our fate when the robbers entered and left, each day and at all times, and at each encounter they hit, killed, and stole everything that fell into their hands, and the Jews moaned in silence, and the misery was unbearable. And now, when those bandits didn't enter, it caused horrible distress, so who could understand that? And who could solve this complicated question? And most important, from whom and from where would our salvation come? The most worrisome question in those days was, How could we survive, and would our lives return to a normal course? Powerless, we sat on our ruins waiting for the end, without knowing what kind of end: the end of our miseries, or the end of our lives?

[Page 263]

Was it true that this distraction was taking place with the same anger in each town occupied by the Nazis? If so, this was a total extermination. Meanwhile, our life was becoming harder to bear, and the rope thrown around our necks was getting tighter and tighter. At these moments, I remembered that before the war broke out, Hitler, may his name and memory be blotted out, not once and not twice promised that the day he captured a certain country, the Jews would no longer live there. Was it true that now he was planning to carry it out?

There was no end to the chapter of our miseries, and every day, liquidation was becoming more and more prominent. When a few Jews gathered and went through the incidents that had happened to us since the occupation, they found many conflicts in the attitude toward us so, they thought maybe this time it would only pass with fear. Having no choice we waited to see what the day would bring, so day after day passed without any change, meaning that the ban on going out to work wasn't lifted, and not even a single robber dared enter. We used the opportunity to talk to them and hear their opinion of what was happening around us. A certain kind of inner fear started to take over each ghetto residents and grew from moment to moment. Was this a total liquidation? You can't compare our life at that time to a dog's life, because dogs' owners let them lick the bones under their legs, and we weren't allowed to do even that. The fear that prevailed in those days within the ghettos walls made the days longer, and the fear of what the day would bring dried out our brains. Day after day passed, and a few more days, until Saturday, August 8, 1942.

That afternoon, black clouds gathered in our town's sky. It looked to us as if the clouds had come to bring us the horrible news of the upcoming danger. The uproar among the ghetto's Jewish residents increased from moment to moment. Without saying a word to each other, they wandered crazily. Fear and shivering took hold of everyone, grievance and sorrow was set on each person's face, and no one knew what was going to happen. We received the impression that the murderers were planning an action like none they'd ever done before. In addition to the dark clouds that covered our town, evening started to fall with its darkness, and all together this affected and depressed us. And like every day in the evening, most people didn't wander in the ghetto street. A strong rain came with the evening and didn't permit anyone to stay outside. It was impossible to find out anything from the murderers, who usually came in every once in a while to take something out and lie to us, because none of them had come in the last few days. Meanwhile, we heard gunfire through the sound of rain. At the echo of the shooting, of which no one knew the meaning, everyone went into his hiding place. The shooting didn't stop, and together with it, fear increased. There isn't a pen or enough ink to describe the sights of that night. It was impossible to look at the mothers' and children's faces, which were full of sorrow and grief. The shooting lasted almost all night, and the next day we were informed that nothing bad had happened to any Jew. This time the Jews didn't calm down, and the unrest didn't leave their hearts.

[Page 264]

Early in the morning the next day, not a single Jew dared to leave his hiding place. We heard voices talking in the Ashkenazi language [German], and it was the only Nazi who stayed in our town all that time. He asked us to come out to collect the bodies of those who had been killed by mistake, and we must do it quickly to prevent epidemics, and he guarantees that such incidents wouldn't be repeated, and nothing would happen to any of us.

Having no choice, we left our hiding places. Next to the rabbi's home, which was also a synagogue, we started to dig a mass grave for the victims who had fallen that evening. It was impossible to know who and how many had died in the evening, because when we'd collected a large number of bodies, and before we could cover them, the murderers started to fire at us with their guns, and each of us escaped to save his life. Again, they went homes and went into their bunkers, and they waited. We stayed in hiding on Sunday, August 9, 1942. In the evening, when it was quiet, the echo of steps walking on the sidewalks by my house reached my ears. I risked my life and quietly got closer to a hole in the wooden planks. The walker was one of the murderous Ukrainian policemen, and I called him by his name. Surprised, he turned toward me to see who dared to call him while danger was hovering over these people .He directed his steps toward me, and I asked him to tell me what was happening around us, I also told him that I knew he couldn't help me, but at least maybe he could give me a hint, maybe he knew why there was such a sudden change. He told me we had nothing to be afraid of. Kremenets had informed them that Jews had shot at the Nazis, and they were ordered to check the ghetto for weapons, and if they didn't find weapons, everyone would return to their places. The lie showed in his eyes, but I had to believe him. After that, he continued to walk, and I remained standing on my knees, because the hole through which I talked to him was very low. I left the place and entered the bunker. There were 32 people in that room, women and children. Halfway through the first day, we started to feel the lack of air, and some started to suffocate, but what, where would you go to look for different air? The air was suffocating us in all corners of the world, in the whole world's eyes, the modern or the democratic, and no one paid attention to the horrible tragedy that would end with a whole nation's destruction. Where was the smallest part, let it be the smallest of the small, who always dared to raise their voices even from one corner of the whole world during times of trouble? Was it true that the country was full of violence and murder, and the whole world stood on the civilized European killers' side? Don't mention the righteous of the world, because they don't exist. From the way it looks, my life was saved by the murderer of 5,000 Vishnevets Jews and 1,000 Jews from the town of Vyshgorodok! One day, the murderer mentioned above took a known amount from our town's murderous policemen, traveled to Borskovits, and with his own hands butchered Moshe Venshil's whole family. It was worth knowing that the village of Borskovits was in the Lanovits district, but it wasn't enough for him to only hear that they were already dead and had been killed cruelly, but he had to be sure to fulfill the holy work himself.

The first day passed without any incidents. The lack of air grew from hour to hour and moment to moment, and then some people from our home left for the attic, first to decrease the amount of people in the bunker, and second, to look carefully through the cracks and see what was really happening outside the boundaries of our residence.

[Page 265]

Truthfully, we didn't see anything special, because on Mondays, the Ukrainian population was busy with their work. For that reason, there was no movement in the streets, and since the second day passed quietly, some of us slept in the attic. On Tuesday, early in the morning, we woke to the sound of voices getting closer to us. And here we saw with our own eyes about 20 armed killers, each with a gun on his shoulder, singing their national anthem as they approached the ghetto entrance. We didn't have time to climb down and go into our hiding place; we heard men, women, and children screaming and shouting. Before we had time to see what was really happening, we heard the killers' voices in my home, and because everyone was hiding, we heard a few of them say, "There aren't any Jews. Let's go to another house." We were sure that they'd already left. Hiding in a relatively small place in addition to the large bunker were Duvid Kitaykesher's 14-year-old daughter, Yakov Marchbeyn and his wife, and I. We were the first to be taken from our home, and for that reason, around 32 people were saved for now. Duvid Kitaykesher's daughter was sick with typhus, and her fever was surely over 40. Among those who took us out was one Nazi who just showed the murderers what to do, and they moved from place to place by themselves to instruct the other murderers. I approached him with the request that maybe he'd let that young woman stay home because she was sick and didn't have the energy to walk. To that, he answered with the same song that the Ukrainian killer told me: that Jews in Kremenets had shot at them, and therefore they needed to search for weapons, so they were taking us out, and when they didn't find any weapons, everything would return to normal. When he faced me, he realized that I didn't believe him, and then he pushed his fist into my face and said to me, "When I tell you, Yudi, then you must believe me!" and ordered one of the killers: "Take them all down immediately." They led us all to Bath Street, and there they separated the men from the women. What kind of cold blood did these people have, that nothing showed on their faces when they took everyone to their final extermination? They also wanted to remove the thought that this was the final extermination from each Jew. They stood Tsvi Margaliot, Yakov Marchbeyn, and me next to Shike Yakira's factory by the entrance to the ghetto. They ordered us to demolish the wooden wall, something that we did with great care so we wouldn't be among the first to be taken to the other side of the ghetto, where people were loaded on a truck that took them close to the Christian cemetery in the Old City. The sound of gunfire echoed over the river that passed through our town. We began to demolish the wall and sorted the wooden planks without stopping. Meanwhile, a certain car entered and stopped, and two high-ranking Nazis came out. One of them faced us with the question, "What are the Jews doing here?" We told him we were sorting the wooden planks. To that he ordered us, "Leave the sorting and stand in your places."

[Page 266]

At first we stopped our work, but when he was far from us, we again attended to the wooden planks. Suddenly, we heard some noise coming from the corner by Chaye-Tove the butcher's wife's house. It was understandable that none of us dared to get closer to the place from which the screaming was coming, but the policemen with their guns in their hands and without belts (that was also premeditated) started to march over there. One of the two Nazis who had entered walked closer to the corner to see what was happening with his own eyes. It was obvious that they cleared the way for him, so I could also see the sight behind him. From one of the buildings, where the butcher's son lives – he had a son who wasn't mentally well – since he couldn't physically protect him, he started to scream, and the air was filled with these screams. That one Nazi murderer approached him, put his hand in his back pocket, pulled a gun out, and with a shot to the young's man mouth, he silenced him for eternity.

When I saw that, I saw clearly that all hope was lost. Meanwhile, I counted the number of Ukrainian murderers; there were 28. There were around 60 and some men in the place where we were standing. The Nazis who'd come to see how the work was progressing were gone, and the cars left their location loaded and returned empty. The only Nazi who stayed was guarding the entrance gate to the ghetto. It was apparent that he wasn't satisfied with the job given to him. But who could think they might help us? I looked at the sight and saw that very soon we'd have to move from our location and walk toward the murder. I approached a few of the men who were standing with me, and suggested that since there were 28 of them and 60 and some of us, maybe we should storm them. It was clear that we couldn't save our lives, but also that the murderers wouldn't come out alive from our hands. To that, one of the young men got closer to me – I don't know his name. I think his father was Melksnits. He worked as a tailor at Yokil Teslier's, one of his sons worked as a barber for a long time and worked for Bentsi Sherer, and the other brother also worked for Yokil Teslier. He faced me with these words: "I don't want to pay with my life for you. I have a work permit, so I'll continue working, and I'll stay alive." And no more than 20 minutes later, he was already among the dead.

He wasn't the only one who thought that way. The reasons for these ideas were the Nazi murderers' behavior, with the help of the Ukrainian murderers in the Ukraine, etc., who never told us that each time they took some men they annihilated them on the spot by shooting them in the back. They purposely spread the rumor that it wasn't true, that they were living in labor camps, and also that at first they agreed to return the men and then the young women without anything bad happening to them. All that was done in cold blood. First, they took some men in order to decrease the ghetto population's inner strength, and then they starved those who were left, so much so that they couldn't show any resistance. The contagious diseases and epidemics that resulted from slow starvation helped them complete their plan.

[Page 267]

After he said the aforementioned to me, I left the place where I was standing and walked toward where the Nazi was standing guarding the entrance. I took a gold chain from my pocket and told him once, "What you see is yours, and if you take me to my home, I'll give you additional valuable items worth a very large sum, and you'll take the woman standing with the group of women holding a child in her arms with me." Quickly, he took the chain from my hand and shouted at me, "Run away from here immediately." To that I told him, "How can I escape with the policemen standing ready to shoot?" Then he scolded the Ukrainian murderers: "Relax your guns, you pigs," and to that he added, "All this is going to my head, but what can I do? An order's an order." I began running toward the cellar over which the Markhbeyns (the Kuts family) lived. When I was already inside the cellar and had started to climb the ladder to reach the attic, I saw Hirsh Margaliot and Yakov Markhbeyn (Yekil, Eti Rachel's) running after me. We hadn't had the time to think where to go or where to hide when two murderous Ukrainian policemen entered through a door on the other side, one holding a gun in his hand and the other a bayonet. They came over to us and demanded that we give them valuable items, let it be a watch or other items. Then we each put in what we had: I had a watch, and the other two gave each one 20 or 30 dollars. They left, and we decided only out of weariness to stay in the same house, climb to the attic, and later on we'd see. We climbed quickly, first to prevent another meeting with the killers, who later on took people from their homes and killed them. They visited each home to remove everything that came into their hands. When we'd climbed up, we found some people hiding there. For a moment, we each looked for a place in a corner, first to rest after three days without sleep or food. Once we lay down, we immediately fell asleep from extreme fatigue. And afterward, I don't' know how long, I woke up to the sound of screams from the street. Quickly, I got up, and through a crack in a door located behind my house, I saw the first Nazi, who'd given us the opportunity to escape. Next to him stood the two who'd come to inspect how the work was progressing. A Ukrainian policeman was babbling in the Ashkenazi language, which no one could understand, but I understood that he wanted to explain to the two that the people who'd escaped from the place with the help of the guard lived in that house. He ordered the two Ukrainian policemen to nominate one of them as a head leader to find and bring the escapees out. My blood froze in my veins when I saw the sight, thinking that maybe they'd find the room where 32 souls were hiding. It is understandable that we'd be guilty. After a few moments, they came back and promised that they'd searched and checked every corner and hadn't found anything. On the spot, the two ordered two Jewish policemen to enter and bring out those who'd escaped. When they also came out empty-handed, first they beat the Ukrainian murderers because they'd lied to them, and to even things out, the Jewish policemen also received their share. It was worth watching the murderous way they struck the policemen.

[Page 268]

The echo of each strike was heard from 100 meters away or more. With that, the matter ended, and they left the place. We felt as if a hard rock had dropped from our hearts.

We found out that we'd been in a deep sleep for many hours and that we shouldn't waste time thinking about how to continue the rescue, meaning that it wasn't clear if we could save ourselves by escaping from the ghetto's border, but we were sure that it would come to nothing if we stayed inside the ghetto. Therefore, we had to investigate it carefully and escape only where eyes would take us. We stayed inside the ghetto for two more days, and death hung over each step. We sat in the attic, and we saw the tragedy through a crack in the roof: how they took a family after family from each house to be killed. Meanwhile, the carts entered. Their duty was to collect the sick, no matter what age they were, and also the elderly who were too weak to stand on their own legs. They collected them on these carts, with half their bodies were on the carts and the other half almost hanging on the ground, and the horse continued to walk to the sound of their voices, and their screaming reached the midst of heavens. It looked like the times when a certain forest was cleared and the roots were pulled out. The work was done by some Vishnevets residents, not by the police. Until 12:00, on

August 11, 1942, 2,000 or 2,500 souls were destroyed. Their only sin was that their ancestors stood at Mount Sinai.

In the evening, we left the house where we and the 32 had spent the whole day without food or a drink of water. We decided to stay one more day; maybe that day we'd find a hiding place. At night, we decided to leave the ghetto under the threat of death. By chance, when we came to the exit next to Beni Mazur's house, the policeman who was guarding the exit walked in one direction, and we – Yakov Markhbeyn and I – took advantage of the moment and crossed the road toward Zagorodzye. From there, we climbed into the forest that led to Great Zagorodzye. We approached one of my better friends and knocked on the window, and when someone answered me through the window with the question "Who is it?" I only requested that they let us in, without mentioning my name. They recognized my voice and opened the door for us. The two of them, mother and son, stood panic-stricken and frightened, and the first to approach us was the son.

"Believe me, I want to do something for you, but the danger is so great that I'll have to risk my life for you, and today a brother isn't doing so for his brother or a father for his son. If only you knew how Vasil Mindzar is visiting each house, beating with murderous blows those who don't want to go out and dig pits to create a place for the dead, whom they murder with shots in the back."

It is worth explaining here that this was the same Ukrainian young man whom I'd asked through a crack on the day they surrounded us to tell me was happening around us with regard to the fact that we weren't allowed to leave as usual for work. To that, he answered me, "When they check and don't find weapons, each one will return to his place uninjured and healthy." He was one of those who made sure the pits were ready so the town wouldn't run out of space for the number to be slaughtered.

[Page 269]

Even though we talked in whispers, he and his mother were full of fear that maybe one of the neighbors heard our knock, and she offered to let us sleep there that night, but said that the next day we had to leave their home without any excuse. We stayed. Weary and fatigued after four days without sleep, we closed our eyes before we lay down. We didn't want to, and also couldn't, think about what tomorrow would bring and how we'd get out of here. At the time that death hung over each step, we felt: Sufficient unto the day was the evil thereof!

We fell into a heavy, deep sleep, and in the morning, at dawn, the Christian young man climbed up to us. We thought maybe he'd at least brought us a piece of bread with some water, and when I saw that he came empty-handed, I said to him, "Ivan, you know we haven't eaten anything for a few days." To that, he answered, "They say there's going to be hunger this year from a bread shortage."

It was harvest time, and the smell of wheat brought from the fields in those days intoxicated us.

He wanted 20 dollars for a piece of bread. We didn't have a choice; we paid him the sum demanded, and for the time being, he forgot the danger that was still hanging over him – maybe because we didn't mention it to him – and so a few days passed. On one of those days, he returned from town and told us that every day Jews were being taken out of their hiding places to be killed, and they thought that according to the murderers' account, three quarters of the population was already dead. Most left their hiding places and gave themselves up to the murderers so as not to die of starvation.

On August 20, 1942, when he'd already demanded a number of times that we leave him, I made him the offer that tonight he could go to my home. I told him the location where valuable items were hidden, and he could go and take whatever he wanted for himself. All he had to do was go to my two brothers and tell them I was staying with him and take them to his place, and when they arrived, at that moment, we'd leave his house together. He didn't refuse, and that night, he came up and told us he was leaving. By the way, I also asked him to take not much, but at least one or two shirts for me so I could change the one that I hadn't changed for 12 days.

We didn't sleep all night. We waited impatiently; maybe they'd all come together with the shirts. The night passed and morning came, and no one from the house came up to us. We didn't know what to think. We were worried that maybe he'd been caught on the way. Maybe when he returned with the items, he was taken to the police station, and now for sure they'd come to him, conduct a search, and find us. Every moment, a new thought came to our minds, one more horrible than the other, and maybe my two brothers had gone with him, and they maybe they'd caught all of them? Who knew, and if nothing had happened, why wasn't he at least climbing up to let us know how his mission had gone? That day, at 10:00 or 10:30, our savior reported. He told me how successful he was. When he arrived at the place, he opened the small door with one knock, and there behind the doors, he found the items. He couldn't take everything at once.

[Page 270]

When I reminded him that I needed a shirt in order to change the dirty shirt I'd already been wearing for almost two weeks, he answered that he'd brought everything under great fear and needed it all for himself. He didn't give me any shirts, and as for my brothers, he'd found out that they'd been taken out the previous evening, and now they were in the Great Synagogue, and according to whispers in the streets, tomorrow, meaning Saturday, August 2, 1942, they'd be slaughtered. I didn't dare complain that he didn't give me a shirt, because I didn't want to arouse the anger of the owner of our lives, and second, I wanted to ask him to go to the location where the synagogue was and give one of my brothers a note from me. I wrote these words on it:

"Try to take any opportunity you have to escape from where you're staying, even if it involves a mortal risk, because they've gathered you so they can take all of you to be killed at one time, so if you try to escape, you may be able to save yourselves. Any other way, they'll kill you for sure. I'll wait for you until tomorrow at the home of the person delivering this note, and we'll leave together. Maybe we can reach Brody. He won't allow us to stay more than one day."

That evening, he came and told us he'd delivered the note to my brother and promised him he'd give it to the second brother so that they'd try to find a way to leave together, and if they could, they'd come to the designated location in the evening, and then we'd see what we could do. We waited for them all night; it was on Friday, August 21, 1942. The next morning, I asked the young man to go and see what had happened. After an hour or an hour and a half, he came back with the message that the synagogue was empty, meaning that on August 22, they'd taken all of them, a few hundred men, women, and children, to be killed. He let us stay until that evening. We stayed until 8: 30 and left for the road.

Some people remained in hiding, but every day, families gave themselves up to the murderers so they wouldn't starve to death. Two weeks later, we found out that a month or two passed before the final liquidation.

This is all I can write as a witness to the torture, horrors, and cruelty, and how the Ukrainian murderers tortured us. And again I repeat that all the Jews in our town, Vishnevets, along with the Jews from Vyshgorodok, were murdered only and only by the Ukrainians. Without them in our district, the Poles in Poland, and all the Christian population in all their locations, they couldn't have exterminated us so cruelly.

We have to memorialize everything that I testify to here on this paper. It is possible that I haven't revealed all the details about our murderous neighbors' brutality. The generations that come after us should know how and whom we can trust and remember the saying "If I am not for myself, who is for me?"

[Page 271]

The Story of Asher Sofer
by Cherne (Katz) Rabin (Lanovits)

I knew Asher before I saw him. In 1930, I had a Hebrew teacher named Yosef Spirt, of blessed memory. He was a good Jew and a loyal Zionist. He tried to establish the Hebrew language through a variety of methods and using all his skills, because our school wasn't recognized by the Polish authorities and was almost illegal. He didn't have many possibilities, but he did everything to the best of his ability and understanding. He had an idea that I could practice the language by exchanging letters. I liked the idea, but with whom? Surely, could I write letters to people in Lanovits? Then he remembered Asher, a family member and a young man around my age who lived in Vishnevets and knew Hebrew; maybe we'd find common interests to write about to each other. When Yosef Spirt, of blessed memory, explained the purpose to Asher, he agreed to write first, and so he did. After I answered him, we began exchanging letters, and my teacher's goal was met. And so I knew Asher before I saw him.

During my vacation that year, I decided to visit my family in Vishnevets. I wanted a little change from the atmosphere in Lanovits, and I wanted to meet a new group of young people. I already knew one person, and I informed Asher that I was coming. That evening, he came to introduce himself, and through him I met his friends. I spent almost a month in Vishnevets, and obviously I saw Asher and his friends almost every evening.

During our conversations, he told me about his daily activities. I knew he dedicated his days to his movement and Betar. I saw the enthusiasm with which he talked about the movement and how he was connected to it, and saw that he was doing his duties with dedication and great belief. I belonged to a different movement, and the arguments between the movements' leaders were very serious, sometimes involving conflict and hatred, but all these matters didn't interfere with our friendship. We could have a good time together without mentioning our different points of view.

After that summer, when I had such a good time and felt so good among the friends I'd made, I returned to Vishnevets every time I had the chance. I had the opportunity to do so at least twice a year, and each time, I found Asher immersed in the movement's work. His belief in the movement grew stronger when he started to teach younger people, and he did it with great dedication.

The movement started to take away his days and evenings. Some evenings, he joined us late "because the movement was first in everything," and I appreciated him for that.

[Page 272]

He was able to serve as an example to a different group of young people who didn't belong to a movement and were involved in reckless behavior and lacked substance.

Even with all his activities, he never forgot his friends and didn't forget to welcome me the day I arrived in Vishnevets.

There was a kind of rare nobility in him that was expressed in his social behavior, the way he argued with those who opposed him, his relationship with his students at his movement, and mostly the way he treated his family.

***

When the horrible news of Hitler's holocaust arrived, I remembered everyone who remained there, my friends and family. I also remembered Asher, and my heart ached. I mourned all of them, and I also mourned him.

One early evening, I went to visit Yone Ron. The street and the house were covered with darkness – maybe it was a power failure or maybe it was just gloomy – and from a dark entrance I was asked, "Someone has arrived from Vishnevets. Please guess who it is. He's here with us."

I answered in an instant, "Asher Sofer!"

I don't know how it crossed my mind that he'd survived, that he was alive. But my heart told me he'd arrive. He deserved to enjoy the fruit of his Zionist dedication.

The meeting was emotional. There was no end to curiosity: How did he get here? How had he made it? And what was the fate of everyone without whom we thought we'd never be able to live? Asher promised to come to my home and tell me everything.

At the end of 1945, the country was under the whim of the crumbling British rule. Week after week, there was a curfew, and day after day, there were surprises. At night, we went to bed not knowing if they'd declare a curfew while we were sleeping or if we'd have enough time to get food. And look, someone knocked on my door at five after midnight. I was afraid that maybe the British had come to my home. My husband was wanted by them as an active member of an anti-British clandestine movement. With our hearts pounding, we carefully went down to open the door, and Asher Sofer was standing in front of us, dressed in a uniform with Polish insignia.

I was astounded.

What was this Polish patriotism here in our country? When we hated them in their country.

And here is his story, which he told little by little during the six weeks he was in hiding.

When the Germans began bombing Warsaw, he was working at the Betar office in Warsaw. In 1939, he sensed that a war was going to break out. Everyone ridiculed him. He paid no attention to them, packed his suitcases at once, and left for the train station, where to his surprise he found everyone, even though they'd laughed at him a couple of hours earlier. They all traveled to a safe place. He went directly home. It seems that his heart predicted he'd never see them again. Meanwhile, the Russians entered Vishnevets. He felt that his place wasn't there because of his many sins, being the son of the well-to-do Issakher Sofer and an active member of the Betar movement.

[Page 273]

When Asher asked for a job, someone told him cynically, you're not getting a job because we have a long account with you. Immediately, Asher understood his situation and decided to leave town. He said goodbye to his brothers and asked them not to tell their father. When he went to say goodbye to his sister-in-law, Shlome's wife, she was shocked when she heard where he was going and began screaming. Asher covered her mouth so his father wouldn't hear, and with a small suitcase, like one you'd take on a short trip, he quietly and sadly left his birthplace.

After a great deal of hardship, he arrived in Vilna, where he found many friends and leaders of the Betar movement. From there, he was able to inform his family where he was staying. Taking a mortal risk, his brother Yoel came and brought him a little money to live on and reach the Land. Asher tried to convince his brother to stay, but his responsibility to his family and to his father prevented him from doing so.

In Vilna, they looked for ways to immigrate. Meanwhile, they held movement activities in hiding, and to support themselves and cover their activities, they worked in trades.

Among them was a person named Slutski, who was a talented graphic artist. He made counterfeit documents for himself and visas to China for Asher and Shpilberg, without their party's knowledge.

With great fear, Asher handed his documents to the authorities, and everything went through without any problems. They joined a group of 12 illegal immigrants and left for the Land of Israel via Moscow and Turkey.

In Mersin, Turkey, they had to report to the Jewish Agency, and Barlas, its representative. When his turn came, he asked to be alone with Barlas and revealed everything to him – his illegal status and his connections to Betar.

His two friends didn't see anything wrong with what they'd done, but Asher was afraid he was endangering the agency's status and reputation and wanted the agency's men to act cautiously.

But Barlas jumped up and answered him, "You can go back where you came from; we don't want to endanger the agency because of an illegal immigrant."

With great fear, Barlas telegraphed Dr. Yonitsman of Betar and informed him of Asher's dangerous act, but he didn't raise a finger to save him.

Asher was left penniless in Turkey, depressed and without a chance to reach the Land.

Somehow, the news reached his brother Yosef. Immediately, he went to Shprintsak and informed him that he belonged to the Betar movement. To that, Shprintsak answered, "But he's not a Communist?"

And he authorized an immigration certificate.

In 1941, Asher arrived on Israel's shores from Turkey in a rickety fishing boat.

In 1942, he volunteered for the Jewish Brigade, but he was disqualified because of his poor vision. Revenge consumed his heart. He wanted to go to the front lines to shed German blood and avenge his parents, friends, and relatives who'd been murdered. When he couldn't, he enlisted in Anders Army in order to return to Poland, to the burial town of his ancestors and the tragic victims, and to avenge their blood on the various front lines.

[Page 274]

He was accepted into the army as a medic.

He was able to reach Syria, but Asher realized there that he wouldn't be able to fulfill his mission with them. In addition, he saw that they hadn't changed their Nazi anti-Semitic ways, even toward their brothers-in-arms, and he realized that he wouldn't be able to go into battle with them. He decided to leave, no matter the prices. He deserted, and with great difficulty and without documents, he arrived in the Land. The night he arrived, he decided not to endanger his two brothers; maybe the British would search for him at their homes at their Polish allies' request. And so he came to us.

[Page 275]

R' Simche Ayzik Rotman

by M.M.

R' Simche Ayzik Rotman

One of the most outstanding characters in Vishnevets, who left his mark on our town and its way of life, was the great teacher R' Simche Ayzik. He excelled in his great knowledge of the Talmud and all the Holy Scriptures and their interpretations, and his revitalized knowledge and multifaceted education earned him a great name in town.

Today, it is difficult to say how he came to be in our town. Maybe he was among its founders or maybe one of its first builders, but many generations before ours talked about him as a town prodigy. He acquired his knowledge by studying on his own and increased his knowledge of many fields without anyone's help. Everything came to him from himself, and as usual in cases like that in such towns, there's no one to tell us whether he studied on his own because he loved it, because there was no one greater than him to teach him, or because he didn't have the means or any parents to support him, etc.

His multifaceted education in the ways of the world earned him endless appreciation and admiration but also misgiving and distrust.

For three generations, he taught the Torah and good manners to local older boys, and when they finished their studies with him, they were considered bridegrooms in everything. At that time, his cheder was probably called "a school for bridegrooms."

The town turned to him with a variety of requests. He gave his help, and there was no end to the admiration and praise he received. But R' Simche Ayzik Rotman reached the height of his glory when he was asked to compose a petition to the Russian czar to soften his heart so he'd order a pardon for R' Yosile Radoviloy, who had been arrested as punishment for murdering a slanderous teenage boy. His letter, which was embedded with classical celebrated words – as the members of the generation before us related – touched the Czar's heart, and he tore up the evil decree. R' Yosile was taken out of prison, although the fear of a trial continued to hang over his head.

What distinguished R' Simche Ayzik is that then, around 100 years ago, he adopted an advanced outlook on the world and leaned toward the Enlightenment openly and without fearing the difficulties it would bring him.

[Page 276]

His ideas about man and society and about Jewish society in foreign lands outpaced his generation's ideas, and for many years he rebelled against the local people and their lifestyle. The war of opinions he conducted with the public and its leaders wasn't an easy one and caused him a lot of hardship. If not for his great personality and his firm stand as a scholar, who knows if he could have stood it. We find the echoes of this war in his notebook, which he left with one of his dedicated students, Eliyahu Averbukh, of blessed memory, which by chance reached us – completely yellow, eaten by mold, and with blurred writing.

In those writings, we see a man who locked himself in his attic at night, and maybe in his solitude he investigated and wrote down the changes and suffering in his soul and the obstacles he faced when he wanted to live according to the values of those changes.

In the tradition of the intellectuals of that time, he used ornate Hebrew in his writing. Each sentence contained part of a verse from the Prophets and part of a sentence from rabbinic literature. It seemed as if he needed to "base" his ideas on our prophets' words and the proverbs of our sages, of blessed memory. Because of his great familiarity with the style of their phrases, and to give his ideas legal standing, he drew from those who preceded us and those who preceded them.

His notebook is paved with fables, animal fables, events in the forest and the heavens, satirical songs, and epigrams, all in the style of the "logic of the harp," with the harp and the singing helping the logic. There are also letters to an imaginary addressee who probably symbolizes the Jewish institution of those times. He heaps abuse and disrespect on him, calling him "a borrower who pulls his hand from his lender," meaning that he loaned his former students, the tax collectors of wisdom, a great deal of silver and gold, but instead of paying off their loans, they slip away from him, not only escaping the subject once and for all, but also plotting to "swallow him from the face of the earth" and "lower him into a pit."

His long poems, which are rhymed with multicolored dense verses, reflect the era and its leaders. Their actions and the opinions they shared are of great interest for our book.

We can't translate and present all of them. The few we've selected shed light on the darkness in which a generation of Vishnevetsers lived (as did the people of other towns), where they tried to hatch their dream to become a nation not among the gentiles, but in a country where the sky covers the land.

The long poem we present reflects the deep tragedy of a man who fights a war on both sides.

On one side, he provides the local children, his students, with progressive ideas, putting tools in their hands so they can live a brilliant life in the world to come, but as a result, his eagles spread their wings and want to fly out of his cheder, and the danger of losing his source of income hovers over him. And maybe it's not only the lack of income that worries him, but the possibility that all his Jewish teaching might shatter at once against the rock of estrangement.

The poem is directed to his students. He "sends his regards" to them and appeals to his "loving friends who also study together" not to say, "the term is over – it's time to go to the Russian teacher," because this wasn't his intention when he preached for education.

[Page 277]

It is apparent that the Jewish intellectuals' gloomy, miserable drama also broke out in full strength in our town, and its echoes were carried in the hearts of three generations, the students of R' Simche Ayzik Rotman, the generation's most loving and most tragic teacher in our town. And maybe, who knows, he gave them the push to live in a country – not the Kingdom of Heaven, but a real country that isn't waging a war of shadows. On the other side, the short second poem, "On the Enlightenment," testifies to his idealism and the price he paid for his opinions and his idealism, so that "poor and rich/strike me, hit and wound me."

Today, we don't see these poems as harmless or lacking in tension. The echoes of burning souls rise from them, and many of the best of our nation were burned by them. And as their poems become more innocent, the personalities of those who were willing to stand on their opinion grew to the point where they were willing to pay the price for it.

Who knows if the great sacrifice of the people who secretly fought for the "delicate, holy language," the commanding language of the praised sons of the Israel Defense Forces, and their fight to give young men "the knowledge of the world" that today is in its new resurrection is the Weitzmann Institute and many others. Who knows if we could have reached what we have today without them.

The story of R' Simche Ayzik, of blessed memory, is a story of an innocent warrior who fought for a great intellectual conclusion, and we see the results in our nation's life today and …so it started.

His story is the story of our town and its war of opinions, and so it came to an end.

Both deserve to be on a tablet.

[Page 278]

Loving Friends
by Simche Ayzik Rotman

1.

Loving friends who also
study together,
don't be in a hurry to
leave school,
don't learn to lie and
destroy
in insulting language
and beautiful sayings.

2.

"Because it's time for
the term to be over,"
"you're already at the
Russian teacher's."
Surely it is a stupid and
cunning evil way
that sits and waits to
divert you toward
idleness,

to spend your days with
emptiness and your
nights with fear,
and he won't refrain
from evil devices.

    3.

Don't step out of your
bounds, and don't break
the fence;
don't leave the cheder
before your time;
don't extend weekdays
at the expense of the
holy day;
don't touch each other
by a hairsbreadth;
don't come to devour the
holiness inside you
to throw it off you like a
burden, like a load.

    4.

The Torah should not be
your blazing religion,
given to you as a legacy
in those days
as temporary reading
and tasteless plaster
that is easy to read in
an hour or two,
not with great effort and
sweat on your face;
its secrets will be dark
for you, and its
wrappings a fog.

    5.

My hand won't come
down heavily on you so
you can sit in the in a
narrow room of Law

or just study the
delicate, holy language,
because before you I
discovered
and before you my heart
didn't hide
that a young man's duty
is to study his country's
language.

6.

Also the different fields
of science,
knowledge of the ways of
life,
it is good for a young
man to collect it by the
handful;
he will long for the
secrets of the wise
so he won't join them
with an embarrassed
face;
they will be his eyes in
the land of the living.

7.

But only this I'll
comment to your morals
so you won't precipitate
in matters so you won't
sabotage your timing
don't tear the crown of
beauty from yourself
and a maidservant won't
become a mistress.

8.

Then you will bring a
blessing to your souls
and the work of your
hands

at someone who sends
his regards;
I am your teacher.

[Page 280]

On The Enlightenment

by Simche Ayzik Rotman

Because in public
it is called a traitor
that desecrates everything holy
and only being praised
by this, by them,
she is the Enlightenment.

And this is all my sin,
and I could not find
poor and rich
they strike me, hit and wound me.

[Page 281]

My Parents,
Some of the First Immigrants from Vishnevets
by Shlome Rachmani

Our town, Vishnevets, was saved from the pogroms that took place in the towns around us, but the fact that we were saved by a miracle left an unpleasant feeling in me, and I decided to leave.

I immigrated in 1920, and I was one of the first young immigrants from my town.

My father, R' Moshe Derbarimdiker, R' Levi Yitschak of Berdichev's grandson, built a house in Vishnevets, and its atmosphere settled in his son's souls. I didn't rest here in the Land until I brought him here, and then I calmed down.

R' Moshe Derbarimdiker secured a place for himself in Vishnevets on his own accord and never mentioned his origin to anyone in order not to magnify his name. He was resolute in his opinions, gave a lot of advice to those who approached him, and was willing to help each person in his time of distress.

My mother, Nechame, managed the store and enabled Father to deal with his public work, listen to his fellow man's whispers, and delegate his free time to clear matters brought in front of him.

Mother was known for the fact that every day from the age of 12, she woke up early to pray in a quorum and never missed a day of prayer, and here in the Land, she used to pray next to the Western Wall, and as was her custom, she never stopped until her last day.

I was very young when I emigrated, and I suffered as many others did at that time, but it didn't stop me from convincing Father to liquidate his business and immigrate.

In 1925, my parents and their children immigrated. It's a pity that our brother Chayim stayed there and perished with his whole family.

In a way, their immigration forged links between generations. In 1850, Bat-Sheve, our grandmother's twin sister, immigrated after she got married, and established the well-known Olshteyn family here in Jerusalem. Every once in a while, she visited our town with her sons, and her visits served as an awakening to Zion and its forgotten existence.

My parents' immigration at that time was a kind of pioneering renewal, and the impression it left on the people of our town wasn't quickly forgotten. You can say that each immigrant to the Land confused those who remained in town, and the immigration of my father, of blessed memory, also caused changes in our town's way of life, and we preserve his merit along with the merit of the rest of those first immigrants. May his soul be bound up in the bond of everlasting life.

[Page 282]

Bat-Sheve and Zalman Chazan,
of Blessed Memory
by Meir

They were humble in their ways. With modesty and simplicity, they extended help to all who were in need during times of unemployment and lack of a day-to-day income. Those who needed financial aid received it at the Chazans' home. Their home served as a meeting place for people from Vishnevets and towns nearby, such as Lanovits, Shumsk, and Vyshgorodok.

When Zalman worked as a tinsmith and his income was meager, the Chazan family listened to the whispers of those who suffered, and their home was an inn, a friendly, warm corner to those who entered.

Tel Aviv: Greetings from Israel 5691

[Page 283]

Loyal to the renewal of Zion, Chazan's soul was dedicated to the building of the Land and population's suffering from the Mandate's government's restrictions and bloody riots and conflicts with Arab gangs. With their limited funds, they carried a heavy load and brought members of their immediate family to the Land. They gave them financial aid and helped them settle.

After the accident that took Zalman's life, Bat-Sheve was left alone. Many who knew her and enjoyed her kind heart didn't come to comfort and help her. But Bat-Sheve didn't take it to heart or complain during her troubles and loneliness. With her good nature, she didn't despair, and before her death, as we knew she would, she willed all her property to help others, to "Ilan" and the Organization of Vishnevets Emigrants.

The money from her estate, thousands of Israel pounds, served as the foundation and covered a generous part of the publication of Sefer Vishnevets.

Let the page with their picture that we have in front of us be a memorial to Bat-Sheve and Zalman Chazan, of blessed memory.

[Page 284]

In Memory
of the Martyrs of Vishnevets
by Chayim Rabin

May the nation that resides in Zion remember the martyrs of the Diaspora, who took our nation's sorrowful faith on themselves, kept their Judaism in their souls, and paid for it with their blood.

May the son of a Jewish town remember his birthplace, the cradle of his vision, and remember its residents, who under pressure, desperation, and oppression planted in us the yearning to live openly and in prosperity and freedom.

May the Vishnevets survivor remember the town of his youth, adorned with lovely scenery and springs, where he bloomed and where the flowers of his greatest dream, the dream of living in his homeland, blossomed.

May we remember our parents, brothers, and sisters, our friends from school and our neighbors from the Vishnevets alleyways, who died before their time, before they matured, before they became old and their longing for us and life in the homeland wilted.

We will remember our loved ones, victims of evil men, whose tortured souls left them while they called our names.

We will remember that somewhere in the distance, there is an open mass grave shouting at us,

Remember us!

Build a memorial for us!

Together we were slaughtered, together we were cut off, together we lay in a mass grave, flesh to flesh, skin to skin, and our souls as one.

May our tombstone also be one!

May the man from Vishnevets, wherever he is, remember that it is his duty to remember them, to tell and write their stories a book.

Let us bring the memory of our loved ones to each joyful event, and may their souls be bound in our souls and the souls of our sons after us; may it be so!

[Page 293]

Horror and Death

[Page 295]

The Last Rabbi of Vishnevets
by Edna Yafe

Translated by Tina Lunson

Don't look at me that way, dear Rabbi,
don't look with your wonder eyes.
Your penetrating look has no limit
and your face–heart is in my eyes.

I will never forget, dear Rabbi,
how they made you kneel and crawl,
cut your beard into a cross;
your light that last day, dark as night.

Rabbi, your people are shining again.
Jerusalem is ours once again.
The old history will be no more.
We are told from above: Be anew and be!

[Page 296]

Let Us Not Forget
by Mordekhay Fishman, New York

Translated by Tina Lunson

For the memorial book, I believe that it is my duty to write not only my experiences in my home town, but a memorial, so the time itself is not forgotten and won't be forgotten by Vishnevets compatriots, wherever they are.

I'm one of the few Vishnevets Jews who went through Hitler's concentration camps in Buchenwald and in ghettos. It is not my goal to break your heart by telling about my experience. But only to remind. And who can remind? Only one who went through everything himself, several ghettos and concentration camps, until May 1945. Because when you've read descriptions of ghettos and camps by a talented writer, many of them are translated and interpreted in various ways.

So, accept the reality from your Vishnevets brother who went through that hell, from 1939 in the Petrikov ghetto through Camp Buchenwald and the liberation of Theresienstadt (Czech) in May 1945.

The words in the Shavuot poem Akdamus[1]–that if all the trees and rivers were transformed into pens and ink, they would not be enough to describe the holy Torah's worth–are exactly applicable to me when I attempt to describe everything I went through.

I will limit myself to a few facts in order to convey to you that the memorial shouldn't be just a complaint.

With my own eyes, I witnessed the burning of 500 small children in barrels of gasoline. Living people had to do this, and then dig graves for themselves and go into them alive. This was in the ghetto.

In Buchenwald, a camp that had existed since 1934, the Germans denigrated people, shaming the "aspect of God" in them. It happened that people of higher culture, whom I knew personally, went around as naked as Adam and didn't even know they were naked.

Some 400 people a day literally perished from hunger, and those people didn't have to be burned people alive. The ovens couldn't burn so many dead people. Close to the liberation of Buchenwald, they gathered all the inmates in one place. Ninety percent were sent off to be killed.

[Page 297]

All these are just a few facts, so that this memorial will be written with "ink" that can never be erased. So for our towns, the verse "two towns and one family" is fulfilled, since nothing remains of our town Vishnevets either. Against that we deserve to have a beautiful family in Israel, the Vishnevets Association.

You Vishnevetsers in Israel must be the backbone, the continuation of everything good and fine that was cut down and murdered with the demise of our beloved Vishnevets community.

In our Vishnevets Association, I am the Protocol Secretary, concerned with maintaining relations with you in various ways. Be assured that your brothers in New York are ready to do everything to maintain that connection.

Let's all hope that this memorial book about Vishnevets will enter the house of each Vishnevets Jew, so that throughout the generations they and their children remember and teach what Amalek[2] did to you and your town, Vishnevets.

The destruction of Vishnevets should never recur in the history of mankind. If this memorial book is to be a memorial for us, may our children never forget it either, and we will have fulfilled the duty and the last will and testament of the Vishnevets martyrs that resides with us, the remnants of destroyed Vishnevets.

Remnants of Vishnevets ...

Translation editor's notes:

Akdamus, or Akdamut, is a liturgical poem recited annually on the Jewish holiday of Shavuot by Ashkenazi Jews. return

"Amalek" here symbolizes an enemy of the Jewish people (here, the Nazis). Exodus 17 describes the Amalekites attacking the Hebrews from the rear, where theelderly and other most vulnerable members of the community would have been. return

[Page 335]

Mama

(From the book In klem [In Straits])

by Avraham Lev   Translated by Tina Lunson

Mama you're not here now, Mama!

Mama you are no more.

Who will say sweet rhymes,

who will wipe my tear?

Who will read the little letter

that I've sent out to you,

across a sea on big ships,

back now four years ago?

Then did it ever reach you,

arrive upon your doorstep?

Long years, anxious years–

_____ death from you, and cold.

Where is your grave, where is Mama?

Good Mama, white dove.

Body burned away with others,

reduced to dust, to dust, to dust.

Bring me, wind, just carry here,

dusty ash from Mama's body,

come from four–corners' wander–

find her ash, seek out her ash!

What remains is all

of my Mama, woe is me.

I still see her eyes a–sparkle,

I feel, it seems, still in touch.

Maybe then the wind will carry off

a little ash from her body?

Come on, wind, from distant wanders,

hear at night my quiet call.

[Page 352]

My Mother Is Off to Ponar
by Avraham Lev
Translated by Tina Lunson

"They took your mother to Ponar"...
a young friend brought the news to me,
and then the grief boiled up in me:
Mama, you survive only in these lines!
Sharp sorrow convinced me that
my pen had traced out
my mama's path from Vilna to Ponar,
and from Ponar to unknown heights;
that the wind had lifted her ashes up high,
and where had she later rained down?
And maybe carried them to me, too,
falling in drops of rain.
Just like my tear here on my hand,
and I did not understand:
that my mama was wandering like this
around in the countryside...

[Page 387]

Vishnevets 1944
by Simche Hirsh Betener's

Translated by Tina Lunson

The Russians arrived on December 17, 1939. I was working as a salesman for Yosel Averbukh. Although I was a legitimate employee, I decided to leave town so as not to see the happiness that came with the new regime.

I went to my brother's in Butin, where I was elected pretsedatel siel–Sovieta [village elder].

On October 2, 1940, all the Polish settlers in the area were shipped out to Siberia.

I took this in with a calm conscience, because the settlers in our area were not well liked among the Poles.

On April 16, 1941, I was mobilized into the Russian army and transported deep into Russia, 300 kilometers from Moscow. The Russo–German war broke out on June 22, 1941, and as a tank officer, I was in the thick of it.

I relate this because, as I fought the Germans, I didn't know the Germans were murdering and eradicating the Jewish people. I was fighting for my army and Russia.

In 1942, the Ukrainians, betraying the Soviets, fled from the front and went home. It seems that they'd heard about Hitler's victories. They also wanted to take part in the killing of the Jews. But Stalin thought we were all to blame and ordered all the eastern Ukrainians taken from the front, including Jews. I, however, was considered trustworthy, and I stayed at the front.

At the beginning of 1944, the Russians battled their way to Tarnopol. The Russians didn't let soldiers fight near their home province. I knew that I hadn't told anyone [where I was from], and I set of for Tarnopol Zbarazh with the thought that I might see my family, relatives, and friends.

I went to Dubno. On the street, I recognized a Jew: a capmaker whose name was Yenkel Tsitrin.

A conversation ensued. Gradually, incrementally, he told me: in Dubno, where there had been 16,000 Jews, barely 30 Jews remained: broken people who had survived through a miracle.

[Page 388]

In Kremenets, there were even fewer. In Vishnevets? He implied that he couldn't tell me about our town's misfortune. He said only, "Don't go to Vishnevets! Better stay in Dubno."

I couldn't help myself. I went off to Kremenets and from there, to Vishnevets. I counted the minutes until I got there.

I didn't recognize the town. I went to the dike, which led to the Old City. I stopped my truck and said to my captain, "Comrade Maltsev, I was born in this town, and I request 12 hours' leave."

He tried to talk me out of it, but I convinced him. All the vehicles drove away, and I stayed in Vishnevets.

Walking around in the marketplace near Shimon Chayim Shimon's, I met a gentile from Butin, traveling home. He recognized me and said that I shouldn't stay here in town. The danger was great; I might get killed. He took me to Butin with him. I didn't know that the danger of traveling with him was greater than that of being at the front.

In the village, I went to see Tshervinski. Very touched, he kissed me and begged, "Simche, run away from here. You'll be beaten to death here, and no one will know where your bones are."

I was frightened, and I went from there to a place nearby where I had a good friend, Pavele Pientkovski, and his wife, Anelka. But their house was empty; they'd been gone a long time already, out of fear of the Ukrainians.

I went into the stable. I didn't want to stay in the house. I made a hole in the hay, dug myself in, and looked outside.

Gentile men were lustily singing songs, laughing and joking, but they kept repeating one song.

> We've killed off the Jews
> and planted the trees;
> the trees will develop,
> we will turn to the ladies
> the Polish pabirate.

[Page 389]

At four o'clock in the morning, I left there and went to Vishnevets. I covered six kilometers in 40 minutes, running in fear.

In town, I felt better than in the shadow of the singing gentiles.

I walked around until 7:30 and then met a Jew. I recognized him: it was Hershel Margolius from the Old City, a relative of my mother's. It was from him that I first heard about the great misfortune. His fractured "news" was a rain of pain and sorrow–who could bear it?

They had shot the Vishnevets rabbi to death and buried him along Pochayev Road along with the gentile Ivan Volinski, who was a deputy for the Russians. They themselves had to dig the graves.

There were four pits in the Old City where about 2,500 Jews were buried.

I had to rejoin my military unit. I went into the office, and I recognized the same Russian who had sent me away before. He grabbed me around and said with a big smile, "See how lucky you are. If not for me, you wouldn't be alive now either!"

It was true.

There was an unlicensed physician in Vishnevets, Avraham Yenkel, and a gentile, Sheteras. I didn't find the Jew, but Sheteras was still alive, and they called him "doctor." They had killed Avraham Yenkel and Dr. Grintsvayg as well. He was "one in a million," as they say. When I asked the Russian official if I could lengthen the 12 hours to 30 days, he told me to go to the "doctor" and tell him I wasn't well, I wasn't in good health.

I went to the unlicensed doctor, and he recognized me right away. He used to visit Yosef Averbukh every day. I said nothing. He examined me and said that I was 100 percent healthy and didn't need 30 days. I understood his intention and got very angry. In my anger, I grabbed my revolver and was going to shoot him. He was shocked and started shouting, and the officer came in. He grabbed me by the hand, winked at the "doctor," and we went out. Afterward, he signed me up for 90 days.

[Page 390]

Before I left I said, "Look, your son is alive, as are you and your family. My entire family is gone. How can you act like this?"

I met with Hershel Margolius again. There was another Jewish woman with him, from a village whose name I don't remember. They both told me horrifying facts that made me shudder. But a lot of Jews from Vishnevets will not want to read them, because they took part in them. Now they're going around in Israel disguised, as if for a Purim ball.

I also saw entryway steps made of Jewish gravestones. I saw floor coverings and boots made of parchment from Torah scrolls.

On the graves in the old cemetery, the bones of our brethren and elders were thrown around, uncovered by earth.

In the Great Synagogue, I found the names of our near, dear, Vishnevets friends, which they had managed to inscribe on the walls before the final death march, so that generations later one could know that it was from here that they went to their gruesome slaughter.

[Page 391]

I can't describe so well what I saw and heard in Vishnevets. The town's destruction was wiped away, but the traces of the mass murder couldn't be wiped away. Everything in the town spoke of the worst things that our dearest had to bear.

I met with Anelkin Piontkovski's wife, who told me:

"Even before the Germans arrived, they took 70 Jews and threw them into the cellar at Shimon Chayim Shimon's. They gave them axes and shovels and told them kill one another with them. The Jews didn't want to do this, so they killed themselves in the most horrible ways. With stones, iron bars, and bullets. Only one of them was left, Hershele Sender's. He had had a tavern. All the gentiles used to go there to drink. He was thrown in with the dead, and their stones and bullets missed him. At night, he got out, bloodied and drenched in his neighbors' blood, and related what had happened.

My father was among the first victims. He was coming to her in Poland, near Butin, to ask for bread and potatoes for his family members, who were hungry. At night, Ukrainians from Vishnevets came and talked with glee about "snatching Jews." She begged my father to stay the night at their house, but he answered that his wife would be apprehensive and worried. And he left.

He never saw his family or his world again.

Chayim Kornfeld–we called him Chayim Shmeline–Mordekhay Boytiner's brother, was caught by gentiles in Mishkovtsy and beaten to death. My father–in–law, Moshe Rozental, buried him in the little valley behind Katsap's woods, because they wouldn't allow him to take him into town.

Yashke Badeysiuk, a shoemaker, became a police officer for the Germans and killed hundreds of Jews. When I was there, he hid in a well, and I dragged him out of there and brought him to court. I saw that murdering Jews wasn't a serious crime in the world for any gentile, and told Hershel Margolius that he should be a witness and say that he had killed Russian parachutists. Hershel did as I asked. The prosecutor jumped for joy and said, "Scoundrel, confess. If you tell the truth, we'll shoot you, and if not, we'll hang you, and you'll suffer."

[Page 392]

Badeysiuk replied, "Do with me what you will. There are plenty of Ukrainians here. They'll get even with you for me."

I've recorded what I remember. It's difficult to remember more; it's even harder to return to and describe it.

[Page 401]

Our Poor Town

[Page 408]

Vishnevets–Historical Dates

by Chayim Rabin

Translated by Tina Lunson

1. Universal Encyclopedia (Published 1867)

... a small town in Volhynia province, Kremenets district, lies on the right bank of the Horyn [River] between two large lakes ... known for its ancient fortress, and its history is closely tied to the history of the famous princedom of the Wisniowiecki Korybuts.

Near the fortress that was built, the town of Vishnevets was established in 1395 by Dymitr Korybut, the Sewacy prince, whom Prince Witold drove out and gave areas with estates in Volhynia; and there he built the nest for his dynasty.

Some ascribe the founding of the fortress to his grandson, who was named Soltan.

The town itself and its peripherals appear only in the light of the fires of wars. It was first mentioned in 1494, when a small Polish unit was based there by Crimean Tatars.

In 1500 it was turned over to Ivan the Terrible, as the Tatars had ruined some of his towns, among them Vishnevets, which the Tatars had totally burned, and they had taken 5,000 people from the area captive.

In 1502, the same chronicler relates, 9,000 Tatars attacked it at the point of Mongolian arrows, and destroyed the entire area surrounding Vishnevets with fire and sword.

Only on April 28, 1512, did the Poles repay the Tatars for their two defeats, when a Polish army of 6,000 under Hetman Mikolai Koniecpolski's command penetrated the Tatars' 24,000–man army lines two miles from Vishnevets, near Lopuszyna. They killed many and took 16,000 soldiers as prisoners.

From then on, the enemy did not dare approach the walls of Vishnevets for more than 100 years.

In 1672, the fortress was restored by Jeremi Wisniowiecki, after which he fell into the Turks' hands because of the Jews' betrayal.

[Page 409]

In 1744, after the death of Michal Serwacy, the last of the Wisniowieckis, his estates went to his daughters, Oginska and Zamoyska.

In 1781, King Stanislaw August visited Vishnevets for the months of October and November to conduct discussions with Prince Pawel of Russia. It is said that the town rabbi entertained him with passionate speeches in Latin.

In 1867, we find Vishnevets as a town built of wood, rich in trade, and poor in industry. There were one fabric factory and a few tanneries. The population was then 5,000.

2. Jewish Encyclopedia, edited by Dr. Katsnelson and published 1908–1913

... In 1765, the Vishnevets community registered 475 Jews in the Old City, 26 in the New City, and another 163 Jews in the surrounding villages.

As it is told, the Jews in Vishnevets were slaughtered in 1653 by the Tatars, who had returned from Berestechko, and their homes were totally destroyed.

In New Vishnevets, the Jewish community numbered 3,178 in 1847 and 2,980 in 1897, out of a population of 4,196.

3. Register of the Council of Four Lands

1. In the Register, Vishnevets is called Vishnits, which is in the Volhynia voivodeship.

2. In 1597, a rabbi writes there:

"... and with God's help I didn't give up, and the conference in the holy community of Vishnits, Lutsk province, when all the leaders (heads) of the four holy communities traveled to meet. Those are Ludmir, Kremenets, Lutsk, and Ostra. Also, on 18 Adar we ventured there to renew the curses and decrees."

Here he refers to boycotting rabbis who purchase their seats (positions) for money and rabbis who are preoccupied with Kabbalah.–Chayim Rabin

4. Volhynia Anthology Reveals (Source Unknown)

From a treatise in the Council of Four Lands over Volhynia, which took place in the town of Vishnevets in 1635, we learn that Rabbi Y. T. Lipman Heler (the commentator Yom–Tov), town rabbi of Ludmir, laments heavily that there are too many pretenders to rabbinic "posts" here in various towns and that the provincial governors and village elders are making a business of selling such posts and getting rich from it.

[Page 410]

The commentator Yom–Tov received compensation from the Volhynia Jewish Community Council to set restrain this and prohibit the sale of rabbinic posts, which was having a detrimental effect on the various communities.

The meetings of the Council of Volhynia Assemblies took place in Kozin, Korets, Kremenets, and Vishnevets.

The chief business of the elected was the just distribution of taxes.

Guide to Volhynia
Composed by Dr. Mstislav Orlovich

Translated by Tina Lunson

Sources:

Antiquities of Volhynia, by Dr. Zigmunt Mormits; Art and Antiquities of Volhynia, by Dr. Yozef Piotrkovski, originally written in 1923 and published in 1929.

The Town

... In the broad valley of the upper Horyn, 22 kilometers from Kremenets, lies the town of Vishnevets, with 3,500 residents.

... The road from Kremenets to Vishnevets is very surprising. It goes through wide, fruitful fields along the foot of the high plains with no trees or forests. About midway along the road, we travel through the village of Horynka, at the source of the Horyn River Volhynia's large, beautiful river, which flows from it.

... You can see Vishnevets distinctly only when you come down the last hill before the town. From the hill, we come down into a deep valley. Then the town shows itself as exceptionally paintable, as the Carmelite church steeples rise over the roofs of the small houses.

History

Vishnevets is the nest of the mighty Wisniowiecki family principality, which stems from

Prince Dymitr Korybut, son of Algirdas.

At the end of the 14th century, he founded the town of New Vishnevets near the village of Old Vishnevets.

[Page 411]

The land estates of Vishnevets belonged to the family until its demise with Michal Serwacy's death ... the governor of Volhynia province, who died in 1744. Then Vishnevets and all its possessions went from the Wisniowieckis, as a dowry from his granddaughter Katarzyna, to the Mniszech family. The gift consolidated their family and remained in their hands until the beginning of the 19th century. Then Vishnevets and its periphery went over the Plater family and in 1852 was sold by Baron Andrzhei Plater to the Russians.

The Vishnevets principality extended over an area of 900 square kilometers and included several towns and 16 villages. Vishnevets is located on the most northerly bank of the Horyn, which creates a lot of small lakes, which are dirty, muddy, and mostly overgrown with thick aquatic plants.

Just like Kremenets and Pochayev, Vishnevets possessed very old buildings, characteristic of Volhynia towns in the 18th and 19th centuries. The houses were built in the classic or empire style, of wood covered by brick on the outside, the roofs high and the fronts decorated with balconies and balustrades. The small houses that ring the market square and spread along the little side streets are among the loveliest houses in Volhynia.

The Palace (Zamek)

The most excellent bit of antiquity in Vishnevets is the palace. It was built by Michal Serwacy in 1720 on the ruins of Jeremi Wisniowiecki's old fortress. At first, the palace was built in the late Baroque style. In the Mniszech era, it was enlarged and rebuilt in the rococo style. According to the memorial plaque hanging in the entryway courtyard, the rebuilding was completed in 1781 with money from Michal Wandalin Mniszech and his wife, Urszula, of the Zamoyski family. The Mniszech family also had an exhibition of the most famous paintings in the world there.

The receiving room, the stairway, and the ballroom upstairs were adorned with 45,000 Dutch porcelain tiles, framed by figurative garlands. In one room was a gallery of portraits of the Polish kings, and in another, likenesses of various local governors and other famous people. The rococo room with its mirrors was wonderful, as were the dining room, some of the lower salons, and the special libraries, whose shelves were decorated with artful paintings and portraits; in the rooms where Stanislaw August and Pawel I had stayed, there were framed plaques on the walls.

[Page 412]

Until the first half of the 19th century, when the palace was occupied by the Poles, it was really a kingly palace, but under the Russians it gradually went to ruin.

The contents of Marina Mniszech's famous art gallery were sold to Moscow and Kiev, and along with that they let go the largest part of its artistic magnificence. The remaining art collection was saved by General Demidov, who owned the palace at the beginning of the 20th century. Although he himself was Russian, he honored the historic and artistic memories of Vishnevets.

During World War I, Baron Grocholski bought up the estate and the palace.

In 1920, with the Bolsheviks' invasion of Vishnevets, the palace was completely ruined and its beauty stolen. All that remained of it were empty walls. The last artistic decorations were gone, along with the valuable collections, and on the lower floor they ripped the valuable porcelain tiles off the walls.

After the war, the Kremenets District Committee bought the palace for $40,000 and restored and redecorated it for use as a trade school, orphanage, and hospital.

The huge orchard at the palace–planted on a hill that sloped down to the Horyn and broadened into an area of about 3,000 dunam–was one of the largest and most beautiful orchards in Volhynia.

The palace stands on the site of the Vishnevets fortress, whose protective ramparts and dugouts are still there to this day. Prince Jeremi Wisniowiecki, the king's father, was born in the fortress. In 1640, he built a protective palace on the fortress site; in 1672, the Turks completely destroyed it and uprooted all the town's residents.

On that bank of the Horyn, opposite Old Vishnevets, a village of 1,900 replaced the former settlement.

[Page 413]

A Treasure of Memories

by Avraham Blum

Translated by Tina Lunson

Even if a man dies on a ship, his soul goes to his ancestors.–Rabbi Tanchuma

Just as it is important to know a person's roots when you talk about him at his funeral, it is also important to know the history of the land of your birth, especially when it has been destroyed along with its martyrs. And we can never hope in a hundred years to make the traditional Jewish request of our children–to "lie with our ancestors"–because there is no sign, no tombstone, where our precious, dear ones lie buried, or where you can go to an ancestor's grave to shed a tear or murmur a prayer with a heartbreaking wail for their holy souls. And just as a blind person is prohibited from reciting the "Creator of lights" blessing because he can't see the light of day, we can't fulfill the commandment to pray at the holy spot or near some clearing in the woods where their scattered bones found their rest, or measure their graves and absorb the same air that their soul does.

Yet there is salvation for the soul, a consolation that we can claim to redress their souls, along with the souls of all the generations who were murdered as martyrs to God–by binding our hearts with an eternal flame for their holy memory, and through charity, lovingkindness, and brotherly love, which is the ethical and noble concept of remembrance and an allusion to the saying "to break your heart is to open it." Time and life cannot extinguish the sacred yahrzeit candle because it belongs to the eternal light of God–the human soul.

I won't and can't add to this lamentation–"do not blame me in my grief"–because I don't possess the wealth of words to express in human language the tragic extinction of our beloved ones: the feelings of our great loss are too deep and the wounds too fresh for words to comfort. To depict such destruction of humanity, one must be the God–blessed mourner who possesses the great religious pathos of an Avraham Ibn Ezra or an Ibn Gabirol, who could bewail the void in pain–clad verses, and I believe that one can only rarely find a comforting word about the great Jewish catastrophe of all time and generations in all the penitential poetry since the beginning of time.

[Page 414]

The unique "Be comforted, be comforted, my people" is spiritual nourishment for Zion and a healing that our ancestors' souls live on in the sanctity of our holy land in the Land of Israel, which we have with the help of the authorities who helped redeem and strengthen the belief that "the Eternal One of Israel does not lie."[1]

*

Having finished my weeping and my funeral oration for our victims and martyrs, I accept the invitation to share a few memories. They, too, are not about material matters, and occupy an honored and respected place in our experiences of the old home–and of Vishnevets in general.

My memories stroll with me, away from the American hustle and materialist hubbub to Vishnevets, to my grandfather Noach, may he rest in peace.

To a certain Friday between the suns, when one throws off the day–to–dayness and prepares to welcome the holy Sabbath–the Sabbath queendom. Each time the enchanting "Come, my beloved"[2] song rings in my ears, my fantasy carries me back to Vishnevets. Before my eyes float the distinguished figures of our parents, may they rest in peace, whom Heinrich Heine so masterfully portrayed in "Rabbi von Bacharach." It's amazing that in all my travels over the great world, I haven't found a single town with so much Jewish charm and people so folksy and dear, on whose faces was etched the symbol of "blameless, honest, and God–fearing" as though they were transfigured from the descendants of Rabbi Shlome Alkabets, the popular Kabbalist and author of "Come, my beloved." No wonder their children have inherited their good characteristics and the lovely ethical intention to "pursue justice and loving–kindness."

As we prayed the afternoon service, the sun shone on the cherry trees as it continued to sink, darkening from the rare, lovely, enchanted, fiery sunset heat, and the prayer leader–a simple–hearted Jew from town who longed for the joy of the Sabbath so he could throw off the weekday yoke–began to sing "Come, my beloved" with enthusiasm and joy. And the others praying caught up the sweetness of the words and sang along: "Sanctuary of the King, royal city, arise and depart from amid the upheaval; too long have you dwelt in the valley of weeping".... And the singing carried them to other worlds and brought balance to their Sabbath souls.

Another glorious image will not leave my memory.

[Page 415]

That is after eating on the Sabbath, when lovely women and charming girls went for a stroll with their husbands and fiancés in the fine, natural landscape around Prince Wisniowiecki's old, historic castle and sang Yiddish folksongs with great feeling. And a few–under the influence of the romantic surroundings–even allowed themselves to sing a Russian love song by Pushkin or Lermantov. And since love doesn't know time or look at a clock, they dallied until the sound of their fathers and grandfathers singing "God, Master of the universe" after the second Sabbath meal reached their ears. They then had to sacrifice their romancing under the starry heavens and the perfumed environment of the forest and trees and hurry home, only to arrive for the last words–if only not to grieve their parents, because respect for elders is held even higher than personal happiness.

Speaking of Vishnevets, I regret that I was only able to find a few sparse facts about the history of the town in Russian archives, and these are as follows:

Prince Michal Wisniowiecki, who drew his lineage from the ancient 13th–century Polish dynasty, inherited the old castle and settled there with his three sons in the 16thcentury, gave the settlement the name of "Vishnavits," after his family name.

In 1640, Vishnevets almost became the capital of Ukraine when Prince Michal and his three sons organized huge Ukrainian armies and marched to Petersburg, conquering Podolia, Kherson, Poltava, and Kiev provinces and half of Moldova.

ing from his triumphs, one of his sons lost his mind over a Jewish girl (her name was not given). Soon after that, Michal left to do battle against the Tatars, Khazars, and Karaims and brought many of them back to his castle in Vishnevets as slaves.

He had a friendly trust in the Karaims–who practiced certain Jewish customs and recited their prayers in Aramaic (Targum)–and befriended a few of them–the Pney–and allowed them to settle in the town among the Jews, whom he dealt with in friendly and respectful terms.

[Page 416]

The population of Vishnevets of that epoch was small and very dear, it seems, not only to the Wisniowieckis, but also to certain Polish and Ukrainian poets, for example Taras Shevchenko. In in his famous poem "Day of Judgment," he depicted a righteous Jew named Moshe who bore the whole pain of his people, but his heart was full of consolation and hope for redemption. The thought that a Vishnevets Jew had found a reverberation in his poetry indicates that the Vishnevets Jews lived in peace, had respect and a means of earning a living, and were under the Wisniowiecki dynasty's protection and later that of other rulers.

Even at the hands of the terrible Ukrainian tyrant and thief Bogdan Chmielnitski, the Vishnevets Jews suffered less than elsewhere in Ukraine, because members of the Wisniowiecki family were always ready to use their influence to help them. It is believed–though without substantiation–that the Jews immigrating into Vishnevets were mostly Ukrainian Jews–right after the Spanish Inquisition (1494). That is an indication that many of our elders prayed in the Sephardi style, while a smaller number used the Ashkenazi style.

Relying on information from our scholars, of blessed memory, that "a man respects his place," Vishnevets can be very proud that the world–renowned saint and miracle worker R' Avraham Baal Shem Tov, the righteous one of blessed memory, lived in the town for a time and used to go every morning to immerse himself in a river deep in the forest. Under the shade of the trees, he would often sit deep in holy thoughts and devotions and, in his solitude, try to bring redemption closer and bring the Messiah. Pious Jews often traveled from Vishnevets to that river–still known as the Baal Shem's Spring to this day–to make requests and drink water from the crystal–clear spring made holy by the Baal Shem.

We're also proud of the fact that the parents of Avraham Goldfaden–father of the Yiddish theater–were born in Vishnevets. And that the famous poet Yitschak Ber Levinson, may he rest in peace, spent nearly every summer in Vishnevets visiting his sister, and while there wrote his purely poetic or everyday songs.

To close my treasury of memories, I'd like to ask my dear fellow Vishnevetsers to forgive me if I stumble into the sin of imprecision or defect in my writing.

[Page 417]

My intent–to create a work of love–was certainly clear, and I hope to find a reward for my work in celebrating your golden jubilee with you today, and the millennium if God wills it, the joy of the 75th in proportion to the joy I have felt while editing the journal, because, in that atmosphere of kindheartedness and brotherly love, I have long sought to recognize the soul of my father, may he rest in peace, and to find my own redress.

His faithful grace will comfort me from all my sighs and griefs; the memory of a good name will be given to me in my house and in the congregation of the Lord. My first property is my inheritance to my children and the children of my children; Eternity forgives, and amen.

Translation editor's notes:

"Be comforted, be comforted, my people" is from Isaiah 40:1. It is recited on the Sabbath after the 9th of Av, which commemorates the destruction of the first and second temples. "The Eternal One of Israel does not lie" is from 1 Samuel 15:29. return

"Come, my beloved" [Lekha dodi] is a liturgical song recited Friday at dusk, to welcome the Sabbath. return

[Page 418]

Vishnevets

by Avraham Averbukh (Todros's)

Translated by Tina Lunson

Which Vishnevets shall I recall?

The Vishnevets of the quiet summer days, out in nature in the misty evenings?

Or the Vishnevets in clouds of smoke from the flaming fires of its destruction?

The Vishnevets of past settled times, with a few well–established town proprietors and the rest of the town half– or full–fledged paupers?

Vishnevets on a holiday. Ayzik, unique in his generation, with his sharp pen; the entire Talmud and Bible in his head, which we, his students, used to beg for: tell him the first word on a page of Talmud, and he could finish the whole page by heart.

Or the Vishnevets of youth longing for the larger, laughing world, to save themselves from poor, lonely bachelorhood?

The Vishnevets of Arke Little Key, who ran the banking system in town, sitting by himself in the kloyz[1] with a chapter of Mishna verses, or the Vishnevets of the Sabbath Jews who wondered, who's taking me for the Sabbath?

The Vishnevets of the Russian police commissioner, the local police, or the Vishnevets in terror of Petliura's pogroms, the highwaymen, and the brave young men who used several methods to avoid being murdered, and succeeded ... better than in other towns and districts at that time.

Or even the New York Vishnevets, with its own four–point program just 30 years before Truman: help for our own from our own, help from society for those who have none of their own.

And Mordekhay Rosivkier "the holy," the joker of Vishnevets, characterizing the help from America so succinctly.

Yisrael from Gatovitse built a fine house with money that his wife's brother sent from Chicago and etched his name in Polish letters.

Mordekhay Kheslivker said, "You see where he built the house–Coolidge Street" (Coolidge was president at the time).

"So maybe the Vishnevets in New York–made up of the lucky ones who left in time–thinks to mention the name from time to time and to save the last remnant."

[Page 419]

And maybe the less–eminent Vishnevetsers, those who might sit near me in a subway car, on a bus, or even in a theater a seat away from me, and we don't know the relationship between us; is it entirely possible that both our grandfathers got a maftir[2] in the kloyz or drank a toast together for the rabbi's yahrzeit?

Which Vishnevets should I think about: the uprooted one, with no hope of rising? Or its rise in America, with no hope of "roots," floating in the air, with no attachment to the past–no aspiration for a future, no spiritual enrichment ... which? Which? Without a clear answer, a voice still calls out: "Vishnevets! Vishnevets!"

Translation editor's notes:

A kloyz is a small synagogue. return

Maftir refers to the honor of being the last person called up to the Torah on Sabbath and holiday mornings and reading from a related section of the Prophets. return

[Page 420]

Vishnevets, My Town

by Yehoshue Zeyger

Translated by Tina Lunson

A little town, the midpoint of a productive, blessed region, dripping with the juice of fruits and vegetables in summer, the fields in autumn heavy with grain and bread aplenty for the population and for export, fine and nicely warmed through the previous winter's snowy incubator–here Jews set up their tent for long generations and lived hand–in–hand with the Ukrainian population–mediated, traded, and developed a standard of living, established workshops for all kinds of trades, current and necessary for their agricultural goals, did not strive to be rich, dealt honestly with their customers, and led a separate life. Who can forget our hardworking craftsmen and village traders, who spent the whole week in the villages subsisting on a piece of dry bread and water, and on Friday returned home on foot for the Sabbath. Summer in the heat and winter in the cold and frost! And thus the threads of life's existence were woven; some had something for the Sabbath, some really had nothing, and so Jews established family homes, bore children, taught them, reared them to a purpose, married them off, grew their families, and got help from grown–up family members. There was light in the Jewish tents. Friday evening bore the sounds of songs of praise; the Sabbath candles burned on the table, and the pure white tablecloth and white challah provided light and a shine, courage and strength to go back into harness for the coming week!

And a short little episode:

[Page 421]

When the Slovak nationals ruled the town for a short time and declared a rebellion against the war, our family had three people lying sick with typhus, and we weren't allowed to go to Rashevski's pharmacy in town to get the medicines we needed for the sick. The patrol was posted near Avraham Lemish's house. I went in and approached the soldier and pleaded for mercy so they'd let me through, but the answer was "Go away. No." It was forbidden. Standing there in despair, I called out, "Comrade Rebel, if you let me go through, I'll give you a gift." "What kind of gift?" one of them asked me. "A white roll, very fresh," I answered. It was a Friday after candle lighting. So, a deal. "Go through quickly and come right back." I went, came back, called the soldier to our house, and gave him the promised gift. That wasn't enough for my mother, of blessed memory, and she said to him, "You have a gift for your humane deed. Now you get another: a cookie sprinkled with cinnamon; and put out the lamp for me, too." "Thank you, thank you." He did so and said happily, "A good night!"

* * *

Yes, regardless, the town's Ukrainian population developed, in a cultural sense. The young people were relatively educated, and they became aware of antisemitic echoes in the land, especially Pochayev Lavra's[1] hateful propaganda or Vitaly Ilyador's pogrom leaflets. But there was no particular expression of this sentiment.

World War I broke out during that time, and that also contributed to the storehouse. In every case, the outward beastly hatred weakened during the occupation of Poland, which put the Poles in the position of a minority, so they were hanging their heads.

Times began to normalize. Trade grew due to greater use by the Ukrainian population, and Jews made a living.

With a penny in the pocket, yours or someone else's, you don't have to fret and sweat about the Sabbath, and Jews began to consider practical goals. Young people especially–some went away to study at yeshiva or university; some took jobs in larger towns.

[Page 422]

Those who stayed in Vishnevets also got organized and did general social and cultural work in the national and Zionist spheres, creating Zionist organizations, a public library, a theater group, and lectures under the name "Week to Week," carried out with their own energies. They founded "Lovers of the Speech of the Past" in which the members spoke Hebrew among themselves–of course, in an Ashkenazi dialect–on the street and in the open. There were even a few extreme members who spoke only Hebrew to servants and Christians. Others in the household had to translate their words, so they taught Hebrew to gentile girls.

I recall that once when returning home from a stroll, I was suddenly ordered by a policeman to go to the police station with him. The police chief received me on a high note, thinking that he knew that I was the organizer of the seditious group that spoke a seditious language among themselves: "I'll present you to the director of investigation according to the paragraph concerning operating an alliance against Tsar Nikolas."

"Your honor, Sir Chief," I answered, "that's incorrect. We're not politicals. We study our Bible. And since we have to learn many chapters by heart, we listen to one another so that we're ready for our examination." "Oh, the Bible," the chief said. "You're really learning the Bible? If so, go home, young man, and sit and study, and recite the Bible with your friends in your language."

Who among us doesn't remember the Sabbath evening strolls near Demidov's "castle"– it, the castle, seemed orphaned and lonely then; the gigantic building with its mirrored salons stood hollow and empty, lifeless and without vitality. The huge park and its fine, tree–lined avenues issued their chords and sighs solemnly and jealously in their solitary aloneness from human steps; the Sabbath evening sun moved off the complex of buildings once a week and came to walk with Israel's sons and daughters for the holiday, here on the winding and flowing pathways. The river opposite was calm and clear, and reflected the strollers. The chapel to the right of the hill stood mute and small, and the young birch trees waved their little leaves, half green and half white, with grace and sympathy and did not even listen to Alter the Convert from Zarudnia with his wooden leg, who was just coming from his work; he crossed himself and bowed to this dummy.

[Page 423]

This had gone on for generations. Because Jews had not only built themselves, but also raised the non–Jews from level to level, higher in everything.

Until Hitlerism came and extracted the latent poison and hatred from the Velokhs, Ivans, and Maxims. They took their portion hand in hand with the arriving murderers. Their action was carried out precisely ... they all killed, burned, and robbed our homes and possessions.

Who doesn't remember ... near Demidov's "castle"

There at the prince's place, where we ran to receive Austrian officers and soldiers, bringing bandages to bind and heal their wounds. There where we brought them milk and food, gave them food and drink, where they lay in the district schools under the cushions and quilts we had collected–there they all dug a hole and threw in suckling children and pregnant women. There is where they murdered the town of Vishnevets …

Not one of you Ulans and Maxims could hide just one Jew, as we now read in Jewish community records how Christians hid whole families of Jews, even though doing so might lead to the death penalty.

[Page 424]

Today you are "Jew free." But the angry winds will root out and carry away our soul, our spirit, and our footsteps from every corner. Demons and witches will rule over our ruined habitations. Jackals will reside there at night. Drunks will loll in your gutters and, unable to bring the word "Jew" to your lips, you will kill one another. The angels of destruction will come down from heaven and will write in red with bloody knives and axes, "God has numbered the days of your kingdom, and it is finished."

And you, Vishnevets brothers and sisters, lie in peace there in your temporary grave. We have registered you as Israeli citizens. A portion in Israel calledB, Yad Vashem has been created for you. The time will come, as soon as possible, when we will also carry your dry bones into your land.

We have etched the Jewish town Vishnevets on parchment and installed it in the state museum of the Land of Israel among all the hundreds of destroyed communities. It remains the property of the people of Israel and the Land of Israel.

Afula, 6.8.1956

Translation editor's note:

Pochayev Lavra is an Orthodox Christian monastery in Pochayev. return

[Page 425]

I See My Vishnevets

by Zeyde Kamtsen (Chicago)

Translated by Tina Lunson

I see my Vishnevets from great America, and I long for it.

I am called Arthur Walker now; I live in a suburb of Chicago. In Vishnevets, they called my father Yisrael "Ally."

I have been in America since 1937, having left as a 21–year–old youth, but I remember Vishnevets even though I studied in Kremenets for years and came to Vishnevets only for

Jewish holidays and vacations.

It was a small town, named for the palace built nearby by a Polish prince named Wisnowiecki. Others explain it differently: it was called that because of the cherry trees planted all around the town, which in Polish are "vishnie."

Vishnevets street, May 3

In the years after World War I, when I was just a child, Vishnevets was a small, sleepy town with unpaved streets covered with a thick layer of dust. In spring and autumn, the streets were full of mud.

[Page 426]

I remember that once, as I child, I couldn't cope with the thick mud, and an older boy had to pull me out; once I lost my boots in the mud.

In the winter, it was very cold, and most of the boys sledded over the snowy, hilly streets on their little sleds. Others skated on the frozen stream that divided Vishnevets in two: the Old City and the New City.

To get from one Vishnevets to the other, you had to walk over a little bridge, which we called the dike. In summer people went swimming at the dike.

Jews went strolling to refresh themselves. They strolled back and forth near the palace (zamek).

Vishnevets was small: only two or three people had a telephone, and a total of one had a radio. But it had a very broad spirit.

I recall numerous Zionist organizations, from the most leftist to the most right. The spirit for Zion was high, and many Vishnevetsers for whom the Land of Israel was a dream now live in the free Jewish state, Israel.

The Jewish population of Vishnevets was materially poor. A few were tailors, a few shoemakers or capmakers; others had shops where they sold various merchandise, especially to Ukrainians from the surrounding villages.

Once a week, there was a market day. The peasants came into town to sell their grain, cows, chickens, and geese and to buy clothing fabric and grocery items.

My father used to buy small red baskets, which he later delivered to Warsaw, where the women used them as shopping baskets.

I don't know why, but I often think about a vivid figure of the town, Shimon Lifshits, a man with a beautiful beard who lived in the center of town. He spoke Polish and always represented the Jewish population to the local administration.

*

Nowadays, in America, everyone talks nostalgically about life in the small towns, especially since the performance of the play "Fiddler on the Roof."

[Page 427]

I remember life in Vishnevets well, but I doubt very much whether my children–born in America–or my friends' children, born in Israel and Argentina, would ever understand what that was like, the little town of Vishnevets.

[Page 428]

Synagogues in Vishnevets

by Meir Or

Translated by Tina Lunson

In talking about synagogues and study halls, one must emphasize their importance not only in religious terms, but also as institutions with a role in social and private life.

That's because each person's private life was tightly bound to traditional obligations, detached from the general way of life by parents and grandparents, creating a traditional life across many generations, as was appropriate for a religious order.

Socially, for hundreds of years, the synagogue was the sole institution for solving various current problems in the Jewish community. And even in our own time, the first quarter of the 20th century, the synagogue was a kind of miniature parliament. The synagogue was the central point in a circle of community affairs that had a social character. Some of the community's most important undertakings were free discussions and dealings during the intermissions between prayers, which were specifically held or prolonged (especially between the morning and additional services) because of the importance of pressing problems, and to crystallize a unified opinion among the members. In many cases, matters were decided according to what the – probable outcomes for the synagogue would be.

According to historical notes, the Christians of those times saw in the synagogue only an old, sacred, traditional religious institution; therefore, the Christian world related to it very favorably. In most cities and towns, the prince, the owner of the town, or a government representative donated a place for synagogues in the town center. So we see how synagogues became concentrated mostly in one place and then became a synagogue street or complex.

That probably happened in Vishnevets, too, where we have all the synagogues in one place.

* * *

The synagogue complex was enclosed by a high brick wall, with the entrance through a wide iron gate with iron doors on both sides. Upon entering "the gate," the majesty of the synagogue was revealed. The synagogue complex sometimes hired a cantor with a choir made up of a couple of dozen young boys.

[Page 429]

In the Great Synagogue–that is, under one roof–there were several small synagogues: the vestibule with a minyan of paupers, and another two small synagogues for tailors and various other handworkers.

There was another synagogue in the synagogue complex–Smoky Arki's kloyz. R' Arki, of blessed memory, lived inside the kloyz. It can be said that R' Arki was the only concession of the kloyz. Himself a learned Torah scholar, he studied with a small group of students from wealthy homes and carried out the commandment of "Torah and service" because teaching was not his source of income. People called him "Arki Little Key," based on a well-known notion of the small town. He practiced the lending of money for interest, and for as little as one week. There was no bank in Vishnevets.

There was a narrow passage between the Great Synagogue and Arki's kloyz through which you entered R' Itsi's Synagogue, named after R' Itsi, of blessed memory. His Hasidim–faithful followers–prayed there. In R' Itsi's synagogue, the members were continuous owners of "seats" handed down from generation to generation. The congregants were from various population strata. On the east side, especially, sat merchants, the wealthy, and those who honored Torah, and the rest were also mostly people of means.

ווישניוויצער גרויסע שוהל

Vishnevets cantor with choir boys

(Inscription on photo: Vishnevets Great Synagogue)

[Page 430]

R' Itsi's Synagogue had given a special permit to R' Levi Yitschak of Berdichev's three sons. Each had unlimited privileges to pray at the cantor's stand during morning or afternoon prayers and also for the rich liturgical poems during the Days of Awe.

R' Matus Segal, of blessed memory, the holy servant, had a claim not much less than those. He distinguished himself by praying with great intention, separately and with intimate intuition. His fine approach and style stirred sympathy to God's service.

The Study Hall was the noble synagogue, as measured by size and number of people praying there. On the sides, in the vestibule, only young people–progressives–prayed and maybe chatted about matters of the day, politics, and other important subjects, talking more than praying.

The Tshaner synagogue, under Rabbi Leybush's leadership, was distinguished by having more services than all the other study halls. They began praying at dawn and ended later than any other synagogue. People prayed there when they were late to their businesses or on their way to the markets.

* * *

Life in the synagogues was suited to each person's position, interests, knowledge and abilities. In Arki's kloyz, on a visit between afternoon and evening prayers, you could see a group studying Talmud, with Leyb Zeyger leading; he was also the one who envisioned and founded the Talmud group in Tel Aviv, in the Nordau synagogue on Bugrashov Street. From time to time, we heard from Zeyger about a celebration on finishing a section of Talmud. In R' Itsi's Synagogue, a group studies daily verses from the Mishna. In the Handworkers' Synagogue, a group studies Â¬Ein Yakov with the teacher Yosele Erlikh. Yosele Erlikh also taught the "Torah portion of the week" each Sabbath in the Tailors' Synagogue. Yosele Erlikh was of those who, as they say, was "for God and for folk": a teacher in the Tarbut schools, an excellent pedagogue and speaker, who brilliantly adjusted to any audience before him. R' Yosele was a wise scholar and knew many things by heart.

Besides the synagogues inside and next to the synagogue complex, there were a few others of a certain character: those of the town rabbi and R' Yosel Margolis, of blessed memory, which people usually called by his wife Sore's name–"Sore Ostrer's Synagogue"–under the oversight of a respected fearer of heaven and learned scholar, R' Chayim Aba Segal, of blessed memory.

Sore Ostrer's Synagogue was founded through a private initiative by a wealthy, childless couple, owners of a big manufacturing business, goodhearted people who supported the needy with a warm heart and generous hand.

[Page 431]

The Ostrer Synagogue was in the town center, which was the main trade center–it served many congregants, some of whom belonged to other synagogues, but because of its proximity to their businesses, they could "hop in" to recite various prayers or a Kaddish. Also a good opportunity–it was close to business.

The Town Rabbi's Synagogue was distinguished by the fact that it housed the yeshiva, directed by the rabbi's son–in–law, Rabbi Itsikel Vayngarten. R' Itsikel was deeply knowledgeable in Talmud and advanced in life practices. He was really progressive in his outlook, and thanks to him, the rabbi's two daughters, his wife, Chanele, and his sister, Rachel, were independently disposed and part of the town's intellectual milieu.

They said that when Rachel was in Lvov for a lengthy medical examination, she befriended members of the intellectual circles there and was in the society of the poet Uri Tsvi Grinberg, who himself stemmed from rabbis, ancestors also claimed by the Vishnevetser rabbi Meir Nachum Yunger Leyb, of blessed memory.

The Rabbi's Synagogue was not unlocked for just the regulars. The yeshiva students prayed there, and visitors who wanted to be with the rabbi prayed there, as he was considered a higher authority under heaven. A number of Vishnevetsers, especially from the Old City, prayed with the rabbi during the Days of Awe.

* * *

Speaking of synagogues, I must mention my rabbi Froyke Shayer, of blessed memory, a scholarly Jew, Bible researcher, and Jewish history expert.

R' Froyke explained to me that the synagogue was not for just praying. In Aramaic, beyt keneseta also signifies a gathering or meeting place. The purpose was to remain a united nation in Exile. In the synagogue, people perform prayers collectively, study Torah together, and the trope is set collectively, so more than prayer is required, since the goal of the synagogue to unify Jews and keep them together, not only to petition God and to study, as each person can do that by himself at home.

[Page 432]

Thus the point of praying collectively was informed and set by the sages of the Mishna and Talmud to protect the unity of the Jewish people.

As we indicated at the beginning, the synagogue was later turned into an arena and forum for forming opinions and making decisions about the community's current problems–all together.

Without the synagogue, the crystallization of a people and society for the purpose of returning to Zion would not have been possible.

[Page 433]

My Contribution to the Memorial Book

by Misha Koren, Cordoba, Argentina

Translated by Tina Lunson

Misha wrote a diary for himself in memory of Vishnevets. These excerpts are so heartfelt that it seemed they should be in the Memorial Book, with the permission of the author.–The Editors

As an Introduction

We all remember our sweet childhood years, when our fathers would send us out of the synagogue into the vestibule during memorial prayers, and if someone then opened a door to the synagogue, then what seemed to us a heartrending lamentation flooded out–Jewish mothers spilling hot tears at the memory of their own dear, departed relatives.

Then how much heartrending it is for those few, fated–to–be–privileged survivors, who mourn whole families, an entire town that was full of the ebullient life of men, women, and small children, wiped out by murderous, persecuting hands.

The surviving Jews from the devastated cities and towns wanted to unify the memory of their birthplaces and fellow citizens with memorial books–a kind of collective memorial monument for their hometowns.

Reading the Yiddish newspapers published in Argentina, where I have lived since 1922, I found out from hundreds of fellow countrymen that memorial books had been written about their hometowns. My residence is Cordoba, the second–most significant city in Argentina. Only one person from the same place lives in the same city as I do–Yisrael Mafshit, and there is local correspondence with the newspaper The Press, but in Buenos Aires there is a large Vishnevets compatriot society with numerous wealthy people who can easily publish a memorial book, but … for such a long time there has been "no call and no answer" from our town's offspring. So I decided that however it was with me, I would take on the work myself so that at least my own memories would remain for my children to read.

I proceed to this very responsible task, including material by my compatriot mentioned above, Yisrael Mafshit.

[Page 434]

He left Vishnevets five years after I did, and although five years in the life of a town is perhaps a small amount of time, it's also large depending on the viewpoint and circumstance from which you observe.

It is also worthwhile to underscore how remarkable the ways of fate are.

Yisrael Mafshit's grandfather was called Yosil Fodem, and that Fodem and another Jew, Berel Zekharye's, as well as my grandfather, Aharon Mekhel, were sponsors for his six terms as local governor in Vishnevets (they were his sponsors for 18 consecutive years, fighting like lions for their starosta candidate every three years in all the reelection campaigns).

Memories, experiences, they gather themselves and flow like a kind of never-ending spring.

What can you write about a modest town like Vishnevets; we didn't have any popular movement leaders. For example, Kremenets, our district seat, 20 versts away, had its Yitschak–Ber Levinzon, father of the Jewish Enlightenment in Russia. Of course, we also had our Talmud experts and Bible teachers–Rabbi (teacher) Simche Ayzik, Yankel Harun Mekhel's, Froyke the teacher, and so on.

I believe that I can do best with the help of memories experienced as a long–term starosta's grandchild, in whose home, logically, much was said and heard.

The language I'll use is a pure Volhynia voice of the people, not polished, but as it was used by us–Yiddish, Hebrew, Slavic. The examples, episodes and narratives, light and shadow, happy and sad, as they were–life itself, in our little town Vishnevets.–The Author

Vishnevets

A little Jewish town, at the beginning or the very end of the great and powerful Russia: It depends on what geographic point you viewed the town from: the first town starting from the Austrian border, traveling through Ukraine to great Russia, or the last town, hard by the same border. Across the border you could count the proper Galician towns and cities: Zbarazh and Tarnopol, and in another border direction, Zalozce and Zloczow, all on the beaten path, landmarks.

[Page 435]

What did our town look like? Like an artistic picture, one in which, as you approach and get closer, you see only colored specks, but as you look at the same picture in perspective at a greater distance, you perceive the loveliness of the same.

A Vishnevets resident saw the same surroundings, the landscape, every day, and for him it created a sleepy feeling: there was a river, so a river! There was a forest, it's a forest. But sifting through it in memory, that appearance, the landscape from a perspective, enlarged by the distance, you see first of all what charm Mother Nature has most bestowed on this little town.

Hills, not especially significant ones, circle the horizon. Toward the road to Kremenets, the Horynka (in Russian it is probably "Gorinka") hills; toward the Zarudye road (from the word "Zagorodye") all the way to the Kolodnoye road, everything was uphill or downhill, depending on the direction. Forests, which encircled the town like a crown–the Zarudye forest, which was a continuation of the enormous park by the castle (zamek in Russian), Luzer, Bidake forests. The river–Horyn is its name–calm, proprietary, snaking along, dividing the Old City, which has only a few dozen houses, from the main Vishnevets with a dike (a kind of bulwark bridge). The "principal" Vishnevets, by my "imaginative count" (no one practiced statistics in Vishnevets) amounted to about 300 houses, with 500 or 600 families (two families often lived together; in Yone Nets's house, five or even more families lived together). All the inhabitants were Jews. With a small exception: the pharmacist, Rashavski (a Pole); the beer tavern owner, Batsavski (a Czech); the monopolishtshik (government liquor seller), a Russian; the Russian tea shop, where not–so–observant Jews bought kipyatok (boiled water to make tea) on the Sabbath; and finally, the ruskaya lavka (Russian shop) owner, a Russian.

Then which elements served to make the town painterly lovely–hills, forests, river, and the surrounds dipped in gorgeous green blooming gardens?!

During World War II, a Spanish journal in Buenos Aires commenting on the German idée fixe "the push for the East"–meaning a productive Ukraine–presented a picture of a street from an Ukrainian small town as an example, and it was our Vishnevets, and although you could see only a part of a street in the early morning of a market day, I could recognize our well-known Zeydenokhi and one of his sons; Shmuel Machit, on his porch; Hertsel Face's house; and after that the house where I was born and reared with the usual glazed sukkah up on the top floor (I kept the picture and treasured it for years).

[Page 436]

Where did the name of our town, Vishnevets, come from? I don't have any certain, specific date, but Russian history records the name of Count Wisnowiecki, contentious and sullen per the history writer–why such a proper Russian as Wisnowiecki changed his coin and became a true-blue noble and dressed like a country squire, and the only one who was successful, it says there, against the Hetman Bogdan Chmielnitski and his haidamaks, may his name and memory be blotted out. Thus, we Jews certainly do not have any complaints....

The previously mentioned castle is just by the town, separated from its surrounds by a park inside a high brick wall, with iron bars and gates that would open only when their proprietor, Demidov, with his chin held high as if her were in the king's court–"stallmaster yeva dvora"–came to spend the hot summer months in his court and park.

[Page 437]

Before his arrival, he let someone from the public know when to expect him, and an audience of men, women, and children would greet his gleaming black automobile with him and his family inside. For us, then, the automobile was something unique, and served only to terrify the horses. After that, the Rakovitser Count, who had previously driven in to Shimon Chayim Shimon's inn in a coach with a livery and six horses in tandem, also exchanged the steaming horses for a smoking automobile. As I said, Demidov arrived, covering all of us with stinking blue smoke, and we, his loyal citizens (the town land belonged to him and we paid him rent), thanked him with applause and shouted hurrahs. A cannon boomed, all for the sake of honoring Demidov.

Disregarding the fact that the Orthodox church was located just opposite the park– not such a homey place for our brothers, the children of Israel–the Jewish youths used that place between the park and the church for their Friday evening and Sabbath afternoon strolls. As the air there was delightfully perfumed, and there were nightingales on moonlit nights, it brought forth their sweet tears. Let us appreciate here that the noisy walks of our youth were never disturbed there.

The castle–the town–the landscape

[Page 438]

It was different when an arriving Jew, a wealthy Jew from a nearby village, one Moshe Rozental, and his son–in–law, Duvid Chinik, bought an estate from a formerly wealthy woman, Frenkeliavakhe, whose property line touched the park and the place opposite the entrance to the church; then Demidov and the church overseer raised a protest and robbed the Jew of half of his land through chicanery, since Demidov had organized the police and a week of dragon–riders because people were afraid of peasant unrest then.

I Go to Study with Simche Ayzik

The great scholar–teacher Simche Ayzik is worth a special chapter.

Boys who were almost grown, almost ready to lay tefillin, went to Simche Ayzik to study, and my parents performed an almost "revolutionary" act by sending me to study with him when I was just 10 years old, and I really had to endure trouble from my older fellow pupils, who only called me "little snot." Studying with him was like entering a university right from middle school. Everything there was different. The pupil had to study by himself, and the rabbi called on him only once a week–himself, not at school–and his study was completely on another level. We especially enjoyed studying a little of Or hachayim [Light of life] with him, as we had to show quick conceptual power, our own intelligence. He was a great Hebraist and wrote letters and even poetry in the old–fashioned flowery style. We were told that he had written a petition (in Hebrew, of course) to none other than the tsar himself, and here is the reason for the petition.

As you recall, Shaul Krupnik lived on Yatke Street. He had a granary, a millet mill. It was known as the Shualekhe. Years ago, it had belonged to a family, a member of which converted. It was a terrible blow for the entire family, in both heartbreak and shame. Especially in making a marriage match, it happened in some cases that someone quietly whispered in an ear that there was a convert in the family.... Once a drowning victim was pulled from our Horyn River–not such an unusual event in the summertime when people often swam in the river. The difference was that the drowned person had large stones tied to his hands and feet. Looking at his face, one in the crowd screamed: oy, it was the Shualekhe's convert. This was the Ariadne who understood Yiddish, and there was a great uproar among the authorities–a religious murder! And if a murder in a religious bath, they promptly arrested the Old City rabbi.

[Page 439]

The respectable people of the town quickly mobilized so as not to allow such a desecration–the rabbi in jail, of all things. He was released on bail until the trial, guaranteed by their homes. The rabbi "considered" this; he was old, he took pains to collect evidence, and he died before the trial began. And because their homes were at stake and they could lose them, they turned to the tsar himself in their desperation, gathering to write the letter.

Of course, since they were all pupils, they wanted to have an example of his beautiful writing. I came up with a new idea. I brought a thick notebook to my rabbi and asked him to write an inscription on the cover, and here I quote that inscription as I preserved it in my memory:

Here are gathered all the letters

I so loved and loved

I write them to my friends

My relatives, my father, or my brother.

Afterward, I asked him to renew my notebook with one of his poems. He looked outdoors, where a heavy snow was falling, and wrote:

Here are gathered all the letters
I so loved and loved
I write them to my friends
My relatives, my father, or my brother.

Afterward, I asked him to renew my notebook with one of his poems. He looked outdoors, where a heavy snow was falling, and wrote:

The mountains of snow and frost
Ice and cold giants
Descendants of the haunch of autumn,
You are heroes of war
That a girl is avenging,
You fought a great man
And reinforcement troops
From man to animal and bird.
Their portion of chain
And their bow inflects
Even the infant, even the aged.

[Page 440]

To Cheder

There were a lot of teachers among us, beginning with the alef–beys teachers and ending with the Talmud teachers; I will consider them on a graded scale: Mekhel Shames, Asher Yoel, Moshe Asher Yoel's, Teacher Yenkel, Moshe Fuks, Nachum

Tarberider, Froyke, Yankl Harun Mekhel's, an uncle of mine, and the greatest of them all in scholarship, Simche Ayzik.

From Mekhel Shames's cheder, I went over to Moshe Asher Yoel's, who had prepared us by teaching us pupils M. Krinski's The Hebrew Language, Part 1. It was also mumbled about that between afternoon and evening prayers, he stopped over in the kloyz and asked for translations of Hebrew words he didn't know.

But with the help of his son Shmuel, he knew what was going on in our local Russian schools, how to make our cheder more interesting. Very simply, all the pupils, children of dry–goods vendors, had to bring boards from crates that merchandise was shipped in, and he, Shmuel, cleverly cut out little swords and rifles from them. So girding himself and our loins, he used to take us out to the street and muster us under his command: "Echad, shtayim, sholosh," one, two three.

From Moshe Asher Yoel's, I moved up to Teacher Avrahamtsi, where we were taught the Five Books with Rashi's commentary. It was characteristic how they tried to keep children constantly busy studying so they had no time to joke around. Even on the Sabbath during the day we studied with the rabbi– Ethics of the Fathers in the summer and Proverbs in the winter. The nights were not free from Torah study either– accompanied by a little kerosene lantern or a candle, children waded through deep snow or treaded the pre–Passover deep mud. In winter, the nights were very long ... with lantern in hand, its glass sometimes decorated with colored paper, a troop of little boys hurried home accompanied by a specific song, sung in a chorus, that remains in my mind: To build, to build, ducklings including those who go by night, Yosele the shÂ¬_ _ _r, Berele the f _ _ _r...

From Avrahamtsi I went over to Yenkel Harun Mikhel's, where I began to look into the Talmud. I wasn't there long before they brought me to R' Simche Ayzik. That "cheder" was the holy of holies, and I will write about that separately.

[Page 441]

Weddings

Happy weddings. The weddings were a source of joy not only for the groom and bride, in–laws, and guests, but for the entire town: on Saturday night, the musicians and their instruments arrived at the betrothed's home to play an overture. The day of the wedding, the couple was led through the whole town to the synagogue courtyard, accompanied by deafening music. Returning from the wedding, the groom and bride were stopped at the entrance by a boy–an educated boy from the groom's or bride's side–who usually gave a speech in Yiddish, Russian, or Hebrew; people would run ahead to grab a place, and sometimes the greeter went smoothly, and sometimes, oy vey, he began to stammer or forgot the words he had known so well by heart at home. Then a hot–headed in–law eager for the chicken soup would displace the boy and open the way for the groom and bride. I remember one of the greetings in Russian:

We greet those newly married

and wish will all our hearts

an ocean of happiness and love,

full health and splendid days.

At dawn, the whole town awoke to the grinding music with which the musicians led the in–laws back home.

Leading the bride to synagogue on the Sabbath was a lovely picture in and of itself: Well–to–do homemakers wearing long, floor–length dresses and trailing long heavy trains of thick black silk or plush fabric, hats on their heads. Sometimes they lent to one another, according to a new fashion that had come about. They were draped with the best and finest jewelry they possessed: strings of authentic, not manufactured, pearls; brooches with diamonds or gems; gold chains with watches; chains that went around the neck once or twice and still reached to the belt. They would go through the streets to and from the shul, accompanied by observers on every balcony, themselves enveloped in a cloud of dust raised by their long dresses, unintentionally stirring up the streets.

[Page 423]

Who were the musicians? This was a family comprising several brothers, and they had a right of possession to the trade. They were called the Hertskes, and no one knew if that was only a nickname. There was a hunch it came from the musicians' term haritsem bom. The eldest brother, the most capable (he played several instruments), moved up in the army in World War I: he was designated to lead a band of musicians and apparently given the rank of ensign, so the soldiers had to salute him. We became aware that he was not named Duvid Hertske but Mandelboym, a very fine family name. As I said, his band was, for that place, not bad at all, but they were surpassed by the fame of the Tshaner (Teofipol in Russian) musicians. But to bring them in was a luxury item, and the only one to do so was Fradele the orchard–keeper's husband, who was a contractor. You could really lick your fingers at their playing.

A Rabbinic Wedding

Our rabbi, Yunger Leyb, or Gur Arye, as he will be called here, had such a stately appearance, a beard of such volume, that his fine appearance could put Rembrandt's Jews of Holland in the shadows. But he never let himself be photographed because of the commandment "Do not make any graven images." Our handsome rabbi made a wedding for his eldest daughter, Chanele, to a rabbi's son in Berdichev. This wedding was differentiated by the greeting of the in–laws: the young man traveled out, riding on a horse and in a made–over Cossack uniform. People carried on all week about the visitor, especially Jews in fur hats. He accepted a seat by the eastern wall in the Great Synagogue and a call to the Torah, for the promise of a contribution to the synagogue;

no one ever gave one groshen. I recall my father remarking–he was beadle at the time–
"Those who are used to taking all the time are not accustomed to giving...."

A Tragic Wedding

I remember that a marriage to a young man from Radzivilov was arranged for the
teacher Moshe Fuks' widow's daughter. A number of in–laws from the groom's side
arrived, among them one of the groom's brothers, a 10–year–old.

[Page 443]

Since it was a hot day, the boy went to bathe in our Horyn River and was pulled
out later as a drowning victim. People went to ask the rabbi the question, what to do?
To which the rabbi replied, the music–meaning the wedding–must go on.

The Little Shoe

Before the Days of Awe, we cheder boys would steal into the kloyz and throw
ourselves onto the shofar to try to pull from it the harsh sounds of the tekiyas,
shevarim, and teruas [shofar blasts]. We always encountered a remarkable thing:
beside the shofar, in the same holy place where it rested, was a black kerchief, and
near it an odd–looking little shoe: it was made of black leather, without a heel, like a
little sock and woven around with straps.

We had no idea what a shoe was doing there in the hidden, most holy place in the
kloyz until someone told us that it was a shoe used in the ritual of refusing to marry a
brother's childless widow.

From then on, we were drawn to the shoe with reverence, even more so than the
shofar; such a small thing when a shoe can cause a misfortune to happen to a widow,
and her tragedy without the shoe could be, heaven forbid, doubled. As children, we
wanted to see the shoe in use sometime, and our little hearts throbbed and waited for
such a moment.

And one day it did happen.

I myself was a witness to the painful procedure in which the shoe played a major
role.

I myself did see my people in a dark hour.

Nachum Lekhetitser lived in a house in front of Rashavski's pharmacy. His
daughter married a young man named Moshe from near the Kremenets Road. The
young man died suddenly and left his wife without children. Only with a one–year–old
brother–in–law.

The young widow had to wait 12 years until the little brother–in–law could free her
and tell her that he did not want to marry her. Twelve empty, lonely years the poor

woman suffered in her widowhood, bound to the caprice of that little child and dependent on his good intentions. But he could not grow any faster. She had to wait.

[Page 444]

Until God's help came, when she was old and made ugly by her life those 12 years, the man–child became a bar mitzvah and could "free" her and determine her fate. He released her, and the little shoe came into play.

Many of the singularities of the procedure have escaped my memory, but what I remember, I remember as if it were today.

The kloyz was packed with people, the judge led the ceremony, people held their breath; people clapped for quiet, now people were not talking; each wanted to show his mastery of the matter, not even thinking that here are clever people witnessing something from hundreds of years ago, tying us to primitive, half–wild hordes of people. Each person enjoys it when he can mention a citation from the Talmud that the other does not know, but we wait like wild creatures, enjoying it in a way I hadn't experienced before.

The moment arrives, the widow is separated from everyone else with the black cloth, like someone with mange; the judge speaks to her through the black linen "wall." Who understands now what the dark Aramaic words mean? The little brother–in–law, the main actor of the overly crafted spectacle, understanding the least of anyone present. Suddenly it is quiet, they name the devastated widow again, and the mysterious shoe falls, thrown by the child's little bar mitzvah hands, right at her, and she is free.

Vishnevets actors and musicians, and their sponsors

[Page 445]

The Beginning of Theater in Vishnevets

For us, the forerunner of Jewish theater lovers was Yosel Boykis. He had recently returned from Warsaw, where he was a trade employee and had become absorbed in the impressive presentations of Ester–Rachel Kaminski when she was at her most productive.

In Vishnevets, with homegrown energy, Yosel carried out several dramatic performances with great success.

People in Vishnevets got accustomed to theater. After him, we young students founded a theater–lovers' circle, and under the direction of Fayerman–the ritual slaughterer's son–who had come home from Kishinev, we drew the dramatic thread further, playing "Yiddish King Lear" and "The Wild Man," among others.

The presentations usually ended with general festivity. The musicians went out onto the balconies of the village mill, where we had the theater salon, and the streets came alive under their merry tunes. It's let's all be merry and gay for Jews, we're playing the theater!

The Little Cemetery and "The Dybbuk," or Anski in Vishnevets

On a hot summer day, a noisy clock clanged, and a phaeton (a large britshke) harnessed to two completely exhausted, glistening black horses drove into the market square. In the phaeton was seated a middle–aged man with a short beard, dressed in a Perets shoulder–cape and wearing a soft, black hat on his head. The street was startled; children looked around at one another uneasily. Perhaps it's a license inspector again, maybe it's worth putting some merchandise aside for a while and making the shop look a little pitiful.

But then, when the honorable young man drove to Shimon–Chayim–Shimon's inn, everyone was at ease and hurried over to the inn.

We saw the young man get out with Bunim Shimon–Chayim–Shimon's, and both set out in the direction of our shop. Calmly, at a smooth pace, the mysterious traveler came into the shop, gave a hearty greeting to my father, and said,

"I've been told that you are the beadle of the Great Synagogue."

[Page 446]

"I want to ask you to make it possible for me to visit the synagogue. I'm from the Petersburg Jewish Museum, which purchases and collects unusual items of a pure Jewish character and keeps them for the museum."

My father sent me to call on Mikhel the sexton for the synagogue key, and we went off to the synagogue. We opened the heavy door, studded from top to bottom with fat–

headed iron nails, and the whole entourage, with the guest in the lead, went down the stairs of the "deep depths" and into the synagogue.

The guest strolled slowly to the cantor's desk and stood there astonished: on the desk lay a gigantic book, a kind of prayer book from hundreds of years ago. The outside was covered with leather and artistically ornamented with gold engraving. The pages were all parchment, very thick, and all around was a halo of light–teardrops from generations of long nights during which Jews wept their woes and troubles into the book.

He turned some pages of the book and was astonished. All the chapter headings were written in large, artistic letters. A real rarity, the only one in the world. Regarding this rarity thoughtfully, the guest turned to my father and the others: "Jews, I am Sh. Anski. How much would you want for this prayer book, or will you sell it to me?"

But the Jews could not agree; they could not part with such a treasure. In no instance. For no price.

Anski was not put off; he walked on and stopped by the artistically carved Torah–reading desk with its gilded chains at the ends, from which hung two golden hands spread out as for the priestly blessing.

He was prepared to buy the desk. But they would not agree to sell it.

Anski remained calm, keeping to himself, and looked around some more.

The synagogue was large and beautiful. It was two stories high. Light shone in through individual windows with colored panes. The ceiling had several cupolas, and there was a large, prominent dome in the center. In the center of each cupola was a small, round opening from which hung a brass filigree hanging lamp on thin, shining brass chains.

The middle lamp was huge. Anski was a customer for them all, but they sold him only one side lamp. It was also ingeniously crafted with hammered–out flowers, buds, little roses, and cherubs, but a lot smaller and less valuable.

[Page 447]

Anski was happy with it.

They wanted to leave. But Anski suddenly spied a stone emerging from the wall with its smooth side to the wall. He asked someone to turn the stone around; he wanted to look at it. He would pay to repair the wall. His request was fulfilled, and all were astonished when they saw that on the other side of the stone were carved blessings for the town and its residents; the stone appeared to be very old, and who knew why they had to hide the inscription. Its history was lost. Hopeless. From then on, you could see the stone with the letters facing outward. We didn't sell the stone to him either. But from all this, Anski saw that there a long, deep history silently existed in our town, and he asked us to tell it to him.

Then we led him out behind the synagogue, near Yisrael Niuk's house, and showed him the little cemetery, which was walled in like a well, overgrown with thick wild grass and neglected. And we told him that women had been coming here for generations and tossing garlic in, just as at a real cemetery, because according to the legend, when Chmielnitski's gangs came into the town, seething, unruly, and wild, they encountered a wedding entourage. Jews were leading a young couple to the canopy, and the thugs grabbed the groom and bride and threw them into the well alive.

* * *

Anski could not beg us to clean out the weeds and set up a stone, an inscription; perhaps there was still a witness around. Vishnevets did not want to disturb the dead.

But after that story, Anski wrote his famous Dybbuk, and in it vividly depicted the story of the couple that had been taken from the canopy and thrown into a well, and knew no more of life.

Our Own Trotsky

A Jewish high–schooler from Kremenets, from the first Ukrainian regional high school, and a fellow student of mine whose family name was Goldshteyn, arrived in town. He had grown a short beard in order to look a little older and had started calling himself Orlenka–"a Christian." He had done that according to instructions he'd received while organizing the official civil authority for us.

[Page 448]

Since the potential enemy could be the Poles on that side of the current border, and the Central Government could not send an army because it was maintaining many fronts, it was on him, using capable propagandists, to create a peasant militia that would maintain a watchful eye on the trenches remaining from the recent war. The reason for such an army was that it ostensibly cost the government coffers nothing; there were plenty of abandoned weapons around. The peasant was happy to hide out in the trenches and keep watch; he grabbed some food from a house nearby, or his family brought him food from home.

Furthermore, the Poles who had decided to attack our area had sent their own propaganda specialists from their side, and knowing and understanding the dark ignorance of the masses, they began to use the Jewish motif as their propaganda medium, putting out a rumor that "the Jews had carried off four bags of communion bread from the Pochayev monastery."

For such a "crime," their first reaction was to make a reckoning with the Jews in Vishnevets.

I saw my schoolmate Goldshteyn–Orlenka among them, carried between two armed peasants. When he recognized me, he asked me to find him a cart to Kremenets. I went immediately to do his bidding–but really, he who rules and commands was only looking for an opportunity to get to Kremenets through me.

Only after those events were over did I consider what life–threatening danger he had put me in, just by turning to me.

As expected, the peasants from the nearby villages abandoned the trenches and came into town, gathering near the bailiff's office.

I slipped in unnoticed, and I overheard one of the town peasants, who was known to be a little left–leaning, apparently answering a previous speaker.

"No, we've lived with our Jews in peace for hundreds of years. When it rains on us, it rains on them too; if the sun burns them, it burns us too. If Jews have done something wrong, it was some other Jews in other places."

I wanted to keep standing there and listening, but suddenly a non–Jewish woman called to another, who was standing near me:

"Divisia etlin sinok."[1]

[Page 449]

Look, I understood that it would be the same for me as for Etel's son …

The crowd listened to the speaker who said not to bother the Vishnevets Jews. They set out for Kremenets, taking Goldshteyn with them, whose young life they very unfortunately ended in the Horynka forest, where they also covered it up.

Tovye Shag and His Steam Mill

Neighbors and friends used to come to our home in the evenings after the Sabbath for a glass of tea and an omelet or cakes. They had conversations about the Jews' situation and politics in general.

Among the usual guests was Tovye Shag, a wealthy Jew, who emphasized his wealth with a large gold watch that he frequently took out of his vest pocket and peered at through gold–rimmed glasses. Once I heard him say, "If they want to take me, they'll have to chew through the walls."

I didn't understand the meaning of the words at the time. It was years later that I took in their significance: it was soon after the pogroms. Tovye Shag was afraid they would rob him of his possessions, and he decided to construct a building that then housed a five–story steam mill with gigantic steam boilers and expensive machinery. When the mill began to function, he saw that there was a flaw. It was too good for Vishnevets: in just one month, it could supply the entire region with enough flour for a year, and it ate up an enormous amount of wood, so much that it required its own forest to supply it.

As business went from bad to worse, he hired out the mill to two sisters–in–law, Shifra and Krishtal, who came from Slavuta and quickly became a riddle for the whole town–for everyone, men, women, children. Shifra had a daughter my age named Gitashe, who spoke only Russian and went to school on Friday and Saturday, although they kept a kosher kitchen. In time, we discovered the significance–they were descended from the true Shapiros.

Shifra and Krishtal also lost money on the lovely mill enterprise, and they left Vishnevets.

[Page 450]

Of course, when Shifra left, Tovye Shag was again left with the mill and the huge monthly deficits, until the two Katsap brothers slipped in and bought the mill for a song. They did indeed have their own forest, and then the mill was grinding, even if not every day.

Afterward, Shag fell from his status as a rich man.

Converts

A Jewish woman in Vishnevets converted and married a non–Jew, and as it goes, the gentile disappeared and left her with a nice number of children. No one knew whether she was a widow or a divorcee or a "grass widow." She lived as an outsider, torn away from both worlds, rejected by both societies, but demonstrated her inclination to the society she had abandoned. Every Friday evening, she would set out a candelabra with lighted candles. She lived on a little hill up from the "Ziemsker Hospital" on a completely gentile street that began at Shmuel Balter's house, the last Jewish house.

The lights were like a beacon from a castaway ship in the distance on a great hostile sea, calling out from the sea and begging for mercy and prompt aid. A kind of quiet connection to distant brothers and an open severance from nearby enemies, her neighbors the gentiles.

Who can evaluate the depth of the tragedy that played out in the heart of this simple, primitive woman, who in her innocence thought that a heart–to–heart connection was enough to make folks' mutual hatred disappear.

* * *

Another case of conversion was that of a Jewish man named Alter. He married a gentile woman who did laundry for Jews her whole life and went among Jewish homes while he was alone in the house. But when he encountered a Jew, he would soon come away with a bit from the Jewish holiday prayer book or a verse of cantorial song.

Someone said he said, I did wander far from home, but I did it so that my children should not suffer from Jewishness.

Impossible things. His children did suffer from Jewishness. Their neighbors, good Christian brothers, shouted "vikristi," or manufactured Christians, crafted gentiles, after them, also a tragedy.

[Page 451]

Misha Korin on the left

A view of the Vishnevets Old City

[Page 452]

Love for Me, Too

He was a neighbor, Motel, Mendel the wagon–driver's son, and he was not a sluggish young man, not unattractive, especially in his fine manliness when he would come from his military service to rest up at home, which he had to do for four long years in the Far East. In those in–between times, when he would come home to rest, he fell in love with one of the Karminik (they manufactured flints) sisters.

When Motel returned from service, he wanted to marry his heart's chosen one–but his parents and relatives were set against the match. Not for nothing, but for a reason: he is poor, the girl is poor, so two paupers are going dancing. Moreover, there's a girl in a village, a distant relative of Hershel "Air" (nicknamed because of his stinginess) has a daughter, she's very clever, even a jokester, in any case there's a dowry. But Motel held his own, saying the girl loves me and I love her. One sister–in–law got into the mix, Feyge Yosel the Terek's, and told him that it's obvious that he loves her, but is he so certain about the girl's love, why not test it to see; he should bring a bottle of water and say that it's poison. And if the families won't allow the match, he'll drink some of the poison, and she should drink some and put an end to the matter. He carried out his crafty sister–in–law's trick, and when he presented his girl with the plan to poison themselves, she replied, "If you want to poison yourself, poison yourself, but I'm young and want to live more..." Of course, he married Hershel "Air's" daughter. Love for me, too.

Meir, We've Already Spoken

I don't recall whose idea it was, but it's fixed in the student youth's memory. Since the central authority was concerned about the rise of popular education, we could propose to the instructor that, calculating how many pupils there would be in middle school, we should establish an appropriate educational institution in Vishnevets. Meir Averbukh and I were chosen as the representatives. Averbukh was designated as head spokesman because he had a smooth tongue and was cut out to be a very fine orator. I arrived at the appointed hour at the bailiff's for the audience with the instructor. Meir Averbukh, however, did not arrive on time for some reason.

[Page 453]

When the time for our talk with the instructor approached, I went in alone and gave him the petition from the student youth; he talked to me about it in a friendly way, promising to take steps. Witness to all this was Meir Averbukh's uncle, Shimon Lifshits, who, seeing him arriving belatedly, called out to him in anguish and vexation, "Meir, we've already spoken!"

Embarrassed by His Family Name

The town shopkeepers frequently suffered from paupers–the door knockers, for example, who went through the town begging for alms, some begging for clothes, others wrapping a kerchief around their beards to appear to have a toothache, completing their itinerary, and then changing their appearance and starting to beg all over again. When recognized, they became aggressive and called people names, or swore with curses and oaths.

The shopkeepers came together and selected a commission, of which my father was elected president and treasurer. They imposed a monthly, voluntary payment on themselves. Itsik the Tall (Kremenetski) used to go around with a big basket collecting all the payments and brought them to the treasurer, and that's where the shopkeepers sent the paupers. "Go to the treasury, they'll give you charity from all of us."

Of course, at the treasury they had to produce their personal documents. Once a poor man showed up who did not want to show his documents or even say his name. My father explained to him that he wouldn't be able to get any funds without it, and he responded gloomily "But you won't laugh?! My name is Zishe Krepl..." [little fritter].

The Beadle is Led to the Synagogue

My father served two terms as beadle of the kloyz, where we had a fixed place by the eastern wall and prayed there. But one Simchas Torah (that was the season for choosing beadles) the congregation at the Great Synagogue decided to honor my father with the title of beadle. On Simchas Torah a crowd of Jews filled our house. Avrahamski the teacher went to our oven, clapped his hands, and shouted, "Tas, tas, tas!" I asked my mother what that meant, and she interpreted it as an insinuating suggestion that she take the roasted ducks out of the oven and serve food to the crowd.

[Page 454]

We led my father to the synagogue under a canopy, and the crowd made merry, Simchas Torah style, dancing in front of him until we were inside the synagogue.

About my father's beadle service, I remember that during market days, non–Jews would show up, probably sent by Jews they knew, with some version of this: "Is this where the mayor of the synagogue lives?"

"Yes, what's the matter?"

"Since a horse (sometimes a cow or a sheep) has gone missing, I have already given money for candles at my church, and the horses have not turned up, so I decided that if our god couldn't help, maybe yours will help. I've brought you money for candles."

In such cases, my father behaved well, not wanting to take money directly from a non–Jew; but I would take the contributor to the vestibule of the Great Synagogue, where the letters spelling out "put money through here" were painted over a crevice in the stone wall. The peasant believed with complete faith that the golden coins reached the true messenger.

Translation editor's note:

This sentence has not been translated. return

[Page 455]

Vishnevets in a Trick Mirror

by M. Averbukh

Translated by Tina Lunson

Do you think this is a paradox–to include in a memorial book a town's specific folklore, when it seems to be the laughable, refreshing, comical experiences of the time before the bestial wave of Hitlerism. Yet there's no shame in reliving episodes of day–to–day life, still rooted in that faraway youth that vanished together with that life.

All this happened back then.

When you were a child in cheder and your childhood years were exuberant with impudent energy, here and there you played a few pranks.

With the dew of childhood still on the lips, you can speak silliness with a naÃ¯ve, open heart. Then, when you wove childish fantasies together with the same group of friends, and did things to annoy the teacher or parents and grownups and got pleasure and joy and satisfaction.

Suddenly the world becomes old and sinister. Suddenly you're no longer a child, and you run away and separate yourself from the experiences that everyone around you is having and doing. Then you observe your youthful ways from a great distance and see: it was once joyful, too; humorous, too; dew of youth, too. Upon my soul, it's a shame it will be forgotten by eternity.

Pictures of that grey, prosaic reality flicker endlessly inside you. You grew up in that reality, and however small each of those pictures is, in and of itself, the urge to tell about it is strong ... because that's how it was.

A Tree with Sour Pears

Before you stands a mature tree, a big tree, near the river, close to Shmelke's house. That's why it's called Shmelke's tree. Certainly, Shmelke didn't care for the tree; he didn't water or improve it. It just sprang from pure Nature, covered with many branches reaching out and up. It even covered part of Shmelke's roof. A fruitful tree with sour little pears, almost like poison to eat.

Of course, we cheder–boys were drawn to the tree, and we ran to enjoy it with abandon.

[Page 456]

We also took pleasure from Shmelke's agitation and shouting, because to reach the bitter fruit on the upper branches, we had to throw stones, which, to Shmelke's chagrin, broke tiles on his roof.

Shmelke's tree remained an attraction for us year after year, in our free time from cheder. And, besides the river, it was a gorgeous panorama to behold.

A Wedding in Town

Actually, a wedding in town wasn't just for the groom and bride, the in–laws, and the invited guests. A wedding was for the whole town, because a large part of the population took part in the wedding–uninvited, but it didn't matter. The impression was that the whole town made the wedding, and, without exception, everyone adopted the young couple joyfully and happily.

Already from the Thursday before the Sabbath when the groom would be called to the Torah, everything was about the wedding.

Each thing was prepared with inner anticipation and respect for the honor of the wedding canopy to be set up on Tuesday. By Tuesday, everyone was excited, big and little, old and young, rich and poor, even in the Old City across the bridge over the river. Everyone anticipated together, looking on with wonder at the groom and bride being led in a parade to the Great Synagogue.

Some waited impatiently in the packed balconies, some in a mass on the bridge, and those who had declared themselves progressives had, to avoid the aftertaste of provincialism, pressed to the sidelines, or they were a very passive part of the crowd as they experienced the joyous procession.

After the wedding, young people gathered around under the windows of the wedding house with great curiosity and tried to observe what was going on inside through any crack.

People impatiently awaited the call for the "gift sermon" and especially the main act, the main attraction, when the musicians and the wedding jester, Avrahamtsik, improvised in rhyme; and not in such a refined style, but with great pathos. Himself a trumpet player, he spoke with a strong intonation, and it went more or less like this:

[Page 457]

A Parody of Avrahamtsik's Jesting

One can make a terrific parody
on a stretch from Liz to Zarudye,
or a small one from Rafal Shteyner's steps
to the red walls of Mendel's apothecary.
As Avrahamtsik the accomplished musician
dispenses fiery melodies–
with a pockmarked face
and one useless eye
makes intimate poetic musings
in the language of Vasil Kokorozhe.

The pair of musicians fall silent
at Avrahamtsik's fine–tuned talent;
have mercy on the bride and groom
when he preaches the jester's speech.
But don't just take my word for it:
a masterly wedding jester is like a good poet
who enthrones the bride with flowery verse.
Slowly with pride and without hurry,
the musician, the wedding jester, says:

Dear sirs and esteemed ladies,
you can make rhymes however you like
fine and thin like string
or fat and juicy like rope
that could embarrass gentile soldiers–
for my wedding jester rhymes
will make your face red and flushed. Also, my dear new in–laws,
take off your lacquered shoes,
take off your new socks
when the clarinet blows
and dance nonstop in your bare feet
when I play the sugar–sweet;

all the shops are closed at night
in order to hear the flutes talk,
ruining good mazurkas.

Everyone fill your glasses
when the groom's side turns up their noses,
and when your throats are wet,
listen to Shmelke on the bass,
and show off with the hunchback,
one of the very best drummers.
On the fiddle, Duvid Ritske
always plays like a whirlwind.
With feelings so strong and hot
they can be cooled only
when our God above
makes a musician out of Meir the Deaf.

Everyone, everyone, the greatest and smallest
who are standing right at the window
may listen to Avrahamtsik,
your loyal man from the party hacks.
I am no liar, no matchmaker,
just a real, accomplished wedding jester.

And not always a fool
I make a living at rhyming.
But my enemies be damned;
they make nothing from wedding jesters.
May it also ring in your ears
when I sing for you.
On everyone's account, I will wish for the bride
that the groom have all the important qualities
except for the gift of gab.
No doubt he knows his good luck
in the clever bride Sheyne–Beyle;
of course that speaks for itself

Four horses harnessed to the sleigh,
the rich father–in–law arrives,
the friend Avraham Yakov Freylekh,
the king of grain and clover.
In fine lacquered boots,
pockets packed with money,
a prince, a wealthy man,
so much for me and you.
And his wife Beyle–Yente,
not generally a knock–about,
with a full double chin that trembles as if on a swing,

distributes cash
from between her fingers.
Also better to die discreetly
than like the wife of a king.

For the second in–law, R' Volke,
who lives near the rabbits,
we want to play a merry polka.
For the groom's uncle R' Meir,
we'll play a Jewish sher.
And now, dear guests,
stuff yourself with the best
here in this warm nest;
drink a toast and eat.

We hope there comes a time
when people wish
that mother–in–law Udye–Reyzel
isn't put off
by joy and eyes full of tears.
May she hear the news
in everyone's ears
that her daughter–in–law has a baby boy.

[Page 460]

Vishnevets Discotheque

Properly speaking, in those days no one had any concept of anything called a "discotheque," even in the most modern, avant garde countries in the world. In the early 20thcentury, God protect us, but according to the mode to this very day, in Vishnevets there was a place of amusement suited to that generation's tastes.

The institution was a labyrinth that had fooled hundreds of schoolboys: Froyke the Teacher, Nachum Tunrider, Moshe Fuks, Yankel Asni–Beyle's, and many others from the Tsharner Synagogue, even Leybush Kripke.

The "discotheque" belonged to a couple: he was Volke with the crutches, and she, Matel "Head." Volke, unfortunately sentenced to three–quarter–length legs, couldn't move from his spot without a pair of crutches; he usually sat in his "office," that is, between the columns at the entrance, enjoying the pleasure of God's warm sun and blue sky, and also the cheder boys' tumult.

Matel Head was called that not just because of her clever head, but because it was a head with such virtue. It's not worthwhile to stress that she was a woman of valor, the maker of their livelihood. The couple maintained themselves on "luxury" items:

nuts, bagels, breads, hard candies, caramels, and soda water. During the week, it was from students; on the Sabbath, from the adults.

Mostly the "discotheque" was in a whirl every Sabbath and holiday afternoon. Young men and women gathered together after a week of work to satisfy their Sabbath rest. Catch a word, amuse yourself, blush, crack nuts, spit out the shells, and drink soda water. Together, they sang flaming love songs like "Where are you, under the window my love, my lovely." And juicy, sad songs about the Exile, attraction, and deep longing, such as "Let us say goodbye, the train is leaving."

No money was required, because how could you count kopeks and sixes on the holy Sabbath in the cheder neighborhood on nearby Synagogue Street and other holy institutions. The clients had already taken care to buy chits on Friday: white, one kopek; green, a six; red, a ten. It was called a "ten," but the value was only five kopeks. To make a bustle, they counted the chits like groschen, and the largest coin, a ten, was suited to the craftsmen who earned more and also bought peanuts and Turkish nuts.

Thus, over time, an intimate group developed.

[Page 461]

Also, there was dancing on Motele's earthen dance floor surfaced with yellow sand, accompanied by Feygele the singer, who sang like a canary. The scenery wasn't starry because hearts were warm, because you understood with a wink and the speech of feelings.

We know that very few of today's discotheques have served as starting points for matches, only as leisure, without so direct a path from romance to the wedding canopy.

But the Vishnevets discotheque justified its existence with splendid results. I know for certain four romances that developed there, and the heroes of two met again on the other side of the sea with happiness and joy and with children and grandchildren. I mention this with a special song of praise for the happy inn of their romances–Volke–Matel's "discotheque."

The Recruit

A thing well known, and not an "open secret," is that Jews used any means possible to avoid military service.

Why and for whom would you serve the man, the Russian tsar. It barred the doors to education. But it didn't prohibit you from managing a bulwark, a forest, a mill for a nobleman. You put aside capital, like leavened bread for Passover, and contracted out with a gentile name. In more than one case, the gentile "name" swallowed up the fortune, and at best willed a large part of it as "hush money." So why stretch your neck out for Nicholas?

At different times, different means were employed. He who was a hero chopped his right thumb or ripped all the teeth out of his mouth. That was two generations before us. Afterward, we saw Jews with chopped–off fingers around town: the honorable town starosta Yosel Fodem was none the worse for his condition–anyhow, he held his pen between his middle fingers; but Mendel the tailor had to put a thimble on that stub to stick a needle through, and got used to wearing a tin finger down to the bone, which from a distance glinted like a medallion. So people no longer called him Mendel but the Tailor Medallion.

In our generation, those means remained symbolic traces of the past, and a kind of parody on the old times when the tsar kidnapped Jewish children for 25 years of military service in cold, distant Siberia. In our times, they didn't make such brutal mistakes. Progressive means were used.

[Page 462]

Recruits had several months before they had to appear before the military commission, and they slimmed themselves down with a strict diet, didn't sleep, and wandered all around town in a military parade like an organized group of proud soldiers. Being in town, they could live it up and disturb the quiet night with annoying marching and Russian–Ukrainian songs in loud voices, like "Dubinushka" and "Eini khadi ritsiu," with endless clamor and commotion until morning.

Besides all the recruits' mischief, there were some comical feats. Especially switching the signs. For example, Ostrovski the pork dealer's sign, which had a pig's head and entrails, was re–hung on Sender Kopels' store, and on the door of Mendel's pharmacy, they hung Moshe Shuster's sign, which had a big, black boot and a ladies' high–top shoe.

Everyone suffered in sympathy for Sender Kopels because, for him, the mischief was a bloody joke. Since he was a Talmud scholar, extremely God–fearing, and the town arbitrator, it was literally an offense not only for him but for the community that valued and listened to him. The recruits had gone too far, not quite to scarring the town, but creating pain and shame. It was done on a Friday night in order to last through Sunday morning. That meant a kind of Sabbath demonstration of spiritual pain for Sender Kopels. Feh! But people rushed to Mendel's pharmacy in droves to observe the evil wonder, and they even sent someone to get him so he could see the display, too. He, a progressive, was advanced, even to wearing a short jacket and gold pince–nez for his eyes, like an English lord. He came to behold the sight, stood in front of the pharmacy, and with great annoyance poured out his bitter heart for each wave of onlookers. Mendel the pharmacist was a professional; he had filled prescriptions for the recruits as well, and didn't react in the usual way but in a big way, according to his wisdom, and swore and cursed: "Nitshevo." That is: it doesn't matter; tramps, rascals, scoundrels, they will all serve the tsar.

The recruits heard his wish and began to visit him every night at the second watch. They woke their patient every time, singing and marching.

After a short negotiation, the pharmacist paid five rubles ransom to Yosel Pesi's, president of the orphans' home.

Listen and learn–you don't curse recruits.

How to Learn Respect for the Community and Its Caregivers

It happened in those days of the great anarchy in Russia.

[Page 463]

Kerensky's power wasn't yet consolidated. The Bolsheviks were then based in Moscow and Petersburg, as well as in such distant regions as ours. Ukraine was ruled and rampaged by a bacchanalia of various bands. In Kiev, there was the Ukrainian council with Hetman Skoropadsky. Petluria's pogrom took place in Prokhorov [Proskurov]. There were unsettling events in Krasilov among the local gentiles, the Makhnovists in Vladimir, regular gangs in the Vinnitsa area, and not far from us, the Teofipol pogrom.

With worry and terror, we heard the forewarning and waited for something to happen to us in our town, too. Were we an exception to the Jewish troubles?

On an initiative headed by Shimon Ayzenberg and Dovid Roynik, the "sama oborona"–self-defense–was organized. In the ranks of that group were energetic young people like Vevtshik and Yidel Naftali's, Simchak Zak, Freyde Shantsi's two sons, Yisrael the Red, and Yoke and his friends, who in a Christian manner, using their heavy hands, didn't treat the gentiles well at the markets. So when the drunkards acted up and made trouble, they threw them to the sides and smacked their heads so they wouldn't come back again.

With the help of Vevtshik Naftali's and Zanvel Shnayder, who both served as brave soldiers (even receiving awards under Nicholas), practice exercises were held in Ayzenberg's watermill.

Like loyal and courageous insurance, the self-defense effort was suited to the situation. If only the time would come, and we could resist the temptation. But the time did come, and at that time we were the only authority there. What can you do, alone in the town, isolated from other higher government institutions?

One fine morning, making a wild commotion, a few dozen riders invaded the town on familiar, gentile horses; a few of them were barefoot, in tattered, quilted jackets, looking like a bunch of beggars–except for their commander, a former officer in some kind of military uniform–and they occupied the town. Long-Legged Moshe, the only Jewish messenger in town, was immediately sent to demand that five respectable proprietors call an urgently important meeting.

At the meeting, the commander–who, as it now turned out, was the son of a rich gentile in the Vizherodka area, Petke Slavin–announced loudly that he proclaimed the occupation of the town and presented himself as a department of the Tarashtshantses, the Ukrainian Bolsheviks.

[Page 464]

Until the arrival of the commissar sent from the higher authority, his department was responsible for order in the town and the proper behavior of the population. Until then, having no subsidy from the higher authority and also because of communications difficulties, he demanded a contribution of 12,000 rubles from the Jewish population, which must be paid within 48 hours, and also another small item: 20 pairs of boots and 18 warm jackets.

The messengers called a general meeting, where it was decided to divide the town into regions and to delegate pairs with a list of how much each of those visited could donate to the contribution, according to what they could probably contribute.

Two prominent delegates approached M. Sh., who, instead of 200, grudgingly laid out only 50 and commented in Russian to take it without further appeal. The messengers, ashamed and insulted, turned away empty–handed.

M. Sh. was hard as stone by nature. He dealt in what you would hope not to need. But unfortunately, they were very necessary articles. His business was a gold mine, and he was stingy, so people used to call him, sarcastically, a wealthy man with deep, full pockets but with hands too short to give. They also called him the artificial Zionist. Whenever he was expected to show up to be presented with a share in the Colonial Bank, that is, Dr. Herzl's certificate of Zionism, he didn't. He was distant from Zionism, even when several Zionist parties were already active in town. It was conjectured that he bought a shekel at only one of the three opportunities, with the laconic reply that he had bought it by other means... And at the elections to the Zionist Congress, he claimed that he didn't have voting rights over the shekalim that he hadn't bought "by other means."

M. Sh.'s tactless conduct with the contribution delegation spread around town like an arrow from a bow, with alarm and clamor. He seemed unashamed of his behavior in such a dangerous situation. No wonder, then, that when the bitter report reached the self–defense office, they quickly decided to take stronger measures.

Two brave messengers knocked on M. Sh.'s door late at night. From the other side of the door, inside, came a worried, melancholy question, from a sleepy someone with a trembling voice: "Who's there?"

[Page 465]

The answer from outside was, "Your own people, from the self–defense."

From inside again, "What do you want?"

"Either your money or your life. We want to protect your property and your life. You can't continue your stingy act with our delegation. We want not 200 but no less than 250 from you, and you'll whine, count, and pay us. Open the door and count it out into my hand. Then everything will be OK."

A quiet, closed silence. The delegation was worried and doubtful, and also annoyed, that their brutal passion had shocked the "person," and that something violent would happen, because they heard some kind of mysterious movement inside. Jews are merciful people. A heavy pause. They waited. After a few minutes, they heard a woman's voice, "In the middle of the night and us with sick people, such wild criticism!"

They answered from outside, "M. Sh.'s conduct is beyond any reasonable person's. He sets a bad example for the community. He's a great deserter. You should be ashamed to be under the same roof with such a person."

"We advise you to convince him to bring, as required, 250 rubles by 10 o'clock in the morning." The messengers concluded their visit and left, and tensely anticipated the morning.

It's important to underline how the last monologue by the messengers affected the M. Sh. family, and in the morning–not waiting until 10 o'clock but at 8–he brought the 250 rubles to the self–defense committee.

The incident with the self–defense group was a lesson for M. Sh.'s future community activities. From then on, M. Sh. responded to every collection with sympathy and an appropriate donation: the Foundation Fund, the Jewish National Fund, and as an activist for the orphans' home. In a word, a metamorphosis.

Because one doesn't play games with a community.

[Page 469]

Episodes and Legends

Face Down
(A Bitter Joke)

by Sh. Ayzenberg

Translated by Tina Lunson

In 1914, when World War I began, the Russian Army crossed the Austrian border and took the town of Zalozce. They slandered the Jews, saying that they had burned the military hospital. Then they arrested all the Jews and shipped them out to Vishnevets. There were no jails big enough in Vishnevets to hold so many Jews, so the Russians confiscated the Jewish schools and settled them there.

At that time, at the beginning of the war, all business was interrupted: there was no money, and you couldn't borrow; anyone who owed money didn't repay it, and many Jews remained without a single penny. The situation was very critical, and the Vishnevets Jews had to sustain the Zalozce Jews for weeks with whatever they had. They were given food and drink and clothing until they were sent on to Russia. The Zalozce Jews said that if the situation were the other way around, they would not do as much....

The Russian army sent some of the Zalozce Jews off to work around Kolodno and Zbarazh. Meanwhile, the Days of Awe were approaching, and the Russian army had permitted a few Jews to travel to Vishnevets for the holidays. Among those Jews was one by the name of Shmuel Zolozitser, who stayed with Yosel Ostrer.

Every year at R' Itsi's Synagogue, an Oleksinets Jew named Yisrael Shochet was the cantor. When the Russian Army approached Oleksinets, the Jews fled to Austria (Yisrael Shochet among them), so that R' Itsi's Synagogue had no cantor.

A few days before Rosh Hashanah, this Shmuel Zolozitser came to R' Itsi's Synagogue and said, "I can be the cantor," and appealed to them: "I'll pray for you. I don't want any money, I only want you to give me food, but I won't eat for free." The Jews at R' Itsi's Synagogue l had a little meeting: how could someone they didn't know lead the Days of Awe services? It remained to send Matus the Beadle to talk to him and find out whether he was suitable to lead the community in prayer.

[Page 471]

Matus the Beadle returned, and they asked him, "What did you find out?" Matus shrugged his shoulders and didn't want to talk. "Matus, tell us, what did you find out?"

"I don't want to say anything bad about any Jews, but when I went to him, I found him sleeping face down. This is not a Jewish trait!"

They accepted Shmuel Zolozitser as the cantor, and he prayed well and with much feeling.

The Rabbi and the Police Chief
(Recollection)

by Louis Ratman

Translated by Tina Lunson

I recall what I heard from honorable and observant people in Vishnevets about an event concerning the famous rabbi, Rabbi Yosele, may he rest in peace, that remains etched in my mind and a story that begs to be repeated.

After a drowning victim was found in the town, the rabbi was promptly arrested, and the police chief dragged him by his beard through the streets to the jail.

Twelve men who were owners of stone buildings and houses got him out on bail, posting their buildings as a guarantee for the rabbi's return if he were not released from the libel.

The rabbi became weak and sick from aggravation and heartache. But wanting to protect him from possible incarceration, the good men decided to smuggle him to Austria. Along the way he caught a chill, and soon after his arrival, he died.

Not long after the rabbi's passing, the police chief lost his mind and went running through the streets shouting in wild voices, "This is for the rabbi."

And strikingly, all those who lost their houses in saving the rabbi later became rich, as if through a miracle.

Respectable residents of the town–known as believing people–corroborated the fact that they saw the chief running around screaming "This is for the rabbi" and that they personally knew the people who lost their houses and later became rich.

My grandfather, may he rest in peace, then interceded with the czar with a request, written in a rare Hebrew, and not considering whether the czar would refuse his request, sent the prosecutor to call the Cabinet together and congratulated him and kissed him for his wonderful Hebrew, which the czar praised highly.

[Page 472]

Vishnevets Demons
(A Comic Episode from the Old Home)
by Yakov Sheyngold

Translated by Tina Lunson

Everyone knows and remembers the tomb, the hill of stones that was covered with green grass in the summer and mud from after the High Holidays until Passover. The tomb was behind the Great Synagogue, a place where almost everyone was afraid to go late at night because it was said that the Great Synagogue was lit up in the middle of the night and the dead came to pray then, and that demons came to dance on the tomb because there was once a well there, where in the days of Chmielnitski (may his name be blotted out) the haidamakas threw a whole wedding party–the groom, the bride, in–laws, and musicians–and so were buried there. Children–as well as adults–used to go there and toss in garlic, and on the morning before Yom Kippur, pious Jews would go there right after services to recite prayers.

It was after the High Holidays, when the there was a lot of mud, on a Sabbath night after Havdala. Yitschak Kremenetski (Itsik the Tall)–a tall Jew, a Jew the whole town knew, was a good brother to everyone, even addressing the judge and the rabbi with the familiar "du," and was invited to almost every wedding and circumcision. If you had to come to an agreement about something, he would be one of the mediators.

On such a Sabbath night, when there was plenty of mud, soon after Havdala, he went over to the market square to see and talk with some good friends over a glass of tea and stayed there until late at night. Walking home through Moshe the Blind's alley, which a gentile's wagon had almost completely blocked, he also happened to go by the synagogue and the tomb. Nearing there, he heard strange shouting and handclapping coming from the direction of the tomb. Not easily frightened, and thinking that it was probably a pig (they used to go there to wallow in the mud), he picked up a stone and threw it into the place where the sound was coming from. Just then, the shouting and clapping got much louder, and he began to see more clearly that something was rising and falling back down. Frightened, he gathered all his strength and ran home–which was not more than an American city block away–ran into the house, and fainted from fear.

[Page 473]

There was a big scream from Miryam, his wife, and the children and neighbors came running and together revived him a little.

Coming to, he began asking people to go with him to see what was going on there. A group of Jews formed, holding lights and their ritual fringes in their hands. They were going to ask the demons to go back to their eternal rest.

But approaching Yankel Leybele's, where you could already see the tomb, everyone heard some strange shouting and saw the strange leaping of a creature that terrified them, and they clutched their fringes and started loudly reciting "Shema Yisrael." A few of them began to run back, because who can stand up to a wild demon?

But seeing that more people were arriving, they went closer and found a local gentile, completely drunk, wallowing in the mud. It was Yoske the carpenter, who made benches and cabinets for Vishnevets Jews. And as soon as he received payment, he went drinking, and often he went back, and if someone was not paying attention, he stole the furniture and sold it to another Jew. And if someone caught him at it and said, "Yoske, this is mine, I've already paid you for it," he would say, "It's yours, take it back."

[Page 474]

Hometown Memories

by M. Fishman (Vishnevets–Brooklyn)

Translated by Tina Lunson

The word yizkor had two meanings for me:

Things and events that I remember from my childhood years

Yizkor, which I and none of those who were saved from our town will not and must not forget.

I would like to linger on things that I remember from my childhood years.

I was reared by poor parents, who sent me to study with teachers whom they didn't have to pay a lot of money. And sometimes they'd pay nothing. Since my father had no money, and I was growing up, he sent me to the Vishnevets Talmud Torah, which didn't have its own building. The lessons were presented in the study halls, which they used to call the Tailors' Synagogue, R' Itsi's Synagogue, the Tshaner Synagogue, and so on.

Dear, highly educated teachers sacrificed their time and skills to educate the poor children, most of them boys, who didn't have the opportunity to study in the secondary schools–the Tarbut Schools. The Tarbut School did have its own building and charged tuition. It was a progressive school, as it is called today.

The revenue for establishing the Talmud Torah was due to those dear Jews who devoted themselves to collecting donations from the town proprietors. At the head of those proprietors was Hirsh Matus Segal (one of his sons survived the war and is in Israel). But despite the poor conditions in the Talmud Torah, we Talmud Torah students often achieved a higher level of learning in all subjects than the Tarbut School students.

Finally, the day came, and we merited moving into our own Talmud Torah building, for which sincere Jews had used every means to amass the sum of money required to build the Vishnevets Talmud Torah.

When I write about the Talmud Torah here, I have in mind several areas of Torah. The Torah that for me and other survivors of my hometown Vishnevets, many gave and indicated our path in life. However primitive the teaching was then, in our poor, primitive little town of Vishnevets, it gave us the foundation and source for Jewish and secular knowledge.

[Page 475]

Those dear Jews not only carried the burden of providing the Talmud Torah with books and tuition, they also took it upon themselves to pay the teachers, more than 10 at that time. Among them were such well–known teachers as Issakher Sos, Erlikh, and others. I should mention several names of the dear Jews who volunteered their time and money for the Talmud Torah, not for "publicity" but for a little place in the world to come.

Today this would sound like "social work." Here are some of the names: Shimon Lifshits, Todres Averbakh, Matisyahu Segal, and others whose names I can't recall at the moment.

In modesty, I would like to mention the light–filled memory of my father, Efraim Fishman, may God avenge his blood, who used to make the rounds every week to collect Talmud Torah contributions from the proprietors. May the light–filled memory of the supporters and contributors be eternalized and their names mentioned with reverence.

It is difficult to depict the boundless love and goodness of the impoverished, hardworking Jews in Vishnevets with my poor pen.

As fate would have it, several years before the war, I was torn away from my beloved parents and other Jews when I had to leave to find work someplace else.

The memory of my hometown is holy, sacred to me. My hands shake when I try to mention my hometown. Tears choke me and a shudder goes through my body when the memories of our little Vishnevets community are awakened in me.

May their souls be sanctified in the fire of martyrdom in which they were devoured, and may their light–filled memories never be forgotten by the surviving remnants of Vishnevets.

May God avenge their blood!

[Page 476]

The False Accusation against the Great Saint R' Yosele Radiviler

by M. Chazan

Translated by Tina Lunson

It is important to relate the history of the slander that was made against R' Yosele Radiviler 89 years ago in the town of Vishnevets in Volhynia, where R' Yosele had settled after leaving Radzivilov.

I was told the reason R' Yosele left Radzivilov and settled in Vishnevets, where the accusation took place, by the elderly R' Yisrael Safir HaKohen of Vishnevets, a brave Jew, may God lengthen his days:

It is said that in the dynastic line of rabbis from which Rabbi Yosele drew his pedigree, there was a custom that had been handed down from generation to generation not to stay in the same town for more than 20 years.

So as the 20–year mark for his time in Radzivilov approached, the rabbi let the Radzivilov community leaders and his followers know his thoughts about changing his place, according to the custom of his ancestors.

Generally, many towns would have liked the privilege of having the rabbi settle there and would have been prepared to accept him with honor, but it appeared that Vishnevets held more charm for the saint than other towns, so he decided to settle in Vishnevets.

Thus, Vishnevets became known over all Volhynia and Poland–where the rabbi had many Hasidim who traveled to meet with him, and the Vishnevets Jews considered this a great privilege.

This happened about 98 years ago, in the year 5638 (1877–1878). The Hasidim were happy because Vishnevets and Radzivilov belonged to the Kremenets district, and it was no great distance.

Then the rabbi came down to Vishnevets, where a lovely, spacious, eight–room apartment had been prepared for him. He took four rooms for himself and four for his son Rabbi Sender Shmuel, who a short time later was accepted as rabbi by the Vishnevets town leaders.

And although the rabbi was happy in Vishnevets, all his Hasidim called him Rabbi Yosele Radiviler, and to this day he is called by this name.

[Page 477]

The rabbi had thousands of Hasidim all over Volhynia as well as in other places, and there is much to write about his particular Hasidism, but that's another story. Here I want to describe the accusation made against the rabbi, how he was put into jail when a drowned convert was discovered in the Vishnevets river right after Passover. And because it was a religious murder, how the rabbi was held responsible for it.

And this is what actually happened.

In Vishnevets, there was one Moshe Shuele's, a miller. His wife was named Tsivye; their children were Shaul and Avraham Itsi.

Tsivye had a brother, whom people called Yeshue Lanevitser, who ran a cheder and was a teacher.

Tsivye had another brother who died and left two orphans, Mendel and Avraham Itsi. She took Mendel in and set up Avraham Itsi as a helper for his uncle the teacher.

The whole story of the accusation against the rabbi developed from the teacher's helper, Avraham Itsi, who suddenly converted.

It is not known exactly what brought him to convert, but one fine day he decided that he had had enough of taking children to cheder and instructing them, and he suddenly disappeared from Vishnevets. The whole thing was murky, and people started searching for him. After a short time, when no one had heard from him, the family was worried. But before long rumors spread that Avraham Itsi was in the Pochayev monastery and that he had long since converted.

At that time, he was not quite 16 years old.

You can only imagine what happened in Vishnevets when the sad news reached the family and its relatives. The whole town roiled and talked. They forgot their businesses and livelihood and talked only about the convert. It created great pain and shame for the family. It was a disgrace and an injury.

It was well known that the Pochayev monastery–the largest in the land–was the grandfather of impurities, and it was difficult to save anyone from there even if they wanted to be saved, because "whoever goes in does not come out." It was really dark and bitter for them, and there was no advice to offer them.

[Page 478]

His cousins Shaul and Avraham Itsi–and his brother Mendel–traveled to Pochayev to see if there was something they could do on the spot. Maybe they could rescue him. They were very disappointed to hear that it was impossible to get into the monastery because it was surrounded by a huge fence, and anyone who entered had to have special permission. It was not possible to go any further.

For the family in Vishnevets, the incident was even more painful because people were suggesting that they had not treated him well, and so he ran away. That was like salt on their wound. The problem caused them a lot of heartache, and their hope was to wait for an opportunity to go to the monastery, for better or worse.

Such an opportunity did come quickly, by chance. Although the monastery was completely walled off from the town, permissions were given for tradesmen, including Jewish merchants, to enter and do business.

You must understand that the monastery had many buildings, fields, forests, gardens, and orchards that were leased to Jews as well. The Jew who leased the orchard had a protector there, a Jew by the name of Chayim Anshel Margolis. He also had a lovely daughter who often went to spend time in the orchard.

It was through her that an opportunity was sought to reach the convert, because the converts were allowed to go into the orchards on Sundays to play and enjoy the fruits and trees. A plan was worked out that the daughter would draw him aside, and from there they could get him out and help him.

Exactly how the deed was executed remains a secret, but in fact that they did get the convert out and cross the Austrian border, which was not far from there; he was then taken to a relative in Skala and left there.

The convert was convinced that he should return to being a Jew, because they promised him that the lovely young woman would be his bride.

That seemed to affect him more than anything else, and it appeared that he was truly sorry for what he had done. So he thought about it for a while. But before long, the young man became uneasy, and eventually he once again made a false step.

[Page 479]

It was discovered that he had already been to see the priest in Skala, told him the whole story, and expressed his desire to convert again.

His relative in Skala was fearful of the consequences of sheltering this convert and asked that [the Vishnevets cousins] come and take him away before it was too late.

It was clear that unless they could pack him off to another location, there would be trouble. So when his cousins came to Skala, they first of all took him back to Vishnevets and looked for ways to get rid of him.

To this day it is not known exactly what happened to him or who helped lead him off the path, because everything was a big secret so that no one would know where his remains would end up.

The story of the convert may not have become known so quickly if not for that, by chance, someone recognized him as his body floated by with a sack tied around its neck; the sack contained stones, which had fallen out of holes that fish had bitten in the sack as the body floated.

This happened right after Passover, when the ice had already melted. On a Friday morning, someone noticed a body floating in the river. The news spread quickly all over Vishnevets, and everyone ran to the river. People were curious to know whose body it was, and one fisherman–Itsi Kotliar, a Jew who had dealt in fish his whole life and could tell a good tale–set out in a boat to bring the body in. But when he recognized that it was Avraham Itsi the convert, he took the body to the opposite shore of the river.

But eventually Lyabetski, a policeman, arrived. He could speak Yiddish, and he helped drag the body out. The Jews in Vishnevets quickly sensed that it was better not to get mixed up in this, and one by one they dispersed. The children, however, who were free from cheder on Fridays, didn't go away, and they were the first to recognize Avraham Itsi, the cheder helper.

The policeman who spoke Yiddish learned too much from the children. You know how children chatter. Before long, the police chief arrived on the scene. He was a true enemy of the Jews.

[Page 480]

He immediately had the rabbi arrested. He would be the security until the guilty party was discovered.

The rabbi was in the middle of praying, and this made a strong impression on him. But he rallied, and they took him off to jail for cross–examination. When the Jews saw that the rabbi had been gone for a long time, they understood that he had been arrested, and they prevailed on the police to let him go free for the Sabbath. He would not even discuss it, and the outrage was so great that they had to send to Kolodno for Uri Tsemach, who was a friend of the chief's, and even he was barely able to persuade him to free the rabbi until Sabbath night, after Havdala. In any case, the Vishnevets Jews had a disrupted Sabbath because the authorities also arrested Avraham Itsi's cousins and their parents, plus his brother Mendel. On that same Sabbath, the assistant prosecutor came from Kremenets along with the investigator (the Vishnevets investigator was on vacation at the time).

Also, a doctor came to perform an autopsy on the body.

And from Pochayev came the baptized mother of three converts, his friends. Later, three priests arrived from Pochayev to make the preparations for the funeral, which had been scheduled for Sunday.

They announced to all the village gentiles that they should gather by the church from which the funeral procession would start. They brought the rabbi to the autopsy, and seeing it, he was so nauseated that he could barely be resuscitated. The Jews in Vishnevets would never forget what they through on that Sabbath and Sunday until the ceremony was over.

As soon as the funeral procession ended, the Jews searched for ways to rescue the rabbi. In the meantime, three days had passed, and it was discovered that the rabbi had not prayed for those three days because the arrestees were dirty and the jail was too foul a place for prayer, and consequently he had not touched the food that had been brought from home.

Convincing the police chief that the rabbi needed a separate room didn't come easily. They set up a bed and a table with a bench, brought in some holy books, and made it as comfortable as possible for the rabbi. But releasing him on bail was not up for discussion until the investigator returned from vacation.

[Page 481]

When the Vishnevets investigator did come and took over the papers from the Kremenets investigator, he still couldn't help with bail because, according to the papers, this was a premeditated murder in which the rabbi had taken part.

As Shavuot approached, the Jews tried to persuade the investigator to release the rabbi for the holiday. But he demanded that they lay out 2,000 rubles against his return to jail; they brought him the money, but they never got it back. The rabbi went back to jail after the holiday. Two or three months went by, and the investigator was still afraid to take it upon himself to release the rabbi on bail, but since he was big on bribery, he himself searched for advice on what to do, and after all, the 2,000 rubles was still in his possession, and he was afraid they would demand the 2,000 rubles back. By the time he conceded that he would release the rabbi for 8,000 rubles' bail, it was already the middle of Elul [August]. The sum was paid, and the rabbi was freed from jail until the trial.

During the Days of Awe, many Hasidim came to the rabbi, and everything looked fine and good, one could pretend, but as if for spite, on Yom Kippur the main prosecutor arrived from Zhitomir and asked where the rabbi was, as he had to be set up in Kremenets to begin a new investigation. When he discovered that the rabbi was out on bail, he spoke sharply to the investigator and told him that he must send him to Kremenets posthaste.

The investigator ordered that they should go to Kremenets on the morning after Yom Kippur. But people wanted the rabbi to be in Vishnevets for the first days of Sukkot, so they started negotiating with the investigator, but he couldn't help. He had to obey the prosecutor's orders. He handed over the papers to the police chief as ordered, and they were able to persuade the police chief to deliver the rabbi on the first interim day of Sukkot.

The rabbi traveled to Kremenets on the first interim day of Sukkot, and the Kremenets Jews saw to it that the rabbi had a separate room. They were even allowed to chop up the roof for a sukkah, and as usual that cost plenty of money.

On Shemini Atzeret, they brought a minyan to pray, and even R' Yisrael was there for the minyan with the rabbi, because he was a kohen. The other arrestees were furious that the storeroom had been emptied for the rabbi and that he was given so much respect.

[Page 482]

While the rabbi was traveling to Kremenets, his son Sender Shmuel went to Zhitomir with patronage so that his father could be released on bail, because the 8,000 rubles were still being held by the investigator. He was successful. A telegram was promptly sent to the Vishnevets investigator stating that Rabbi Yungerleyb could be free on the bail that he was holding. When the rabbi's son returned to Vishnevets, he was certain that his father would already be home, but it turned out that the investigator didn't believe the telegram since, he said, anyone could have sent it from Zhitomir. He must have a signed document that he could bring back from Zhitomir.

R' Sender Shmuel had to travel to Zhitomir again and bring the signed document, and then the rabbi was freed until the trial. So the rabbi was free until the second winter before Purim. He happened to be in Teofipol when it occurred to the investigator that he should deliver the rabbi to Kremenets in the Okruzshnoy court for the trial.

When Zverkovska, the secretary for the investigator, read over the papers, he understood that it was looking bad for the rabbi. He put the papers in his hat and went to visit the rabbi's wife, Chane'le, and told her everything, immediately let the Hasidim know of the danger, and then set off for Teofipol.

Meanwhile, the investigator sent for the two deputies and told them to go to Teofipol to get the rabbi and deliver him to the Okruzshnoy court in Kremenets. They departed for Teofipol to get the rabbi. His wife, Chane'le, related to the rabbi's friend what the papers accused him of and how the secretary had warned her of the danger.

There was a certain Chayim Borovitser in Teofipol, a wealthy Jew. He took it upon himself to deliver the rabbi to Kremenets in his horse and wagon, and the two deputies followed behind. The rabbi was sure he was traveling toward Kremenets. His wife was traveling with him. But when they came to turnoff for Volochisk, Chayim took it before the two deputies noticed, and they continued along the road to Kremenets.

Meanwhile, the rabbi was conducted across the border and driven to Glina, where he remained until he passed away. His wife, Chane'le, became ill even sooner and died of pneumonia.

[Page 483]

The trial for the others took place right after Passover: the miller Moshe Shuele's was sentenced to 12 years in jail; his wife, Tsivye, 10 years in jail. The teacher Yeshue Lanevitser got 10 years. All three were sent to Irkutsk in Siberia. Their children were not old enough, and they were set free. Chayim Anshel got two and a half years, and since it had already been two years until the trial, he served the remaining six months.

The young woman was freed as well since she was young. She married, and her name was then Kartman. With that ended the story of the accusation against the great Rabbi Yosele, which at the time roiled the entire Hasidic world and held our region in suspense for two whole years.

The anguish and worry exhausted the rabbi, and the sudden passing of his wife shortened his years and brought his end near. He passed away in Glina in 5641 (1881–1882). May his memory be for a blessing.

[Page 484]

Jewish Benefactors
(A Vishnevets Episode)

by A. Freylekh

Translated by Tina Lunson

At the end of the 19th and the beginning of the 20th century, when thousands of Jews were abandoning Russia and fleeing to America, many–because they lacked money–had to leave their wives and children and travel alone. Later, when they organized their lives and saved a little money, they sent for their families.

Our area was located near the Austrian border, and many emigrants had to pass through our town, and many Vishnevets Jews helped through their words and deeds.

My father, may he rest in peace, dealt with the Russians directly through an authorized contract to deliver certain products for a certain price to the border patrol as well as to higher government officers.

One day, a woman with five children arrived in Radzivilov, which was also on the Austrian border. The woman had been dealing with certain border agents and couldn't come to an agreement on the price they demanded. Only one way remained for her to get out, and that was to leave one or, more likely, two children with good people, because smuggling all of them over the border was impossible. She would not have enough money to reach her husband in New York.

At that time, there lived in Radzivilov a woman by the name of Chaye Apelboym, a cousin of my mother, may she rest in peace. When she learned of this story, she didn't think for long but took the six souls and traveled with them to Vishnevets. And all seven barged into our house.

And after they were made comfortable, the cousin came right to the point:

"Hershenyu! Hershenyu! First God and then you must help these people, a woman and five children, poor, her husband in America! We are Jews after all, children of mercy [benefactors]. We must help smuggle her over the border!"

My father wanted to explain that he didn't want to be mixed up in it, but they didn't give him a chance to say a word.

The two women and children wept and wailed. Just take them on wings and fly them over the border. But my father, may he rest in peace, had been powerfully moved by their first pleas.

[Page 485]

This was on a Friday, so all seven had to stay in our house over the Sabbath.

That Sabbath, my father, along with my mother, worked out a very risky plan. He used to consult with my mother about everything. They didn't even explain what could happen if the plan didn't work.

Sunday at dawn, when the whole town lay in deep sleep, my father climbed onto his horse, galloped to the customs house, went up to the highest officer of the border patrol, and begged for a personal favor–and one without payment: that he should allow the woman and her five children to cross the border without harassment and in the middle of the day, just as if they had a "government pass" but with one difference: the officer at the border would not demand to see the pass.

After a short deliberation, the gentile said, "Hershele! I like your nerve, and since I know you are an honest Jew, I'll be happy to help you. They must, however, come disguised as nobility, and I'll see to it that tomorrow, at a set time, my trustworthy colleague will be at the gate, and they can pass through, no questions asked."

In the morning–Monday–the six people were polished up and dressed in their best clothes, the woman as a lady and the children as gentile princes and princesses. My father hired a coach with bells, as that was the agreement–and they crossed the border in peace, just as though they were the highest government officers.

My father had already been to the customs house earlier (ostensibly on business) to see that everything was in order.

And so a number of families succeeded in departing.

The story was known to a very small number of people. And it remained a secret from the town for many years.

[Page 486]

A Favor for a Favor

by M. Chazan

Translated by Tina Lunson

This episode that I will share happened some 73 years ago, in a village near Vishnevets, in Volhynia.

R' Yisrael Safir of Vishnevets–an old Jew, an energetic man–told me about the event. It is the story of how a gentile fell in love with a Jewish girl, and when he couldn't get their parents to agree, he convinced the Jewish girl to run away in the middle of the night.

That had a powerful effect on the girl's parents, and in their despair, they turned to a relative, Hirsh Bisker, who leased estates from Baron von Pliata, who lived in a palace in Vishnevets.

Hirsh Bisker did indeed help to rescue his relative, but the Russian government persecuted him and sent him out of the village, which was in the Pale of Settlement–some 50 versts from the border. His good heart, and the good that he had done for both the Jews and the Christians, saved him from being transported and allowed him to return to his estates and business. The saying "goodness pays for itself" is applicable. And because his wealth came from the estates he leased from Baron von Pliata, I will begin with the Baron, the great scholar.

Baron von Pliata, who lived in a Vishnevets palace, was a great scholar 55 years ago. He was a well–known astronomer and philosopher.

The fact that he was a tutor for Aleksander III's royal family in Tsarskoye Selo shows that he was considered a great scholar and linguist of the time. Nikolay II, the heir apparent, studied with Baron von Pliata as a youth. He came from an aristocratic family in Poland that was related to kings, from whom he inherited many estates and properties. His forests were valued in the millions of rubles. The palace in Vishnevets where he spent most of the summer was located on a hill, surrounded by gardens and orchards. It was gorgeous. In the summer, the orchards and gardens bloomed and perfumed the whole area.

[Page 487]

He was an art lover, so there were many drawings and paintings by the best artists that had cost him a great deal of money. He also possessed a large library and had classic works by all the foreign writers, which he continued to collect.

When years later they wanted to take away the library, they packed them in more than 40 carts. From that you can imagine how many books there were in the library. It is likely that he knew Hebrew, and he often quoted passages from the Talmud, always a surprise for Jews.

It is said that once, by accident, driving near the Vishnevets synagogue, which was counted among the oldest buildings in the town, he expressed his desire to go inside. Entering the synagogue door, he read an "anonymous charity" inscription, took out a 10–ruble gold piece, and dropped it into the box.

Going inside, he walked around with his head bowed, regarded everything, and read everything on the walls. There were prayer books and copies of the Five Books of Moses on the cantor's stand, each of which he opened and said what it was.

Each year he traveled abroad and brought back rarities and art pieces; if he liked something, he didn't spare any expense to have it.

That's how he was known, and if there was a rarity, someone would bring to him, and he would buy it. Thus, he collected a treasure trove of expensive objects and art pieces.

After the Revolution, the entire collection of antiques fell into the hands of the Polish government, in 1920.

The estates were given out in leases. The leaseholder Hirsh Bisker lived in the village of Butin. It was not far from Vishnevets, and Jews had a lot to say about Hirsh Bisker because he liked hosting poor folks for holidays and was very generous in giving charity. It was known that whoever was traveling through Butin had to eat at his house; he simply would not desist.

There was no greater joy for him than when he himself could treat his guests. When he came into town, he brought with him a wagon full of good things, which he distributed among the poor.

[Page 488]

He supported rabbis and religious leaders with a generous hand. Even the gentiles in the village knew that he dealt fairly with them, so they liked him, and he did many favors for them.

The more Hirsh Bisker gave away, the richer he became. He already had other possessions and mills besides being a partner in other businesses connected to forestry, and he was successful in everything he put his hand to. Although he was not well educated, but really a simple villager, he had a good heart, and his goal in life was to take Torah scholars, Talmud experts, as husbands for his daughters.

Hirsh Bisker married his eldest daughter off to a very wealthy man and gave out charity before and after the wedding. The son–in–law was very fine, exactly what he had wished for, and he took the lease in the village of Rakovets, which belonged to Ragof, the governor in Baku. The governor had another village, Mishkovtsy, not far from Rakovets, where Yudel Mishkovitser had settled as a leasee.

That Yudel had a lovely daughter by the name of Rachel. There was a rich Christian in the village who had a son named Timka. That gentile boy set his sights on the lovely Rachel and became a frequent visitor at Yudel Mishkovitser's.

Meanwhile people in the village had begun talking about this, that Timka might take a Jew, Rachel, for a wife.

He even talked to his parents about it, but they told him to get such foolishness out of his head. And Rachel's parents were not happy, and it turned out that Timka decided to deal with it his own way. One night, he convinced Rachel that she should run away with him, and she agreed.

You can already imagine what happened in the morning when people realized that Rachel had run off with Timka, the gentile.

The parents were devastated and didn't know what to do. Since Hirsh Bisker was a relative, they went to him for advice.

Meanwhile, talk began that Rachel was somewhere in a church, where she was being prepared for conversion.

[Page 489]

A gentile came forward to let Yudel know that his daughter was in another village not far away, where the sheygets Timka had hidden her.

Hirsh Bisker turned to the Vishnevets police chief to help him search for the lovely Rachel, who had disappeared. But he wanted [misprints in original] home to her parents. This was not difficult for Hirsh Bisker to do because he had not spared any effort in spreading money around.

Before long, the police chief went off to the village where Rachel was hidden and brought her to the bailiff in Kremenets, who gave her over to her parents. They promptly took her across the border, because they figured that things would not go smoothly and that the government would come to the aid of the priests of the church where they wanted to convert her. And sure enough, the priest in Vishnevets–an enemy of the Jews–wrote a denunciation to the governor in Zhitomir, who then came down to Kremenets for an investigation. Before long, the bailiff from Kremenets was removed from office.

Also, the police chief and constable in Vishnevets were removed from their positions; they were all arrested until they went on trial, and others were assigned in their places.

At the same time, the priest denounced Hirsh Bisker's son–in–law, since he was from Austria, as was Yudel, and now time had left no other way but to cross the border so as not to fall into police hands.

And Hirsh Bisker couldn't be left unpunished. He was not allowed to be within 50 versts of the border and was transported to Kunev, Ostrog district.

Everything that they had possessed became a ruin, and Hirsh Bisker drew a sentence as well.

Hirsh Bisker was devastated and considered how to reverse the sentence.

Meanwhile, the thing had gone all the way to the Kiev general governor, Trentel.

Baron von Pliata was a good friend of Trentel's, so naturally Hirsh Bisker sought a favor from the Baron: to intercede with General Governor Trentel on his behalf.

[Page 490]

He gave him a letter and told him to travel to see the governor in Kiev.

Hirsh Bisker set off for Kiev and went to the general governor's chancellery to hand over the letter from Baron von Pliata.

Sitting there with a broken heart and waiting for the secretary of the chancellery to take him and his request, he heard the secretary call to him:

"Mr. Bisker, what are you doing here?"

He looked at the secretary and didn't know who he was.

The secretary asked, "Don't you recognize me? Remember when I was secretary to the police chief in Vishnevets and I lost my position, and you lent me 25 rubles? Now do you see who I am? Tell me, what brings you here?"

He handed him the letter. The secretary read it over and said to Hirsh Bisker, "Here, take my calling card. Come to my home this afternoon."

Hirsh Bisker went to his home, and the secretary told his wife who their guest was, and how he had lent him 25 rubles when he had lost his job and didn't even ask for a promissory note.

He was treated very well and was promised that everything would be taken care of and that he should come that night and he would provide him with a document that would free him entirely. And so it was: he wiped out the whole matter with the documents from the governor's desk–he was completely free of the sentence.

He took his leave from the secretary and wanted to reward him, but he would not take any money from him. And he said, "With your 25 rubles I achieved this important office, and if I can do a favor for you now, I'm happy. Go home and give my regards to my friends there."

He also gave him a letter for the new bailiff in Kremenets, stating that he should allow him to go back to his to his businesses in his village, Butin, which his son–in–law Taytelman had been operating this whole time.

Hirsh Bisker turned toward home with a happy heart. He carried home with him all the money that he had taken with him to Kiev to ransom himself. But he gave it all away as charity in the town of Vishnevets.

[Page 491]

Characters

[Page 493]

Chane Malke

by M. Or (Averbukh)

Translated by Tina Lunson

As in all the cities and towns in Volhynia, so it was for us in Vishnevets: all types of people lived among us–each one with his peculiar social character. Like council members, scholars, philanthropists, those with inherited wealth–summer in cloth kapotas, winter in skunk overcoats, and most of the middle–income people with heavy furs and little pelts.

And there was another stratum in cotton coats that begged and did hard labor, ending each day with poverty and want; they had weighty dreams at night about ways to make a living, and in the morning confronted the day of grey life between heaven and earth. They were unfortunate figures with no certainty or hope for betterment. And among them floated, like stars in the clouds, a spiritual piety. There are not many stars (if any others were needed), and one of them was Chane Malke.

Chane Malke–old as a grandmother but with a smile like a child's. In the suffocating atmosphere of gentile jackets and pitch from the wagons at the Monday market, she brought a waft of a juicy blossom that injected everyone with belief in a fine, humane spirit.

[If] Chane Malke, walking by, waved her hand over your forehead, she warmed your heart as with balsam; when from a distance she gave warm, friendly winks of thanks to old acquaintances; and her friends were people of suffering and pain, who looked to her for motherly care and tenderhearted support.

There are some people in the world who, when they appear, make a person calm; their name is goodness. From Chane Malke's forehead, which jutted from her head covered with a "Turkish" kerchief, you could sense her task wherever she went– this was a symbol of goodness. Her sharp eye penetrated every corner of need. With courtesy and deep empathy, she delivered help with silk gloves, and especially anonymous donations.

The elderly grandmother, with light steps like a deer, where is she off to? Someone lacks something for the Sabbath. She moves energetically and very quietly–quick help; a she connects a sick person to the Visiting the Sick Society, she takes part in a funeral for true lovingkindness, and not in the same breath prepares a bride–she puts on her silk kerchief and does what needs to be done, arranges the feast so that, heaven forbid, the bride is not insulted and the family is not ashamed.

[Page 494]

Requesting, claiming, demanding–so that people will participate in the great commandment [to give]. You must give, one with an open hand, another with just the fingertips, because who would dare refuse and obstruct the effort when Chane Malke, the missionary of prompt help, is standing before him? You give even with a frown, so as not to be punished by Chane Malke's dissatisfied though sympathetic look.

There are other women who make the Sabbath for the poor, among them some religious functionaries [wives] and others who do it for show. They do their assignment with a big basket in hand, and with great impetus and pomp on Sabbath eve, and call out the names of the recipients to make a bustle, add salt and pepper to their particular bit (a loaf of challah and a piece of fish), with gossip about the poor family, with no sympathy, so that often their delivery is accompanied by insult to the needy, who are beyond any criticism in the eyes of the giver.

No so Chane Malke, because her deeds are accompanied with deep human feeling and a deep–hearted, free–willing, kindly offer to help the downtrodden.

Hidden deep under her shawl, she carries the gift with great honor and respect to the sufferers.

She heard from a certain source about a case, about a downfallen family in the town, with a girl whose time had come, and only thanks to Chane Malke's initiative did they accomplish the commandment of marrying off the bride in a dazzling and festive manner.

In those days, she collected hundreds of rubles–tsarist rubles, and that thanks to her gentle approach, which opened the hearts of the great families. She stood an entire family "back on its feet," because in time the young couple luckily worked their way up to a good living and reached the level of the great families.

A few donors were jealous of Chane Malke, since they were just givers, because giving is only one third of the commandment, but Chane Malke delivered the cure for the plague to each, taking each mission to its end. For her the reward was fuller. She demanded, she took, and she gave.

Anyone who did not see Chane Malke in action and her mission in a silk scarf did not see the personal procession of old charm and wonderful tradition that demanded recognition of praise and respect.

[Page 495]

Her hands were full of commandments, and she had no doubt in her belief that she was running an account with the Master of the Universe in accumulating commandments fulfilled for the world to come.

She herself was of middle height, but from her forehead shone a royal glow with the special charm of a Mirele Efros[1], not in a scene from the play but literally in life, with heart and soul.

With her warm, wonderful spirit and her good heart for good deeds, a clear countenance with traces of a tender refinement, as they say: one of the brilliant stars in the clouds of the monotonous grey life of Vishnevets was Chane Malke.

Translation editor's note

Mirele Efros is an 1898 Yiddish play by Jacob Gordin.

[Page 496]

Three Generations of Pedigree

by Alef

Translated by Tina Lunson

If you are a Vishnevetser, you know just what "the family" means. It's enough to add your grandfather's name to the term "family," and you have a chain with three generations: the grandfather at the cantor's desk, the father at his prayer stand by the eastern wall, and the boy at his side.

The father dealt in notions or piece goods, and when possible, he was a grain dealer, or even bought forests to chop down, or was a mediator in the sale of an estate; he had his prince, for whom he was the "court banker." He had privileges and could receive concessions, thanks to the prince, which were accessible only to gentiles: selling monopoly items or taking a farm lease.

So, a Jew with a beard and side curls, and perhaps also on the Sabbath with a silk coat with a sash, or conversely already a "progressive," with a short coat. Very busy with businesses and community matters. Achiever of things for the powers that be, where the doors are opened wide, able to ask a favor for himself first of all, but also for the community.

In all the historical dramas that were played out in the town, from power to power and through various transitions, there was an uncrowned advocate in Jewish troubles, who cracked the whip, and whom Jews loved. Synagogue wardens were servers at his celebrations. R' Ploni[1] this, R' Ploni that–literally a legend. He said as much about himself. A prestigious family, a great scholar, a fervent Hasid; when he was a child–at three years old he sat on the Trisker Rabbi's knee, may he rest in peace. A paid–for son–in–law with those who lived in the big house. And moreover, with his own energies, he worked his way to wealth and wisdom and happiness.

When the town rabbi went to visit him at home, it was a procession: the beadle two steps behind, and he himself, the rabbi, the magistrate in his colored silk coat, white stockings, and black lacquered shoes; it was the picture of a patriarch with a handsome, representative long beard in front, like a big, colorful banner–and it all said, proper behavior!

The rabbi went to the "president," the proprietor of the town, who lived in the big masonry house with the wide gates. And the proprietor was no Baron Ginzburg or Anshel Rothschild; nor did he have a rabbinical diploma.

[Page 497]

But he did have his merits: he was honest, a fundamentally honest man and a zealous worker in community matters. Straightforward, precise, knowledgeable in business and in the community. A regular in the synagogue. Every day of his life, he opened or closed the holy ark. On Yom Kippur at the closing service, he stood fast, pale, but with strong character; he stood as a representative of the community, not only for the prince, but ostensibly also for God. Progressively inclined but in the end a fearer of heaven.

*

To welcome the Sabbath, a householder harnessed everyone into the synagogue, like a general with his family brigade in the service of the Creator. The whole week with regular folks, and Sabbath with an extra soul for God. After lighting the candles, the woman stood by the window and looked out with Sabbath joy at how the householder went to pray with their five sons, a commandment, a row, a lovely panorama.

In looking at that scene, a widow–and thus one punished by God–was envious, and spoke from her bitter heart:

"The Master of the Universe has gifted him with more than a quorum for the grace after meals, and after their 120 years they will join him in the true world; he will carry four in his own hands, and the fifth will go right to the Garden of Eden. Five holy ones. Have you heard! A great merit in heaven. Gotinyu, I am not worth that, [but] may my daughters merit that and be blessed with such a fate."

And as the doors of the synagogue open–not as usual for each person but thrown wide open–one knows that the parade is coming.

*

Then came years of "progress," new winds were blowing, the five grenadiers drilled new thoughts into the brain, going to the synagogue not so much to God as for people, dear father! And among them were two in uniform, with shiny visors, who were studying worldly things. And indeed, the Russian language–"opens a window to Europe." Who are Rashi, Rambam, Orach Chayim, holy books. Smitten with Odessa, the new culture. One in particular had seen Bialik with his own eyes, had heard Cantor Sirota with his own ears. It gives one vertigo, neither here nor there, a separated soul–one God abandoned and no new one prepared. Not only the Song of Songs but also Pushkin, Lermontov, Nadson, Turgenev, and Tolstoy. Respect for one's father, the honored "householder," a Jewish merchant, arisen from important Jews with heart and soul, who has donated Torah scrolls to the synagogues. And I wish all my evil dreams on the heads of those who devised that children should betray the parents.

[Page 498]

For the Kedusha, he dances with everyone who is praying, on one foot; for the Amidah, he stands with his eyes open, using the opportunity while his father stands with his face to the east to make a fan, to think about secular words, but ends together with all those who are praying. That's how they pay the tax, a favor to one's father. No matter that it's Ploni's son, and Ploni is the one who, from deep in his heart and with open hands, procures hundreds of rubles for charity. Later, after ushering out the Sabbath, he will call on "the little key"–Chayim–Hersh–to lend him money on interest so that in the morning when the hardworking Jews–who live solely from the monthly fair–come from the synagogue or from Bathhouse Street, he can press them for charity. And if the fair is flat and it's hard to get returns for charity, he doesn't worry, no offense, the "proprietor" will console you, no misfortune, maybe next time the fair will be a success, Antshel Rothschild of Vishnevets adds another 25 and is prepared to wait for an expansion and give to both charitable causes at the same time. There's a greater God in heaven, and as it says in Ethics of the Fathers, "The world is built on three things, and one of those is charitable deeds."

And when the time came for Zionism to spread its wings, the third ring of the chain arrived–from the grandson, the third generation. A new storm arrived that filled the horizon with striving for a new echo of beliefs and content, and life acquired taste and flavor. Everything and everyone in the movement. Sects rose up out of that lethargic sleep, from grey small–town life, and went off in search of things desired.

The chain in Vishnevets was broken.

How could it happen? Gevald!

But the Pioneer spirit gave energy to the overturn, with tearing, with huge power, young temperament and strong will on the way to a new life, with new content and new important concepts.

Translation editor's note

1. "Ploni" in Hebrew is a placeholder for a name, roughly equivalent to "so–and–so."

[Page 499]

R' Levi Yitschak of Berdichev's
Grandchildren in Vishnevets

by M. Averbukh

Translated by Tina Lunson

Such a tribe was among us in Vishnevets, a tribe of merciful people, grandsons of R' Levi Yitschak Berdichev. We called them the "grandchildren." There were three of them: R' Motye, R' Yisrael, and R' Moshe. They grew like limbs of one tree, belonging to the same origin, treasures from R' Levi Yitschak, may his memory be for a blessing. But each one was a different type according to his individual qualities, and all together they were the grenadiers in R' Itsi's synagogue with the family name Derbaremdiker, prayer leaders for the Most High in the name of the community of Israel. And they were:

R' Motye: His standing place in the synagogue was close to the door in the summer, near the vestibule; in winter, he sat behind the oven, and separately carried on his dialog with the Master of the Universe in a suitable style from the bottom of his heart, with bowing and acquittal. Besides that, in his Shema Yisrael and Shema Koleynu he shouted out heartrendingly in a high voice and was literally outside himself.

R' Yisrael: The second in the line, he stood in the middle of the synagogue, near the cantor's desk, praying in a quiet, calm voice but with a deep inner ecstasy, using all the methods of a solid attorney with good spirit to attain everything good for the community and all of Israel. His pose: his right hand by his ear and his half–closed eyes, his left hand stretched out toward heaven. He demanded, he was certain that he would reach it and his hand would come back full.

R' Moshe: The third, a Jew of tall stature, a representative, stood by the symbol on the eastern wall, near the cantor's desk and the holy ark. A learned man, he prayed with a warm heart, striving for the highest level of intent exactly according to the interpretation of the words: his "Please God, save us" was accompanied by arguments, with certainty and sometimes with both his arms stretched out to the Master of the Universe, storming, demanding that complete redemption. Among other prayers, when he recited "Come let us sing" in welcoming the Sabbath, and the Kedusha in high drama, they must have split open the heavens, and his request must have been accepted at the throne of glory. There was no doubt that R' Moshe's proper demands would be successful; one must also take into consideration the protection of R' Levi Yitschak of Berdichev. Yes, he was surely in his service.

[Page 500]

As we see, each of the grandchildren did something in his own way, and all together they stood watch over the faithful representatives of the community with their intensive, solemn petitions.

We had a special sympathy for R' Moshe. He was popular with us because he was able to achieve the commandment of returning to Zion. Listen to how he did it.

This was right after the Balfour Declaration, when our town had become full of the spirit of the Land of Israel. It was then, too, that R' Moshe's son, Shlome Zalman, still a young boy, was caught up by the fresh, young Zionist movement. R' Moshe could under no circumstances agree to allow Shlome Zalman to go to the Land of Israel. How could he tolerate it when three times a day he promised to wait for the "sound of the great shofar of our freedom," how could he allow rebellion against the promise of the Master of the Universe and, just like than, join the ranks of the modern Pioneers. How? No, it couldn't happen. R' Levi Yitschak's grandchild was patient and would wait for the proper visa and the predestined time, with God's help.

However, Shlome Zalman drilled nonstop on the idea of immigrating to the Land of Israel. He wrangled, discussed, trying to convince himself; as far as R' Moshe could clearly see, it wasn't some dybbuk, God forbid, it was simply a vital question for Shlome, maybe a wink from heaven and his opposition was wrong and could lead to rebellion against his father. He then inculcated his son three times a day with the "O may our eyes witness Your return to Zion," not just to say it, but while standing tall with awe for the Holy One with his face to the east and ending with "in the days of old," and possibly remind himself of the return to Zion of the redeemed from Babylon in Ezra and Nehemiah's time, before the Second Temple.

R' Moshe surrendered with the stipulation that Shlome Zalman would vow that he would at all times, in all conditions and in all circumstances, strongly observe prayer and the laying of tefillin.

Shlome Zalman accepted the stipulation, and with his immigration became the pioneer of the Derbarimdikers–and also one of the first Vishnevetsers–to immigrate. And he brought about the immigration, in time, of Moshe Derbarimdiker's large family, which moved directly to Jerusalem.

Over time, R' Motye's and R' Yisrael's daughters immigrated, and from those branches of the Vishnevets grandchildren, a new tribe of Derbarimdikers grew in Israel–in Jerusalem, Tel Aviv, Rehovot, and Ramat Gan.

A multibranched and fruitful tribe–congratulations!

[Page 501]

Hersh Bisker, of Blessed Memory
(Portrait of a Beloved Vishnevets Philanthropist)
by Chayim Baral

Translated by Tina Lunson

Each city and town in old Russia had its wealthy people, its proprietors, and a lot of poor people. Our lovely town Vishnevets was like all the other towns. But among our wealthy men was someone who was famous and beloved by everyone in Vishnevets for his big–heartedness and for giving charity with an open hand. His name was Hersh Bisker.

Hersh Bisker was born in Ostrog; his father, Avraham Bisker, was also known for his good deeds. Hersh Bisker married into Vishnevets by means of Malke, Arye Grinbarg's daughter. Hersh was tall and handsome, with a beautiful face. His good deeds were in harmony with his physiognomy, externally and internally. The man's face reminded you of Moshe Our Teacher, and he had the heart of Abraham Our Father.

His businesses were farms, forests, and mills. His largest farm was in the village of Butin. At various times, he also had farms in Dzvinyacha, Krivchik, Lozy, Maryanovka, and the Vidomka. He lived near the Kremenets hill, on the right side. Hersh and Malke Bisker had two sons, Shlome and Avrom'ke, and six daughters–Rachel, Shprintse, Beyle, Gitel, Blume, and Leye. Blume Toporof, her son Ruven, and her daughter Ester were members of our Society. Avrom'ke lives in Brazil.

Hersh Bisker always had the poor and sick in mind. He provided a doctor and medicines for the ill, and he himself visited the sick. He sent the poor wood from the village and gave them coupons for flour at his mill. Before Passover, he used to ship a transport of Passover foods to the synagogue courtyard, where they were distributed among the poor.

The manager of his mill once told him that he was giving out too many coupons for flour. He got angry; it was not his concern, he said. When people come with a coupon, give them flour. His wife, Malke, who was also good–hearted, told him once, "Hersh, you're supposed to give charity within limits. Don't forget that we have eight children."

[Page 502]

He called her outdoors and said to her, "Do you see those chimneys? Except for the poorhouse chimney, without charity those people would be buried under their chimneys."

On Sabbath, when he left the study hall, he always had a guest with him, and if there were other guests, he sent them to Nisel Shenker at his expense.

Hersh Bisker was a democrat in the full sense of the word. When he helped a poor girl make a wedding, he also sent his daughters to the wedding and had them fill their purses with money, with the promise that they would pay for all the dances and also dance with everyone. And sometimes he went himself to make merry with the in–laws. Hersh was a good dancer.

He married off his own children like royalty. It was not enough to hire Vishnevets musicians, but he brought in Kremenets musicians, with the famous Aharon Shlome, and both groups played. But his greatest pleasure was the dinner for the poor, which he celebrated for the poor people in town. The feast was prepared with an expansive hand. He brought the musicians, danced with the poor people, and distributed alms.

Hersh Bisker also gave to poor gentiles, so he was accepted by the authorities. When someone had a problem, they ran to Hersh Bisker, and he would go and see what the person needed–and very often he could help.

Once he ran across some bad luck for Idel from Mishkovtsy: one of his girls had fallen in love with a gentile boy, and the gentile boy had taken her to the priest in the church to convert her. So, where to go? To Hersh Bisker. Hersh Bisker put on his coat, took his walking stick, went to the police commissioner, and asked him to see to it that the girl was released from the church; the girl was released and saved from conversion, but the police commissioner was sent to jail for that, so Hersh Bisker provided for his family.

Exiled and Lives in Kunev for a Year

Because he lived in the village of Butin, where a Jew was forbidden to live without a special permit, he was exiled to 50 viorsts from the border and settled in Kunev for one year.

[Page 503]

Due to the police commissioner's respect for him, they intervened for him, and the vice–governor annulled the exile. He came back to Vishnevets and resumed his businesses, but under the assumed name of Jaske Termen, a very respectable gentile from the Old City.

Hersh Bisker lived out a materially and spiritually rich life. He was beloved by the entire town. When he died on Monday, January 9, 1905, the whole town mourned him. All the shops were closed for his funeral, and the entire town came to accompany him to his eternal rest.

[Page 504]

Avraham Yehuda Katz
(Excerpt from a newspaper, Vishnevets, December 3, 1926)
by Yoel Akiva Zusman

Translated by Tina Lunson

On Friday, March 12, 1926, a lifelong local resident and social activist, Mr. Avraham–Yehuda Katz, moved to the Land of Israel. Mr. Katz is one of the best and finest personalities that our town could ever produce, one of our most prominent and gifted people, always successful in all spheres, as there was no institution, management, club, or organization that did not benefit from his deft, skillful participation or collaboration–one of the few who continually stood at the watch for all town interests, without exception.

In 1917, when Jewish society was only beginning to organize, A. Y. Katz sprang to life. He became the tone–setter for every deliberation and at every meeting.

He directed committees. He loved that scene; he was ever the organizer of any presentation and himself stepped out as an actor. He founded schools, libraries, evening courses. He sought work, he created, he pursued development.

The class struggle sharpened, and party squabbles flared up. He was measured and understood how to calm the noise. He brought everyone to an understanding, and everyone remained obedient to him.

There was a civil war in the land. Sedition ruled. The town was drawn close to extermination by several competing partisan armies. Forced "contributions" were paid, and supplies were demanded and provided. There was a scarcity of small banknotes, which in some areas led to horrific pogroms–everything was quickly resolved in this exemplary way:

Katz, along with some others, founded a commission, a self–defense unit, to set out to satisfy all the bandits, to make them understand what behavior was expected, and created a kind of reputation, so that all the headquarters marveled at his work and gradually came to respect the committee.

[Page 505]

A. Y. Katz was a collaborator with the Jewish community, a founder of libraries, chairman of the Zionist Organization, colleague of the Jewish National Fund and the Foundation Fund and a constant supporter; as well as founder and member of the local Land of Israel office, founder and chairman of the Tarbut School, founder and vice–president of the local merchants' union, councilman of local Christian society, member of the Kremenets parliamentary district, the local sanitation commission, and all the local benevolent institutions. He was a respected, experienced merchant, an intelligent man, full of general knowledge, who knew four or five languages. He was also a craftsman who excelled in several trades, such as painting, carpentry, glazing, and many others.

He was also beloved by the whole Christian population and esteemed by the administrative authority.

A few days before his departure, he received a farewell letter from the mayor of Kremenets, which could be considered a kind of testament that depicts in glowing hues and thanks Mr. Katz for his faithful, honest, loyal participation in the parliamentary district, for the great utility with which he always worked for the district's development at every time and in every regard.

On March 11 of this year, a farewell evening took place for Mr. Katz in the club for officials and with many Christian friends.

Well-respected guests attended: the entire intelligentsia, various officials, the teaching staff of the government schools, the director of the Polish school in Vishnevets, the local police commandant, aristocrats, all the officials and the board of the local Christian community, which includes the town and 27 villages, and all their other good friends.

He was presented with beautiful, valuable items–presents as mementos: a heavy silver tobacco box with monograms of the society, beautiful albums with addresses, and many photographs with signatures. Speeches were given with toasts, praising his talents, analyzing his magnificent character, and providing an overview of his long years of community activity for the good of everyone, without exception.

During the leave–taking from the evening–which was late at night–everyone kissed him, warmly pressed his hands, and accompanied him home.

A similar procedure took place the whole week before his departure. From early until late in the evening every day, long lines of Vishnevets residents, young and old, men and women, came to bid him farewell.

[Page 506]

On Wednesday, March 10 of this year, the local Zionist youth organized a grandiose banquet in honor of Mr. Katz at the Hotel Brilliant.

The toasts from friends and well–wishers, toasts to health, long speeches of praise and entertainments, declarations, songs and jokes, and Mr. Katz's and his family's responses took up many hours until late at night, and who knew how long the friendly undertaking would have gone on if not for the sudden alarm that one of Yisrael Fayer's houses was burning in a dense part of town.

Although the fire was soon contained, it had already disrupted the evening, and the rattled audience gradually dissipated, leaving the farewells for the last day.

On Friday, March 12, from early morning on, there was heavy movement all along Pochayev Street.

The street was seemingly flooded with people coming to say good–bye and accompany Mr. Katz from the town, although only for one kilometer, and disregarding the significant and hard–blowing snow falling the whole time.

In large, tightly packed groups, they stood in the house and in the street, talking animatedly, repeating all his good qualities and the utility he had always offered in the course of his long service.

Also, many Christian friends were there, and on each face, one could recognize the difficulty of parting from a dear friend.

Characteristic among many scenes was the following:

A young, local, not wealthy peasant who made ropes and sold them to Mr. Katz in his shop stood by Mr. Katz in his house since dawn, very involved, and from time to time put his arms around him, kissed him, and cried hard.

He went with the long lines of those who accompanied Katz to the outskirts of Vishnevets, and then when the youth started heartily singing nationalist songs, he hung his head, and with a serious manner and hardly daring to approach him again, went to him and kissed him.

Mr. Katz remarked on this and pulled away from the crowd, turned to the peasant and asked, "Why are you crying so, Omelko?"

"Because it is very hard for me," he answered, breaking out in a loud wail and unable to talk any further.

[Page 507]

Fund for the Sick in Vishnevets, or History of an Institution

by Miryam Maliv (Frayer)

Translated by Tina Lunson

It seems that Vishnevets had a power of attraction. My father, Avraham Dobtse's, a Jew from deep in Russia, was stationed in Vishnevets as a Russian soldier from 1914 to 1917 and wove himself into its life; he loved the effervescent Zionist youth and took part in all their activities. And he eventually fell in love with a Vishnevets girl–an orphan, my future mother–married her, and became a Vishnevetser forever.

The Vishnevets Jews did all they could so that the solitary bride and groom would not feel lonely. They were accompanied to the wedding canopy by Moshe and Reyzel Flok and Yankel and Etil Ayzenberg.

On the Sabbath, R' Shune Valkes and R' Pesach Gold (Vatnik) came to take the groom to the synagogue and gave him a permanent place in R' Itshe's Synagogue.

My father could never forget it. Vishnevets became an example for him and a command to do good works. He felt a sacred debt to the loving town and made a vow to do something for it in his own small way.

Years sped by, he pursued a livelihood, and he was as a loss for a way to fulfill his vow.

Once on a Sabbath, as he talked with friends, artisans like himself, he decided to create an institution for the sick, a health institution where poor people could be cared for.

Those who took part in the initial deliberations were Zalman Shnayder, Yisrael Chaye Sheyndel's, Mendele Shnayder, Yosef Kopel's, Yenkel Shayklis, Kopel Blekher, my father, Yisrael Nelkis and Kripitser (?).

The meeting was headed by R' Moshe Shoyel's, a very learned Jew.

The committee turned first to the working youth, asking that they use their "Lubitelene Troupe" to put on a play whose proceeds would go to the goal of the project. The youth responded positively.

All those respectable members then went house to house to sell tickets, and no one refused.

[Page 508]

The fundraising was a great success. That gave courage to further efforts, and there was intensive theater activity. The actors, as I recall them, were Elki Tsipe's, Feyge Tsipe's and her husband, Avraham Senik's, Eliezer Shkoler, Manis Fodem, his sister Shprintse Valker, and Moshe Nudler.

They also made it their duty to collect funds monthly as a kind of tax to support the sick. Kind Vishnevets Jews contributed half– and whole zlotys each month, and 11 families even promised as much as five zlotys a month and made good on their promise.

I remember them. We talked about them a lot among ourselves: Aharuli Shag, Rekhil Todreses, Shakhar Sofer, Shimon Lifshits, Dvosye Binimin's, Hikhel Hamut, Maltsye Kleynman, Duvid Gnip, Motye Shpigelman, the Biskers, and the Marders. I remember them, and I mention them because, in addition to their monthly donation, they gave even more money when it was needed.

In addition, they hired Hershel, Moshe Shuel's son–in–law, to collect the money month after month.

They developed a fund for the sick, and it grew. Any shareholder or confirmed council member could make use of medical services and prescriptions on the "Visiting the Sick" account.

It was an establishment, and real expression of immediate help. It made me proud of my town.

Happy with this victory, my father decided to transform it into a hospital and did not rest until he was successful.

There was a place in town, a crooked, hunchbacked building, a "no–man's–land," that had been abandoned since all its former residents had left and moved to their own homes. The council prevailed on the rabbi and got permission from the community to turn that empty ruin into a usable hospital.

They tore the building down. The place was empty, just go and build. But where to get the money? They turned to Vishnevets Relief in America. They sent money to us, and we began to build.

Delegates from American Vishnevets Relief were with us for the groundbreaking celebration, and it seemed to me that one of Rekhil Todreses' children cut the ribbon. The joy grew even greater with the raising of the walls. After that, they hammered on the roof and one hoped, brick by brick, nail by nail, that the project would be completed.

Unfortunately, the dream was not realized. With the arrival of the Soviets, they turned the building into a cinema.

[Page 509]

The Vishnevets Artisans Union dissolved and, with it, the hope for a successful Jewish initiative in a gentile country.

What happened afterward in Vishnevets, we all know. But when I recall the history of the institution, my father looms large before me like a fervent, hardworking Jew, and alongside him, my mother, his wife, as his ideal partner in life, who saw to the comforts of home and family conversations in order to make it possible for him to do something for his fellow artisans and for the poor, always poor Jews.

May we always bless them.

[Page 510]

Mikhel Fishman, of Blessed Memory
From Newspapers
Translated by Tina Lunson

As work on this book began, we received the news that Fishman had died. We provide here some appreciations of his personality–excerpts from the press. He was a great son of Vishnevets.

(Excerpt from The Yiddish Newspaper, Buenos Aires, October 2, 1961)–the Editors)

Mikhel Fishman–builder of the cooperative and the People's House, and president of "Floresta"[1] and the "State of Israel"–and we write both names in quotation marks because they are more than a cooperative, more than a house for the people, and more than a school: they are the expression of Jewish creativity, the result of determination, and the fruit of diligence. They are the striving for greater things, with a concern for tomorrow.

The school was built with love for our children and the Jewish land. The names express a longing, the same longing that led the directors of the People's House and the school to organize the excursion to Israel.

Mikhel Fishman visits Israel

[Page 511]

Thus, we saw it as necessary to interview President Mikhel Fishman, who stands at the head of the large delegation that will spend a month in the country, visit the Land, and reap inspiration that will certainly affect and encourage our national Jewish efforts on their return.

To chat with Mikhel Fishman is to become acquainted with the history of the neighborhood from the beginnings of community work to today's broad explosion of growth. To talk with Mikhel Fishman is also to be struck by his enthusiasm for everything that is Jewish nationalism. We found him in his workroom surrounded by his closest collaborators. It was easy to approach him, but difficult to start a conversation. Long lines of people wait to be received by the chairman of the cooperative. And he must soon receive a delegation from an important activist institution; in a half hour, a group of representatives will arrive from a Yiddish book-publishing concern to request the credit union's collaboration. We see that it is members' habit to personally turn to the president with their problems. It's almost impossible to talk to Mikhel Fishman, whose natural modesty makes the task of a newspaper interview all the more difficult.

But he can't refuse to answer the questions that we pose to him, and so we discover that the excursion to Israel was organized not only for people of secure financial means, but rather especially for those for whom such a trip would be a financial burden. So the Floresta cooperative financed the trip expenses–and they were not high–and handed out the tickets on a payment schedule over 20 months at a very minimal interest rate. The trip is made possible in this way, and the dreams of many are made a reality.

The Floresta credit cooperative where Mikhel Fishman holds the office of president has seen extraordinary growth in the years since he took the helm of the institution. Huge obstacles were overcome. For this difficult task, he has received the satisfaction of doing useful and active community work. Today, we find the cooperative in a gorgeous building. It has 5,800 members and a staff of 27. The cooperative grows from year to year and doesn't stop on its path to progress. Along with it, the neighborhood has been enriched and beautified with new office buildings and industries, especially in the furniture line.

[Page 512]

(Excerpt from the Yiddish Word, Argentina, February 18, 1961)

Mikhel Fishman: he is the still water that runs deep, the spirit and the soul of community activism in Floresta and environs, and the very person who best represents everything the word Floresta means in today's Buenos Aires. His modesty is not in conflict with the popularity that he has won thanks to his effort, energy, determination, and even sacrifice. One sees him in his credit cooperative, the People's House, and the State of Israel school, but one sees him also in institutions and organizations that include the entire settlement of Buenos Aires in their activities: the administration of the community council and in the management of the Jewish hospital, the Society for Visiting the Sick, and others.

There was a slogan within the family of Jewish community activists in Floresta: Let's let the builders build. Thus, Mikhel Fishman was reelected for several terms to the office of president of the Floresta credit cooperative, the People's House, and the State of Israel school. That is a sign of the trust he earned. That is how the 6,000 members of the cooperative understood it, that it was an institution where being chairman means not only giving good advice, occupying an office, and directing meetings. Being the president of the Floresta credit cooperative means acting in it daily, taking on and solving its problems, and being concerned about credit and the economic interests of thousands of people who have backing in the institution for their commercial activities, which are a source of livelihood, a point of support for climbing the economic ladder.

How many thousands of people has the cooperative helped in a difficult situation or, heaven forbid, in case of misfortune; how many thousands of people has the cooperative given the opportunity to take the first step in a new industrial undertaking or business; how many thousands of people has the cooperative helped to move forward, grow, and ascend; how many thousands of people has the cooperative transformed from poor people into wealthy ones who today support our community institutions; and how many people has the cooperative drawn into work for Jewish society.

Translation's note

Floresta is a neighborhood in the city of Buenos Aires.

[Page 513]

Idel Shapiro
The Editors   **Translated by Tina Lunson**

Idel Shapiro must be mentioned among the important figures from Vishnevets as the initiator of cultural and societal accomplishments.

Those from Vishnevets remember him well.

May his memory be for a blessing!

People from Vishnevets called Idel Shapiro the multitalented president.

They valued and accepted his energetic work in various institutions–political, social, and municipal.

He was an activist and strong supporter of the Jewish National Fund and the Foundation Fund, which symbolized fractured Zionism.

As president of the General Zionist Organization when the parties had sharp differences in belonging–ness, Shapiro even accepted a loyalist position to the league for a labor Land of Israel. With words and deeds, he showed his concern about the training kibbutz, which was closed in Klosove–Rokitno.

He was the uncrowned patron.

After he immigrated to Israel, Shapiro declared himself a follower of Mapai in Hadera and continued his activities in their ranks.

[Page 514]

A Story with Duvid Roynik:
How a Pioneer from Palestine Helped the Foundation Fund
(Der tog, April 5, 1926)

by Sh. Sheyner

Translated by Tina Lunson

We received the following letter with a check enclosed. The story is very interesting and we offer the letter here:

Very Esteemed Editors,

I turn to your honorable newspaper and will without the usual introductions simply come to the point. I am sending you enclosed herewith a letter with a check for $7.50, which I received this week from the Land of Israel from a pioneer by the name of Duvid Roynik from Vishnevets, Volhynia province, and kindly request that you turn the check over to the Foundation Fund in his name.

The history of the check is as follows. I spent last summer in Europe as a messenger for the United Teofipol and Environs Relief Society. In Warsaw, I met the abovementioned pioneer and gave him $50, which one of his sisters from Chicago had sent to him through me; and that helped him realize his ideal of traveling to Palestine as a pioneer. The clothing in which I met him consisted of a jacket and a pair of pants made from a coarse salt–sack, dyed black with ink. With great difficulty, I managed to persuade him to accept one of my suits, and now, after nine months in Palestine, he has found work, very hard work, but enough to make a living. And he sent me this money, the value of the suit, which a tailor had valued at $7.50. For as he said, he didn't want to take the suit until he knew its worth, so that he would know how much he should pay me at as soon as he could.

I don't want to make any use of this money and send it to your newspaper for the Foundation Fund in his name, Duvid Roynik from Vishnevets, now in Tel Aviv, Palestine. I think that the story is worth publishing so that the world may know what idealistic souls the pioneers are.

Sh. Sheyner
Manager, Zhitomir Talmud Torah

N.B. Please send the letter from Palestine, and also a receipt for the money, to me at the Talmud Torah's address.

[Page 515]

Makhlye Vaynman (Kremenetski), of Blessed Memory

by M. Alef

Translated by Tina Lunson

Makhlye was an exceptional phenomenon among the women of Vishnevets. She lived to a ripe old age: 93 years. She was born in 1872 and died in 1965, 22 Av 5725, with all her faculties.

She left a many–branched family, two sons, a daughter, and grandchildren.

As did everyone in recent generations, she went through and experienced the chaos and aftermath of World War I.

From Vishnevets, Makhlye married Yekhezkel Vaynman of Proskurov, a respected merchant who was heavily involved in commerce.

[Page 515]

While the Ukrainian freedom movement raged, especially in the Volhynia and Podolia regions, when Petluria's bands and the Haydamaks hit Jewish towns and villages with pogroms, the Vaynman family evacuated to Vishnevets, stayed there for three years, and then emigrated to Argentina and settled in Santa Fe.

In Argentina, one of the sons–Yakov Vaynman–excelled in trade and now directs broad business connections in various countries, including Argentina, Guatemala, Africa, and Israel.

Yakov settled in Israel in recent years and conducts his transactions from there, traveling from time to time to the countries to which he is intensely connected.

He is a sabra, as Yakov Vaynman is prominent in the higher spheres of government circles. We were informed that he was recently invited to and was one of the honored guests at a celebratory reception at the Guatemalan Consulate in Israel.

Yakov Vaynman treasures his dead mother not only for her closeness but especially because Makhlye Vaynman, of blessed memory, was over her long life not only a typical Yiddishe mama with plentiful merits, but also for her outstanding, affectionate and noble relationships with people. She was also a mother to the unfortunate and to those who were suffering. Empathy and help for others were her calling in life.

With her warm heart and devotion, she often helped people in their need, not just for appearances but as a self–evident obligation. It is impossible to manage in a short obituary to express all of her noble acts. It must suffice to give one illustration as fact: when Makhlye by chance visited a Vishnevetser in Buenos Aires and observed her problematic situation, she adopted the young woman for a long time, concerning herself with her existence, and later paid for a lavish wedding.

Yakov Vaynman honors his soulful mother and, in this Vishnevets book, immortalizes her memory with an eternal light for all generations.

May her memory be for a blessing.

[Page 516]

Society

The First Committee of the Vishnevets Society in America
Seated, center, is Mr. Levi Parnas, of blessed memory

[Page 517]

History of the Vishnevets Society

by Avraham Freylikh (Avraham Hirsh Yonteles)

Translated by Tina Lunson

It was a Sunday in July 1912 when I came to New York from Philadelphia. That same day, Zisye Kleynberg took me to a picnic in Liberty Park held by the Vishnevets Society.

That was when I became aware that there was a Vishnevets Society. I was 19 years old at the time.

At the next meeting, I became a full–fledged brother, as the president, Meir Baral, may he rest in peace, assured me at the swearing–in ceremony; and he entrusted me with the password: lev tov [good heart].

At that time, there were just two presidents, Meir Baral, may he rest in peace, and Levi Parnas, our long–serving president. They exchanged places every other year.

World War I broke out in July 1914, and the "Jewish street" stood up to help our unfortunate sisters and brothers on the other side of the sea.

"Peoples' Relief" was created, and committees of young men and women went from door to door all summer to collect support for those suffering from the war.

A movement took shape among our fellow townspeople to set up our own relief fund, specifically for Vishnevets. Until then, most young people from Vishnevets did not belong to the Society.

After some negotiations between the Society's leaders on one side and the leaders of the relief movement on the other, a general relief committee was established under the Society's supervision to help our fellow townspeople in Vishnevets. This was in 1916. The name of the committee was "Young Friends' Aid Fund for War Victims in Vishnevets Volhynia," overseen by Benevolent Society members.

Society meetings were revived. New young members came to every meeting. Although the Fund was independent, all its activities were reported at Society meetings.

The Committee was very active. It collected money in several ways, starting with nickels (which had just become a coin at that time) up to dollars, which most fellow townspeople felt the duty to pay weekly.

[Page 518]

It is worth noting that not only were the committee members not paid for this, but also paid any expenses out of their own money.

1917–Our America was also dragged into the demons' dance that is called war, and many of our young people put on uniforms and went off to save the world for democracy. Of course, aid was halted because of the war.

1919–The war officially ended. Most of our young men turned toward home. The relief fund was renewed, but there was no longer any connection with Vishnevets.

The committee gathered and worked out a plan to send $300 to Vishnevets in the name of three respected proprietors, in the hope that it would reach Vishnevets by Passover and help relieve the needs of the town's poor.

And it was successful. The money reached them in time, and regular correspondence began, with a dual purpose: to bring aid to the town in general and to specific individuals in need, because the Polish government manipulated the exchange of dollars so that there was simply very little money left for them. And secondly, to transfer affidavits from local relatives and about financial opportunities, so that those who had the chance to leave Vishnevets and come to America could do so.

Member Levi Rotman, who was active in the Society and relief fund, decided to travel to Vishnevets personally to bring his family back. The committee came to an understanding with him to act as Society representative and take along as much money as he could so as to be able to meet the needs of anyone who asked.

William Krasnov was to travel at the same time to bring his family back to America, and he would help with the committee's work.

The undertaking ended up as a colossal success. They brought papers–called "legal affidavits"–and cash, which had been collected to a sum of $55,000.

[Page 519]

The relief fund, that is, the committee, also contributed a large sum of money.

I remember as though it were yesterday how he wrapped a money belt containing 55 bank notes, each worth $1,000 American, around himself, as well as some other bundles. This was around July 1920. He went with good fortune and certainly returned with good fortune in November 1920, bringing 262 people with him, except for a few who had to remain on the ship for various reasons until their relatives took care of things; they came a few weeks later.

Of course, most of the new arrivals became Society members, and that gave the Society a broad opportunity for activity and content.

The meetings of that era were much beloved, and the relief committee became more active in additional projects. We created a movement to build a center in Vishnevets, with an orphanage, a school, and also other amusements.

With the Joint Distribution Committee, we also established a loan office on the condition that we, fellow townspeople in America, were obligated to cover any losses the loan office might incur.

But the big obligations did not hold us back from sending certain sums to the town several times a year for general need. For example, matzo for Passover, poor people's aid for winter, and shoes and clothing for poor children and adults. The Society was also helped by set amounts from the Joint, the Hebrew Immigrant Aid Society, and other social institutions. True, it was not easy each time the committee turned to the Society after a layout, each time finding opponents who were not touched by the sanctity of the Society's treasury. But that only lent some color to the meetings, and the majority supported the committee. Otherwise, the Society would have been weakened–and some thought it was–but it became stronger and stronger.

In 1930, our own country became involved in a terrible crisis. Some of our members became impoverished; help was needed in our own ranks. It required a new approach to the situation: we created a Council Committee composed of Society members. Their assignment had to be to ease the problem, as well as other problems that would arise during that time. And, with very small exceptions, the activists on the relief committee joined the Council Committee.

[Page 520]

Their first action was to establish a loan fund within the Society, so that members who were affected by the crisis could receive an interest–free loan on very easy terms.

Some were literally saved by this action. Small businessmen were helped so that their creditors would not pin them to the wall. Some were supported until they could find work again and pay it back gradually afterward. At the same time, Vishnevets was not neglected, and the town received its yearly stipends.

Then came the year 1933. President Roosevelt closed the banks, and sending money out of America was not permitted. And the Jewish Passover drew closer and closer. The committee was very concerned .... Vishnevets Jews might, heaven forbid, have no matzo for Passover, because it had become a tradition to send several hundred dollars to Vishnevets for Passover. We found a way, and our money arrived in Vishnevets in time for Passover.

At that time–that is, in the early 1930s–several members began a movement to create a youth club for our children, with full autonomy to conduct their business in their own way, in English of course and under the Society's oversight. Unfortunately, nothing came of it, which I regret to this day. But instead of a youth club, the Vishnevets Ladies' Club was established; they wanted to define themselves, and I must leave that to those who know more about their activities than I do.

Time does not stand still. We heard sad reports from Europe, and we did everything possible to lighten the need of our brothers and sisters in Europe in general and in Vishnevets in particular. Until 1939, when the great misfortune befell the world, and especially our people Israel. All connections to the old home were severed. Our land was attacked, and the fire spread, ever stronger and stronger. Our children were taken away from us; we saw no ray of hope. The committee came together again. The stronger comforted the weaker. We gathered fresh energies, and the relief committee was revived. People once again collected money for a fund, with the hope that perhaps a miracle would occur and we would hear from a living being. And as one lives, so one carries on.

[Page 521]

The fire was extinguished; the smoke still rose from the embers of our people, but officially the war was over. In time, we found that a couple of hundred souls had saved themselves. The relief committee became more and more active, and between 1943 and 1950 succeeded in raising close to $40,000, which it used to help our unfortunates in various ways.

1948: The State of Israel was proclaimed. From every corner of accursed Europe and Africa, our tragedy–stricken people streamed into Israel. But unfortunately, the newly formed land could not put a roof over their heads. Besides that, each person was worried about other needs. Enormous sums were required, especially American dollars.

The "Jewish street" fumed. There was a tempest in our Society as well. Here our usual support of United Jewish Appeal, whom we paid every year, would not suffice. This demanded an entirely different approach.

On May 10, 1948, the Council Committee met; these were also the activists from the relief committee, and it was decided without opposition that the Vishnevets Society was obligated to create a large enough fund to provide several Vishnevets families with residences in Israel. A home cost $2,500 American. Say and do! And at that very meeting, someone wrote a check for $2,00s, and in a few days United Jewish Appeal received $3,000 along with a promise of more and more. And until this day, the Society collects large sums every year for United Jewish Appeal and can also be proud that we have bought a set amount of bonds for the survival of our new homeland, Israel.

Knowing that the Histadrut collects money, and knowing that their collection brings good results, the Society started a tradition of holding one meeting a year where we collect close to $1,000. The tradition has been going on for about 10 years.

And United Jewish Appeal and other larger and smaller organizations have not been neglected, and the Society has supported them with yearly stipends since its first year of existence.

In 1953, when the Society celebrated its 50th anniversary, I, being a member for the last 40 years and having taken part in almost all charitable activities, said, "I am proud to be a member of the family that calls itself the "Vishnevets Brothers Benevolent Society."

[Page 522]

I hope and wish that the Society continues to exist for many more years and that all current and all newly arrived members live to take part in the 75th anniversary, or diamond jubilee. Amen, amen.

[Page 523]

Vishnevets–Adopted

by Meir

Translated by Tina Lunson

The idea of connecting destroyed Jewish communities with schools in Israel was instituted on the initiative of Gideon Hauser–the former government attorney general and prosecutor at Adolf Eichmann's trial.

A school that pairs with a community teaches its students that community's history, contacts its townspeople, and records the uniqueness and documentary facts about the community before Hitler's occupation, especially from townspeople who are still alive, noting the tragic events that the population experienced during Hitler's regime. The students, based on the reports, write on the topic and obligate themselves to be the immortalizers of the community, a type of living monument to the murdered martyrs and guardians of the memory that recalls the ruined town that perished with its dear Jews.

Already, more than 400 schools have paired with destroyed communities.

We Vishnevetsers have been adopted by the Binyamina public school. A fine "match" was made. Our "father–in–law" is the famous philanthropist who founded the first colonies in Israel, Baron Binyamin (Edmund) Rothschild, in whose name the Binyamina cooperative was founded in 5683 (October 1922) near the Shomron along the road between Haifa and Tel Aviv.

The official and celebratory adoption, marked by the signing of the "scroll" of adoption papers, took place on 21 Adar 5728 (February 15, 1968) in Binyamina, in the presence of local community leaders, all the teachers and students, almost the entire population, and representatives of our fellow Vishnevets townspeople in Israel. The scroll was presented and deposited in Yad Vashem in Jerusalem, the collection point for all historical documents about the Jewish communities that were tragically liquidated under Hitlerism.

A brochure written by the students was published on the proclamation day, full of broad content about Vishnevets. It was amazing how the students, together and individually, collectively dealt with the specific topic, just as though they had experienced all the trials of former Vishnevets, from its beginning until its demise. Thanks to their devotion, they thoroughly researched the treated material and delivered the end product to the audience of Vishnevetsers.

[Page 524]

To be especially emphasized are the initiative and work for the adoption by the teacher from our town, Rochele Kelner, Leyeke and Chayim Volf Brik's daughter and Moshe Shpigelman's granddaughter. And her husband dedicated a lot of attention, time, and trouble to technical work and prepared a beautiful gallery of photo enlargements featuring our town, so that it appeared to be an impressive exhibit, just like Vishnevets when it was alive.

[Page 525]

The Vishnevetsers' Good Name

by Yosef Shatski

Translated by Tina Lunson

Years ago, a stream of 260 of our Vishnevetsers arrived in the free country of America–I among them.

I am reminded of the first meeting of our newly arrived sisters and brothers from Vishnevets in Henington Hall, on Second Street in New York. My father, Meir Blayshteyn, a founder of and active worker for the Society, took me with him; I can still hear the noise and joy that floated through the room. Each of the new arrivals was dressed as if for a holiday in the new clothes their relatives had dressed them in; each felt happy to be in America, their new, free country. However, feelings of joy and sadness were mixed–that is, everyone rejoiced to be in such a free land yet was thinking about the dear and beloved ones who remained on the other side of the ocean and did not have the opportunity to free themselves from that dark place, Poland.

Soon it quieted down. The then–president, Mr. Parnas, banged the gavel and called the meeting to order. It was quiet in the room; each person took his place. The secretary read the agenda, and it was quickly approved.

Later, the president asked for a motion that all new arrivals be accepted into the Society as members for free; that was soon approved by the members. And so all the newcomers became Society members–I among them.

I was very young then, and did not understand the importance and greatness of the Society's work, and I abstained from many meetings. A few years later, I met with misfortune, and only then did I realize for myself our Vishnevets Society members' brotherliness, devotion, and loyalty. A few brothers visited me in the hospital a few times, and through their loyalty and support, I left the hospital, although not yet entirely healthy. And then I began to understand the great human feeling that lies in our password, lev tov [good heart]. I decided then that as soon as God gave me back my health, I would share in our Society's holy, important, and noble work, and I went to every meeting and worked with great zeal.

[Page 526]

At the time, there was a relief fund, with which we helped those suffering from want in Vishnevets and here.

I came up with a proposal to visit our fellow townspeople around New York, such as in Middletown, Connecticut; Hartford; Boston; Chelsea; Lawrence; and other towns where there were Vishnevetsers. My proposal was accepted. I undertook–at my own expense–to travel in my own car. On my first venture, Avrahamtsi Kop came with me. We visited a number of fellow Vishnevets townspeople, and they took us in, in a very noble and good–hearted way, and responded to us very warmly, as only Vishnevetsers can. We brought back a good sum of money. That work went on for several years with other members who participated in this noble work, such as brothers Leybel Rotman and Nathan Worth, who went along with me. We collected a lot of money each year, with much honor.

Yes, our Vishnevetsers, wherever they are, are always ready to help any needy goal and institution. Yes, we may be proud of our Vishnevetser Society's greatness. May God help us all to be healthy and able to celebrate our 75th jubilee.

With pride, I issue this call:

Brothers of the Vishnevetser Society! My call to all Vishnevets members and regular fellow Vishnevets townspeople, join the noble work of supporting the foundation of the great edifice that for many years has had a great name throughout most of the world, and may it be an inheritance from generation to generation.

[Page 527]

Vishnevetsers in Israel and America
(Meditations at My Banquet in Tel Aviv in 1969)
by Avraham Averbukh, New York–Tel Aviv

Translated by Tina Lunson

I am reminded of one of Avraham Reyzin's poems about Jewish immigration to America, which he wrote some 60 years ago. The poem ends thus:

> They are drawn to us
> and we are drawn to them
> and again we are brothers
> in a world split in two.

That was the mood of the Jewish immigrant then. Arriving in a new country without a language, alone, lonely, and depressed, seeking new earth for existence, he turned to the homey, to old acquaintances. He found them only among those from his town, among his or your parents' friends, friends from the old home and in the New World, created from the human melting pot and in the Society, the union of townspeople.

The Society used the opportunity to bind them together and turn them into a human force for helping people; the Society created an address for lonely people in the New World whose aid–addresses were nonexistent or unknown.

At the same time, the epoch of lovers of Zion[1] (without quotation marks) and "return to Zion" was nearly falling apart.

Idealistic young people took wing with the dream of redemption, driven by limitations and excesses. Inspired by the national–human thought of building a home for the plagued people once and for all, they stood up and moved to the Land of Israel.

Vishnevets youth of that same kind were also among those who went to Israel. They knew what they stood for. The idealization of draining swamps, breaking stones, and enduring illness and a difficult climate confirmed all the difficulties in the land of their dreams and confirmed that going there meant putting their youth in jeopardy for an idea that no one knew would come to reality.

[Page 528]

Still they went.

There was an essential difference between the two groups of "world seekers." That is to say, while some went to America seeking a bit of happiness and paid for it with loneliness, those in Israel sought greater happiness for their folk and knew that the loneliness was equal among them; everyone had predicted it and taken it into consideration from the beginning.

* * *

Meanwhile an entire half–century flowed by. A jubilee full of dreadful catastrophes. Bloody events and the most murderous of all world and human misfortunes, the misfortune of Hitlerism; the world still does not know how far its footprints will reach.

And now the Vishnevets memorial book has been written.

It was written by eyewitnesses to the Hitler plague and the Israeli convention of those who delayed the path to redemption and those who contributed to the difficulties of the redemption. Together, brothers from various walks of life write the martyrology of our parents, brothers, sisters, friends, and neighbors. Together they erect a gravestone for the town of their origin and together place themselves again on a path of struggle, work, difficulties, and achievements. While looking forward to the future, they turn their gaze to the huge mass graves, not forgetting them, and in the names of those buried in the graves, the road from redemption in Israel is a necessity, an ideal, a concrete life's creation, the content of a generation that will prepare a better civic life for the forthcoming generations.

The light from this much–delayed book will make vivid the deep differences between Vishnevetsers here in Israel and those in America.

While here in Israel, one felt a deep interest in the object of the book–in Vishnevets' heritage and the growing, warm bond to it–in America one felt an indifference to the sentiment of birthplace. The generation that bore the load of loneliness in America with the Society's help is indifferent to it, as is its new growth, their children–attorneys, doctors, physicists, scientists, rabbis, and successful business people, among them a few millionaires who are not of Sholem Aleichem's cut, but of a certain American tailoring.

[Page 529]

The children, as they would, feel that the older generation did not think about a redemption for generations but ran to make an easier life for themselves; they are also indifferent to the links of the generations, and the Vishnevets Society becomes a place for a good deeds fund and pointless conferences and meetings and endless indifference. Perhaps ... it is an indifference not only to the Society, but perhaps it is a general indifference, as happens to people whose past is suddenly reflected in a similar bright past and it suddenly appears pale, pale, pale.

In Israel, it is a past of beauty, in which there is great interest. Brave citizens, hopeful in all areas with successes earned by blood in all areas, military, political, and economic, literally a miracle among the nations. The world stands in awe, unable to express their surprise at the success. The world is, so to say, not indifferent to Israel as Israel is one and for itself.

And you will say to me: What does it matter that we in America make a Society, with you here? You should elevate us with your spirit of enthusiasm, without your indifference.

And I will paraphrase Reyzin:

May you be drawn to us
and we'll be drawn to you
and we shall be one
equal in two parts of the world.

Afula, 1 October 1969

Translation editor's note

Chibat Tsion (Lovers of Zion) was one of a variety of organizations founded in Europe in the 1880s to combat pogroms. They are considered the forerunners of modern Zionism.

[Page 530]

With Brethren from Argentina
(February 1961)
by M. Alef

Translated by Tina Lunson

A great joy–it is a great joy indeed to spend time with the guests from Argentina. It has been 10 years since we parted ways. Then, we were wandering souls, without a what, without a when, without a where. We were without a perspective on the future, struggling in powerful convulsions to tear ourselves from that environment. Locked up as if in a ghetto, in a grey small–town life, we viewed life's road with dark glasses. Poor in means, doubtful, with no possibility of breaking out into the larger world, and apathy and worry for the morrow. So when I see the beaming faces here, when we have lived to see this Sabbath together, to sit together as brothers in such a situation–one cannot complain. Each of us has come to a liberated place. Once young, separate, without cause, now, as adults, we have spread out like young, trembling little trees over the whole world, and now we see for ourselves a glorious picture, as in the words of the great Jewish psalmist: like trees planted by the water, we have grown from small trembling saplings into multibranched palms. Grandfathers and grandmothers are sitting here with us. A lovely picture, when we now greet our dear guests from Argentina.

It is not nothing that out of 78 delegates from Argentina, 8 are Vishnevetsers.

When I read the three columns in the Argentine newspaper, the reportage about the delegation to the Land of Israel and how they described the actions of our Vishnevetsers in the delegation in such detail, I was infused with warm, heartfelt, intimate joy. One small thing–the Vishnevetser group walks through the newspapers. I quickly made the calculations. The Jewish population at the end of 1958 was 400,000; we know that each delegate represents more than 1,000 Jews. That means that our delegation represents 40,000 Jews. In the golden era, before the great immigration, Vishnevets numbered 3,200 souls. Compared with 40,000, the 2,300 Vishnevets representation is large and considerable.

If I may make an analogy, a comparison, to once in Vishnevets and today as we are together. Once, a dark picture. Very depressing. A grey life, a hollow life, many of the youth idle and empty.

[Page 531]

In the so–called center on Vishnevets Boulevard with the sonorous name Tshetshigo Maya, a boulevard without trees, with a few wooden railings by the town hall, years without care, with open windows without panes, and a Monday fair, and the picture is accompanied by the accordion music of two peasant beggars, and we young souls are straining as if in chains, with fear and doubt about what our end will be. But today, here at the tables, there is a festive picture and an elevated mood. Today, each one has come to his shore; no matter who [lives] here in Israel or who [lives] there in Argentina or America.

It is certainly a rare privilege that the Argentines from Vishnevets are at the event and have the consciousness, and can allow themselves to take the step, to make the trip to Israel. We imagined that in February 1961 we would see such an inspiring picture, and it is delightful indeed. Be greeted, dear guests.

As I said, our joy is great. But do not forget that the joy is not complete. We here are crumbs from a lively, effervescent town. Unfortunately, fate willed that the list of curses in the tokhekha[1] would materialize for our generation. In the words of the great prophet: there will remain in each village only one, and in each town, two.

We are permitted to have an elevated mood, appropriate to old Jewish tradition. We know that, as during Passover, when a Jew sits on pillows celebrating with the best dishes, that it is a commandment to chew a piece of bitter herbs combined with matzo, remembering the practice in the Temple according to Hillel. At this opportunity, let us remember those souls.

The Hitler–flood ferociously drowned millions of lives, among them thousands of our dear and beloved who gave us life with sacrifice and faith; with no reason, the flood made them into a burnt offering for Ashmoday as martyrs to their faith.

The only comfort for the Vishnevetsers who were each transplanted to a new place is that they will forever carry the memory of the Vishnevets martyrs. We are forbidden to forget them; we will not forget, and we cannot forget. It is thanks to that not–forgetting that we are all here together.

And now to our dear guests, about our organization, Irgun yotsey Vishnevets b'erets yisrael–the Organization of Vishnevets Emigrants in Israel.

We felt that we were obligated to be in one collective. Then Vishnevetsers from the concentration camps started to arrive, and they brought personal particulars about the great destruction in Vishnevets. At first, the meaning was sentimental–for each price we set up a memorial for the martyrs. We planted 1,000 trees in the Martyrs' Forest on the hill of Jerusalem, erecting a tombstone.

[Page 532]

Each year on the day of the great inquisition–action in Vishnevets (29 Av), we gather for a memorial prayer. But it was not enough. We had all turned into a living tombstone. We are all from one origin, from the same place, from the same cradle, where we heard our mothers' sweet voice for the first time singing the classic lullabies "Raisins and Almonds" and "Red Pomegranates," when they wanted to wake us from sleep to life, and our fathers with knitted brows pondering their goals for us children.

We carry the feel of our town within us, as though a strong pulse beats there for civic work in every stratum of young people. We remember fruitful work for the Jewish National Fund and the Foundation Fund, the strong organizations Youth Guard, Brit Trumpeldor, Pioneer, Young Pioneer, Zionist Worker–and the general league for labor in the Land of Israel. We were determined to exist for the living as well. Thanks to the townspeople society in America, the Parnas Fund was established and became a necessary institution for productive, constructive goals. We were powerless more than once, so the more multibranched the activities could be, the better we could face our needs.

We want the Vishnevets collective to, as much as possible, gather all the Vishnevets societies in the world into an organized group with its center in Israel, because here is the only place for Jewish independence.

I will end with three wishes.

The first wish is:

You have come–come often.

The visit was a concept of appeal and flavor.

The match with Israel's one flaw is a great gift. The Jewish state is a new land, a bat mitzvah. Youth grows and develops. You cannot be pioneers from a distance. Rather, Israel has built your state. Whoever has built a new life has also built the country. I hope that you will be happy and can allow yourself to come here and organize yourself in a good way. The time for a match has not come–become betrothed, in the meanwhile.

The third wish:

Come to Argentina, be inspired by what you have seen, and give us a warm, heartfelt brotherly greeting from all of us.

[Page 533]

Turn your townspeople society into an active unit of the Vishnevets collective, strengthen our hand, be in continuous contact with us, and cooperate with the American townspeople society; make it possible for us the conduct constructive, productive work for Vishnevetsers. And for Vishnevets, where we have left our childhood and our youth, and where the martyrs' bones rest.

Translation editor's note:

The tokhekha refers to Deuteronomy 28:15–68, where Moses outlines the curses for disobedience to God.

[Page 534]

Vishnevets Townspeople Societies in America and Israel Afterword from the Organization
By Meir Averbukh
Translated by Tina Lunson

The "Society" of Vishnevets sisters and brothers in America and the Vishnevets organization in Israel (irgun yotsey Vishnevets) are a kind of Siamese twins that cannot be distinguished, if only because of their close, cooperative activity and mutual understanding in their social content and of their existence.

The Society has the right of primogeniture because it was founded at the initiative of a few people headed by Louie Parnas, of blessed memory, in 1903, while the Vishnevets organization in Israel first began its activity in 1949, that is, two generations later.

But it is not only the earlier date that places the Society on the right side of the coin and in advance in general, but the material backing and the moral support that have made it possible for us to create the loan fund and provide productive help and constructive support to the dozens of families that remain after the Hitler–flood and came to Israel. Those merits crown the Society with honor and respect on the long road of collaboration, brotherly concern and mutual activity as brothers in America and us here in Israel.

The good deeds fund named after Louie Parnas, of blessed memory, is an exemplary institution for townspeople societies in Israel. The Vishnevets organization in Israel has sympathy for our organizations that perform its activity for its members' welfare; we may hope that we will be true followers of the old tradition of the Society.

We also hold up as an example the great relief activity of 1920, which the Society undertook under the leadership of Leybele Roytman, of blessed memory, and made possible the mass emigration from Vishnevets to America. More than 350 people–then 10% of the Jewish population–left Vishnevets and went to America.

That happened after the dramatic experience of World War I, the Russian Revolution, pogroms in Ukraine, oppression from several regimes, and anti–Semitic propaganda. I recall how mass immigration was for a Vishnevets wage earner, a Talmud scholar, allegorically like the times of Ezra and Nehemiah, and that could only have happened thanks to the Society.

[Page 535]

Easily Recognized Vishnevetsers ... Society Committee

[Page 536]

It would not be right, and it would be more than naive, if we ignored or did not mention a particular way or the earnest local undertakings by Vishnevetsers in Israel. The organization succeeded independently in creating objectives of historical significance in the sense of immortalizing the martyrs and the ruined town.

There were three: Planting a forest of one thousand trees in the Forest of the Martyrs on the hills of Jerusalem, as we erected a tombstone under the oversight of the Jewish National Fund, and arranged for a memorial plaque in the Chamber of the Holocaust in Volhynia province. And Vishnevets was adopted by the Binyamina School (see the separate article about that). Besides that, it is important for us to live morally in the social arena in the organization's framework.

In a short list, it is difficult to deal definitively with all the branches of a social institution's activity when the private and the general need to be arranged through tasks for the whole community and to satisfy the particular according to personal needs, within limited possibilities. We were more or less successful in helping to objectively handle each matter and need. We also kept in mind the critic of social convention that community workers take on themselves, so if the miracle is accomplished, and we regulate the activity with equilibrium, it is only thanks to the care and work of both directions here and across the sea, because the whole time there was full understanding and sincere concern for actual problems, which were dealt with materially and on schedule.

It should be mentioned that the greater Vishnevets colony in Argentina made a sincere beginning in 1965 to come into close contact with the Society in America. We were especially certain of that when a large group of Vishnevets tourists from Argentina headed by Yakira, Fishman, and Tshaytshinetski came to visit; unfortunately, there was no follow-up to that beginning, not even a successful bond through correspondence. Again today, we are considering a possible collaboration with the Argentines and hope that with time we will renew the initiative and, it is hoped, be able to carry it out.

Important to all of us is the general community midpoint of trying to create an atmosphere in which Vishnevetsers may come together to honor their murdered martyrs and immortalize the ruined town, and also live together in intimate brotherly loyalty, as we are all from one birth town, one place of childhood and youth years, all of one fate, all one family.

[Page 537]

Of course, with these short lines about the townspeople societies in Israel and overseas, we want to wish and hope that warm, faithful, brotherly relations dominate them and the community in general. Amen.

We do not forget Vishnevets–at the forest named for her in the Forest of the Martyrs

[Page 538]

A Last Word

Vishnevets 1956

by M. Malev (Frayer)

Translated by Tina Lunson

I visited Vishnevets in 1956, after the extermination. After the destruction, I was in Valbezhikh, ready to travel to Israel, and I decided that before I abandoned Poland forever, I would visit our little town.

I also wanted to visit my poor, unfortunate sister.

I procured a tourist visa, and arrived in Kremenets in the afternoon. I did not travel to Vishnevets right away because the whole area was full of gangs, and it was very dangerous. I had to calculate my every step very carefully.

I was in the area for three months. I was in Vishnevets for a total of three days; I stayed there only one night and slept there.

Our house was between the rabbi's house and Yakov Chachkis's, which was already gone–all the ghetto streets were destroyed, the houses all demolished, totally destroyed. I found only three families in the town: Avraham Rosenberg, Duvid Gnip, and Zev Sobol; the first two are still there today.

A few houses that remained were occupied by Ukrainians who had collaborated with the Germans. Where Shapiro's house had been, Ostrovski, the well–known pig farmer, had put up a house with a brick wall, made of bricks he had collected from Jewish houses. Lerner's house was completely sunken into the ground, why I don't understand, but the windows were blown out and covered with pieces of wood. The house was not usable, yet a local Ukrainian was living there.

The Tarbut school building, which had belonged to Shmuel Melis, was whole and being used as a government hotel.

The Great Synagogue remained whole. Changes had been made so it could serve as residences and for offices. It was all just divided spaces and doors. It was hard to imagine that this was where Jews had united and gathered together with their entire soul and faith.

My purpose in coming was to go to the graves of the unfortunate. I was afraid to go alone, so Zev Sobol went with me, and together we arrived at that holy place that so sacred to us in our hearts.

[Page 539]

The grave was in a valley along the road to Zbarazh. Going into the valley, I could see human bones strewn about, skeletons taken apart, without attachments between one bone and another, bones from thighs, parts of skeletons scattered like toys in the wind; all the bones that were so precious to us were strewn all over.

I wanted to cover the bones with earth, but I did not have any tools, and there were too many bones scattered around–I put earth over as many as I could, and my heart burst ...

Who knows whose bones I covered with that unholy earth? Who knows whose body they belonged to? At that moment, it seemed to me that they might be the bones of my dear father or of my good mother, brother, sister, and maybe my friends from school, I had an attack of hysteria and, wailing in lamentation, I went around collecting the bones, and each bone cut into my heart.

The valley with the scattered bones stretched on for more than a kilometer.

I was told that every time someone comes to the valley, they cover the bones, but the water flows strongly through there, and it rinses the earth away and uncovers the bones again and washes them from place to place. After death, they still have no rest.

To our great woe and shame, the Germans did not trouble to cover this mass grave, and the precious bodies lie freely one atop the other, without protection from wild animals and violent storms. It makes the blood run cold to see the bodies violently pulled apart for eternity.

Across from there, Zev showed me the hill from which the murderers fired on the unfortunate victims and killed them wholesale; according to what Zev told me, they lined up our dear ones on the brim of the valley in the dust and then threw them into their common grave, which waited openmouthed.

On the road back, I recognized familiar faces of Ukrainian neighbors and acquaintances, and I had to pretend I did not see the expressions of joy at our tragedy beaming from their eyes.

[Page 540]

Shoshana Agsi, of Blessed Memory
Born December 24, 1914; Died July 22, 1969
(From a memorial booklet)

Translated by Ellen Garshick

Shoshana, daughter of Henche and Dov Zak, was born in Vishnevets, Volhynia region. From an early age, she received a Zionist education; members of her family immigrated to Israel in the 1920s. And when she completed her studies at the Tarbut School and high school, she decided to immigrate.

In 1935, she was trained at the kibbutz in Kovel, and despite her physical weakness, she endured all the hardships of training well.

In summer 1939, she immigrated on the famous ship "Colorado." The ship was detained by the British, and the people were put into a detention camp at Shemen Beach in Haifa. After a month's stay and many investigations, the pioneers, including Shoshana, were liberated.

When the people were released, Shoshana's health was very poor. She accepted her relatives' request and went home with them to recover. After recovering, Shoshana went to live in Kibbutz Plugat Hayam.

For many years, Shoshana was devoted to working hard in the laundry, at headquarters, in the children's home, and in clothing stores, and we were surprised when illness overtook her.

It was in 1958, the day before the Fast of the Firstborn, that Shoshana was working at headquarters to prepare baked goods to serve to guests at home during the holiday, and in the middle of her work, she kneeled and fell. The hospital determined that she had had a cerebral hemorrhage.

For two weeks, Shoshana struggled for her life and remained paralyzed. She asked that she be allowed to heal and rehabilitate at home, not in the hospital, and her request was granted

It was pleasant to take care of Shoshana–she was grateful for any help. The hours spent in the library at Shoshana's were hours of conversation about world events, literature, art, politics, etc. She always had something new to say and shared her impressions of others.

Medicine could not save Shoshana. She had come home 3from the hospital to continue to get devoted, complete care at home. And now the day had come for her to be transferred to the hospital. Those were her last days. And the thread of her life was cut off.

Name Index

This is the name index for this English translation.

Please Note: This index does not include the names appearing on pages 9 – 24

A

Abramovits, 151

Aharonson, 203

Alef, 368, 384, 395

Alkabets, 298

Anotova, 142

Arye, 4, 153, 198, 329, 373

Asni–Beyle, 344

Averbakh, 353

Averbukh, 39, 171, 285, 298, 338, 340,
366, 371, 393, 398

Avrahamtsi, 328, 392

Aytsikel, 40, 177, 188

Ayzenberg, 4, 40, 80, 161, 205, 206, 207,
208, 209, 230, 347, 349, 378

B

Ba'almelakhe, 171

Badasiuk, 258, 259

Badeysiuk, 298

Balmelakhe, 194, 195

Bal-Melakhe, 195

Barak, 202

Baral, 373, 386

Barbak, 184

Barkay, 4, 235, 236, 237

Beker, 183

Ben-Tsvi, 202, 234

Berdichev, 5, 72, 290, 319, 329, 371

Beren, 127, 158, 159, 171, 183, 184, 210

Berstovski, 104

Betshinsky, 187

Binimin, 378

Binyamin, 113, 204, 391

Bisker, 4, 123, 213, 214, 362, 363, 364,
365, 373, 374

Biskers, 378

Biv, 53

Blekher, 378

Blinder, 171

Blum, 298

Boneh, 206, 246

Borovitser, 359

Boykis, 332

Boytiner, 298

Brik, 164, 214, 236, 391

Brimer, 62

C

Chabas, 191

Chachki, 158

Chachkis, 155, 194, 226, 234, 402

Chatski, 112, 170, 171, 189

Chazan, 3, 39, 108, 291, 292, 354, 362

Chinik, 104, 326

Choish, 123, 124, 125, 146, 255

D

Derbarimdiker, 62, 65, 158, 222, 290, 372

Dobromdiker, 184

Dobrovitker, 158, 159, 184, 192

Dzhigen, 137

E

Elyovich, 52

Emden, 139

Epshteyn, 251

Erlikh, 74, 159, 161, 164, 196, 259, 320, 353

F

Fayerman, 183, 184, 185, 332

Fefer, 4, 183, 184, 195, 196, 197, 198

Feldman, 70, 76, 250, 251, 259, 260, 266

Feygeles, 83

Fishman, 126, 133, 164, 294, 352, 353, 380, 381, 382, 400

Flok, 378

Fodem, 322, 346, 378

Frayer, 155, 377, 402

Frenkel, 96

Freylekh, 343, 360

Freylikh, 386

Fridland, 202, 204

Froyke, 158, 321, 322, 328, 344

Fuks, 92, 327, 330, 344

Furman, 250

G

Garshick, 2, 404

Geler, 131, 133, 141, 173, 179, 185, 218

Gilboa, 206

Gnip, 63, 127, 128, 155, 378, 402

Gold, 378

Goldberg, 170, 205, 206, 208, 242

Goldfaden, 298

Goldman, 170, 171

Goldshteyn, 136, 334, 335

Goldshub, 4, 71, 239

Gorenshteyn, 196

Gosol, 222

Grinbarg, 373

Grinberg, 76, 320

Grinboym, 85, 165

Grintsvayg, 298

Grocholski, 36, 268, 298

Gruber, 128, 130, 146

Grubian, 140

Guber, 123, 126, 127

Gufman, 250

H

Hadari, 4, 226, 227

Hakohen, 354

Hamut, 378

Head, 344

Heilperin, 185

Heker, 190

Heler, 38, 298

Honerchuk, 98

I

Itsi, 318, 319, 320, 350, 353, 355, 356, 357, 371

K

Kagan, 6, 133, 184

Kahan, 44

Kaminska, 183, 185

Kamtsen, 314

Kantor, 139

Kardash, 136

Kartman, 360

Katsap, 298, 336

Katz, 4, 158, 159, 183, 184, 215, 216, 280,
  375, 376, 377

Kecholy, 207

Kechum, 218, 220

Kelner, 391

Ketaykisher, 171

Kheslivker, 298

Kirshenboym, 83, 86, 179

Kitaykesher, 83, 184, 274

Kitaykisher, 179, 180

Klayn, 66

Kleynberg, 386

Kleynboym, 165

Kleynman, 378

Klinman, 77

Kolmbren, 101, 102

Kop, 392

Kopel, 158, 159, 184, 192, 193, 196, 219,
  378

Kopels, 346

Koren, 27, 321

Korenfeld, 216

Korin, 129, 158, 159, 183, 196, 337

Kornfeld, 158, 161, 171, 180, 298

Korybut, 35, 37, 298

Kotliar, 357

Kovalski, 259

Kovilis, 82

Koylenberner, 80, 94, 263

Krasnov, 387

Kraus, 86, 87, 88

Kremenetski, 339, 351, 384

Krepl, 339

Kreshitska, 83, 88, 89

Krigsehver, 126

Kripitser, 378

Kripke, 344

Krupnik, 326

Kubrik, 4, 202, 203, 204, 209, 228

L

Landesberg, 77

Landsberg, 4, 196, 261

Lanevitser, 355, 360

Lanovits, 6, 26, 79, 147, 149, 213, 274,
  280, 281, 291

Layter, 79, 95, 147, 183, 265

Lekales, 184

Lekhetitser, 330

Lemish, 298

Lerer, 158, 159, 250

Lerner, 155, 250, 402

Leshed, 176

Lev, 297, 298

Levanon, 41

Levinson, 298

Lifshits, 100, 123, 127, 128, 317, 338, 353,
  378

Lunson, 294, 297, 298, 314, 317, 321, 340,
  349, 350, 351, 352, 354, 360, 362, 366,
  368, 371, 373, 375, 377, 380, 382, 383,
  384, 386, 390, 391, 393, 395, 398, 402

M

Mafshit, 322

Mages, 2, 28, 61, 72, 83, 92, 98, 108, 112,
  123, 127, 129, 135, 143, 146, 149, 154,
  155, 192, 200, 222, 228, 245, 250

Malev, 402

Maliv, 377

Mandelboym, 329

Marchbeyn, 231, 252, 265, 274, 275

Marders, 378

Margaliot, 80, 275, 276

Margalit, 123

Margolis, 320, 356

Margolius, 298

Markhbeyn, 79, 80, 171, 176, 276, 278

Matis, 25, 112, 127, 128

Mazur, 79, 135, 141, 157, 184, 265, 278

Meir, 3, 28, 29, 39, 60, 65, 154, 171, 195,
    199, 229, 231, 235, 237, 238, 239, 247,
    291, 317, 320, 338, 343, 344, 386, 390,
    391, 398

Mekhel, 322, 327, 328

Melis, 402

Meliv, 155

Melksnits, 276

Mendelboym, 184

Miler, 102, 128, 140

Mindzar, 278

Mishne, 4, 222, 223

Mniszech, 35, 36, 298

Mofshit, 161, 162, 184, 251

N

N.-S, 250

Naftali, 347

Nek, 255

Nelkis, 378

Nets, 323

N-S, 217

Nudel, 127, 189

Nudler, 378

O

Ochitel, 140

Or, 154, 210, 229, 231, 235, 237, 238, 239,
    247, 317, 366

Orlovich, 34, 298

Osherovits, 140

Osterer, 218, 219

Osterers, 158

Ostrer, 320, 350

Ostrovski, 65, 71, 129, 155, 259, 346, 402

P

Parnas, 386, 392, 397, 398, 399

Pientkovski, 298

Piontkovski, 298

Pliata, 362, 365

Plotkin, 228

Poslevski, 71

Presman, 196

R

Rabin, 29, 194, 231, 232, 238, 280, 293,
    298

Rachmani, 290

Radiviler, 33, 354, 355

Radoviloy, 285

Rashevski, 298

Ratman, 350

Remez, 205, 206

Reyzels, 141, 171, 188, 191, 194

Ron, 29, 163, 183, 185, 200, 218, 220, 282

Rosenberg, 402

Rosivkier, 298

Rotenberg, 158, 164

Rothschild, 203, 369, 370, 391

Rotman, 4, 284, 285, 286, 287, 290, 387, 392

Roynik, 4, 157, 208, 209, 210, 229, 230, 241, 242, 347, 383, 384

Roytman, 399

Rozen, 226

Rozenberg, 51, 108, 111, 155

Rozenhek, 160

Rozental, 4, 165, 184, 200, 241, 242, 298, 326

Rozin, 216

Rozumny, 219

Rozye, 136, 194

Ruach, 72, 255

S

Safir, 354, 362

Sana, 165

Segal, 25, 29, 112, 319, 320, 353

Senders, 165, 187

Sendler, 75, 261

Senik, 378

Servetnik, 146, 171, 184, 194

Serwacy, 35, 37, 298

Shag, 67, 123, 128, 194, 335, 336, 378

Shames, 327, 328

Shantsi, 347

Shapiro, 3, 78, 93, 127, 155, 158, 159, 160, 164, 184, 194, 214, 382, 383, 402

Shapoval, 259, 263

Shats, 41, 143

Shatski, 202, 391

Shayer, 321

Shayklis, 378

Sherer, 276

Sheyndel, 184, 378

Sheyner, 53, 383, 384

Sheyngold, 351

Shimkovits, 76

Shimshelevits, 202

Shkoler, 378

Shlayen, 161, 180

Shnayder, 347, 378

Shniribeker, 208

Shochet, 350

Shoyel, 378

Shpigelman, 236, 378, 391

Shpiglman, 128

Shpilberg, 283

Shprintsak, 283

Shteynberg, 168

Shuele, 355, 360

Shulder, 184

Shumakher, 137

Shuster, 346

Shvarts, 98

Shvayke, 151

Shvedki, 70

Sirota, 219, 370

Sklod, 241

Skoropadsky, 157, 347

Sobol, 61, 63, 92, 155, 402

Sofer, 4, 72, 128, 131, 147, 179, 189, 222, 245, 247, 249, 255, 280, 282, 378

Sos, 353

Spirt, 280

Stefanski, 102

Storozh, 129

Sudman, 251

T

Tarberider, 328

Tenenboym, 63, 146, 184, 251

Ternikov, 157

Teslier, 276

Teyer, 255

Todreses, 378, 379

Todros, 128, 298

Trumpeldor, 170, 171, 177, 186, 192, 397

Tshaytshinetski, 400

Tsimberg, 165

Tsimbler, 76, 79, 80, 101, 258, 261

Tsinberg, 63, 64, 127, 165, 213

Tsipe, 378

Tsizen, 251

Tsur, 4, 224

Tsvi, 71, 140, 156, 157, 158, 171, 184,
    202, 204, 215, 228, 233, 234, 275, 320

Tsvik, 149, 151, 252

Tunrider, 344

V

Valdman, 150, 252, 254

Valkes, 378

Vayngarten, 320

Vaynman, 384, 385

Vays, 93

Vaytsman, 258

Venshitska, 83, 88, 89

Verdi, 171, 174, 188, 191

Vilinski, 129

Vilsker, 171

Vitels, 159, 217, 218

Volinski, 298

Volk, 159, 184

W

Walker, 314

Wisniowiecki, 35, 36, 37, 46, 298

Worth, 392

Y

Yafe, 61, 203, 294

Yakira, 85, 100, 184, 187, 259, 275, 400

Yenkel, 298, 327, 328, 378

Yenkevits, 87, 88

Yevdokim, 70

Yonitsman, 283

Yonteles, 386

Yosef, 4, 63, 74, 78, 127, 131, 133, 159,
    164, 170, 184, 217, 245, 246, 259, 280,
    283, 298, 378, 391

Yuger, 71

Z

Zak, 4, 164, 166, 237, 238, 245, 347, 404

Zaloshtsy, 84, 85, 87, 88, 89

Zaltsman, 182

Zamoyski, 35, 298

Zbarizher, 200

Zekharye, 322

Zelber, 251

Zeyger, 166, 167, 184, 197, 231, 233, 234,
    298, 320

Zimbel, 76

Zinger, 98, 184, 219

Zolozitser, 350

Zusman, 375

www.ingramcontent.com/pod-product-compliance
Lightning Source LLC
Chambersburg PA
CBHW082006150426
42814CB00005BA/237